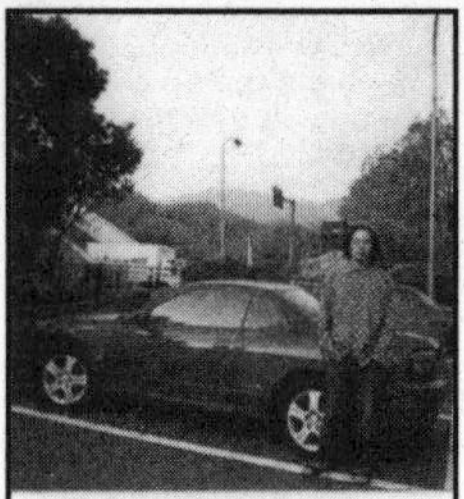

武井宏之

I grew up as part of the robot generation, so now I'm obsessed with my car. I mean, I **really** love it. I love it so much that it causes me stress. Ah, love is complicated.

—Hiroyuki Takei

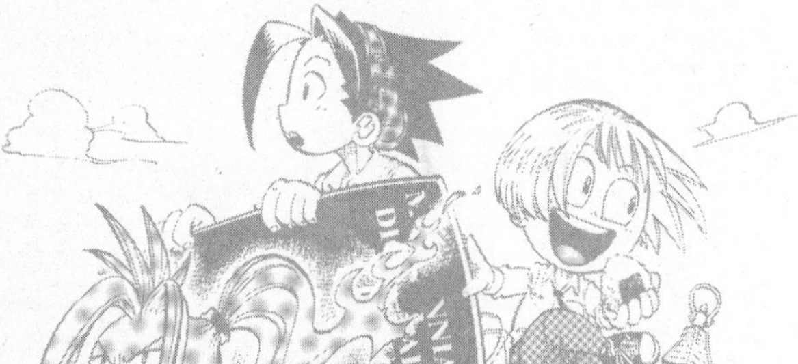
MANTANNIAN

Unconventional author/artist Hiroyuki Takei began his career by winning the coveted Hop Step Award (for new manga artists) and the Osamu Tezuka Award (named after the famous artist of the same name). After working as an assistant to famed artist Nobuhiro Watsuki, Takei debuted in **Weekly Shonen Jump** in 1997 with **Butsu Zone**, an action series based on Buddhist mythology. His multicultural adventure manga **Shaman King**, which debuted in 1998, became a hit and was adapted into an anime TV series. Takei lists Osamu Tezuka, American comics and robot anime among his many influences.

SHAMAN KING VOL. 15
The SHONEN JUMP Manga Edition

STORY AND ART BY
HIROYUKI TAKEI

English Adaptation/Lance Caselman
Translation/Lillian Olsen
Touch-up Art & Lettering/John Hunt
Cover Design/Sean Lee
Interior Design/Nozomi Akashi
Editors/Joel Enos & Carol Fox

Editor in Chief, Books/Alvin Lu
Editor in Chief, Magazines/Marc Weidenbaum
VP of Publishing Licensing/Rika Inouye
VP of Sales/Gonzalo Ferreyra
Sr. VP of Marketing/Liza Coppola
Publisher/Hyoe Narita

Printed in the U.S.A.

Published by VIZ Media, LLC
P.O. Box 77010
San Francisco, CA 94107

SHONEN JUMP Manga Edition
10 9 8 7 6 5 4 3 2 1
First printing, March 2008

viz media
www.viz.com

RATED T FOR TEEN
PARENTAL ADVISORY
SHAMAN KING is rated T for Teen and is recommended for ages 13 and up. This volume contains violence.
ratings.viz.com

SHONEN JUMP MANGA

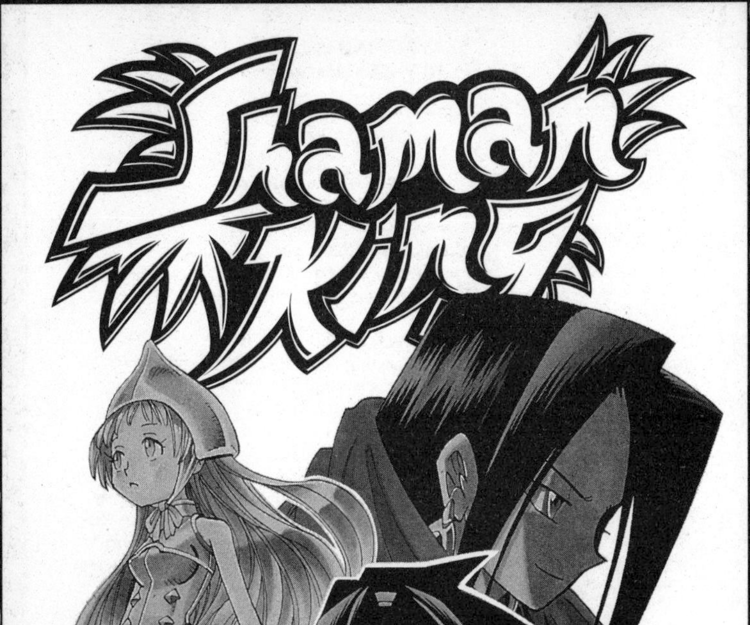
Shaman King

VOL. 15
NORTHERN PRIDE

STORY AND ART BY
HIROYUKI TAKEI

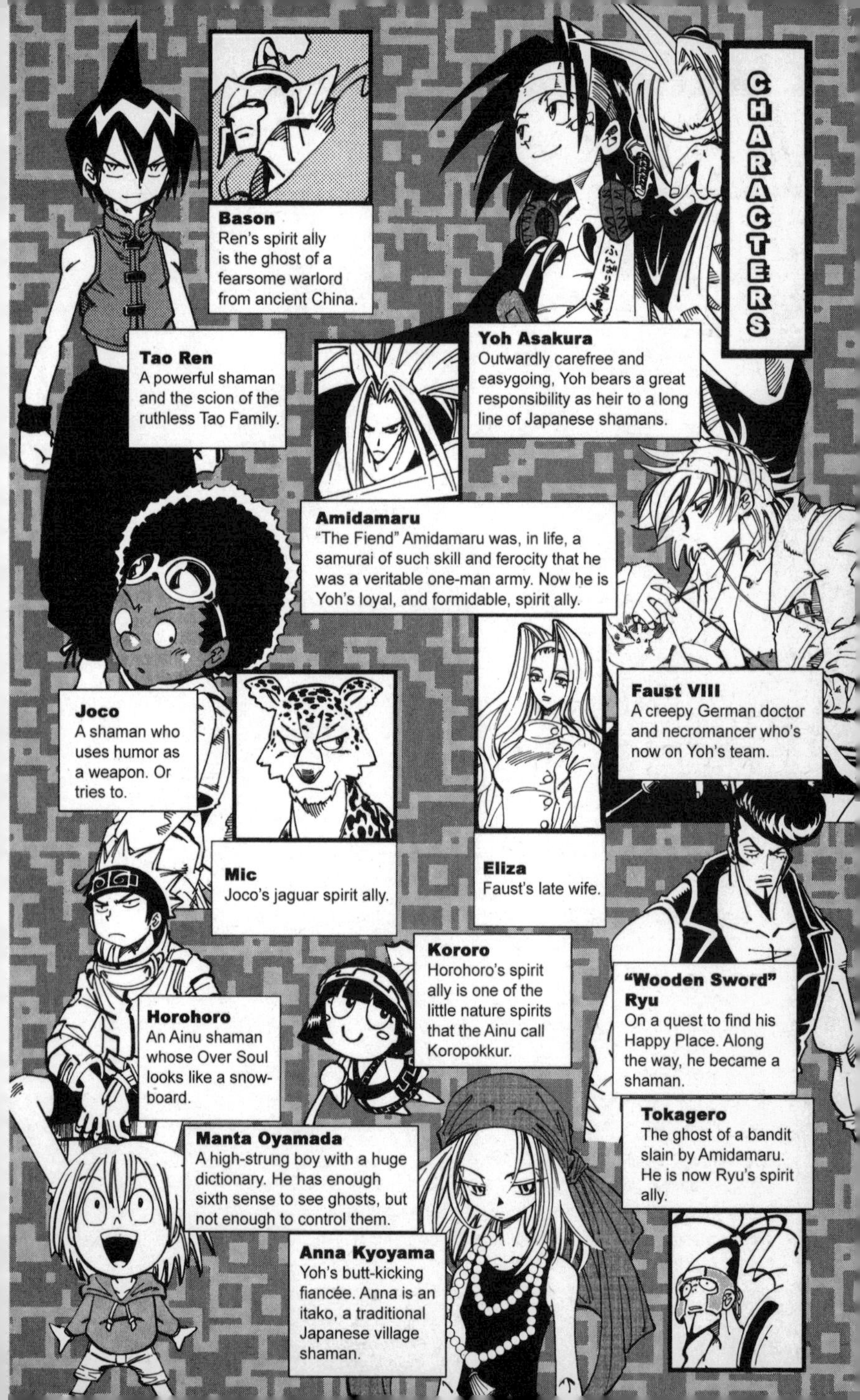
CHARACTERS
Yoh Asakura
Outwardly carefree and easygoing, Yoh bears a great responsibility as heir to a long line of Japanese shamans.
Bason
Ren's spirit ally is the ghost of a fearsome warlord from ancient China.
Tao Ren
A powerful shaman and the scion of the ruthless Tao Family.
Amidamaru
"The Fiend" Amidamaru was, in life, a samurai of such skill and ferocity that he was a veritable one-man army. Now he is Yoh's loyal, and formidable, spirit ally.
Faust VIII
A creepy German doctor and necromancer who's now on Yoh's team.
Eliza
Faust's late wife.
Mic
Joco's jaguar spirit ally.
Joco
A shaman who uses humor as a weapon. Or tries to.
"Wooden Sword" Ryu
On a quest to find his Happy Place. Along the way, he became a shaman.
Kororo
Horohoro's spirit ally is one of the little nature spirits that the Ainu call Koropokkur.
Horohoro
An Ainu shaman whose Over Soul looks like a snow-board.
Tokagero
The ghost of a bandit slain by Amidamaru. He is now Ryu's spirit ally.
Manta Oyamada
A high-strung boy with a huge dictionary. He has enough sixth sense to see ghosts, but not enough to control them.
Anna Kyoyama
Yoh's butt-kicking fiancée. Anna is an itako, a traditional Japanese village shaman.

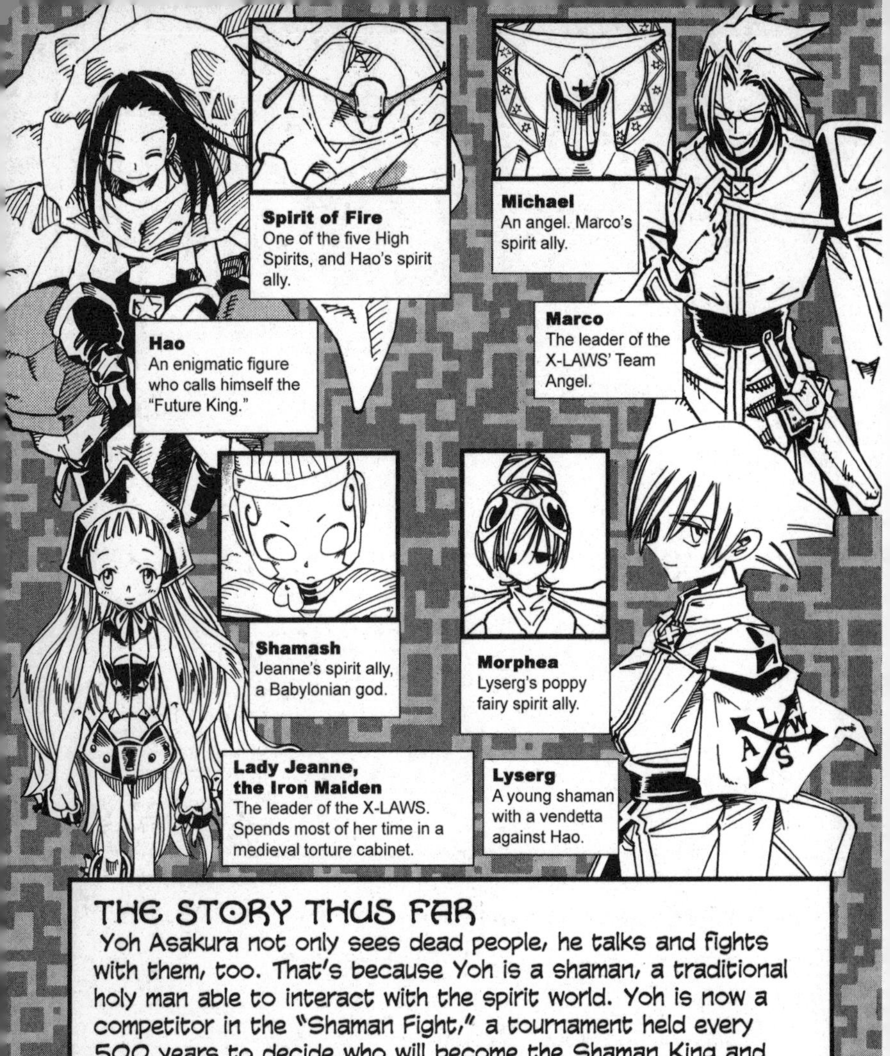
Michael
An angel. Marco's spirit ally.
Spirit of Fire
One of the five High Spirits, and Hao's spirit ally.
Marco
The leader of the X-LAWS' Team Angel.
Hao
An enigmatic figure who calls himself the "Future King."
Morphea
Lyserg's poppy fairy spirit ally.
Shamash
Jeanne's spirit ally, a Babylonian god.
Lyserg
A young shaman with a vendetta against Hao.
Lady Jeanne, the Iron Maiden
The leader of the X-LAWS. Spends most of her time in a medieval torture cabinet.

THE STORY THUS FAR

Yoh Asakura not only sees dead people, he talks and fights with them, too. That's because Yoh is a shaman, a traditional holy man able to interact with the spirit world. Yoh is now a competitor in the "Shaman Fight," a tournament held every 500 years to decide who will become the Shaman King and shape humanity's future.

In the first round of the Shaman Fight, the shamans must separate into teams of three. Team Ren--Ren, Horo, and Joco--defeats a team made up of Hao's minions. Then X-I faces off against Team Nile, and Yoh and company are shocked to discover that Lyserg has joined the X-LAWS! In the fight that follows, the mysterious Iron Maiden makes her appearance, with deadly results. But the cruelty of the X-LAWS only solidifies Yoh's determination to win it all!

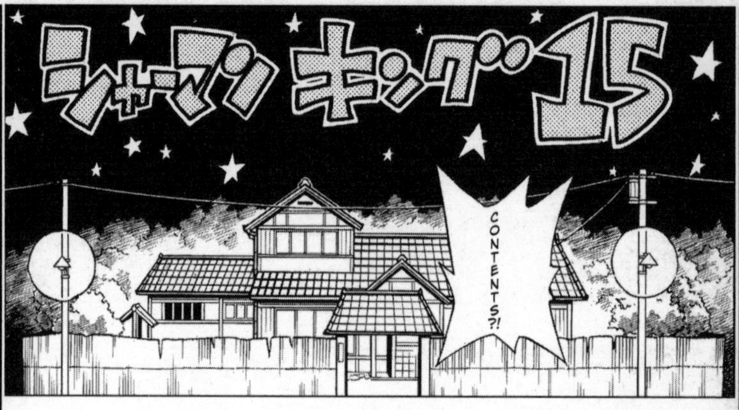
シャーマンキング15
CONTENTS?!

VOL. 15

NORTHERN PRIDE

CONTENTS

Reincarnation 126: Stand up, Team Funbari Hot Springs

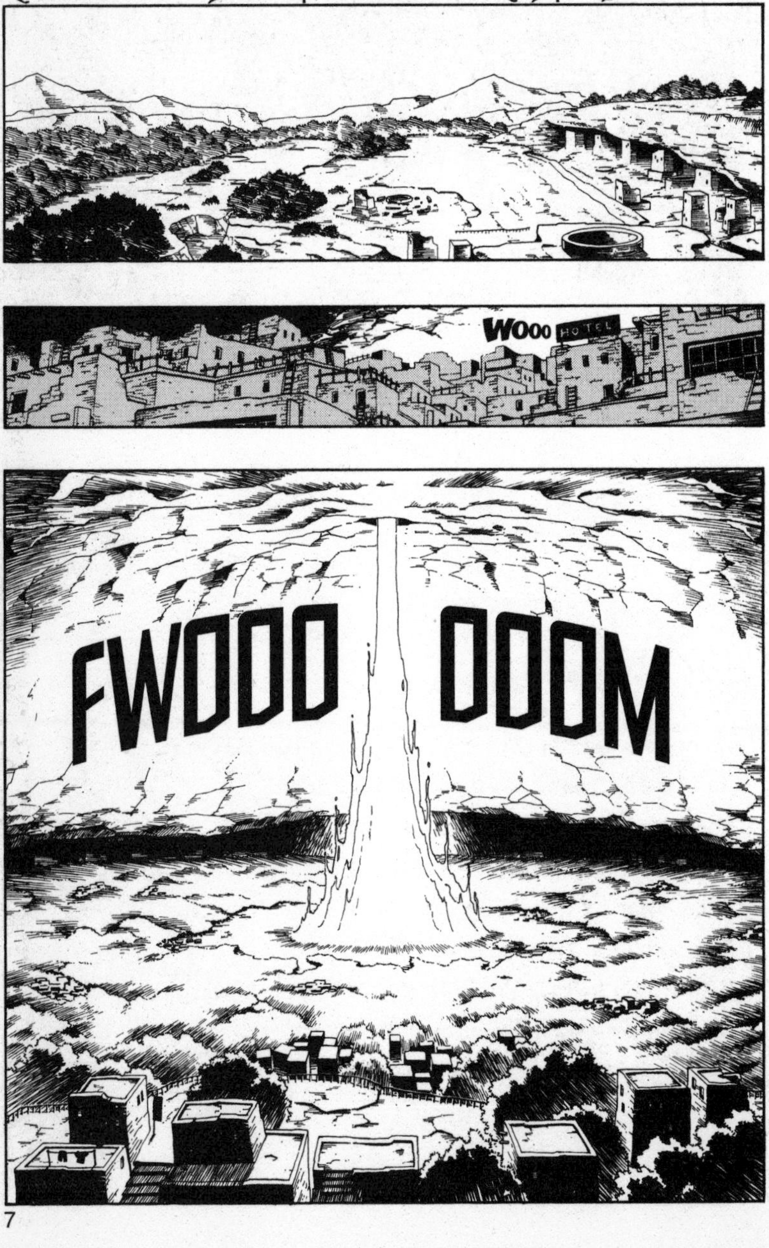
HOTEL
WOOO
FWOOO OOOM

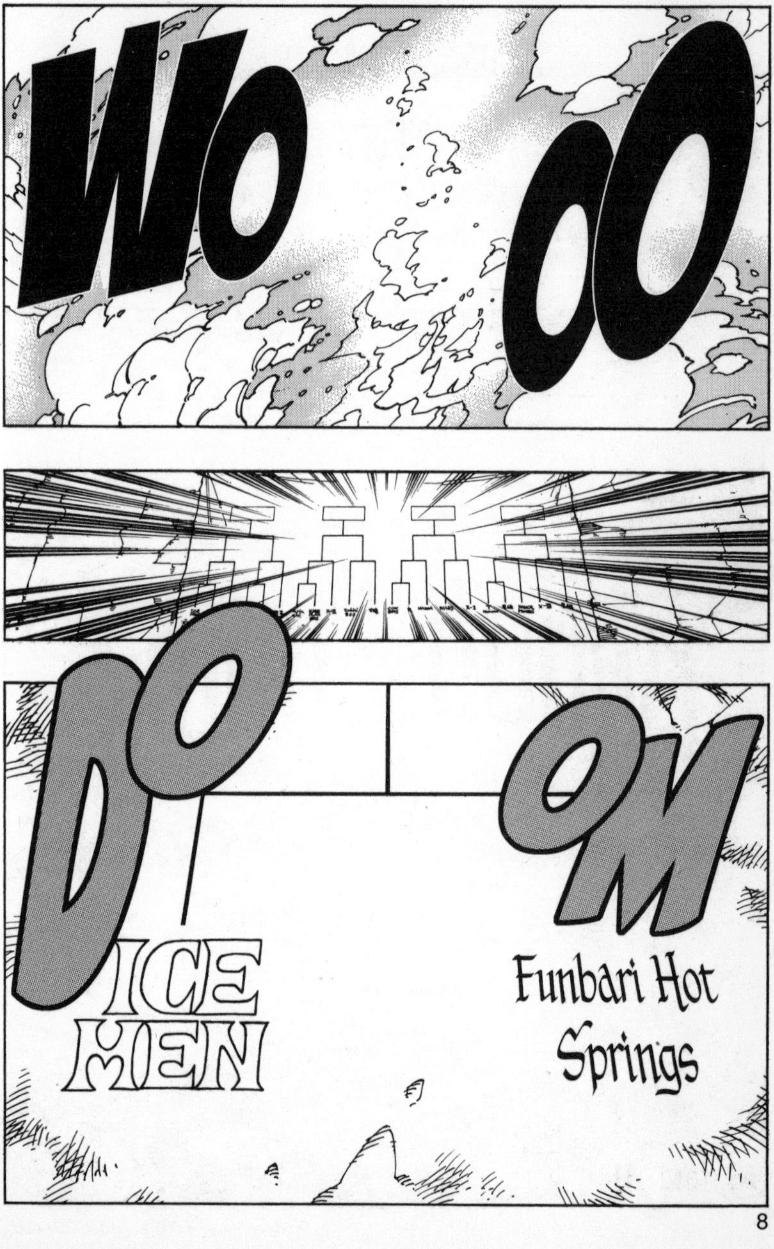
WOOOO
DOOM
Funbari Hot Springs
ICE MEN

Reincarnation 126:
Stand up, Team Funbari Hot Springs

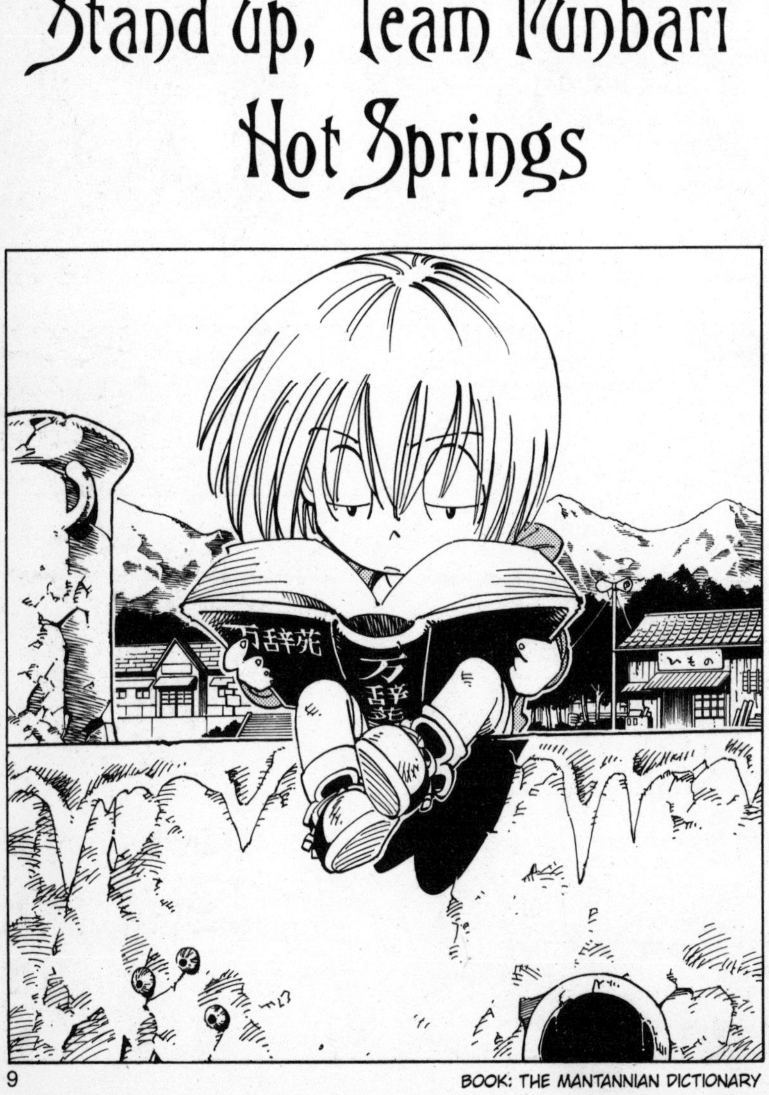
万辞苑
万辞苑
いもの

BOOK: THE MANTANNIAN DICTIONARY

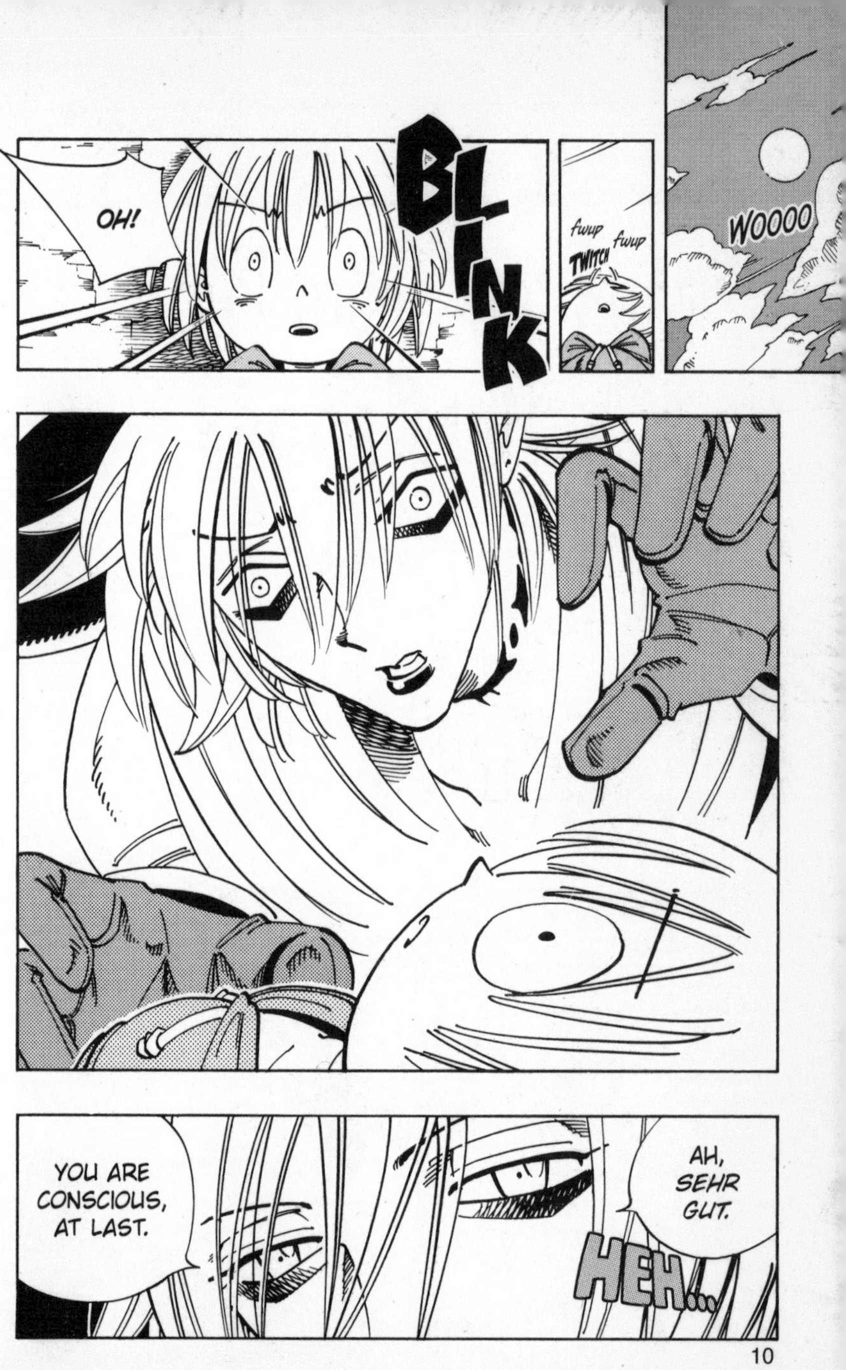
WOOOO
fwup
fwup
TWITCH
BLINK
OH!
AH, SEHR GUT.
HEH...
YOU ARE CONSCIOUS, AT LAST.

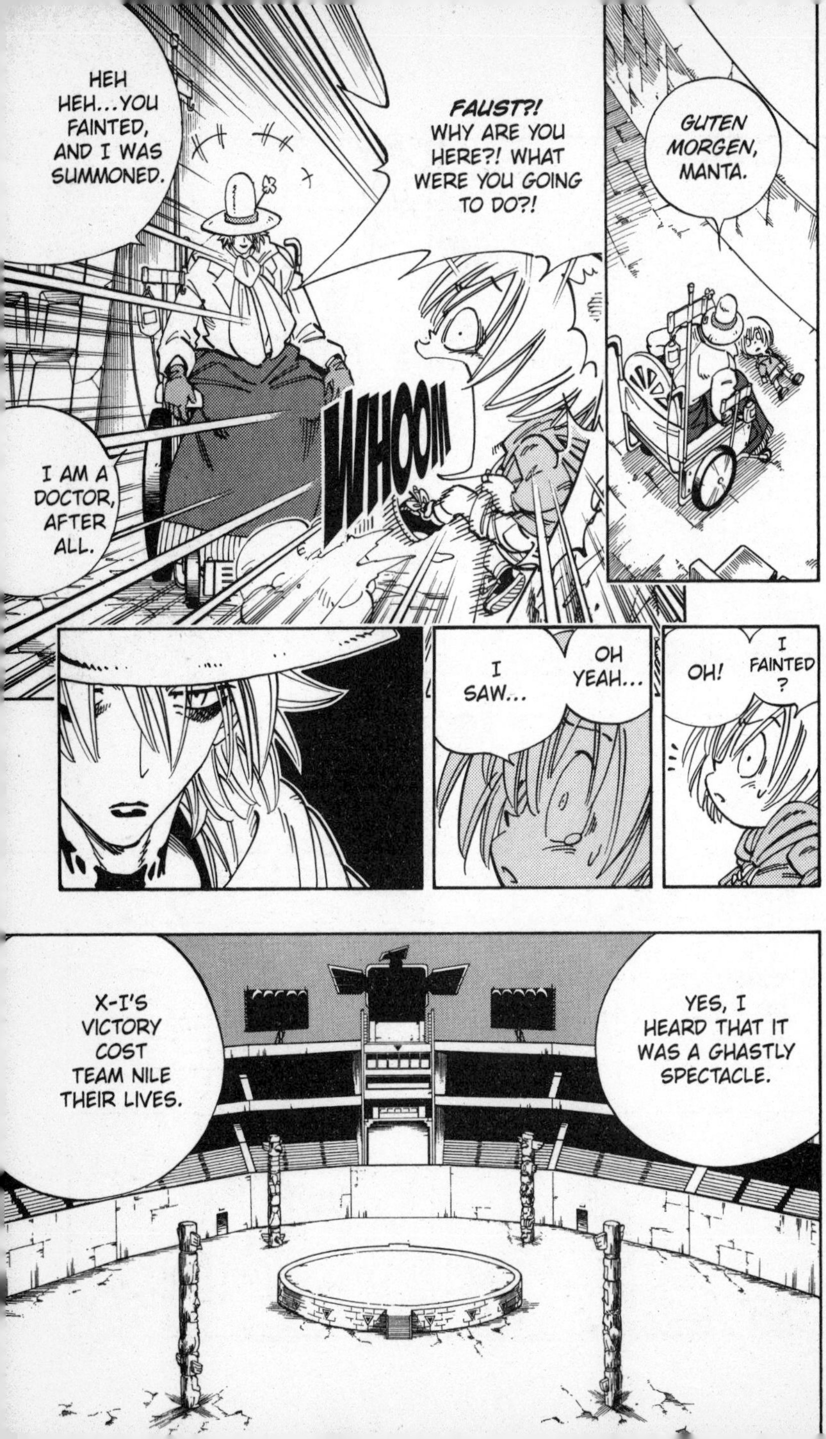
GUTEN MORGEN, MANTA.
FAUST?! WHY ARE YOU HERE?! WHAT WERE YOU GOING TO DO?!
HEH HEH...YOU FAINTED, AND I WAS SUMMONED.
WHOOM
I AM A DOCTOR, AFTER ALL.
I FAINTED?
OH!
OH YEAH...
I SAW...
YES, I HEARD THAT IT WAS A GHASTLY SPECTACLE.
X-I'S VICTORY COST TEAM NILE THEIR LIVES.

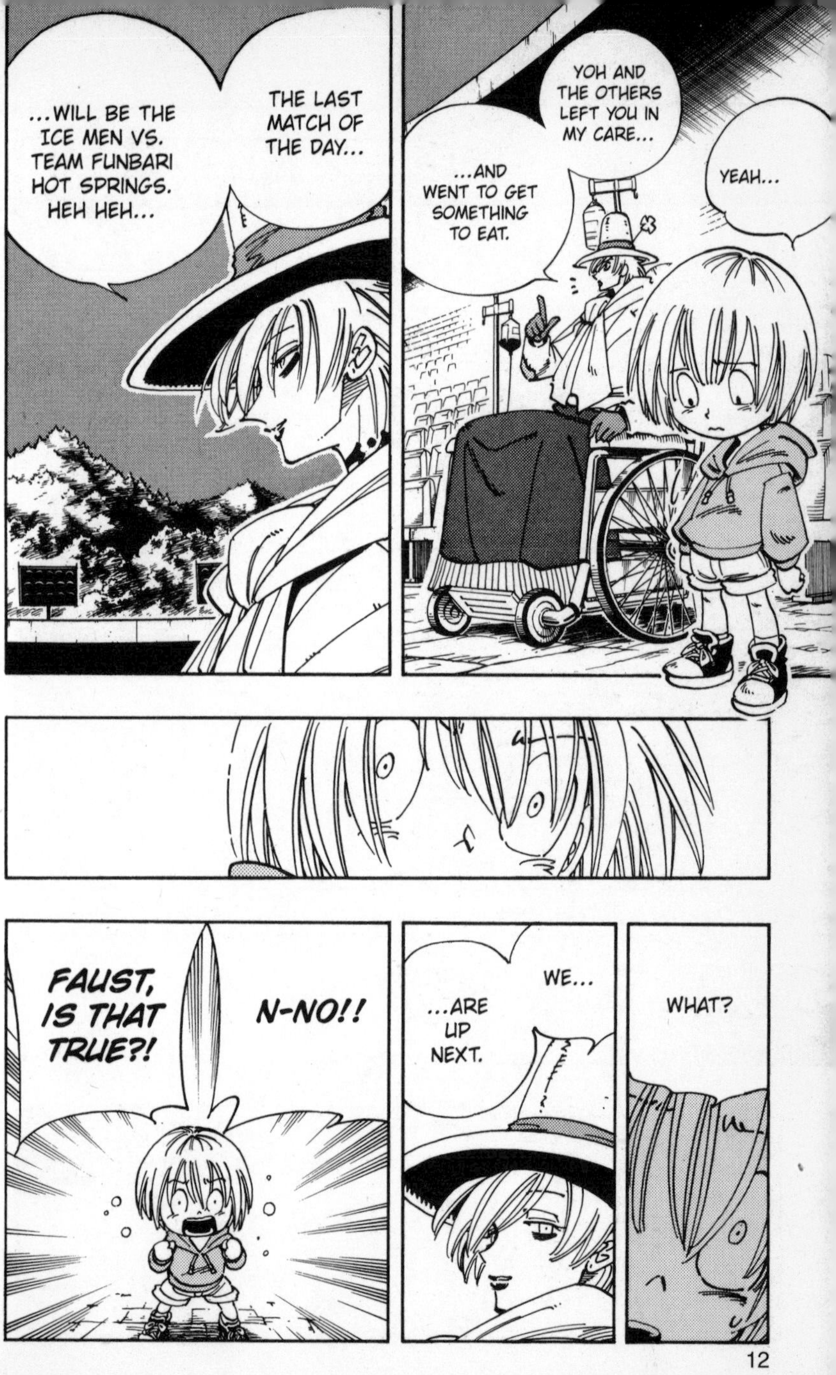
YOH AND THE OTHERS LEFT YOU IN MY CARE...
...AND WENT TO GET SOMETHING TO EAT.
YEAH...
THE LAST MATCH OF THE DAY...
...WILL BE THE ICE MEN VS. TEAM FUNBARI HOT SPRINGS. HEH HEH...
WHAT?
WE...
...ARE UP NEXT.
N-NO!!
FAUST, IS THAT TRUE?!

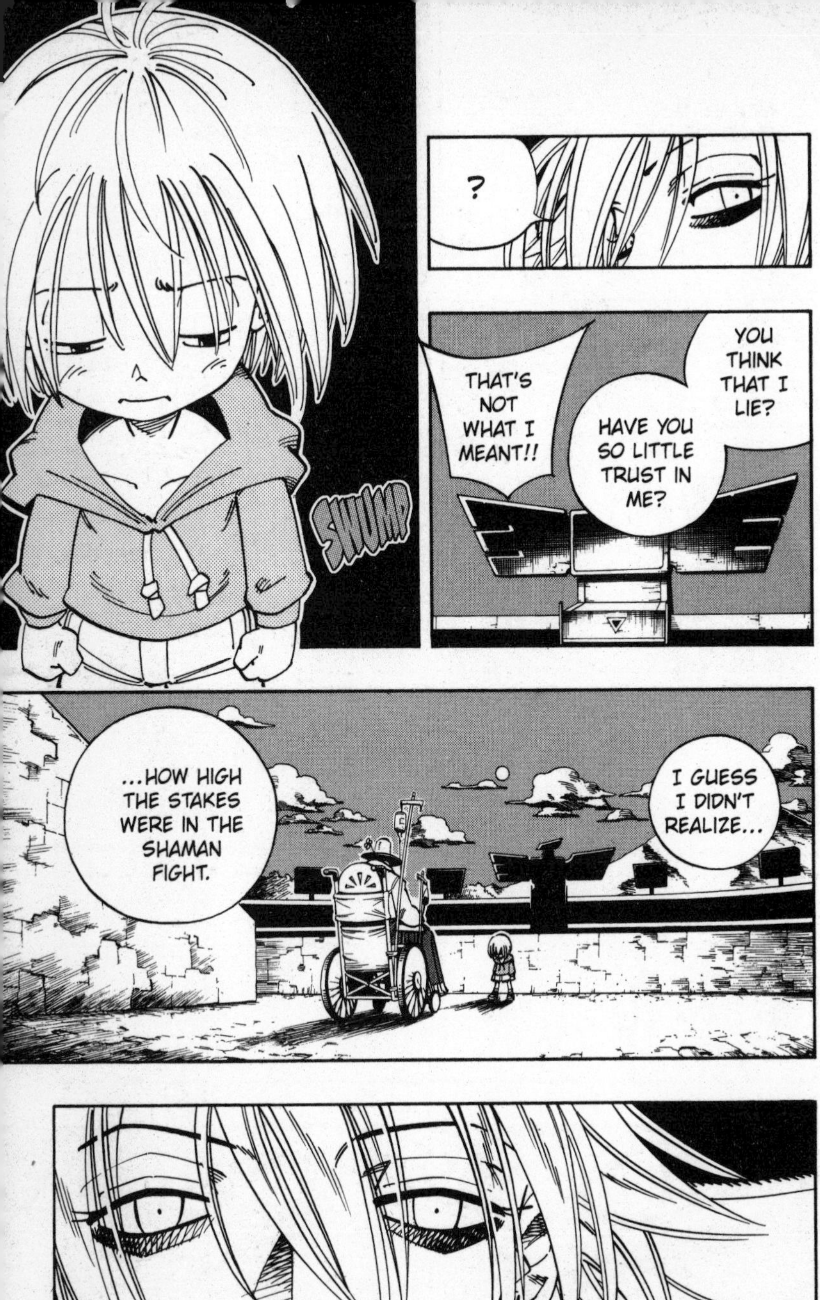
?
YOU THINK THAT I LIE?
HAVE YOU SO LITTLE TRUST IN ME?
THAT'S NOT WHAT I MEANT!!
SHUMP
I GUESS I DIDN'T REALIZE...
...HOW HIGH THE STAKES WERE IN THE SHAMAN FIGHT.

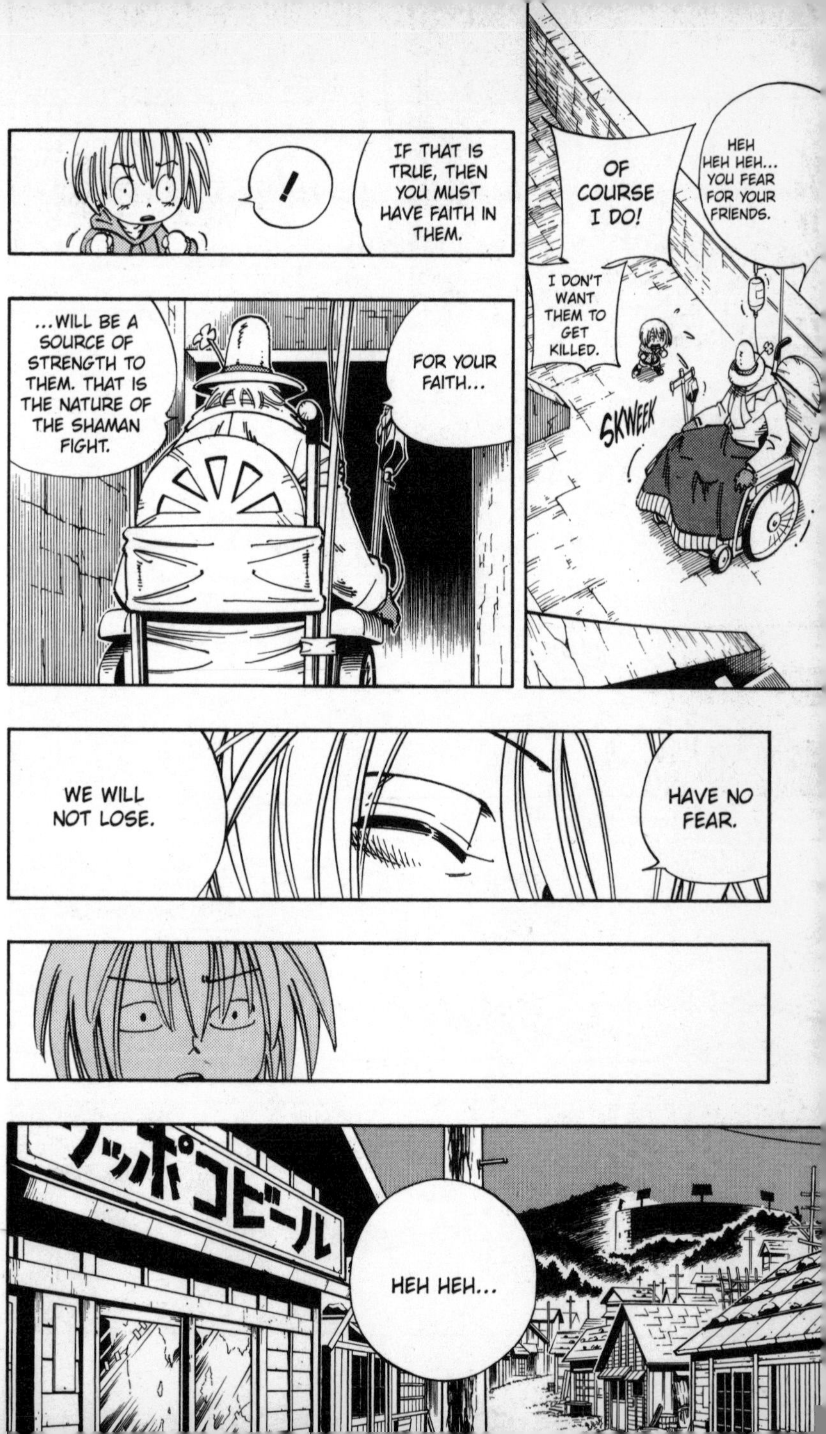
HEH HEH HEH... YOU FEAR FOR YOUR FRIENDS.
OF COURSE I DO!
I DON'T WANT THEM TO GET KILLED.
SKWEEK
IF THAT IS TRUE, THEN YOU MUST HAVE FAITH IN THEM.
!
FOR YOUR FAITH...
...WILL BE A SOURCE OF STRENGTH TO THEM. THAT IS THE NATURE OF THE SHAMAN FIGHT.
HAVE NO FEAR.
WE WILL NOT LOSE.
ッポコビール
HEH HEH...

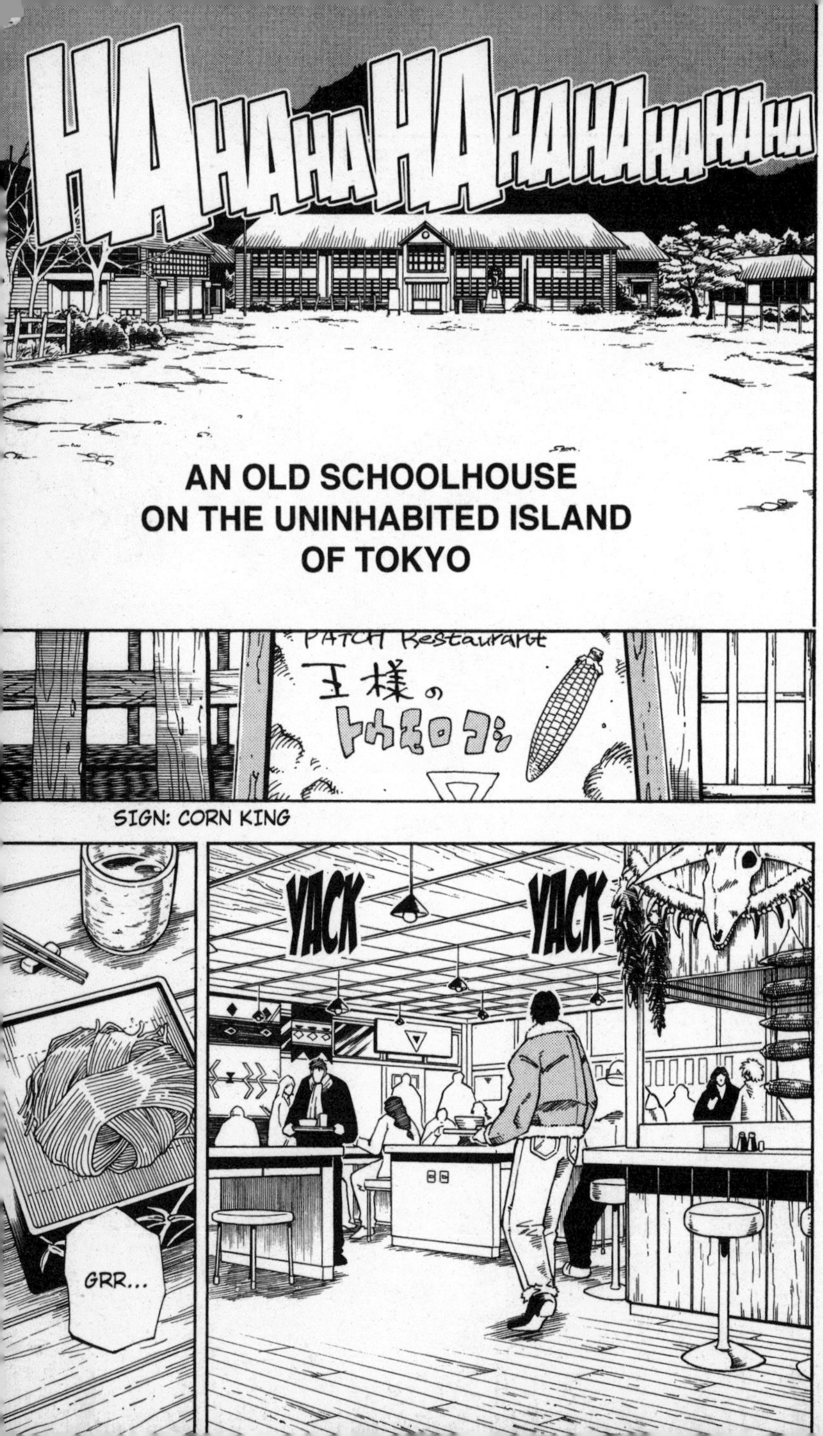
HAHAHAHAHAHAHAHAHAHA
AN OLD SCHOOLHOUSE ON THE UNINHABITED ISLAND OF TOKYO
PATCH Restaurant
王様のトウモロコシ
SIGN: CORN KING
YACK YACK
GRR...

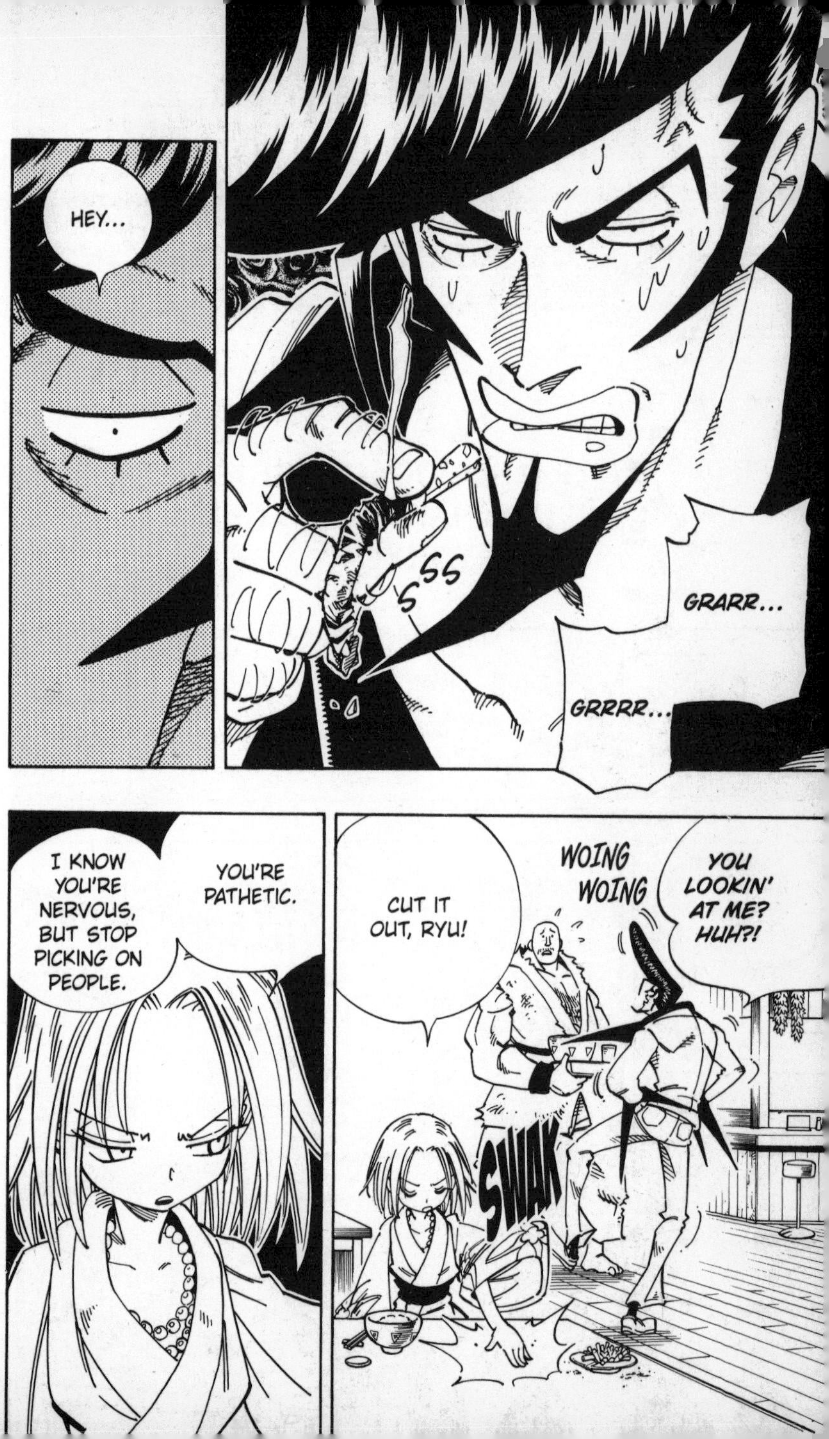
SSS
GRARR...
GRRRR...
HEY...
YOU LOOKIN' AT ME? HUH?!
WOING WOING
CUT IT OUT, RYU!
SWAK
YOU'RE PATHETIC.
I KNOW YOU'RE NERVOUS, BUT STOP PICKING ON PEOPLE.

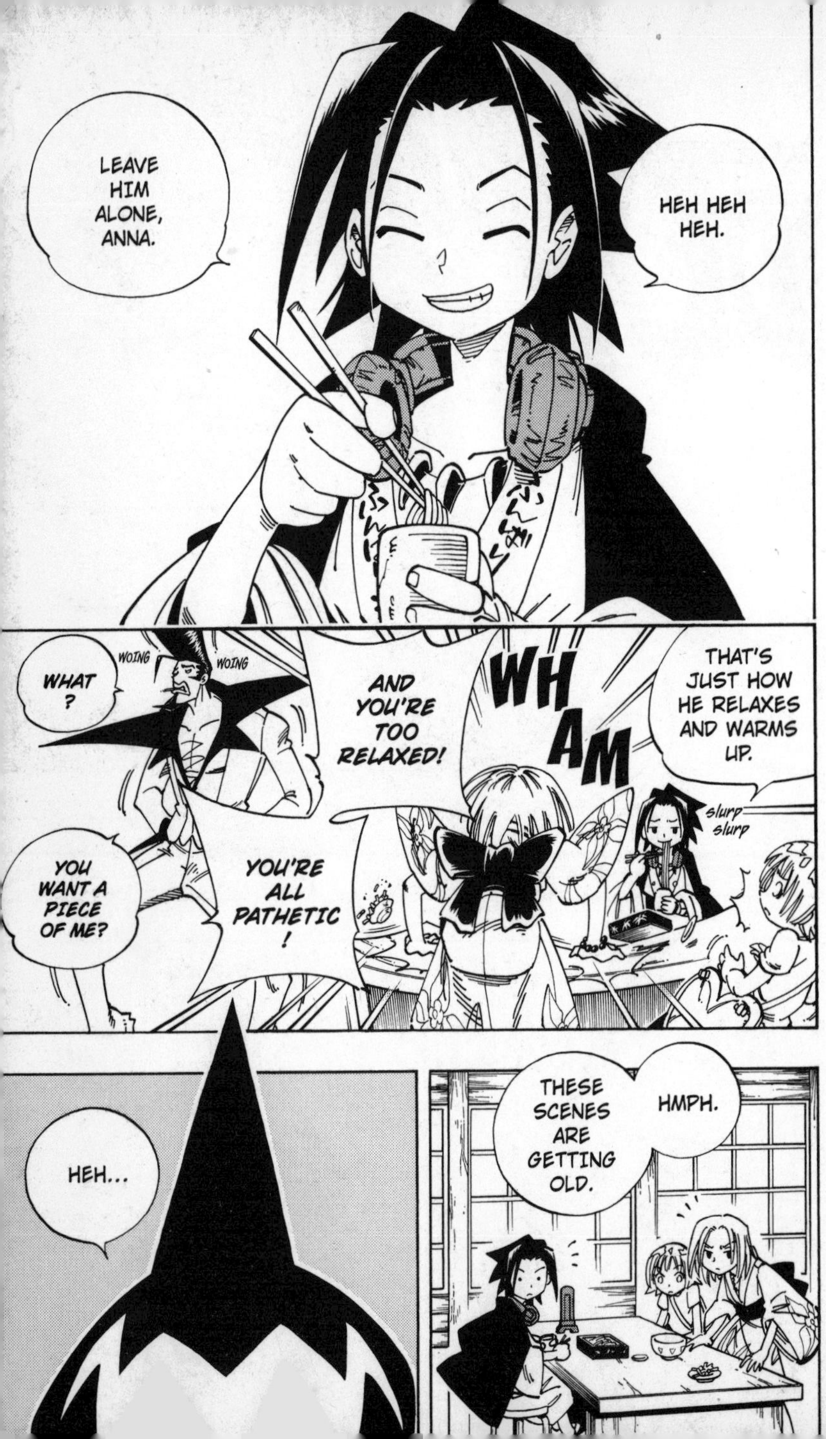
HEH HEH HEH.
LEAVE HIM ALONE, ANNA.
THAT'S JUST HOW HE RELAXES AND WARMS UP.
WHAM
slurp slurp
AND YOU'RE TOO RELAXED!
YOU'RE ALL PATHETIC!
WOING WOING
WHAT?
YOU WANT A PIECE OF ME?
HMPH.
THESE SCENES ARE GETTING OLD.
HEH...

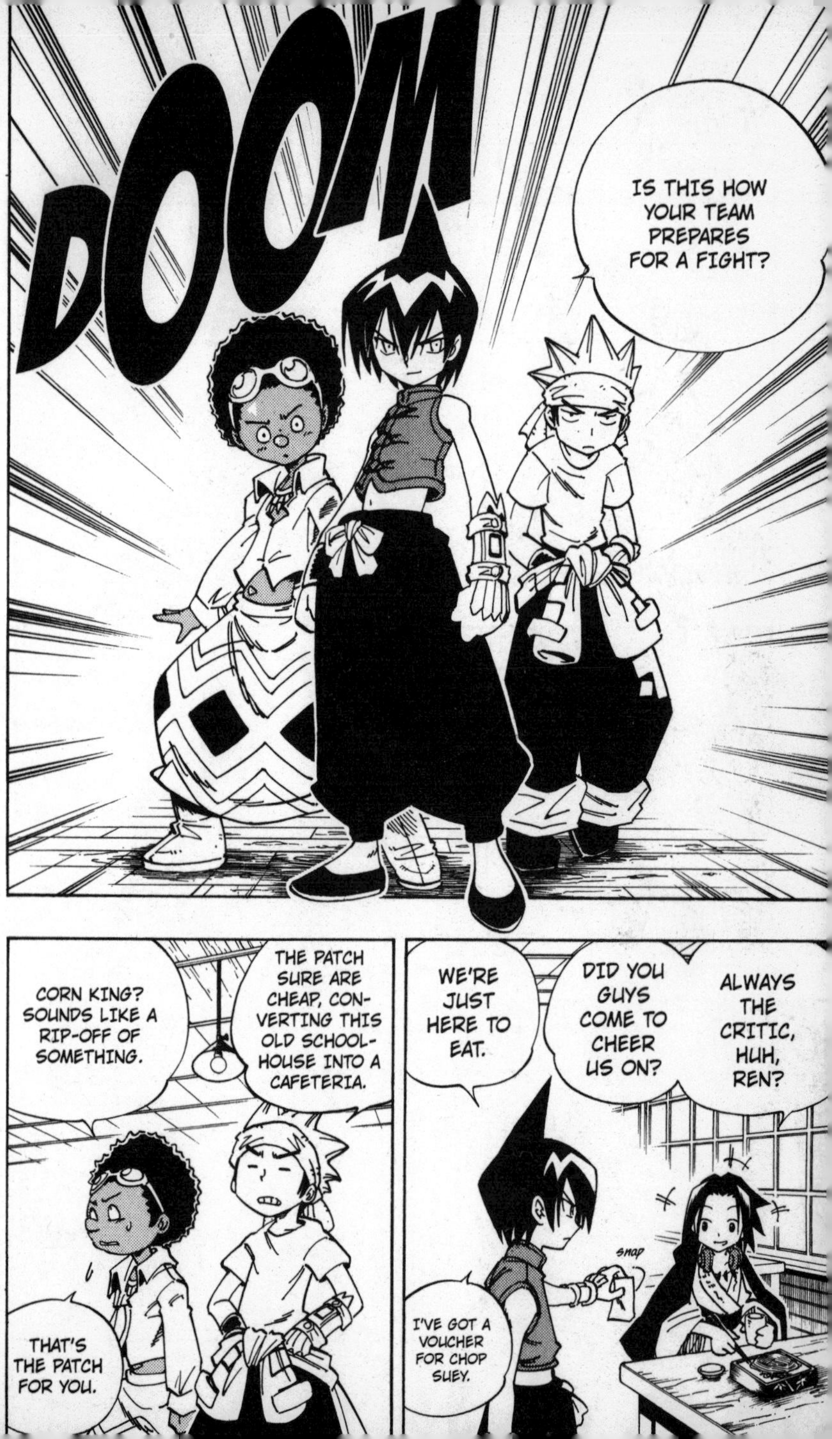
IS THIS HOW YOUR TEAM PREPARES FOR A FIGHT?
DOOM
ALWAYS THE CRITIC, HUH, REN?
DID YOU GUYS COME TO CHEER US ON?
WE'RE JUST HERE TO EAT.
snap
I'VE GOT A VOUCHER FOR CHOP SUEY.
THE PATCH SURE ARE CHEAP, CON-VERTING THIS OLD SCHOOL-HOUSE INTO A CAFETERIA.
CORN KING? SOUNDS LIKE A RIP-OFF OF SOMETHING.
THAT'S THE PATCH FOR YOU.

READ THIS WAY

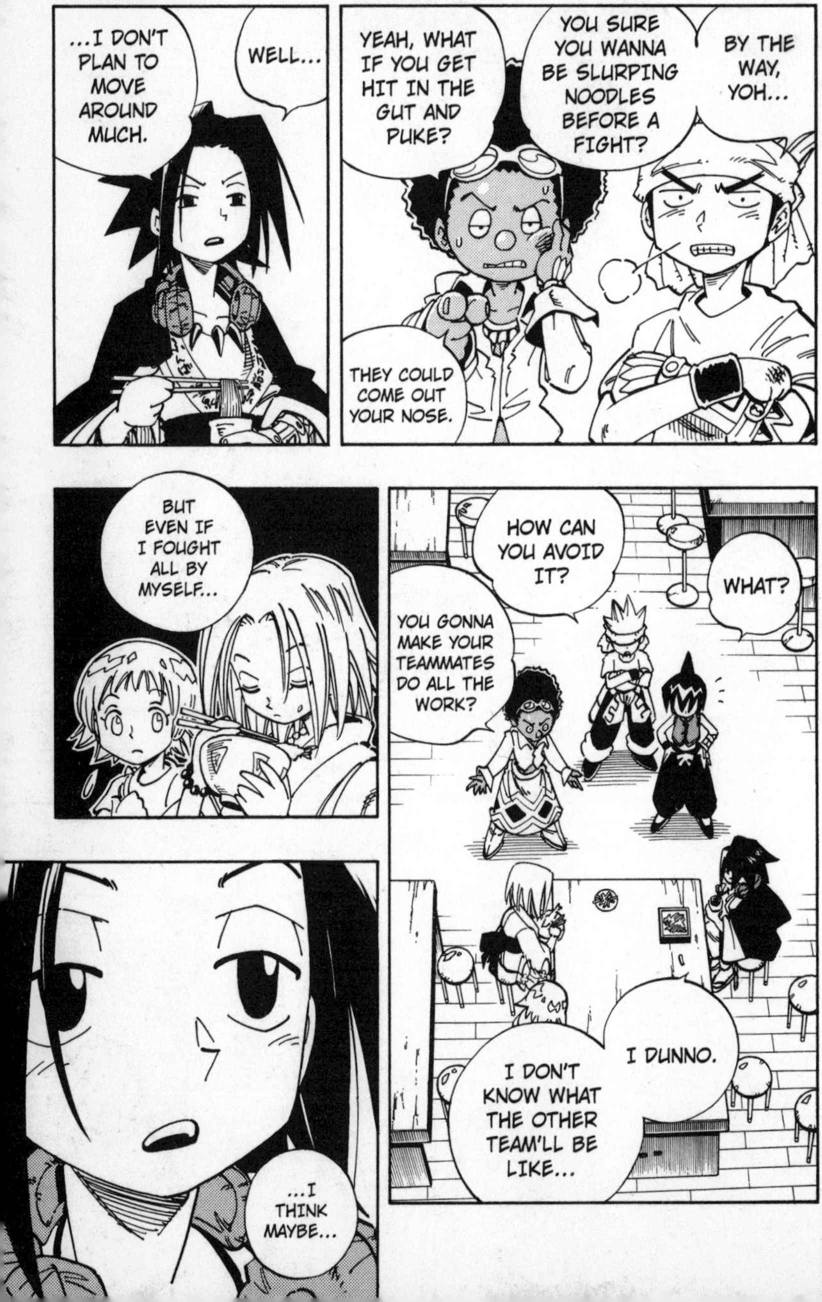
BY THE WAY, YOH...
YOU SURE YOU WANNA BE SLURPING NOODLES BEFORE A FIGHT?
YEAH, WHAT IF YOU GET HIT IN THE GUT AND PUKE?
THEY COULD COME OUT YOUR NOSE.
WELL...
...I DON'T PLAN TO MOVE AROUND MUCH.
WHAT?
HOW CAN YOU AVOID IT?
YOU GONNA MAKE YOUR TEAMMATES DO ALL THE WORK?
I DUNNO.
I DON'T KNOW WHAT THE OTHER TEAM'LL BE LIKE...
BUT EVEN IF I FOUGHT ALL BY MYSELF...
...I THINK MAYBE...

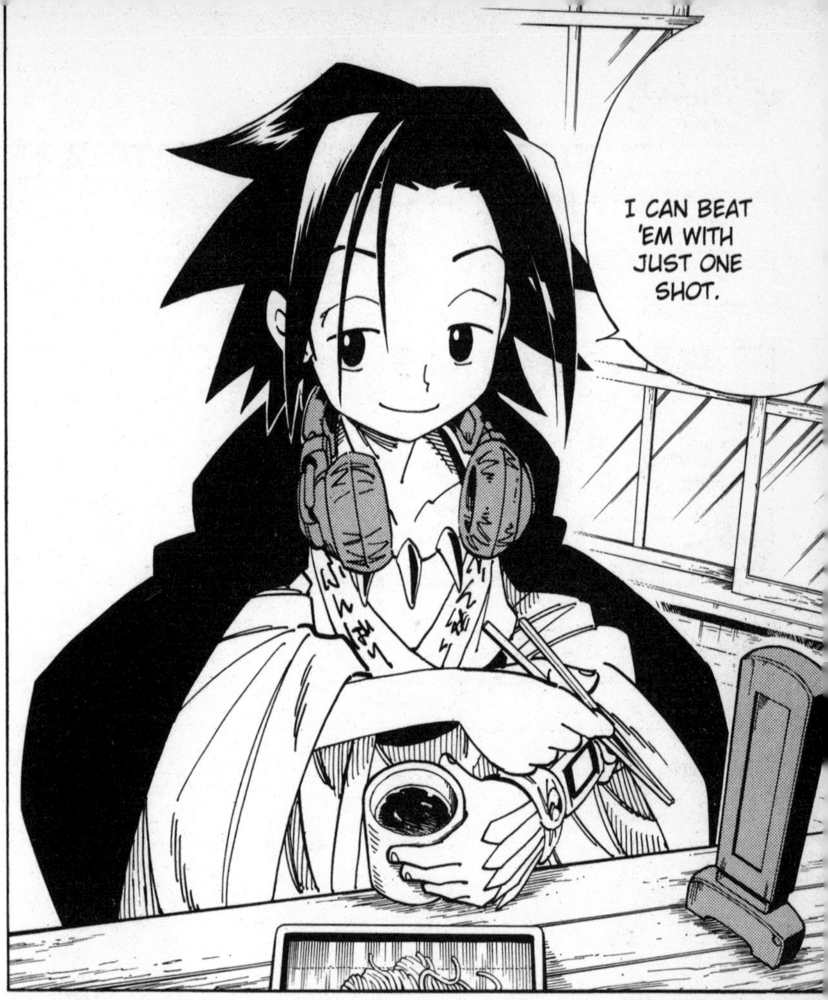
I CAN BEAT 'EM WITH JUST ONE SHOT.
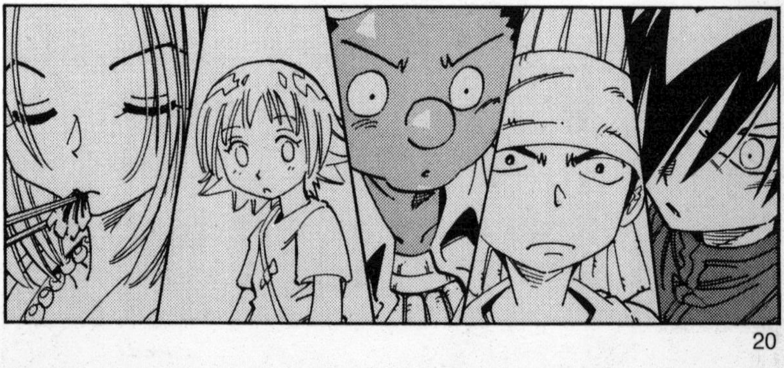

READ THIS WAY

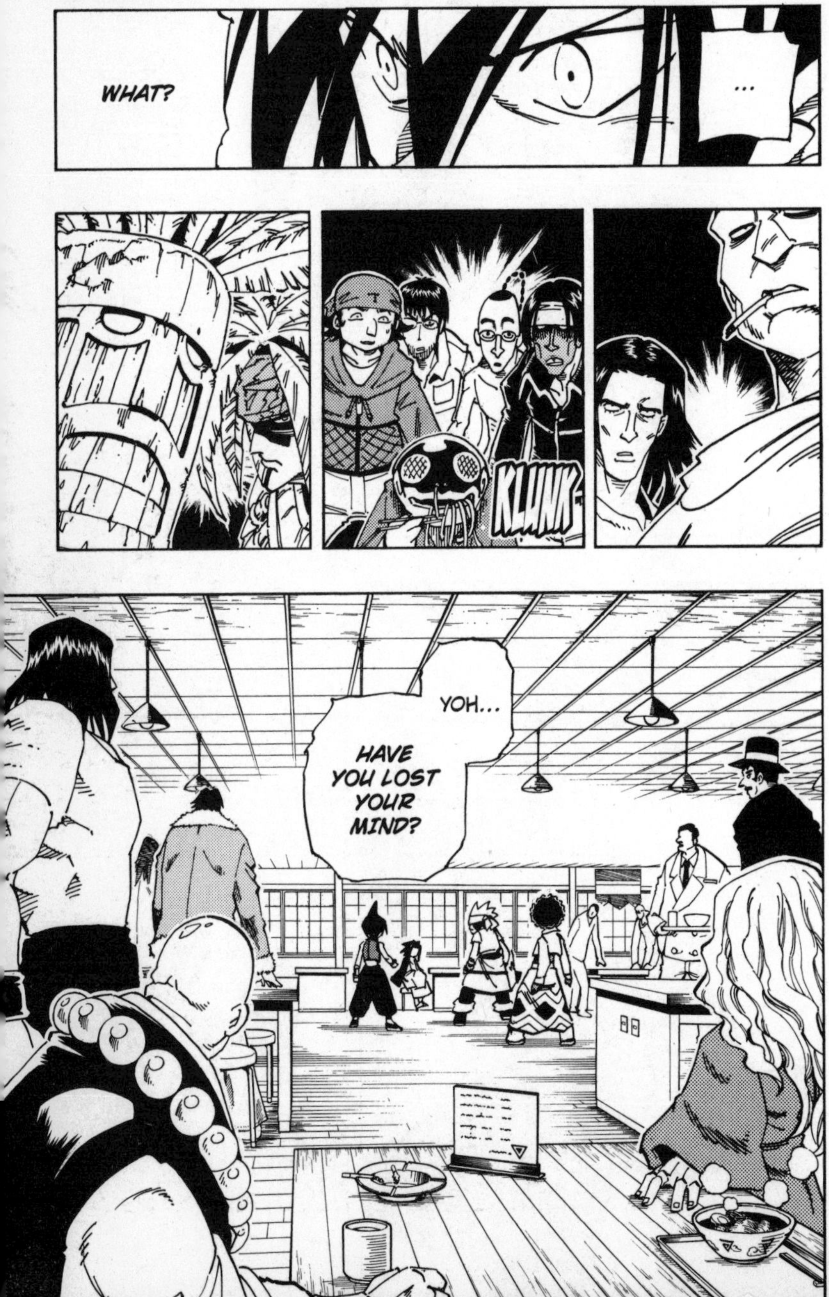
...
WHAT?
KLUNK
YOH...
HAVE YOU LOST YOUR MIND?

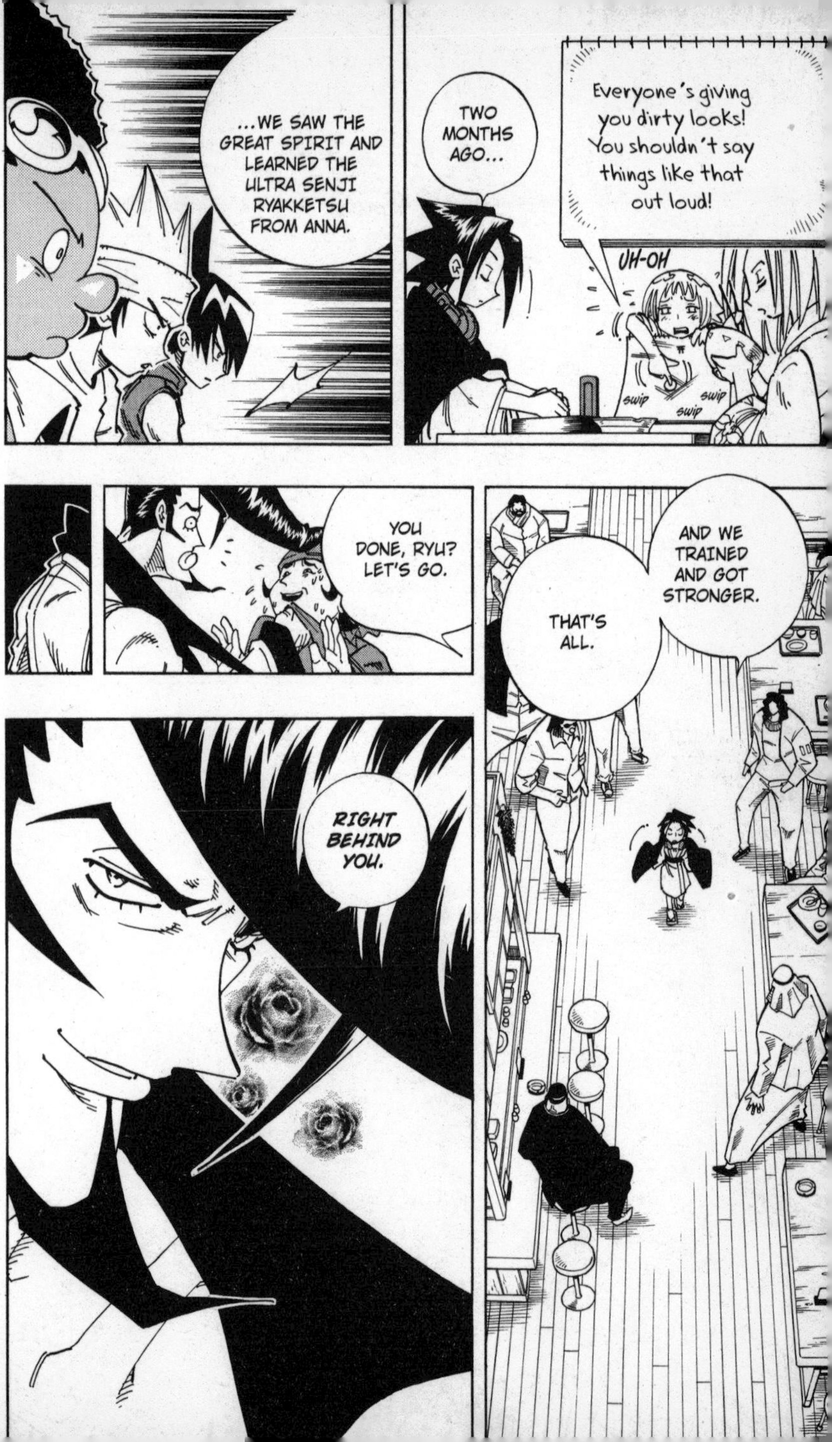
Everyone's giving you dirty looks! You shouldn't say things like that out loud!
TWO MONTHS AGO...
UH-OH
swip
swip
swip
...WE SAW THE GREAT SPIRIT AND LEARNED THE ULTRA SENJI RYAKKETSU FROM ANNA.
AND WE TRAINED AND GOT STRONGER.
THAT'S ALL.
YOU DONE, RYU? LET'S GO.
RIGHT BEHIND YOU.

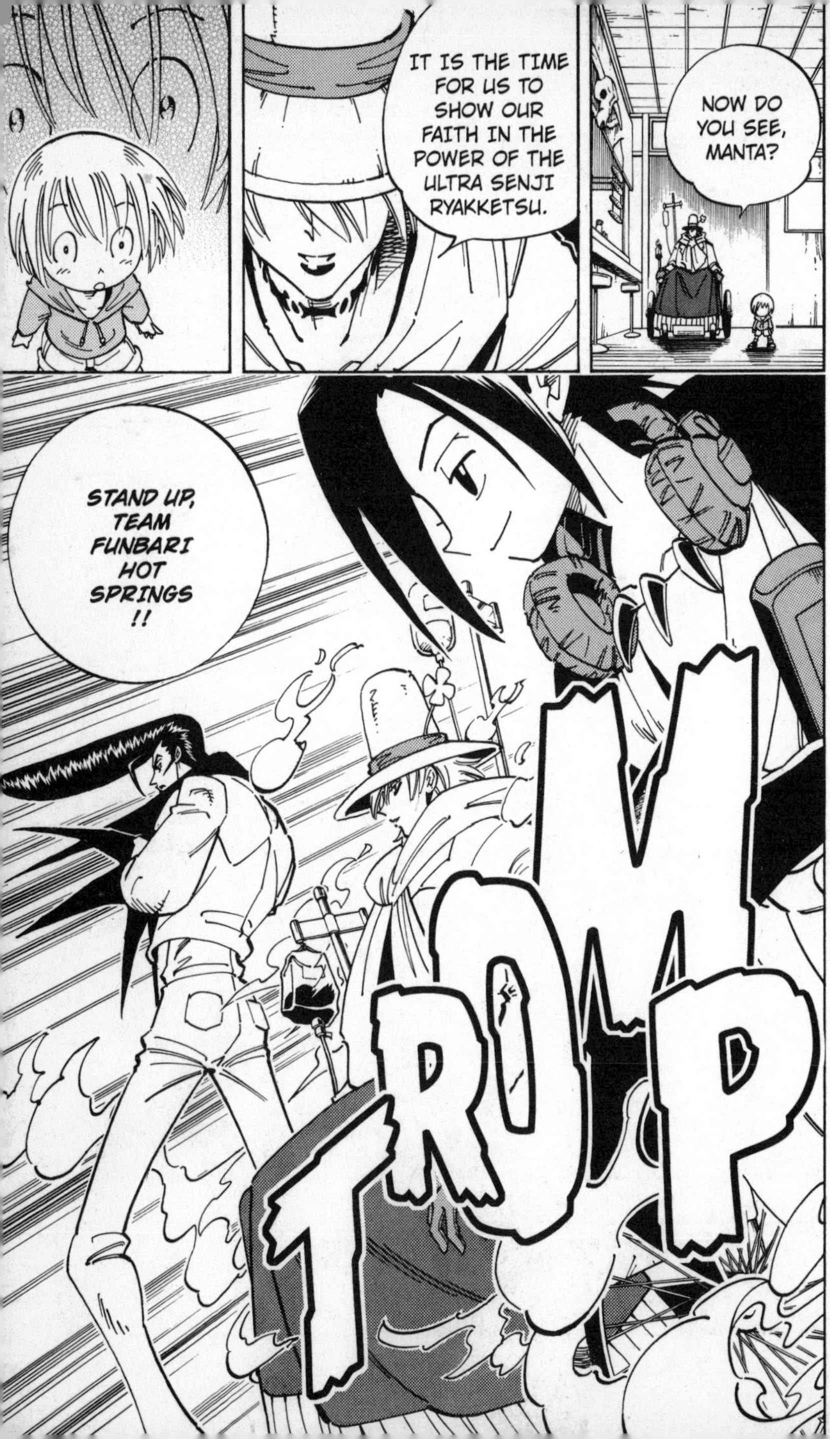
NOW DO YOU SEE, MANTA?
IT IS THE TIME FOR US TO SHOW OUR FAITH IN THE POWER OF THE ULTRA SENJI RYAKKETSU.
STAND UP, TEAM FUNBARI HOT SPRINGS !!
TROMP

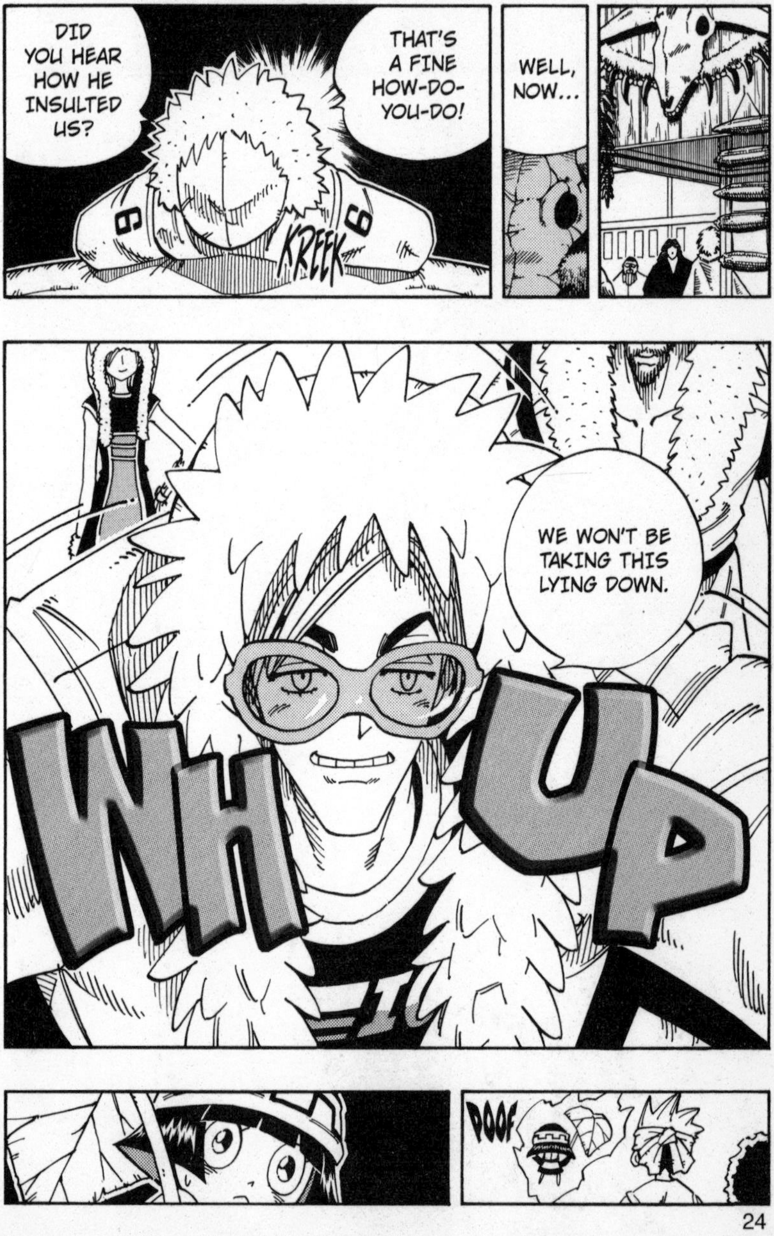
WELL, NOW...
THAT'S A FINE HOW-DO-YOU-DO!
DID YOU HEAR HOW HE INSULTED US?
KREEK
WE WON'T BE TAKING THIS LYING DOWN.
WHUP
POOF

Shaman King

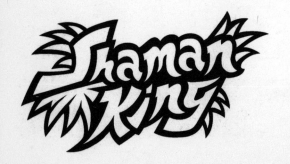

SHAMAN KING CHARACTER FILE No.70

ピノ
PINO

2001
(JULY)

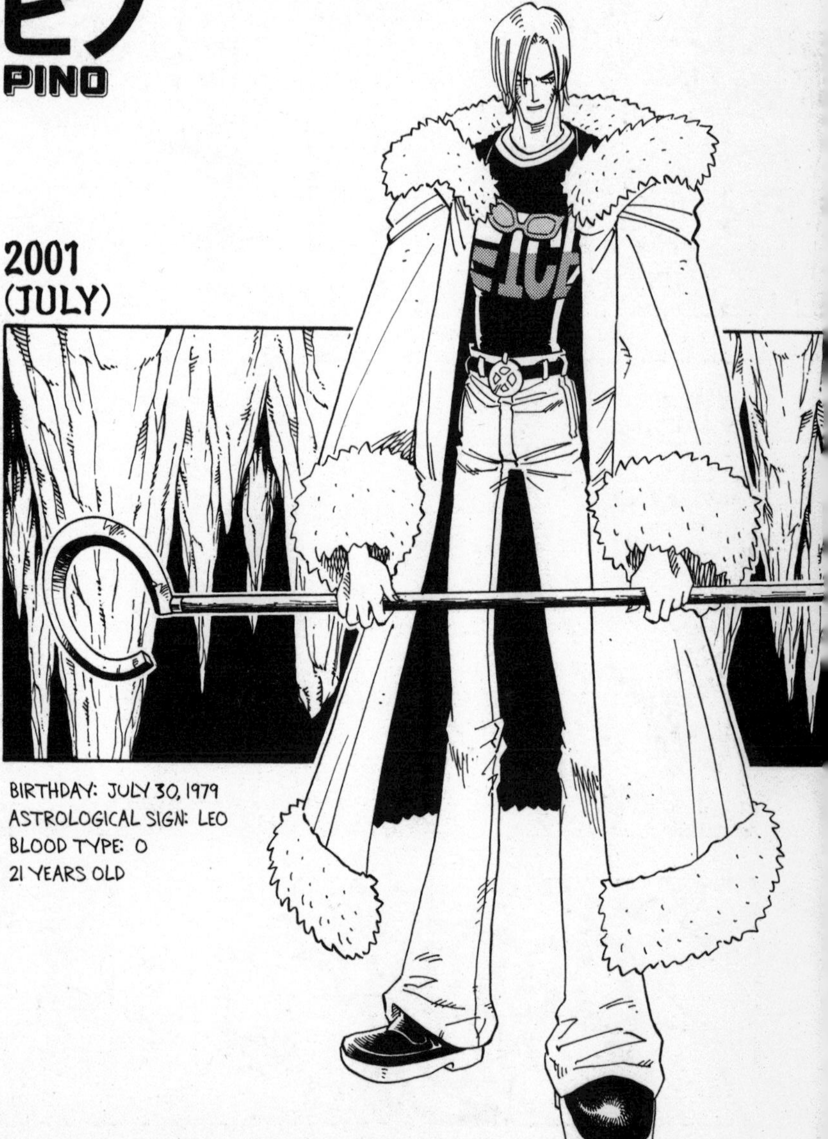

BIRTHDAY: JULY 30, 1979
ASTROLOGICAL SIGN: LEO
BLOOD TYPE: O
21 YEARS OLD

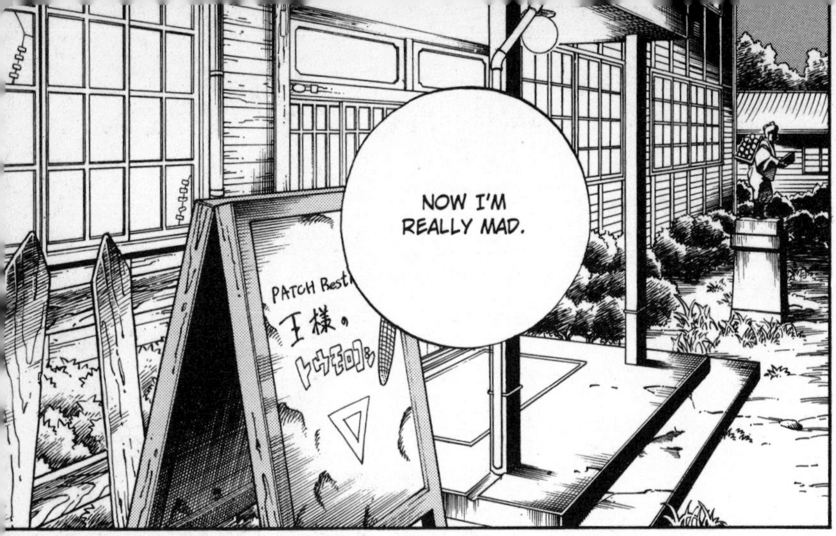
NOW I'M REALLY MAD.
PATCH Best
王様の
トウモロコシ

SIGN: CORN KING

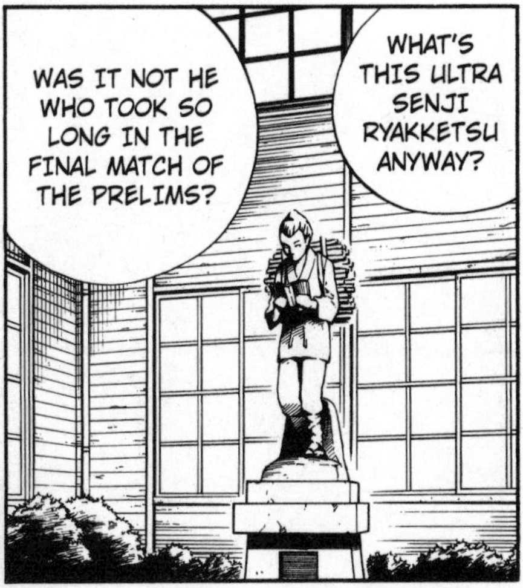
WHAT'S THIS ULTRA SENJI RYAKKETSU ANYWAY?
WAS IT NOT HE WHO TOOK SO LONG IN THE FINAL MATCH OF THE PRELIMS?

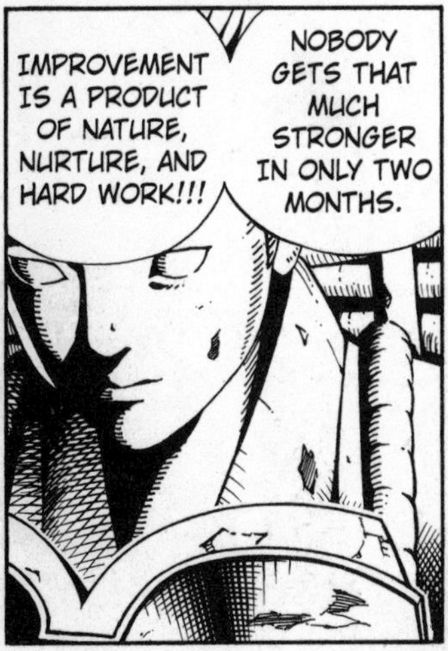
NOBODY GETS THAT MUCH STRONGER IN ONLY TWO MONTHS.
IMPROVEMENT IS A PRODUCT OF NATURE, NURTURE, AND HARD WORK!!!

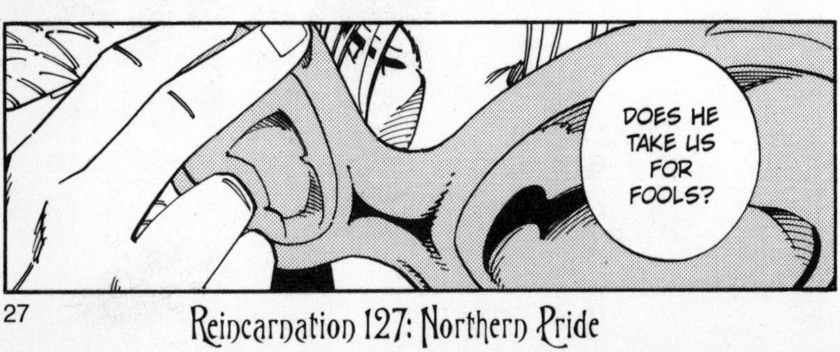
DOES HE TAKE US FOR FOOLS?

Reincarnation 127: Northern Pride

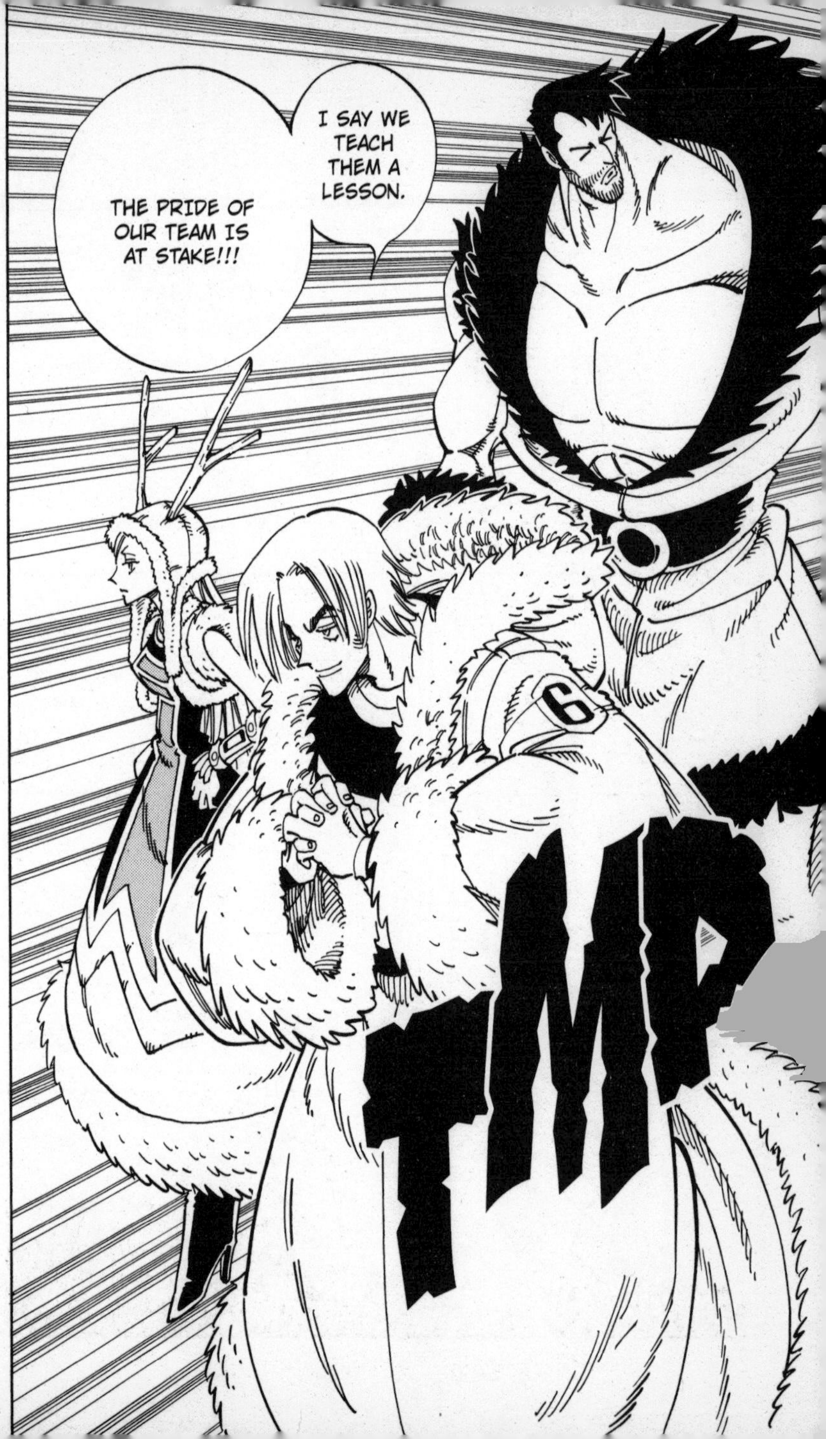
I SAY WE TEACH THEM A LESSON.
THE PRIDE OF OUR TEAM IS AT STAKE!!!
TMP

Reincarnation 127:
Northern Pride

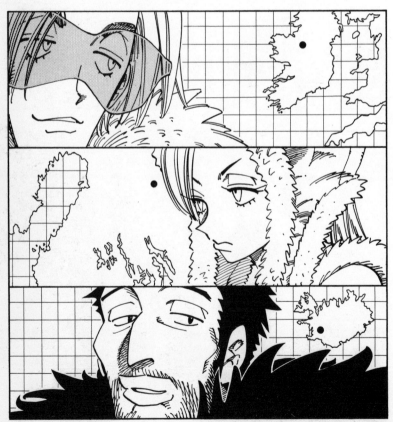

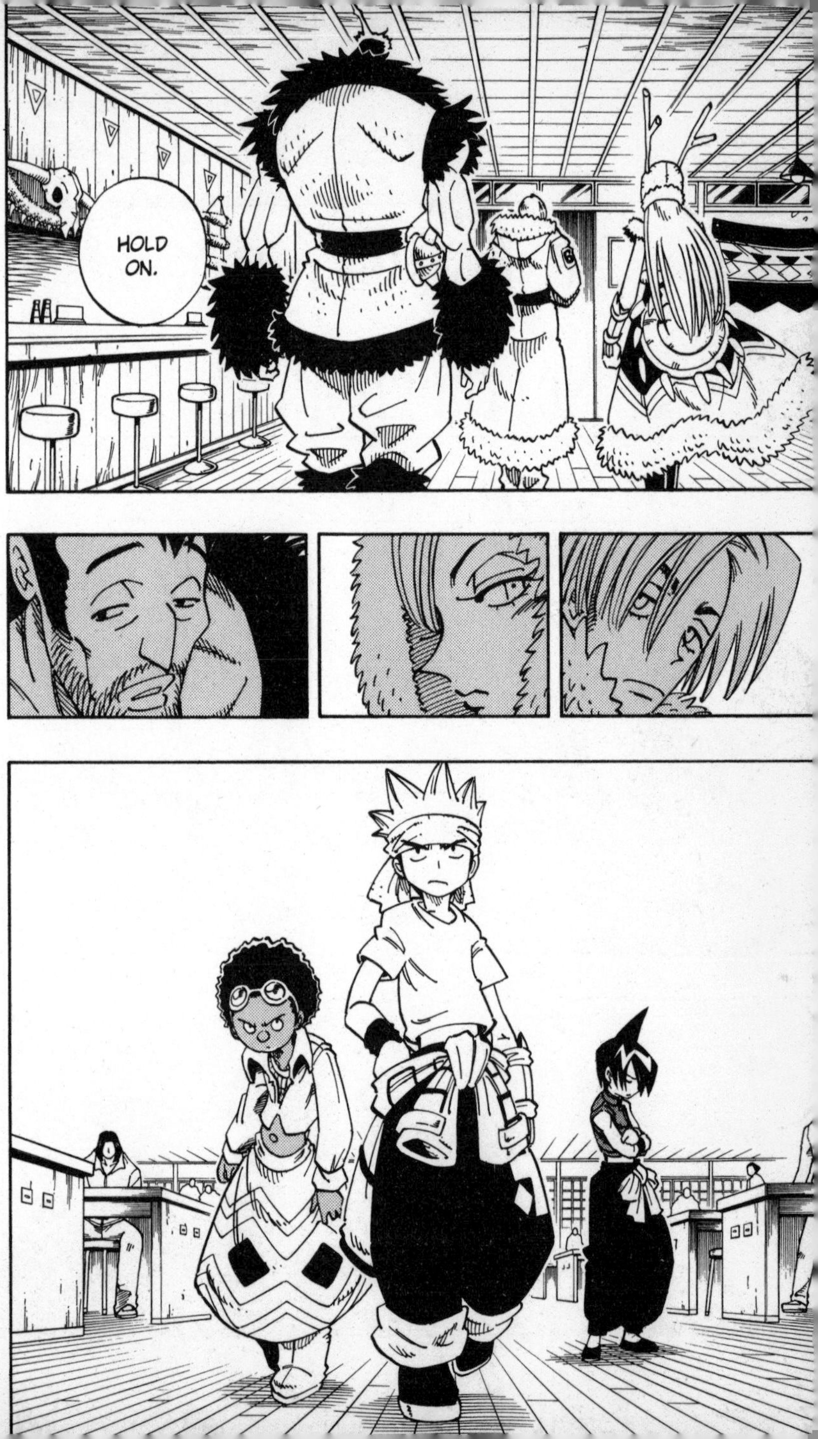
HOLD ON.

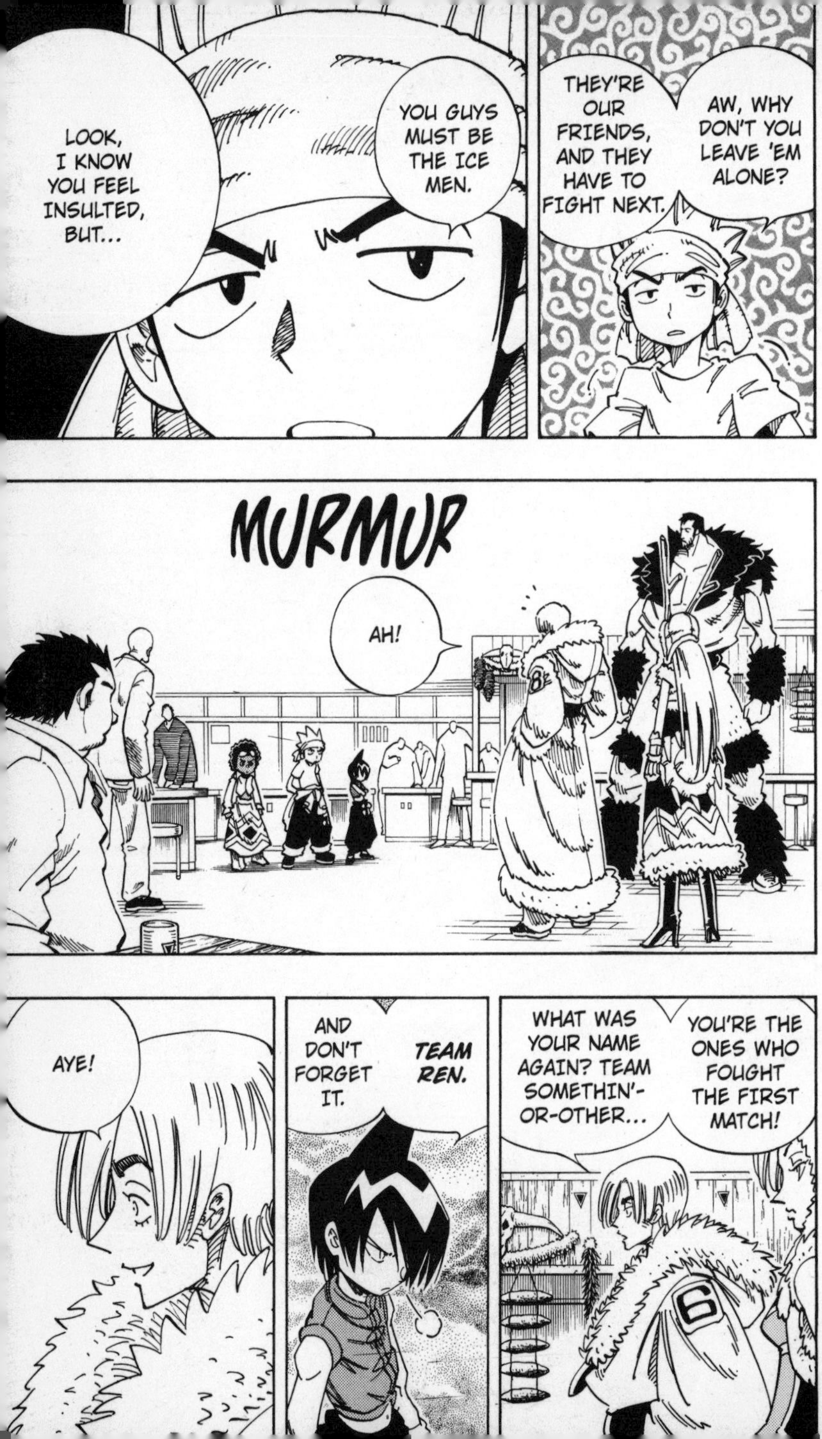
AW, WHY DON'T YOU LEAVE 'EM ALONE?
THEY'RE OUR FRIENDS, AND THEY HAVE TO FIGHT NEXT.
YOU GUYS MUST BE THE ICE MEN.
LOOK, I KNOW YOU FEEL INSULTED, BUT...
MURMUR
AH!
YOU'RE THE ONES WHO FOUGHT THE FIRST MATCH!
WHAT WAS YOUR NAME AGAIN? TEAM SOMETHIN'-OR-OTHER...
TEAM REN.
AND DON'T FORGET IT.
AYE!

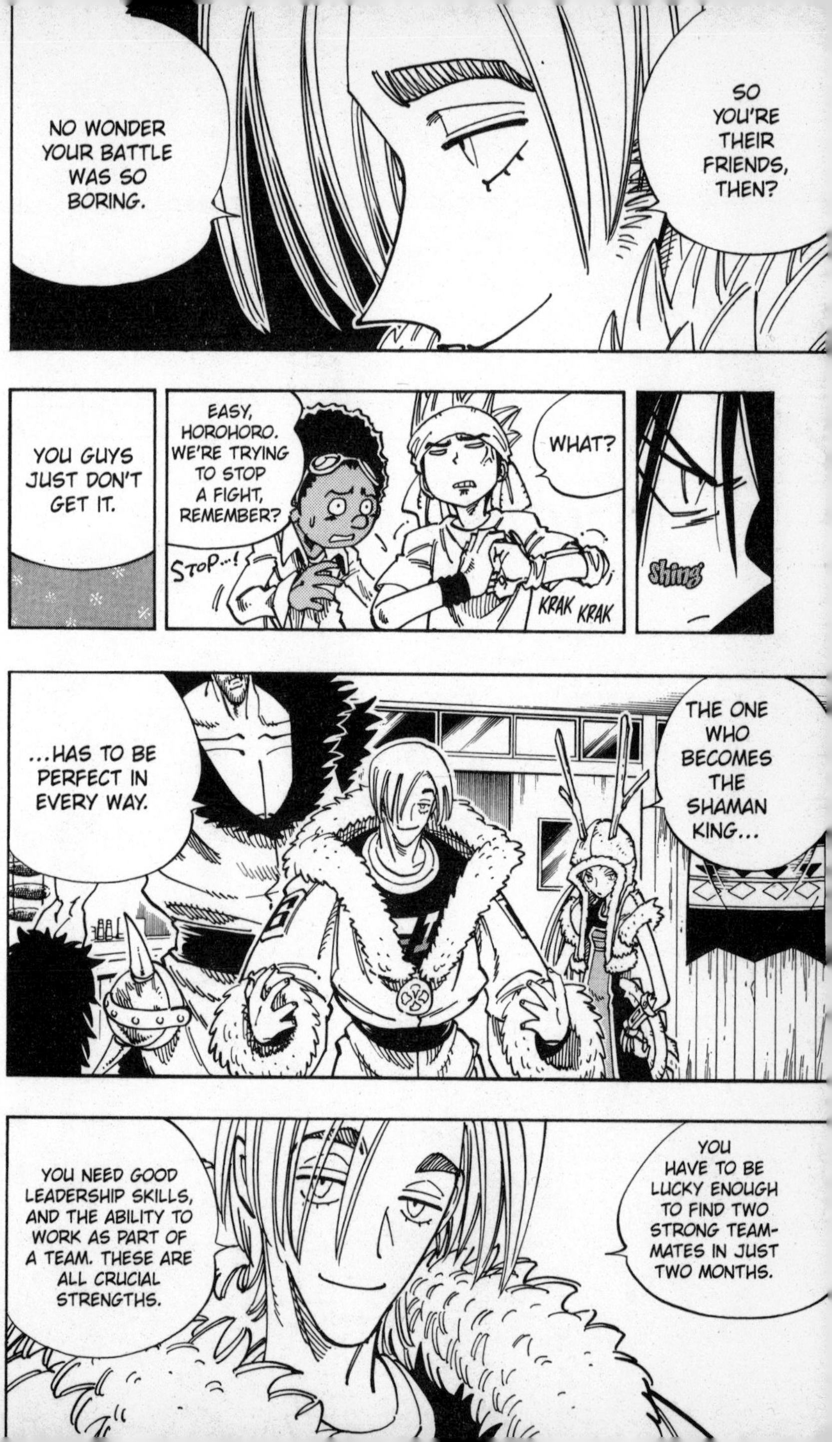
SO YOU'RE THEIR FRIENDS, THEN?
NO WONDER YOUR BATTLE WAS SO BORING.
Shing
WHAT?
EASY, HOROHORO. WE'RE TRYING TO STOP A FIGHT, REMEMBER?
KRAK KRAK
STOP...!
YOU GUYS JUST DON'T GET IT.
THE ONE WHO BECOMES THE SHAMAN KING...
...HAS TO BE PERFECT IN EVERY WAY.
YOU HAVE TO BE LUCKY ENOUGH TO FIND TWO STRONG TEAM-MATES IN JUST TWO MONTHS.
YOU NEED GOOD LEADERSHIP SKILLS, AND THE ABILITY TO WORK AS PART OF A TEAM. THESE ARE ALL CRUCIAL STRENGTHS.

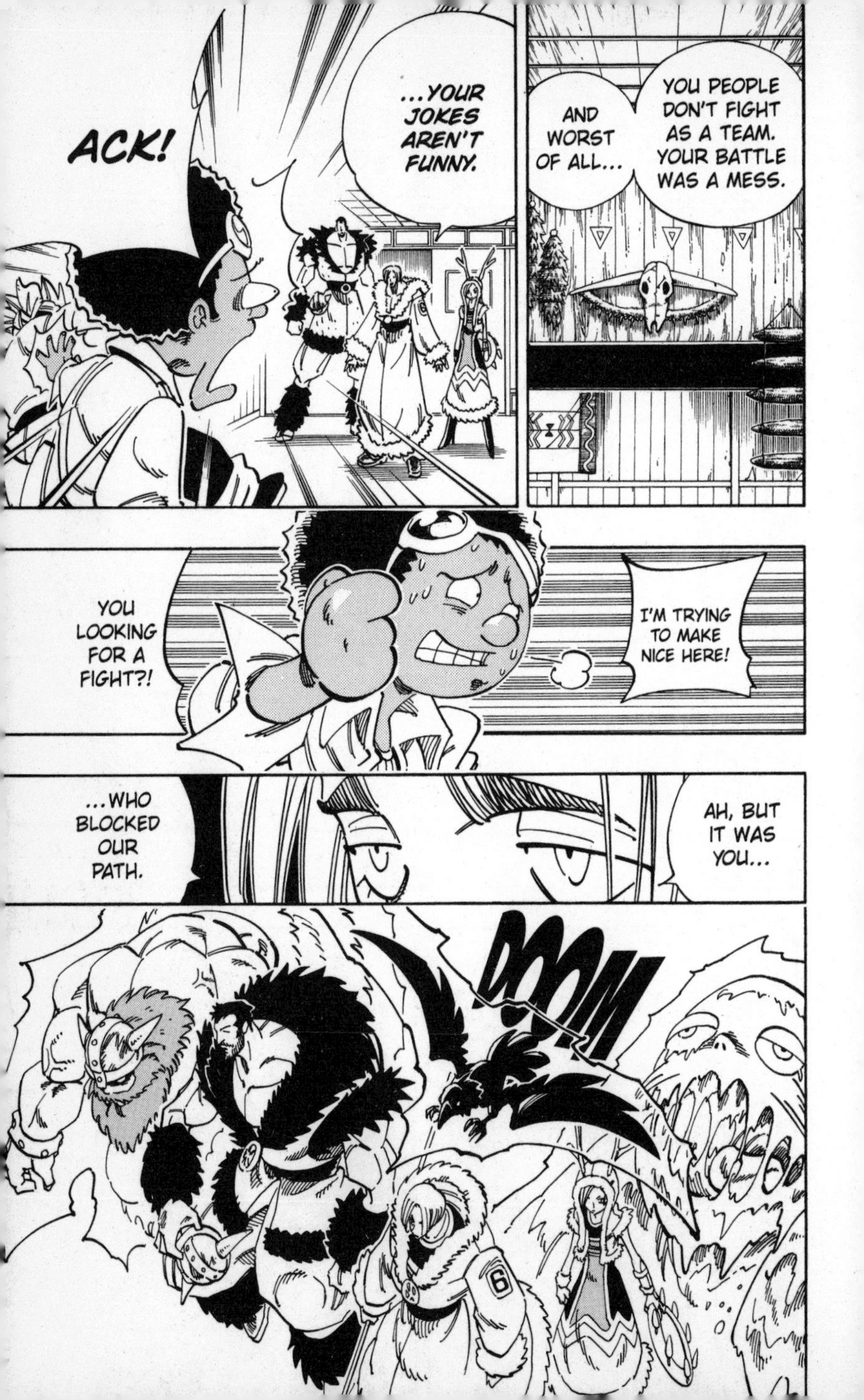
YOU PEOPLE DON'T FIGHT AS A TEAM. YOUR BATTLE WAS A MESS.
AND WORST OF ALL...
...YOUR JOKES AREN'T FUNNY.
ACK!
I'M TRYING TO MAKE NICE HERE!
YOU LOOKING FOR A FIGHT?!
AH, BUT IT WAS YOU...
...WHO BLOCKED OUR PATH.
DOOM

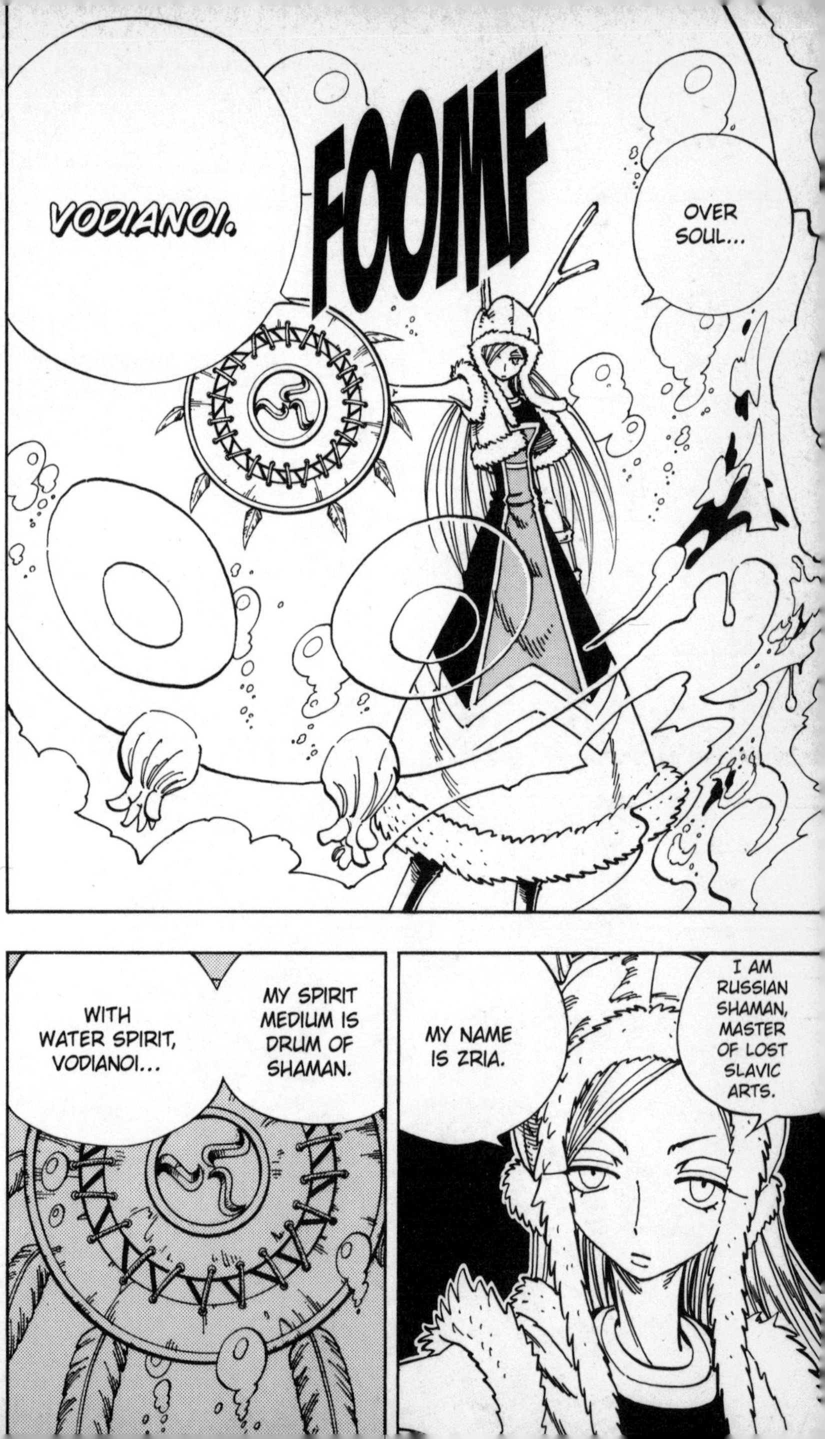
OVER SOUL...
FOOMF
VODIANOI.
I AM RUSSIAN SHAMAN, MASTER OF LOST SLAVIC ARTS.
MY NAME IS ZRIA.
MY SPIRIT MEDIUM IS DRUM OF SHAMAN.
WITH WATER SPIRIT, VODIANOI...

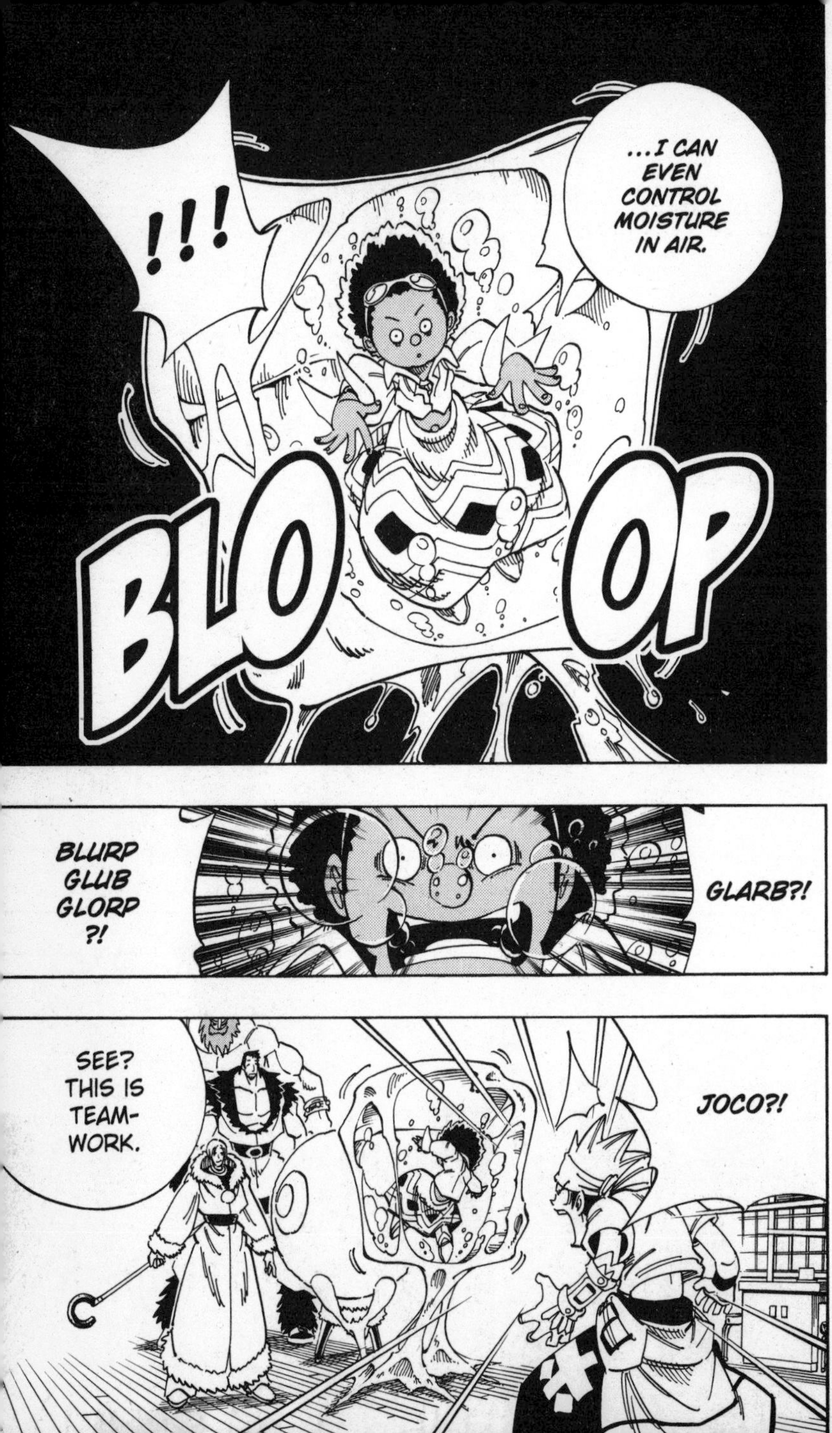
...I CAN EVEN CONTROL MOISTURE IN AIR.
!!!
BLOOP
GLARB?!
BLURP GLUB GLORP ?!
JOCO?!
SEE? THIS IS TEAM-WORK.

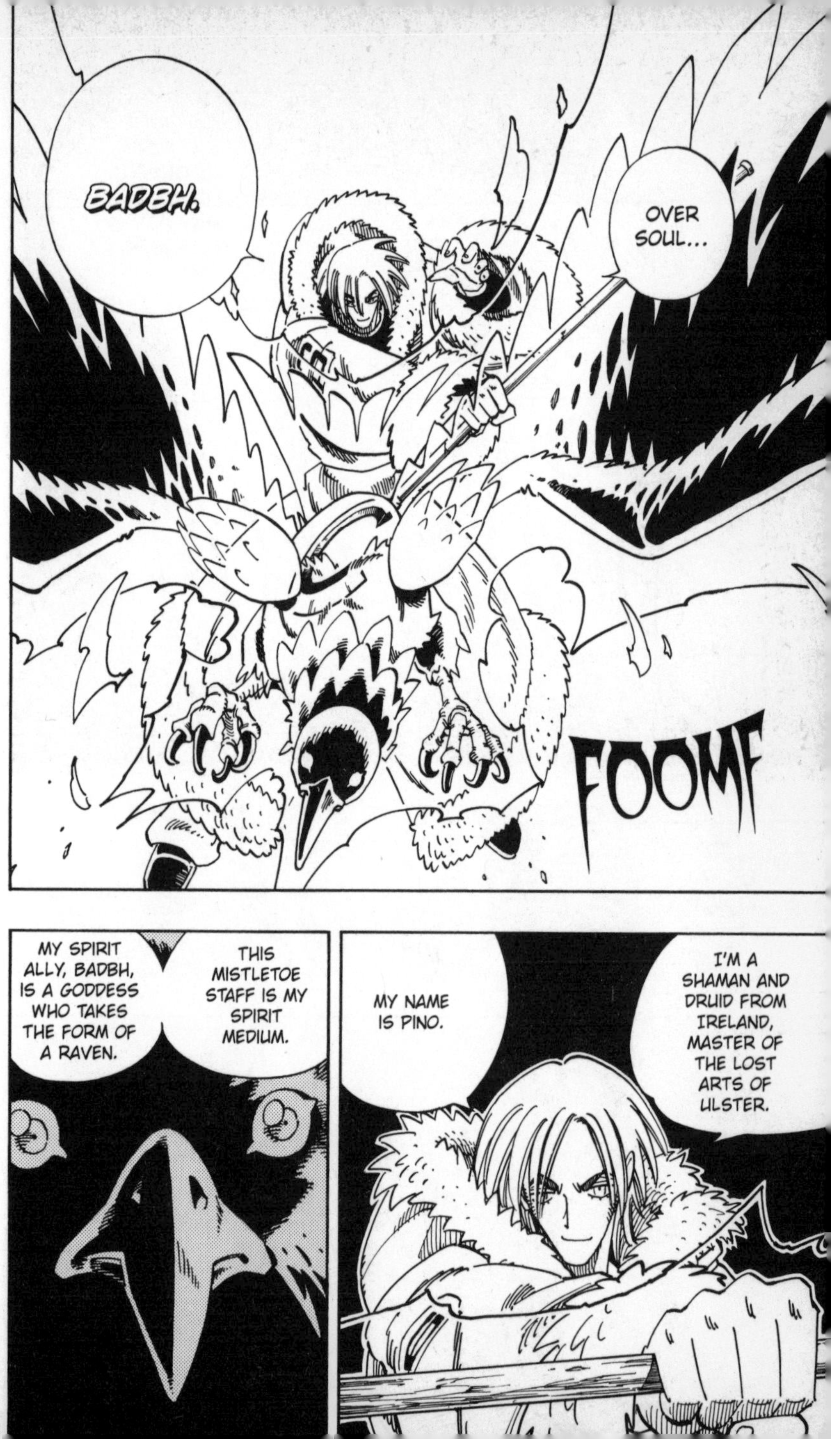
OVER SOUL...
BADBH.
FOOMF
I'M A SHAMAN AND DRUID FROM IRELAND, MASTER OF THE LOST ARTS OF ULSTER.
MY NAME IS PINO.
THIS MISTLETOE STAFF IS MY SPIRIT MEDIUM.
MY SPIRIT ALLY, BADBH, IS A GODDESS WHO TAKES THE FORM OF A RAVEN.

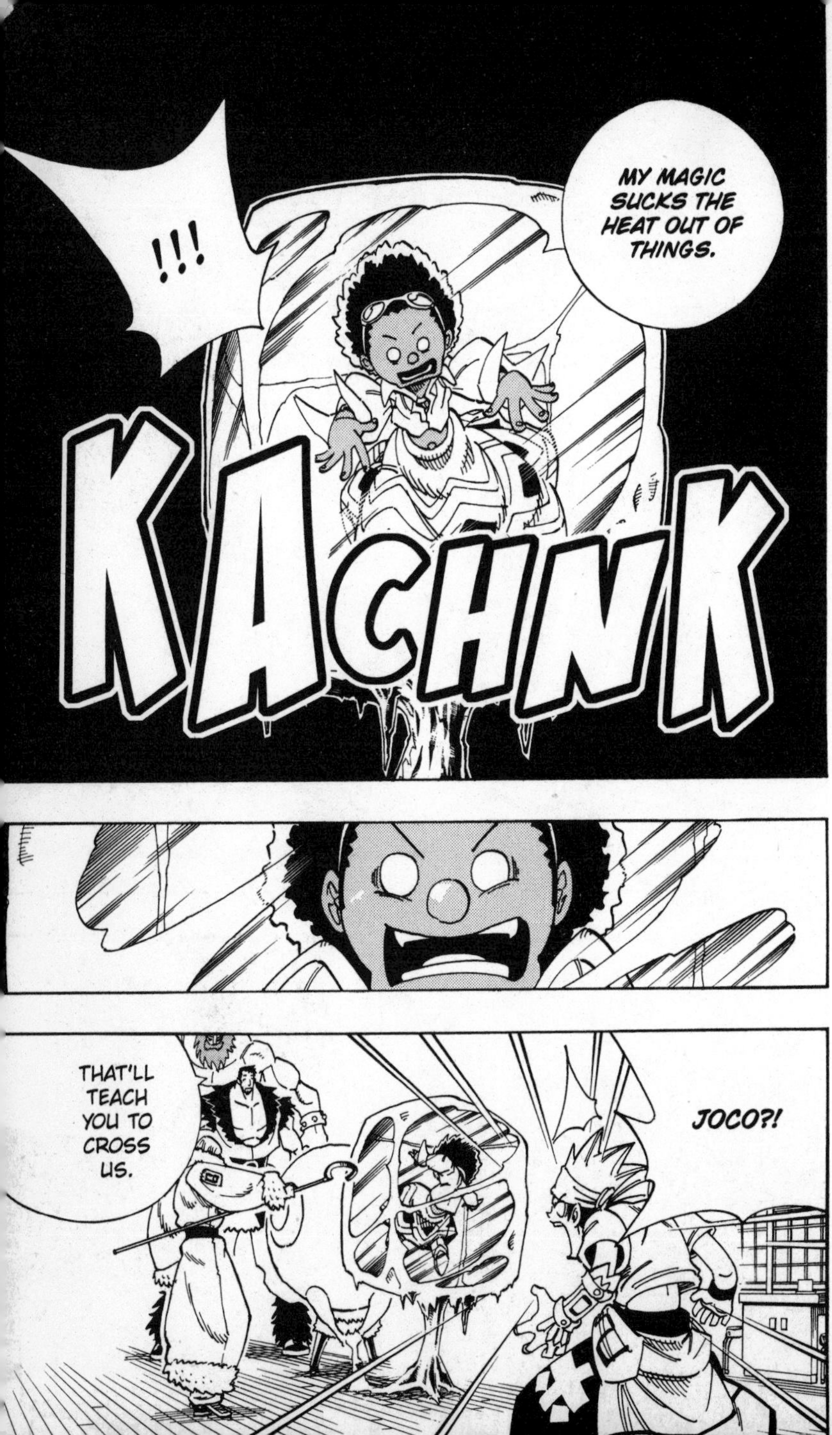
MY MAGIC SUCKS THE HEAT OUT OF THINGS.
!!!
KACHNK
JOCO?!
THAT'LL TEACH YOU TO CROSS US.

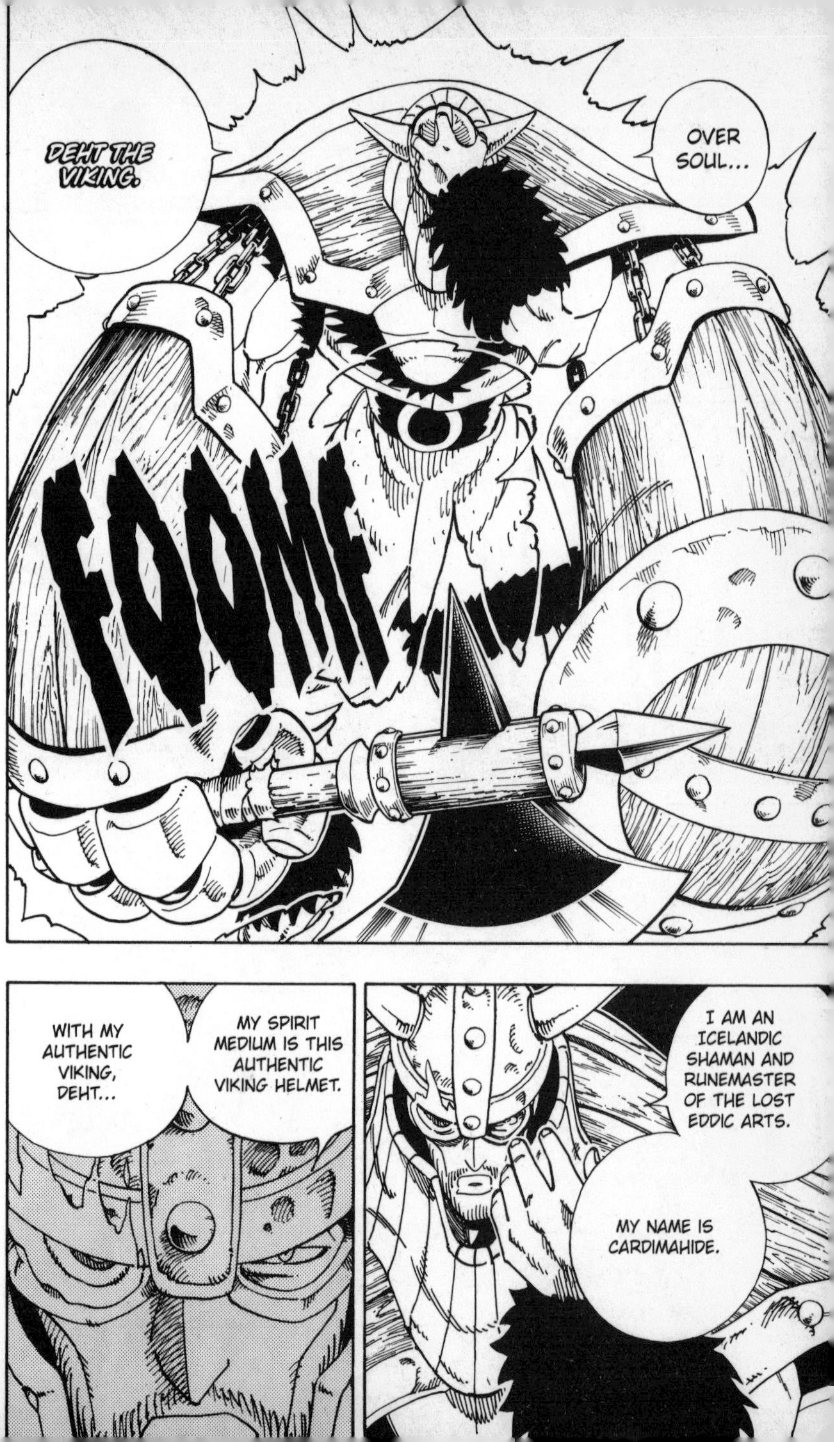
OVER SOUL...
DEHT THE VIKING.
FOOMF
I AM AN ICELANDIC SHAMAN AND RUNEMASTER OF THE LOST EDDIC ARTS.
MY NAME IS CARDIMAHIDE.
MY SPIRIT MEDIUM IS THIS AUTHENTIC VIKING HELMET.
WITH MY AUTHENTIC VIKING, DEHT...

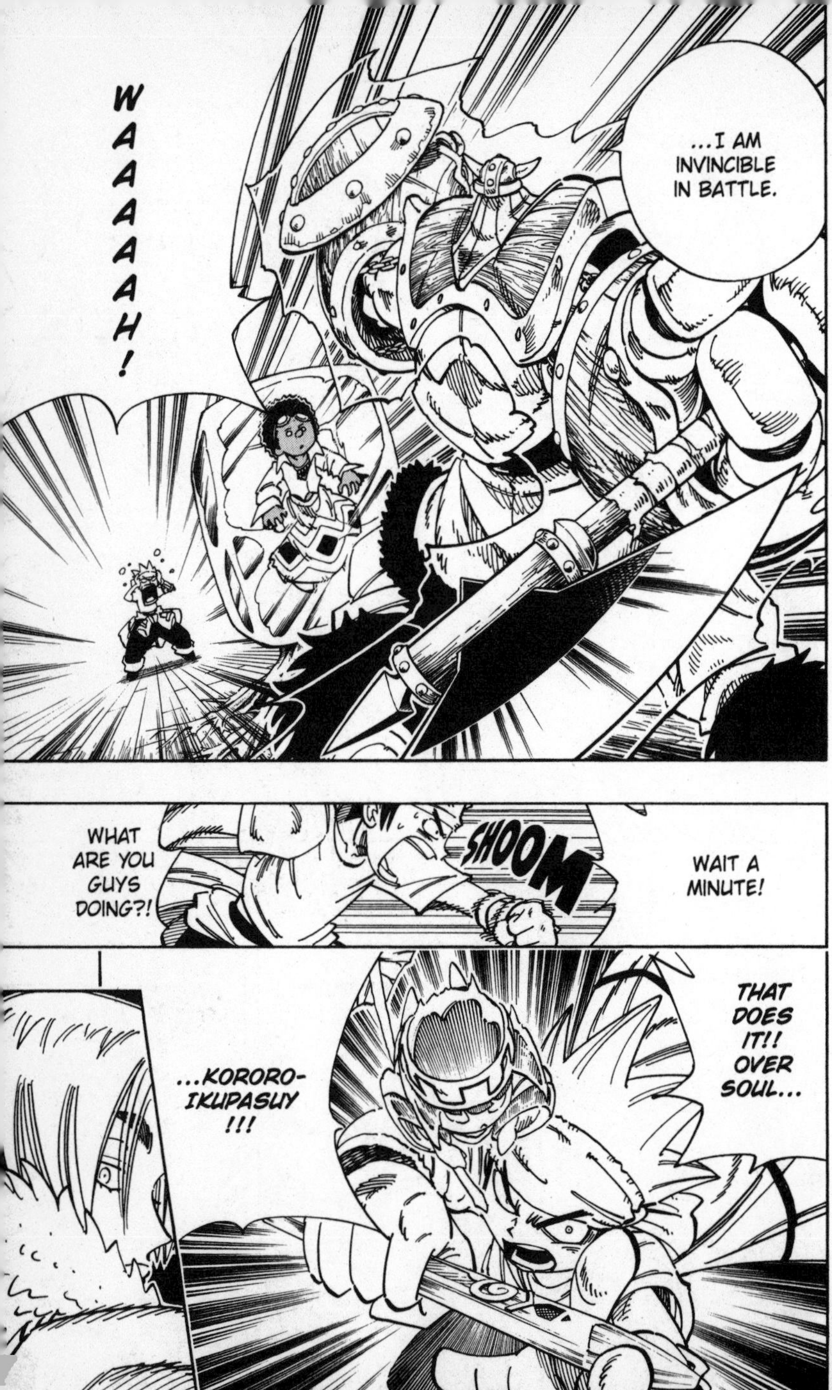
...I AM INVINCIBLE IN BATTLE.
WAAAAAH!
WAIT A MINUTE!
SHOOM
WHAT ARE YOU GUYS DOING?!
THAT DOES IT!! OVER SOUL...
...KORORO-IKUPASUY!!!

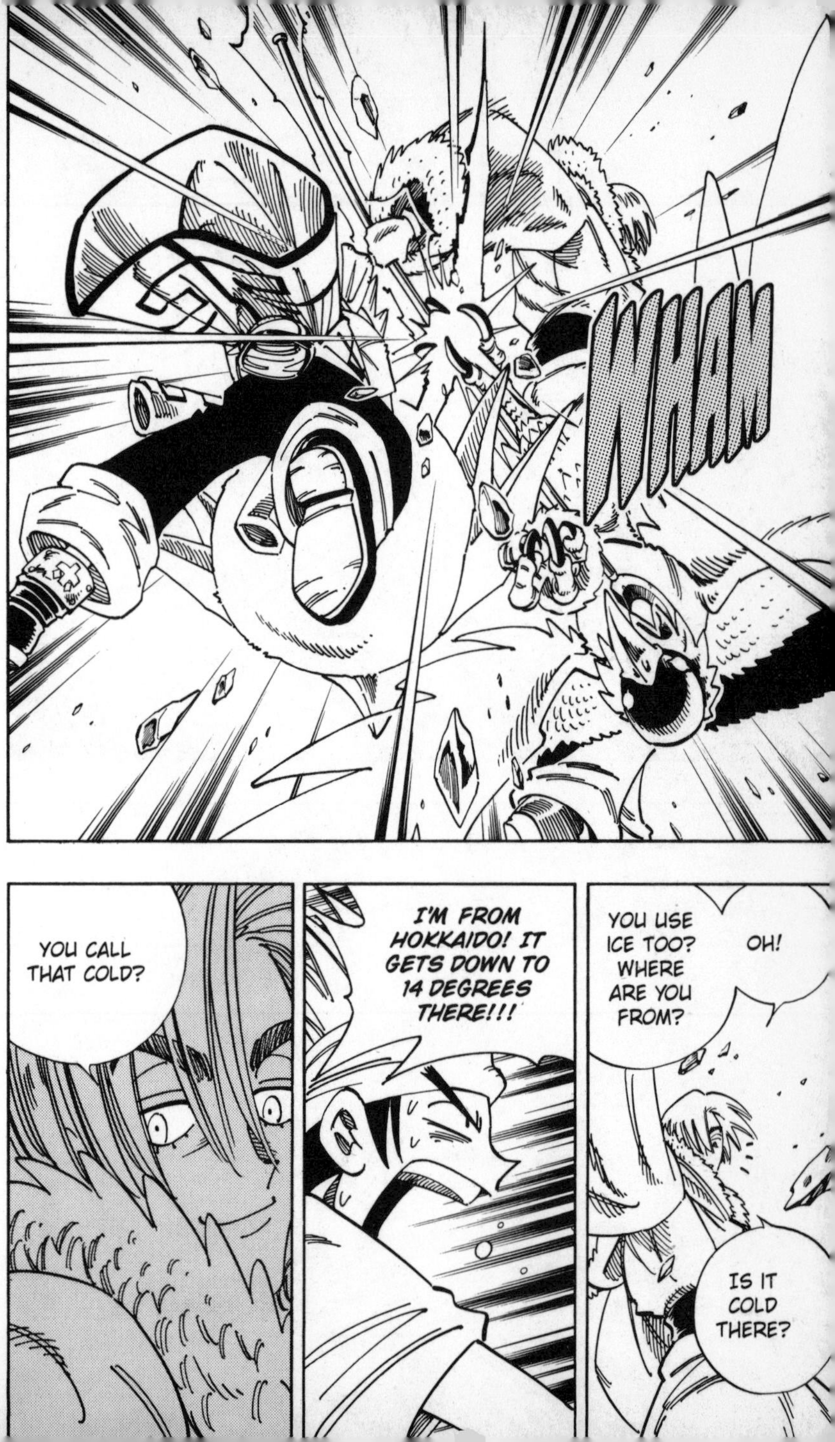
WHAM
OH!
YOU USE ICE TOO? WHERE ARE YOU FROM?
IS IT COLD THERE?
I'M FROM HOKKAIDO! IT GETS DOWN TO 14 DEGREES THERE!!!
YOU CALL THAT COLD?

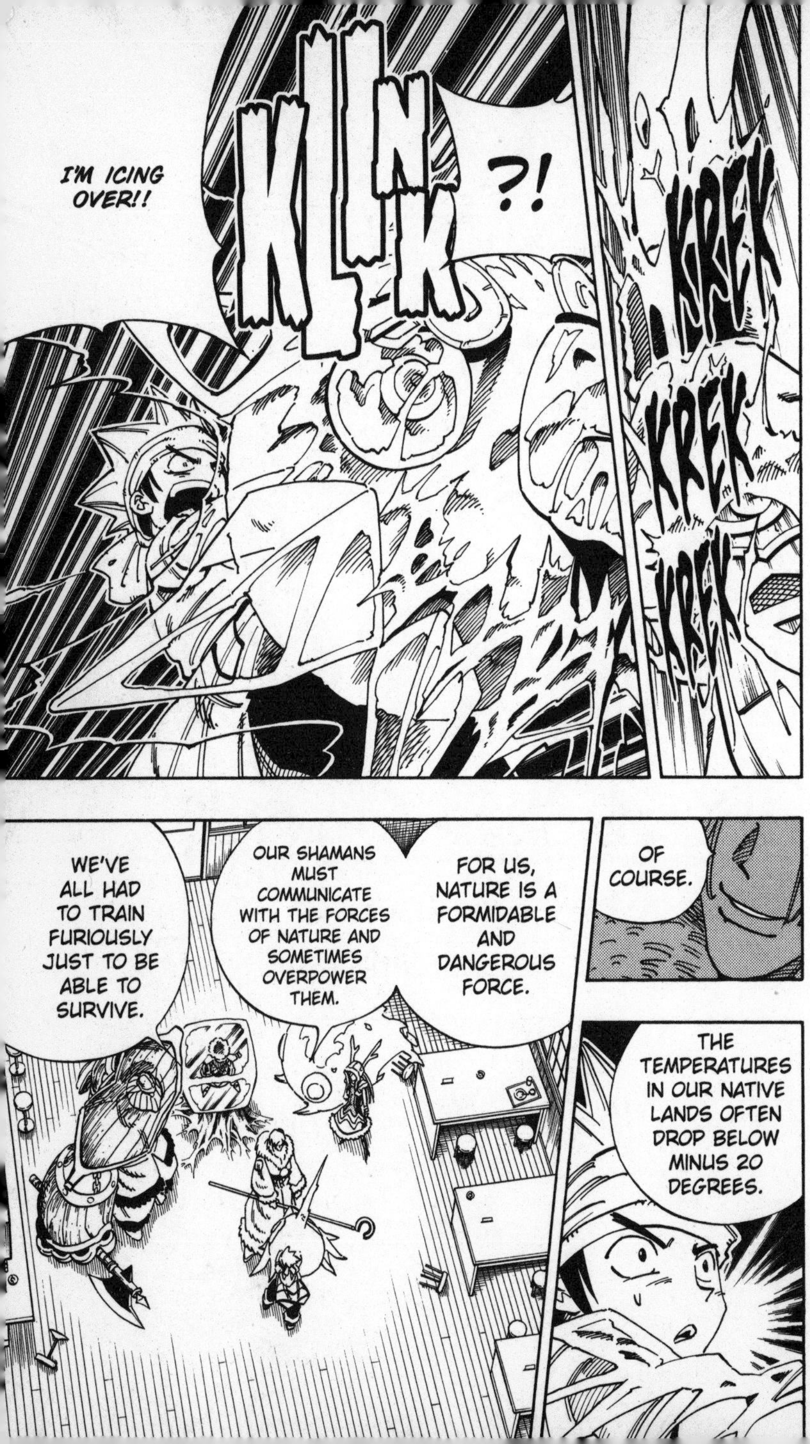
KREK
KREK
KREK
?!
KLINK
I'M ICING OVER!!
OF COURSE.
THE TEMPERATURES IN OUR NATIVE LANDS OFTEN DROP BELOW MINUS 20 DEGREES.
FOR US, NATURE IS A FORMIDABLE AND DANGEROUS FORCE.
OUR SHAMANS MUST COMMUNICATE WITH THE FORCES OF NATURE AND SOMETIMES OVERPOWER THEM.
WE'VE ALL HAD TO TRAIN FURIOUSLY JUST TO BE ABLE TO SURVIVE.

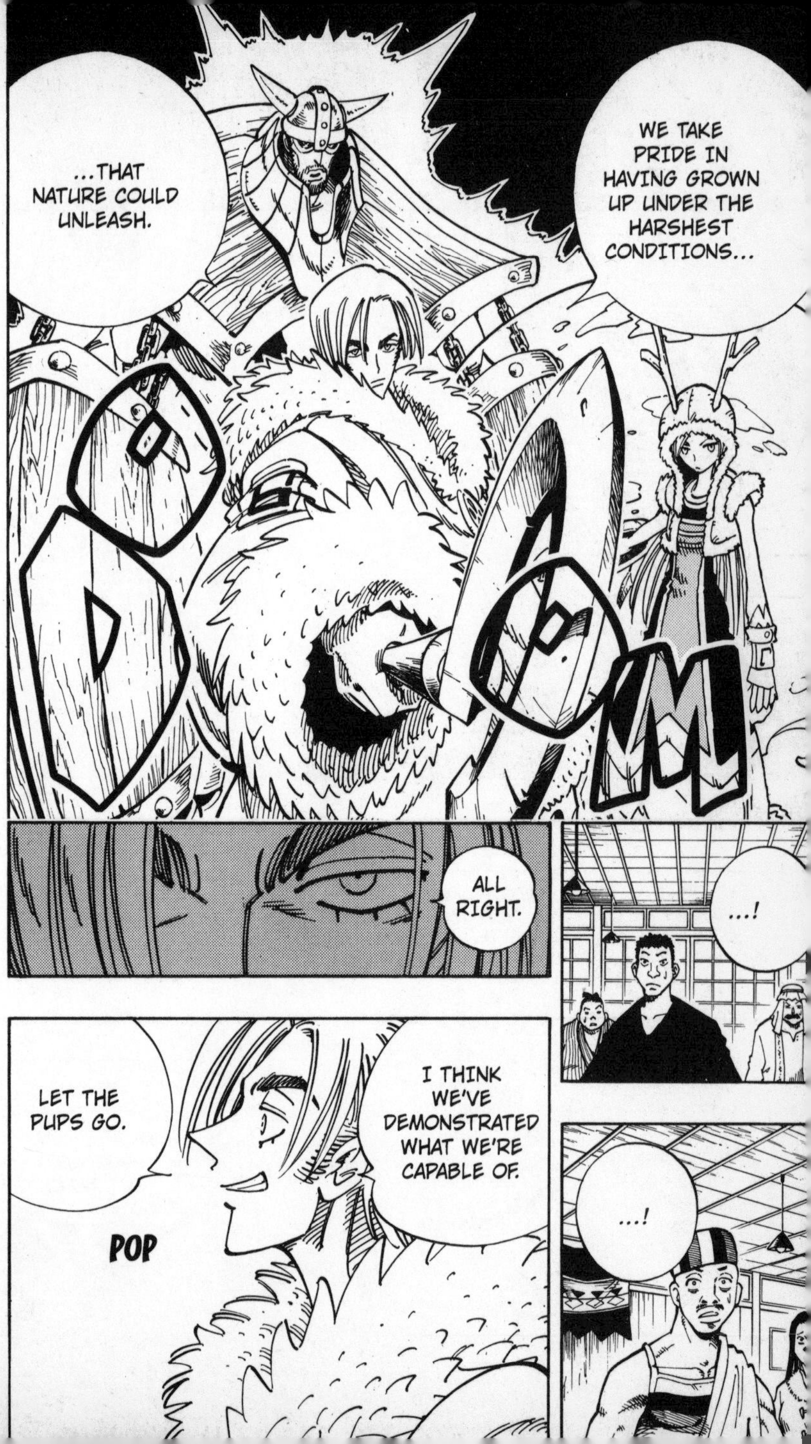
WE TAKE PRIDE IN HAVING GROWN UP UNDER THE HARSHEST CONDITIONS...
...THAT NATURE COULD UNLEASH.
DOOM
...!
ALL RIGHT.
...!
I THINK WE'VE DEMONSTRATED WHAT WE'RE CAPABLE OF.
LET THE PUPS GO.
POP

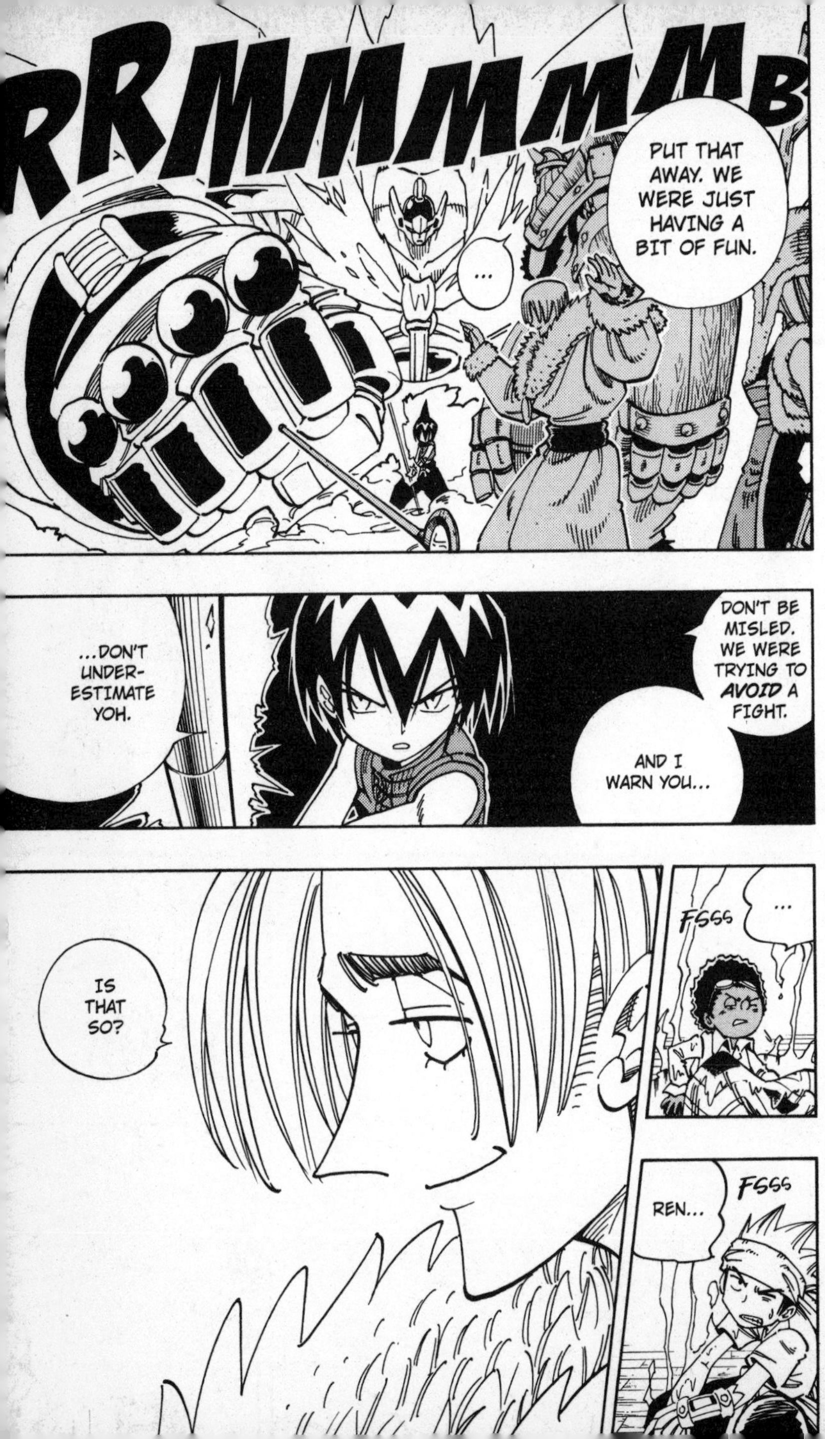
RRMMMMMMB
PUT THAT AWAY. WE WERE JUST HAVING A BIT OF FUN.
...
DON'T BE MISLED. WE WERE TRYING TO **AVOID** A FIGHT.
AND I WARN YOU...
...DON'T UNDER-ESTIMATE YOH.
...
FSSS
REN...
FSSS
IS THAT SO?

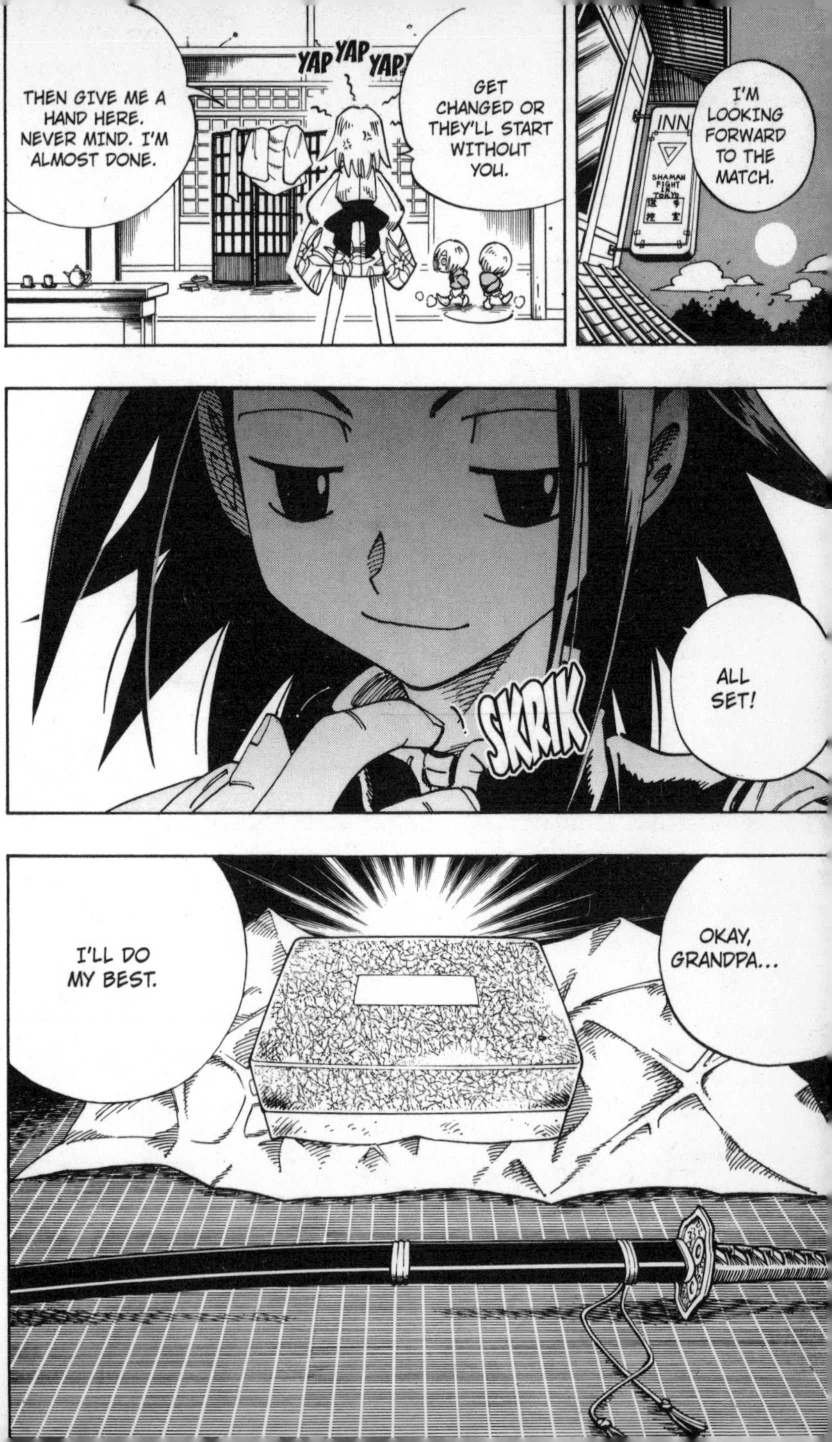
INN
I'M LOOKING FORWARD TO THE MATCH.
GET CHANGED OR THEY'LL START WITHOUT YOU.
YAP YAP YAP
THEN GIVE ME A HAND HERE. NEVER MIND. I'M ALMOST DONE.
ALL SET!
SKRIK
OKAY, GRANDPA...
I'LL DO MY BEST.

Shaman King

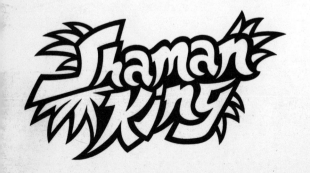

SHAMAN KING CHARACTER FILE No.71

バズヴ
BADBH

2001
(JULY)

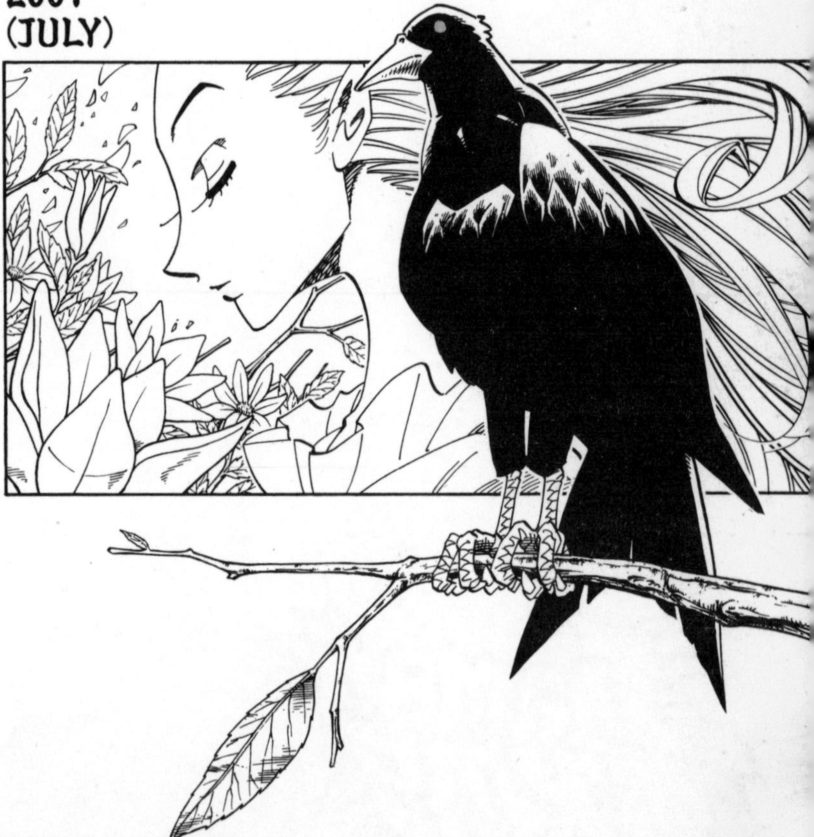

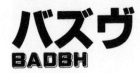

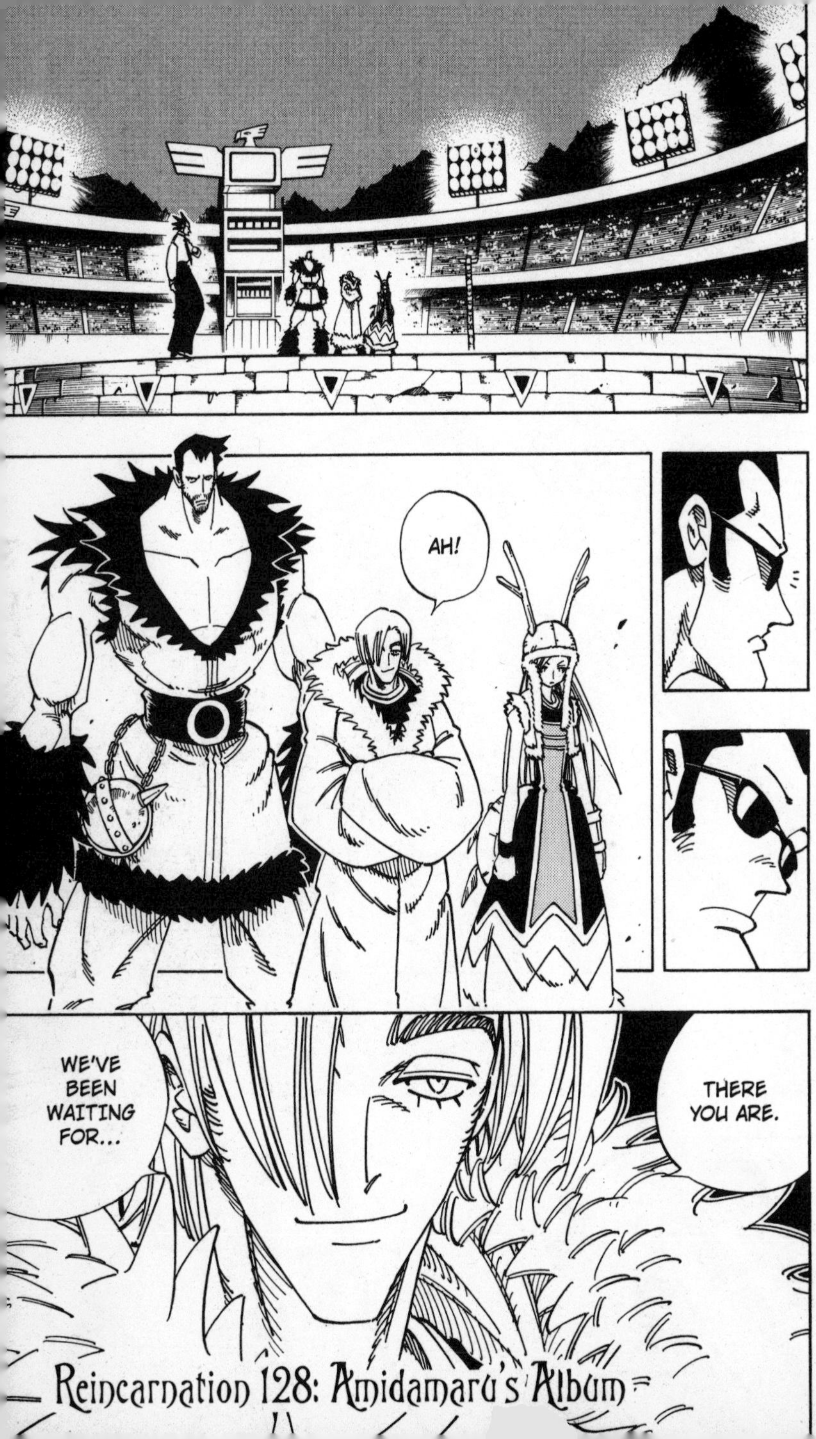
AH!
THERE YOU ARE.
WE'VE BEEN WAITING FOR...

Reincarnation 128: Amidamaru's Album

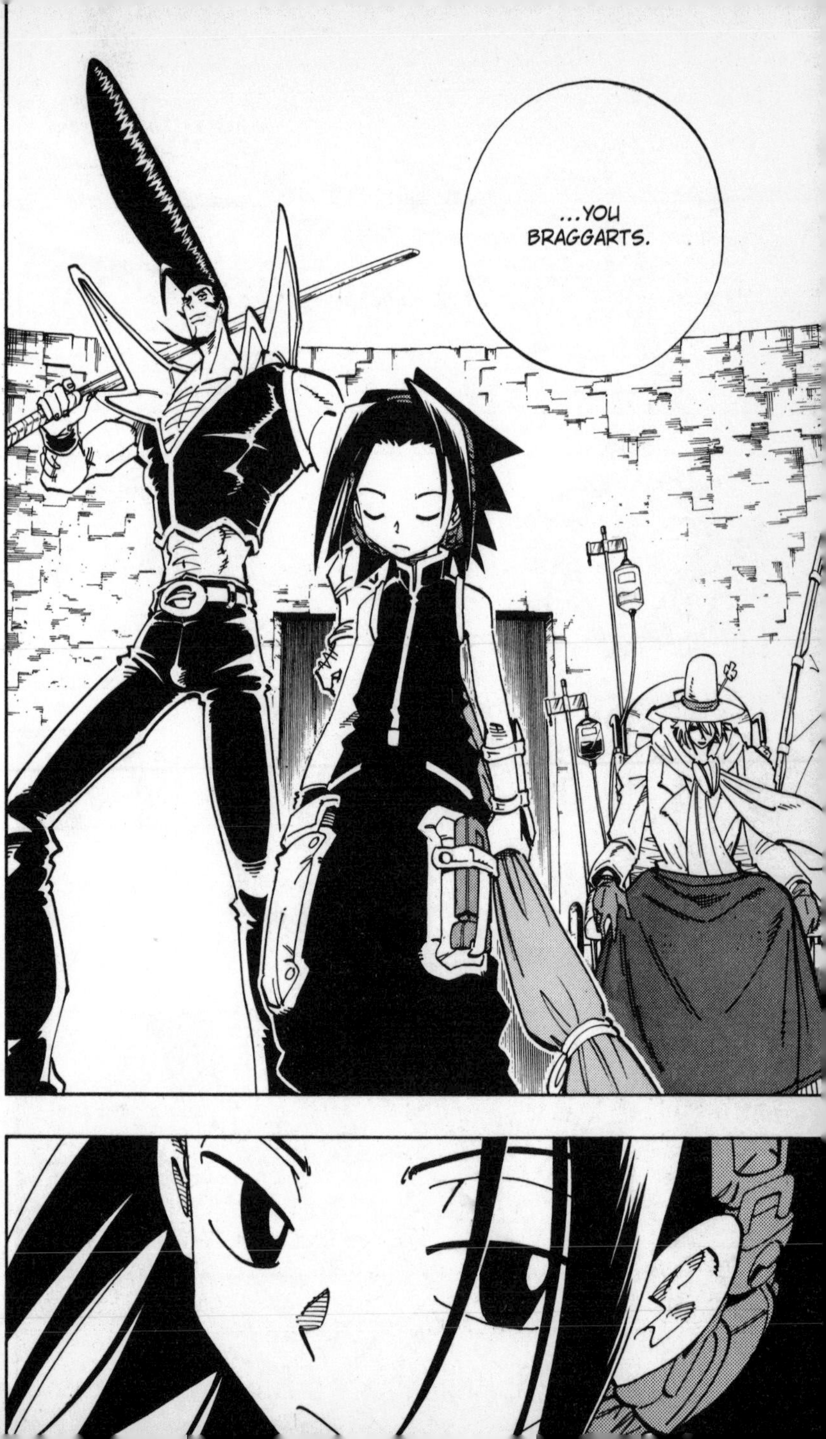
...YOU BRAGGARTS.

Reincarnation 128:
Amidamaru's Album

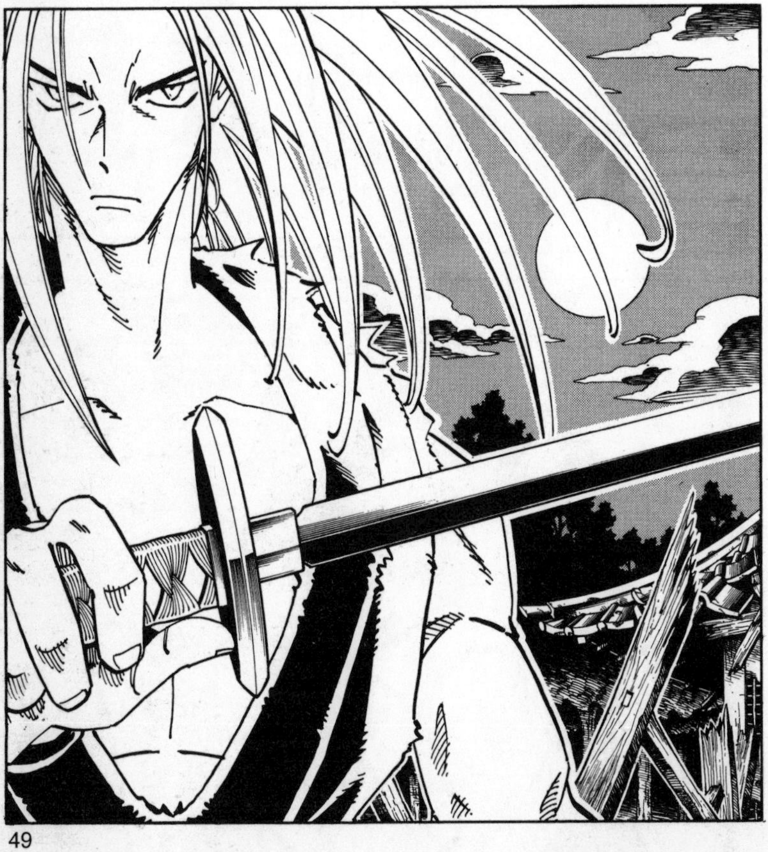

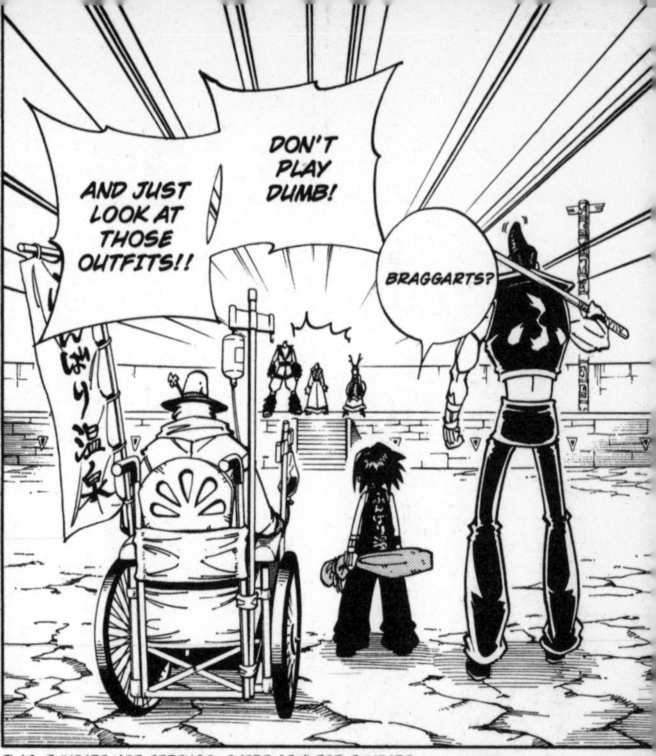
BRAGGARTS?
DON'T PLAY DUMB!
AND JUST LOOK AT THOSE OUTFITS!!
FLAG: FUNBARI HOT SPRINGS. SHIRT: "FU" FOR FUNBARI

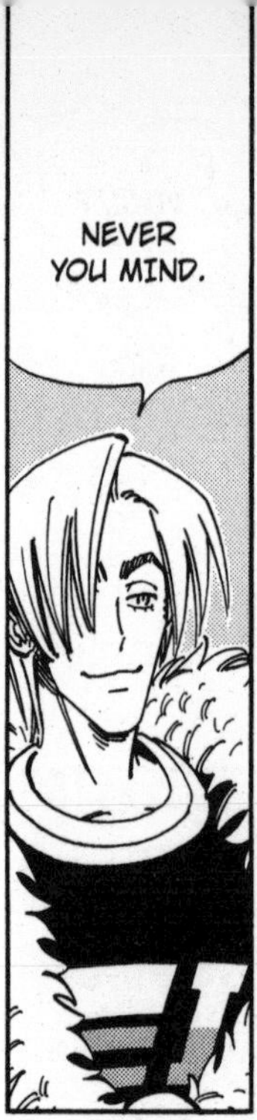
NEVER YOU MIND.

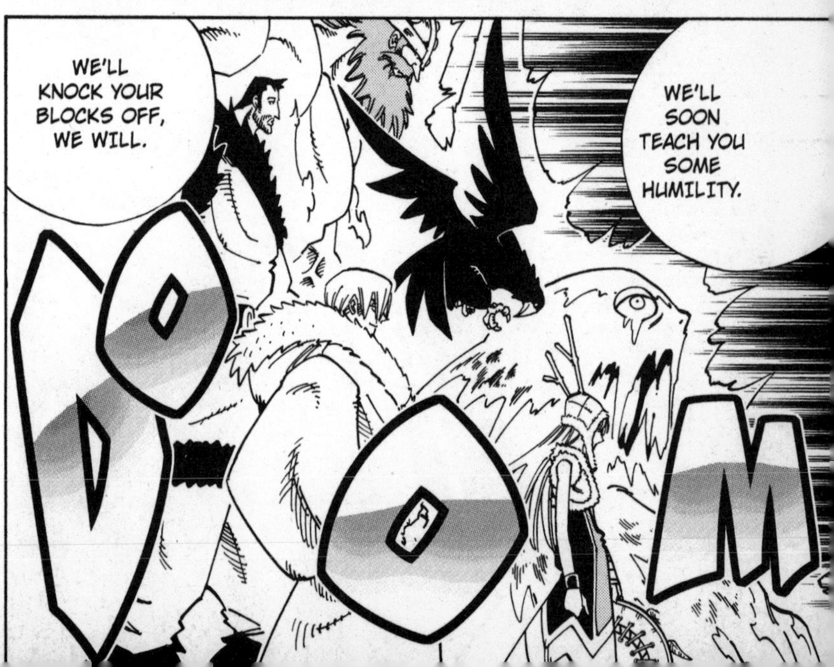
WE'LL SOON TEACH YOU SOME HUMILITY.
WE'LL KNOCK YOUR BLOCKS OFF, WE WILL.
DOOM

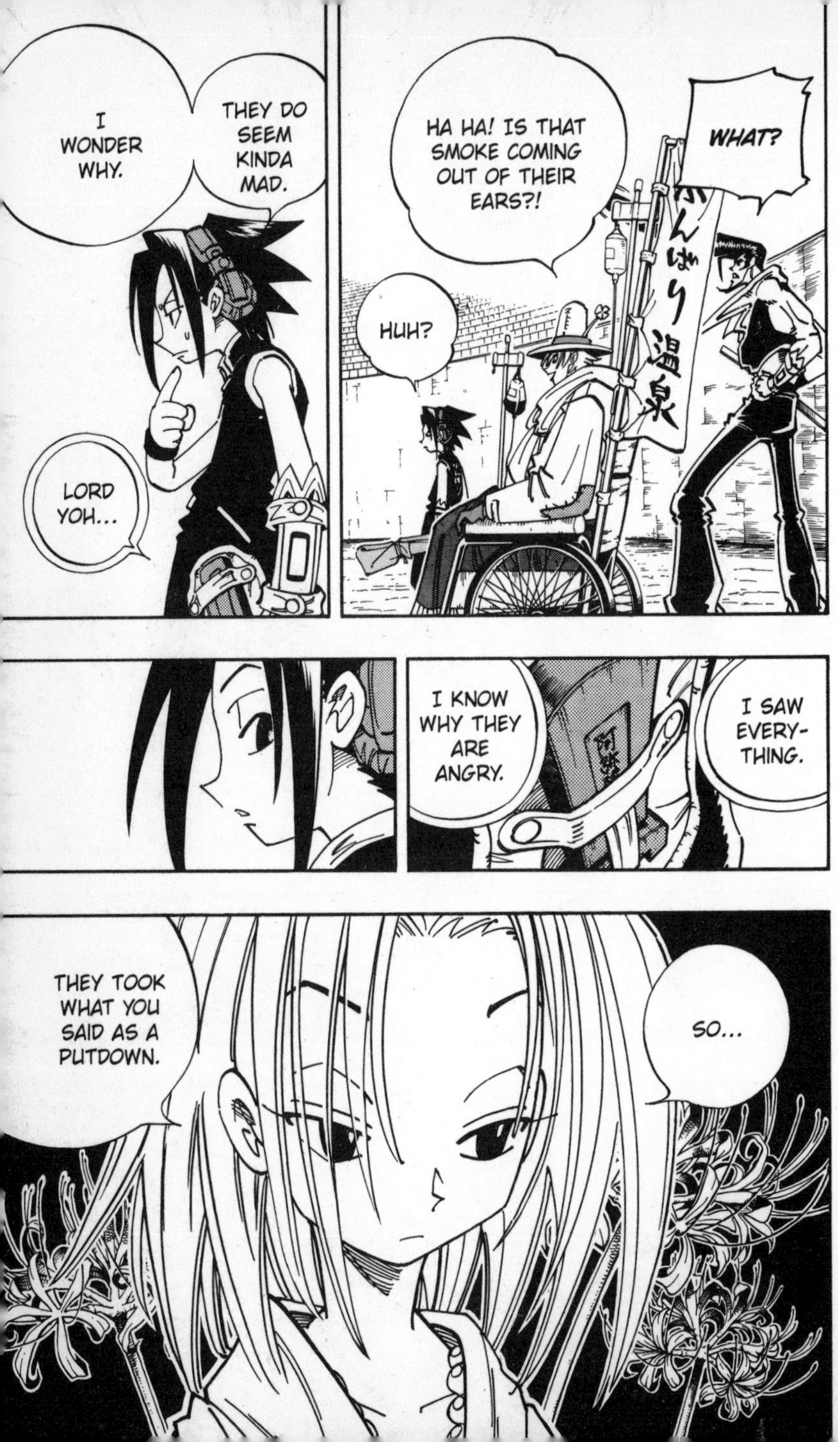
WHAT?
ふんばり温泉
HA HA! IS THAT SMOKE COMING OUT OF THEIR EARS?!
HUH?
THEY DO SEEM KINDA MAD.
I WONDER WHY.
LORD YOH...
I SAW EVERY-THING.
I KNOW WHY THEY ARE ANGRY.
SO...
THEY TOOK WHAT YOU SAID AS A PUTDOWN.

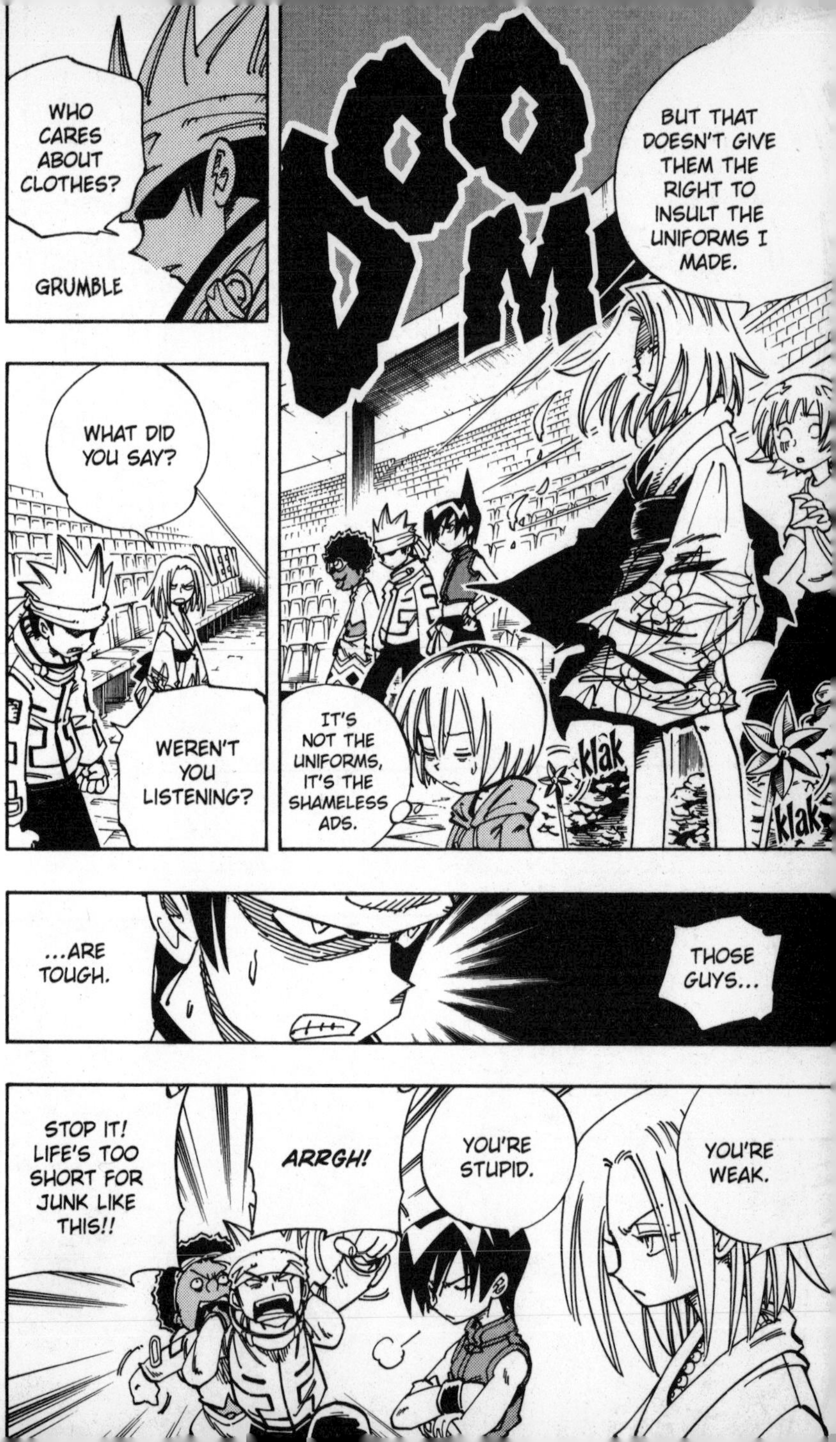
DOOM
BUT THAT DOESN'T GIVE THEM THE RIGHT TO INSULT THE UNIFORMS I MADE.
klak
klak
IT'S NOT THE UNIFORMS, IT'S THE SHAMELESS ADS.
WHO CARES ABOUT CLOTHES?
GRUMBLE
WHAT DID YOU SAY?
WEREN'T YOU LISTENING?
THOSE GUYS...
...ARE TOUGH.
YOU'RE WEAK.
YOU'RE STUPID.
ARRGH!
STOP IT! LIFE'S TOO SHORT FOR JUNK LIKE THIS!!

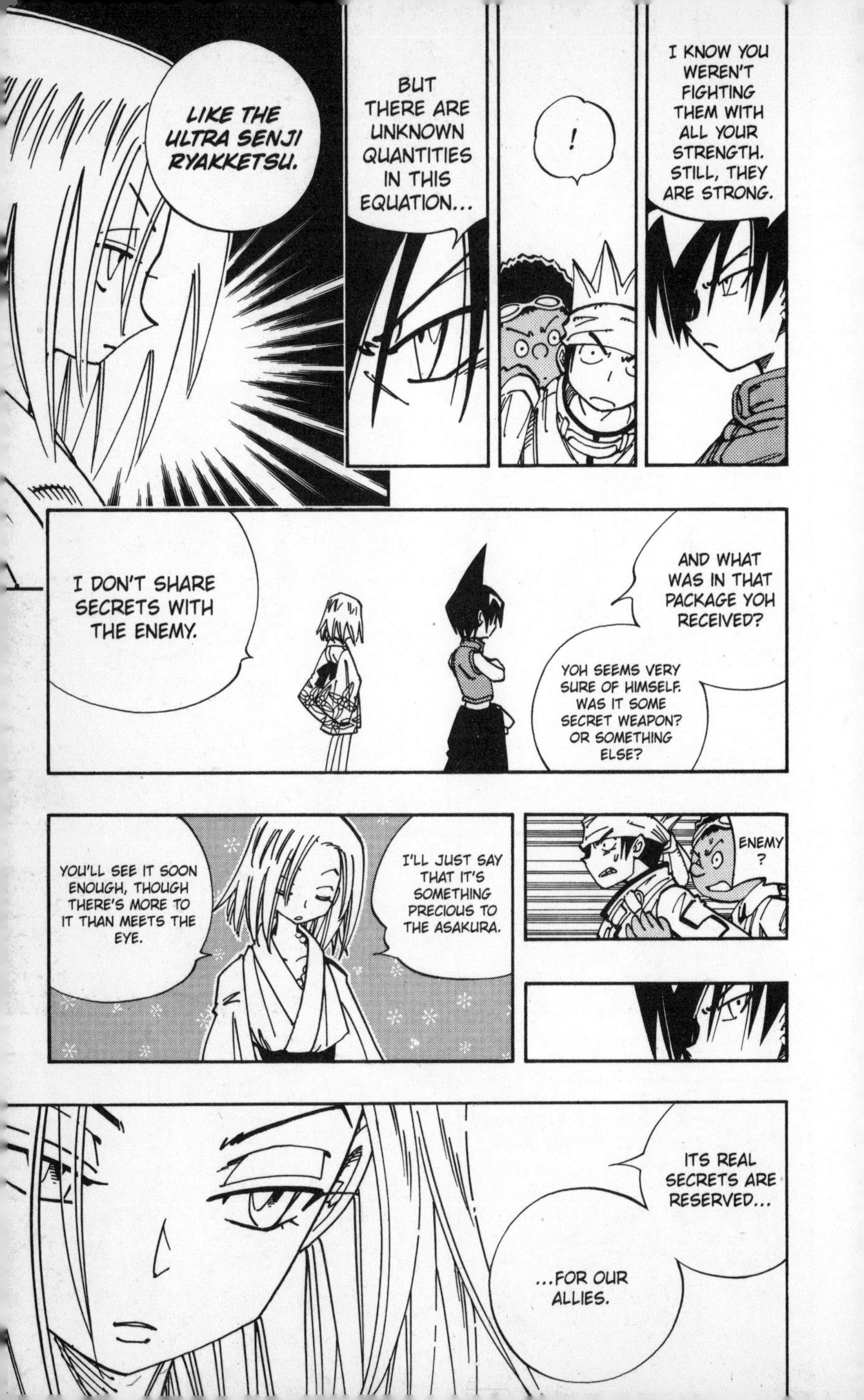
I KNOW YOU WEREN'T FIGHTING THEM WITH ALL YOUR STRENGTH. STILL, THEY ARE STRONG.
!
BUT THERE ARE UNKNOWN QUANTITIES IN THIS EQUATION...
LIKE THE ULTRA SENJI RYAKKETSU.
AND WHAT WAS IN THAT PACKAGE YOH RECEIVED?
YOH SEEMS VERY SURE OF HIMSELF. WAS IT SOME SECRET WEAPON? OR SOMETHING ELSE?
I DON'T SHARE SECRETS WITH THE ENEMY.
ENEMY?
I'LL JUST SAY THAT IT'S SOMETHING PRECIOUS TO THE ASAKURA.
YOU'LL SEE IT SOON ENOUGH, THOUGH THERE'S MORE TO IT THAN MEETS THE EYE.
ITS REAL SECRETS ARE RESERVED...
...FOR OUR ALLIES.

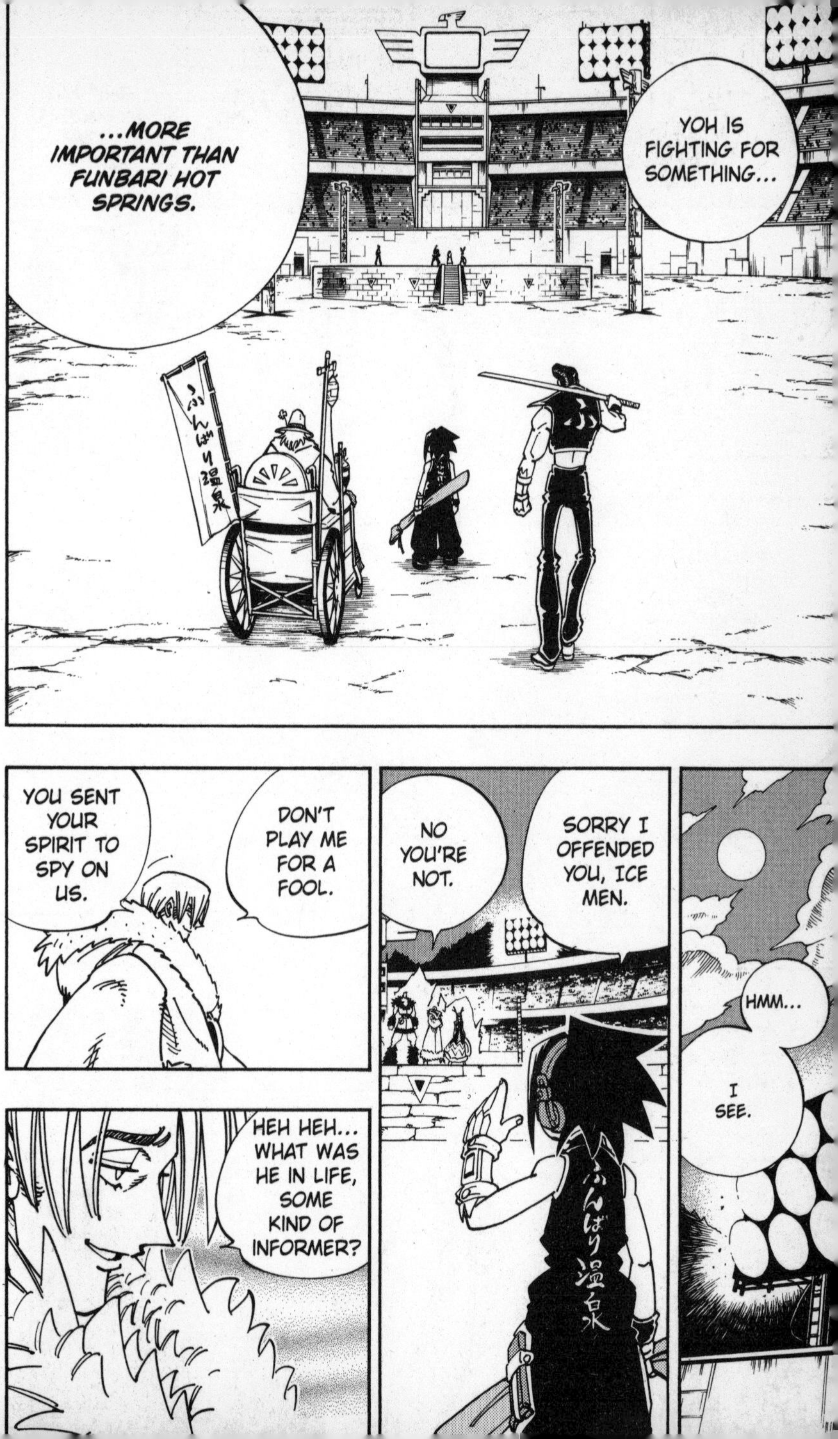
YOH IS FIGHTING FOR SOMETHING...
...MORE IMPORTANT THAN FUNBARI HOT SPRINGS.
ふんばり温泉
HMM...
I SEE.
SORRY I OFFENDED YOU, ICE MEN.
NO YOU'RE NOT.
ふんばり温泉
DON'T PLAY ME FOR A FOOL.
YOU SENT YOUR SPIRIT TO SPY ON US.
HEH HEH... WHAT WAS HE IN LIFE, SOME KIND OF INFORMER?

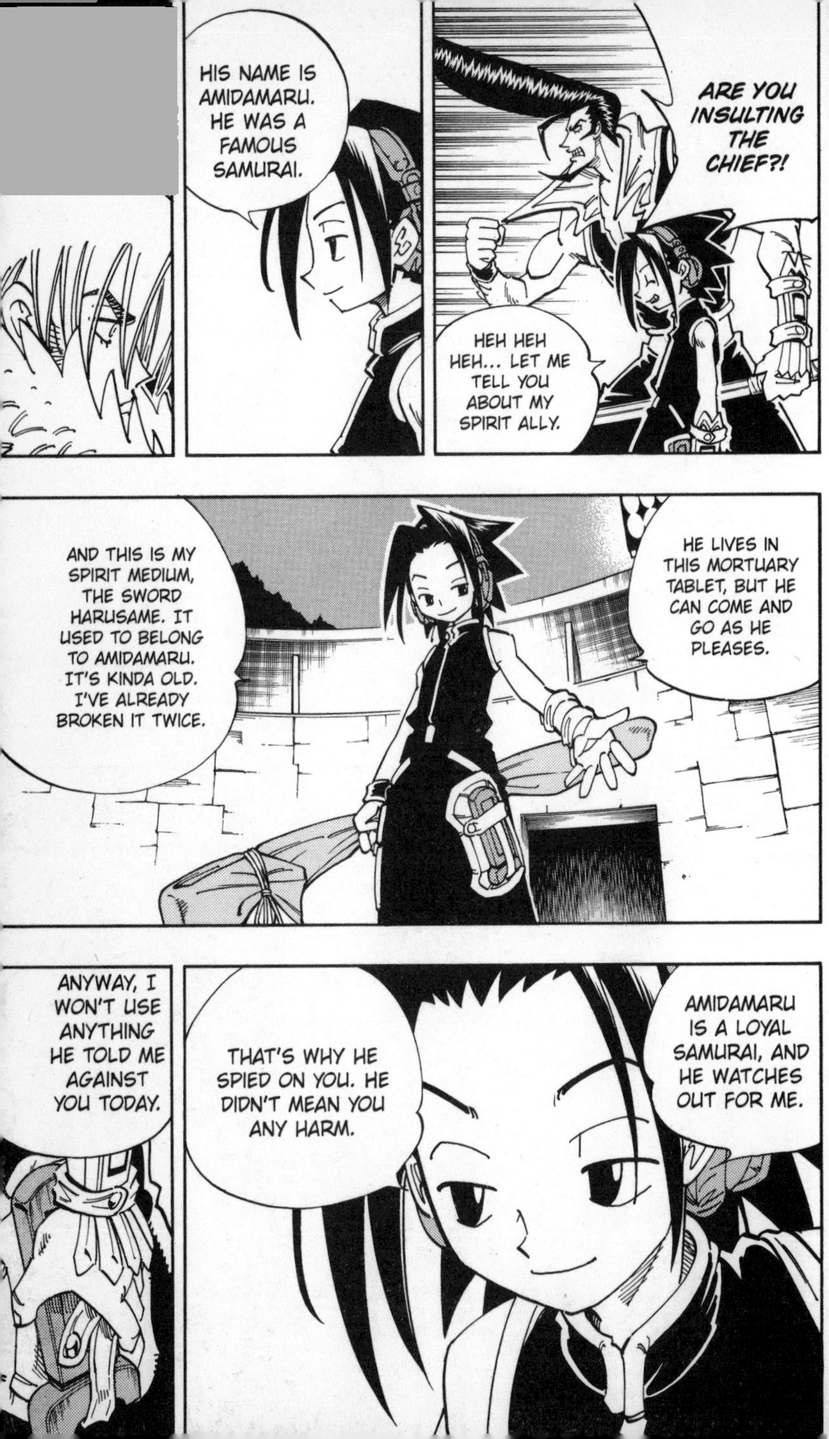
ARE YOU INSULTING THE CHIEF?!
HEH HEH HEH... LET ME TELL YOU ABOUT MY SPIRIT ALLY.
HIS NAME IS AMIDAMARU. HE WAS A FAMOUS SAMURAI.
HE LIVES IN THIS MORTUARY TABLET, BUT HE CAN COME AND GO AS HE PLEASES.
AND THIS IS MY SPIRIT MEDIUM, THE SWORD HARUSAME. IT USED TO BELONG TO AMIDAMARU. IT'S KINDA OLD. I'VE ALREADY BROKEN IT TWICE.
AMIDAMARU IS A LOYAL SAMURAI, AND HE WATCHES OUT FOR ME.
THAT'S WHY HE SPIED ON YOU. HE DIDN'T MEAN YOU ANY HARM.
ANYWAY, I WON'T USE ANYTHING HE TOLD ME AGAINST YOU TODAY.

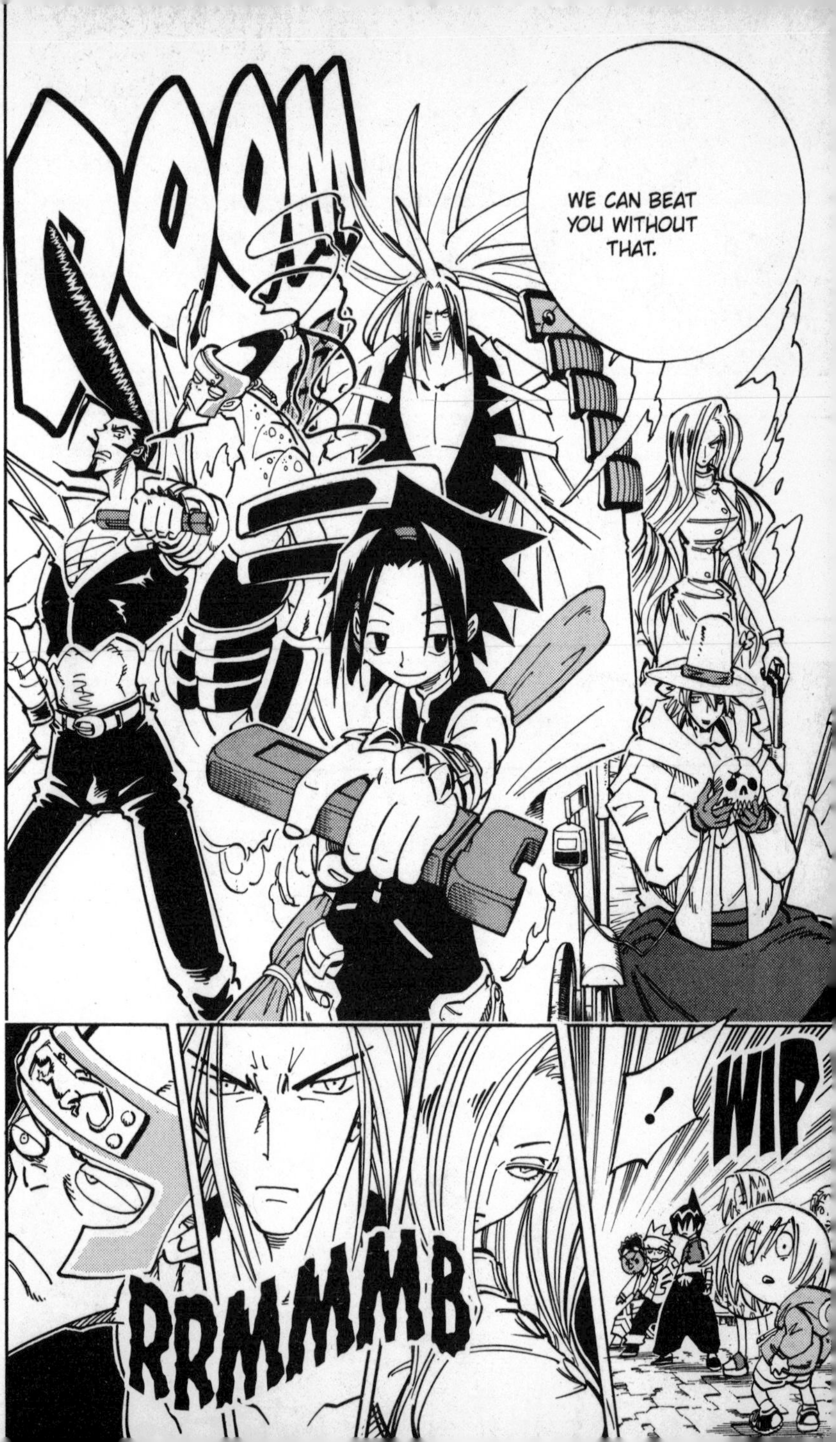
WE CAN BEAT YOU WITHOUT THAT.
DOOM
WIP
!
RRMMMMB

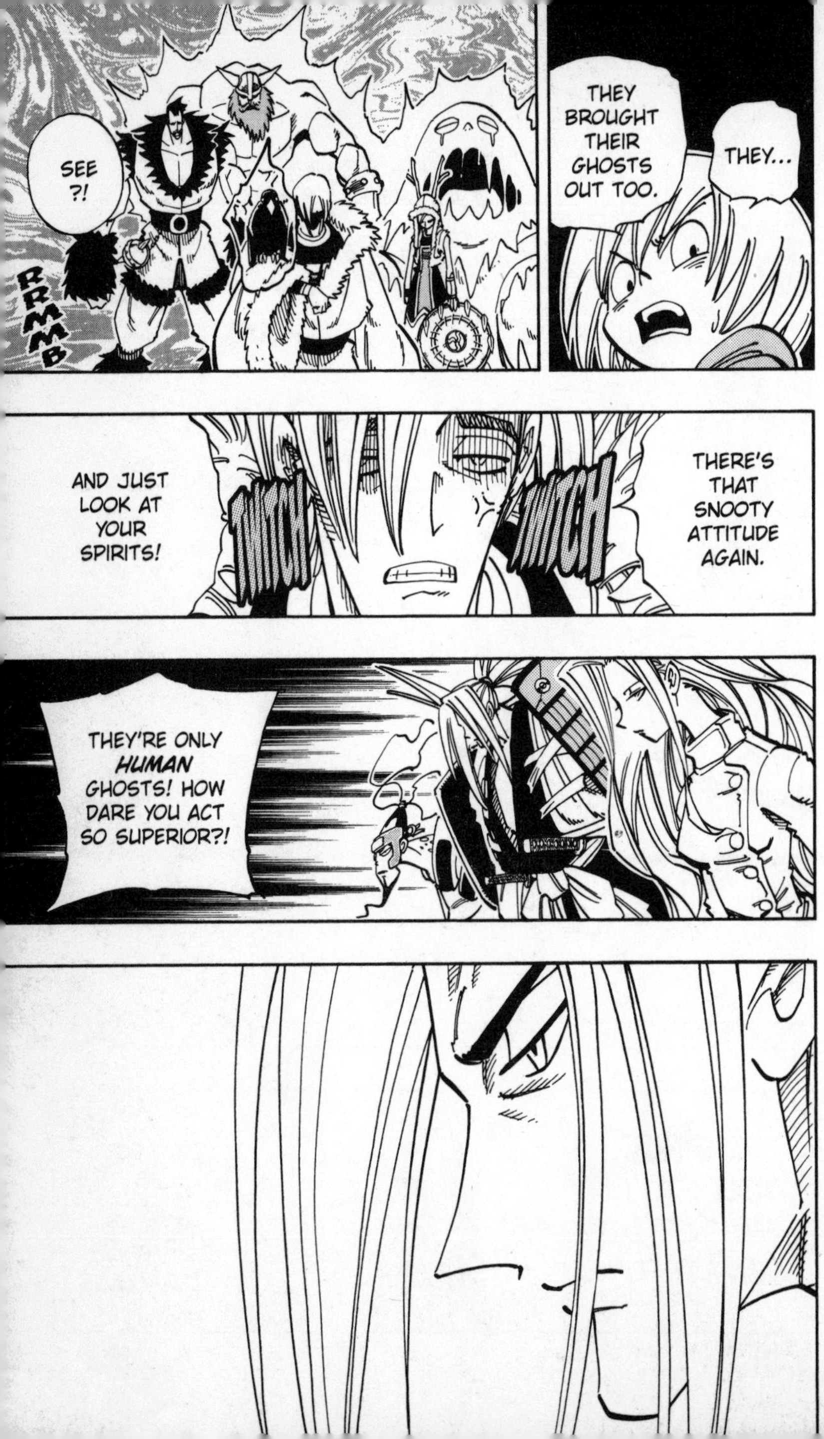
THEY...
THEY BROUGHT THEIR GHOSTS OUT TOO.
SEE?!
RRMMB
THERE'S THAT SNOOTY ATTITUDE AGAIN.
TWITCH
TWITCH
AND JUST LOOK AT YOUR SPIRITS!
THEY'RE ONLY *HUMAN* GHOSTS! HOW DARE YOU ACT SO SUPERIOR?!

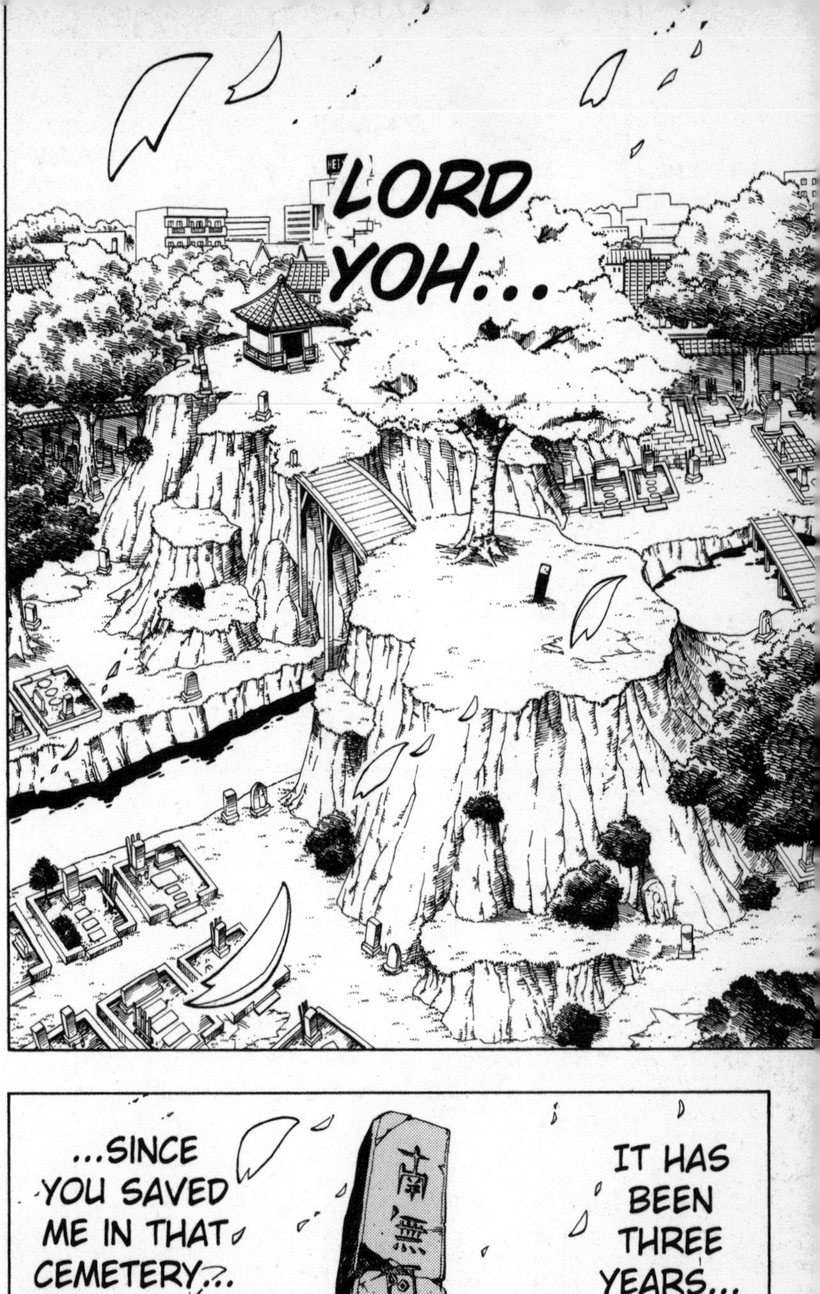
LORD YOH...
IT HAS BEEN THREE YEARS...
...SINCE YOU SAVED ME IN THAT CEMETERY...

TOMBSTONE: AMIDAMARU

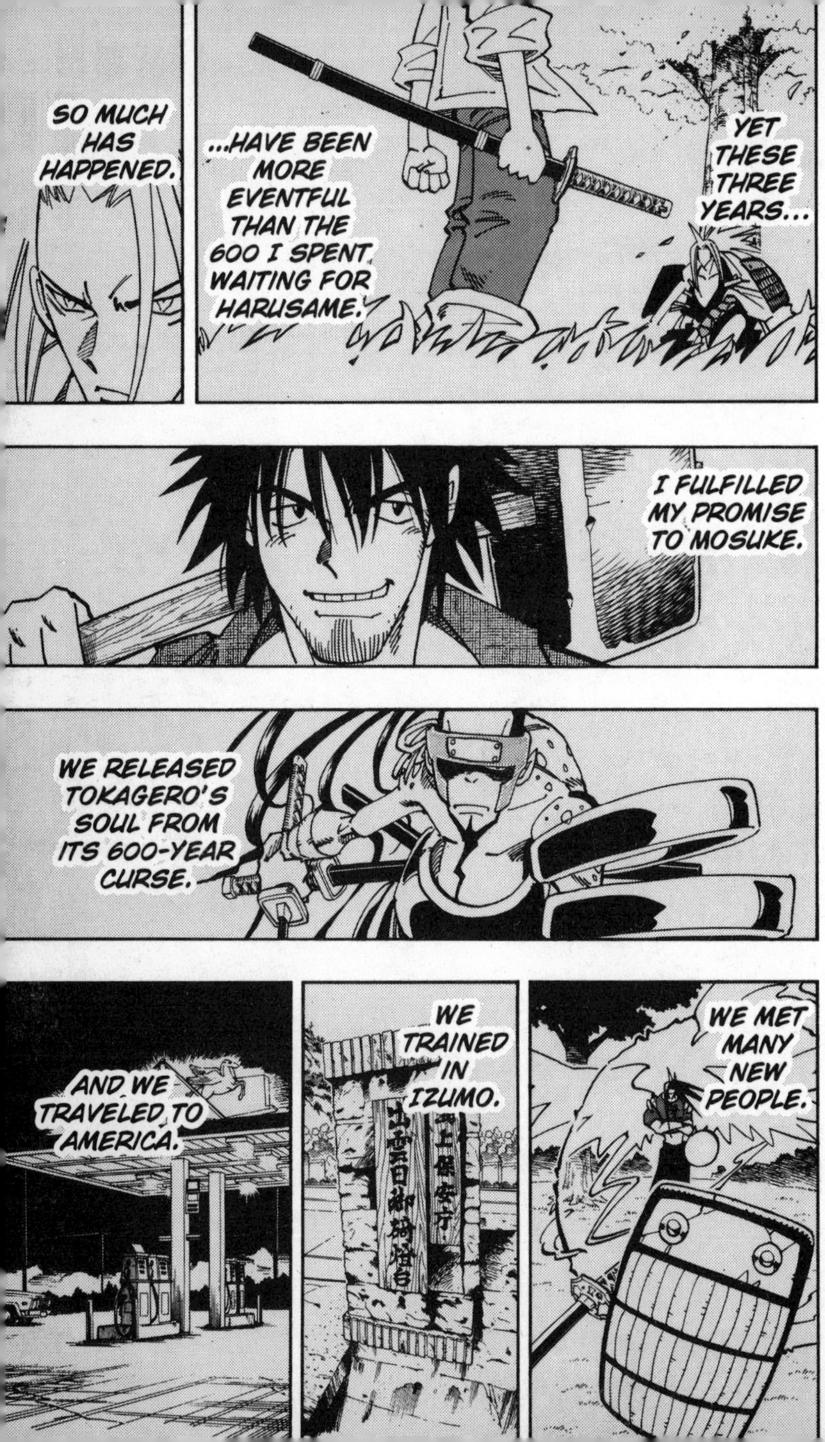
YET THESE THREE YEARS...
...HAVE BEEN MORE EVENTFUL THAN THE 600 I SPENT WAITING FOR HARUSAME.
SO MUCH HAS HAPPENED.
I FULFILLED MY PROMISE TO MOSUKE.
WE RELEASED TOKAGERO'S SOUL FROM ITS 600-YEAR CURSE.
WE MET MANY NEW PEOPLE.
WE TRAINED IN IZUMO.
上保安庁
出雲日御碕燈台
AND WE TRAVELED TO AMERICA.

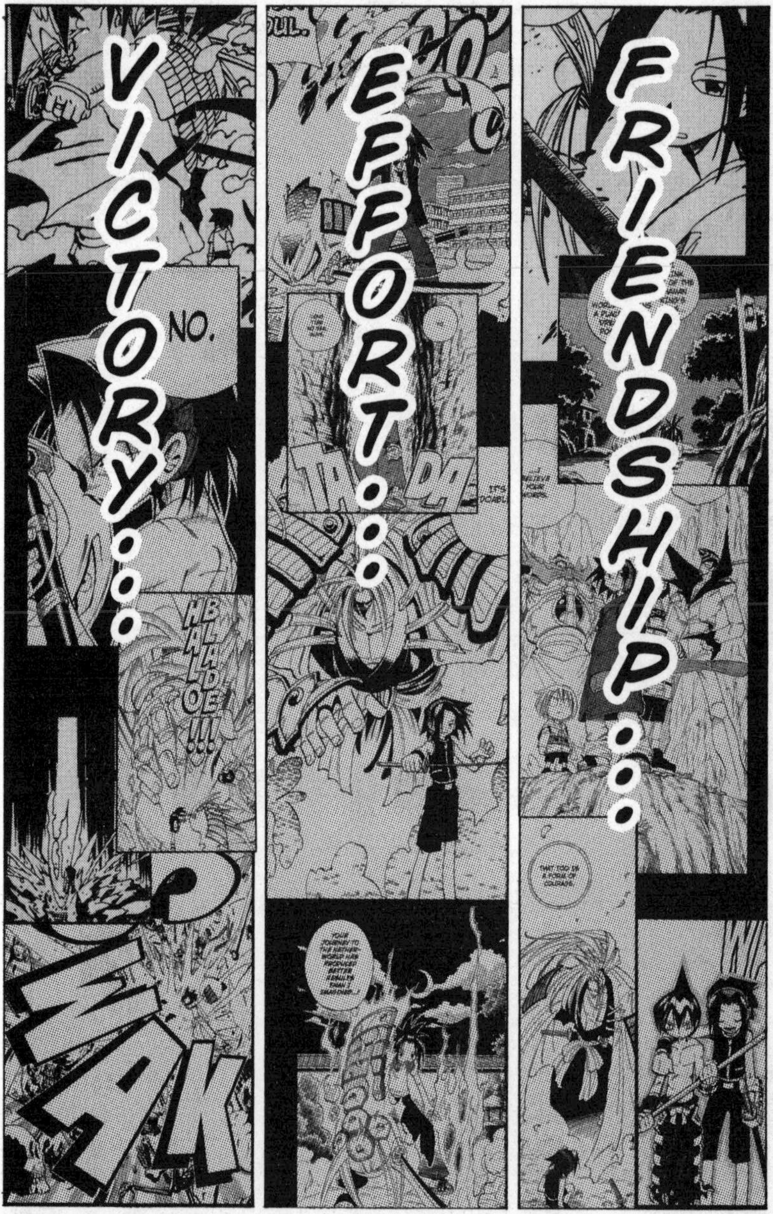
FRIENDSHIP...
THAT TOO IS A FORM OF COURAGE
EFFORT...
VICTORY...
NO.
HALO BLADE!!!
WHAK

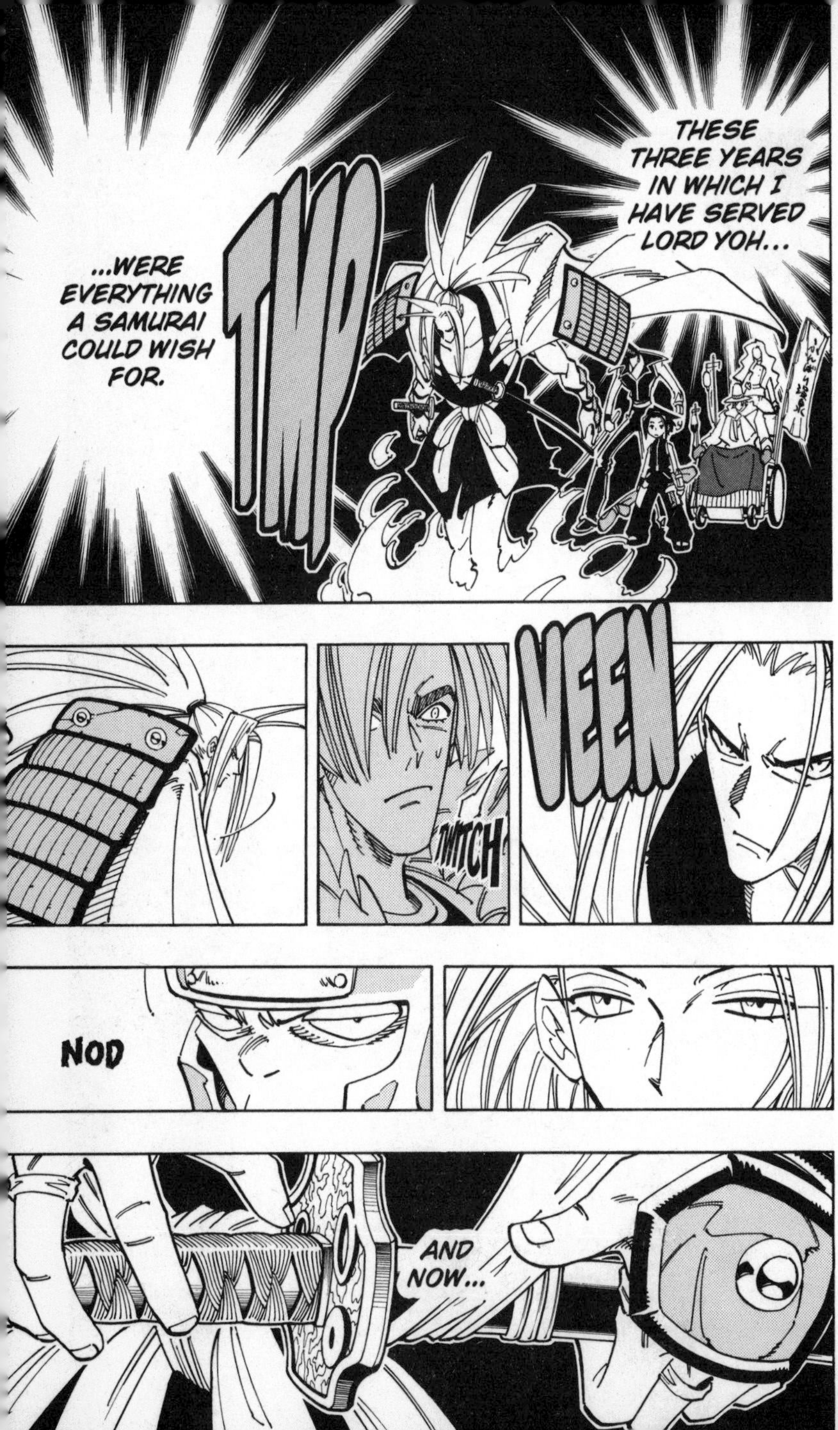
THESE THREE YEARS IN WHICH I HAVE SERVED LORD YOH...
TMP
...WERE EVERYTHING A SAMURAI COULD WISH FOR.
VEEN
TWITCH
NOD
AND NOW...

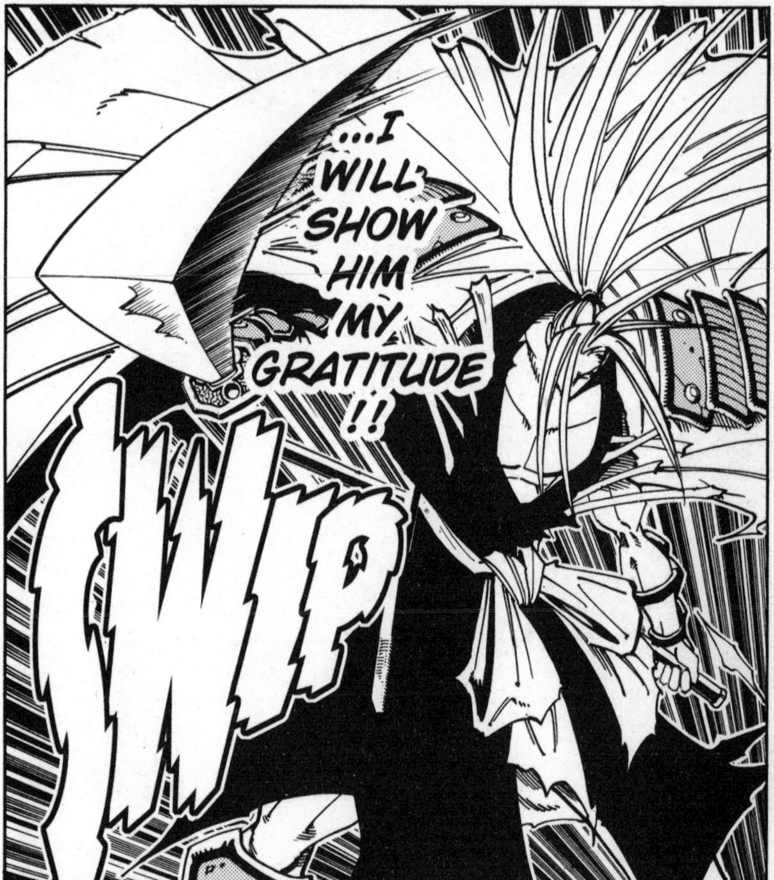
...I WILL SHOW HIM MY GRATITUDE!!
SWIP
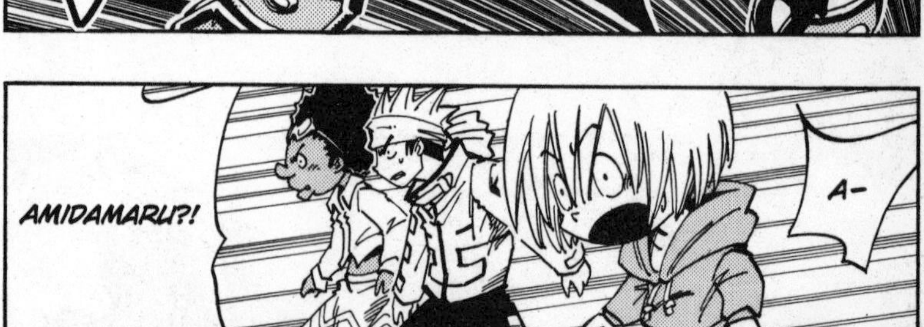
A-
AMIDAMARU?!

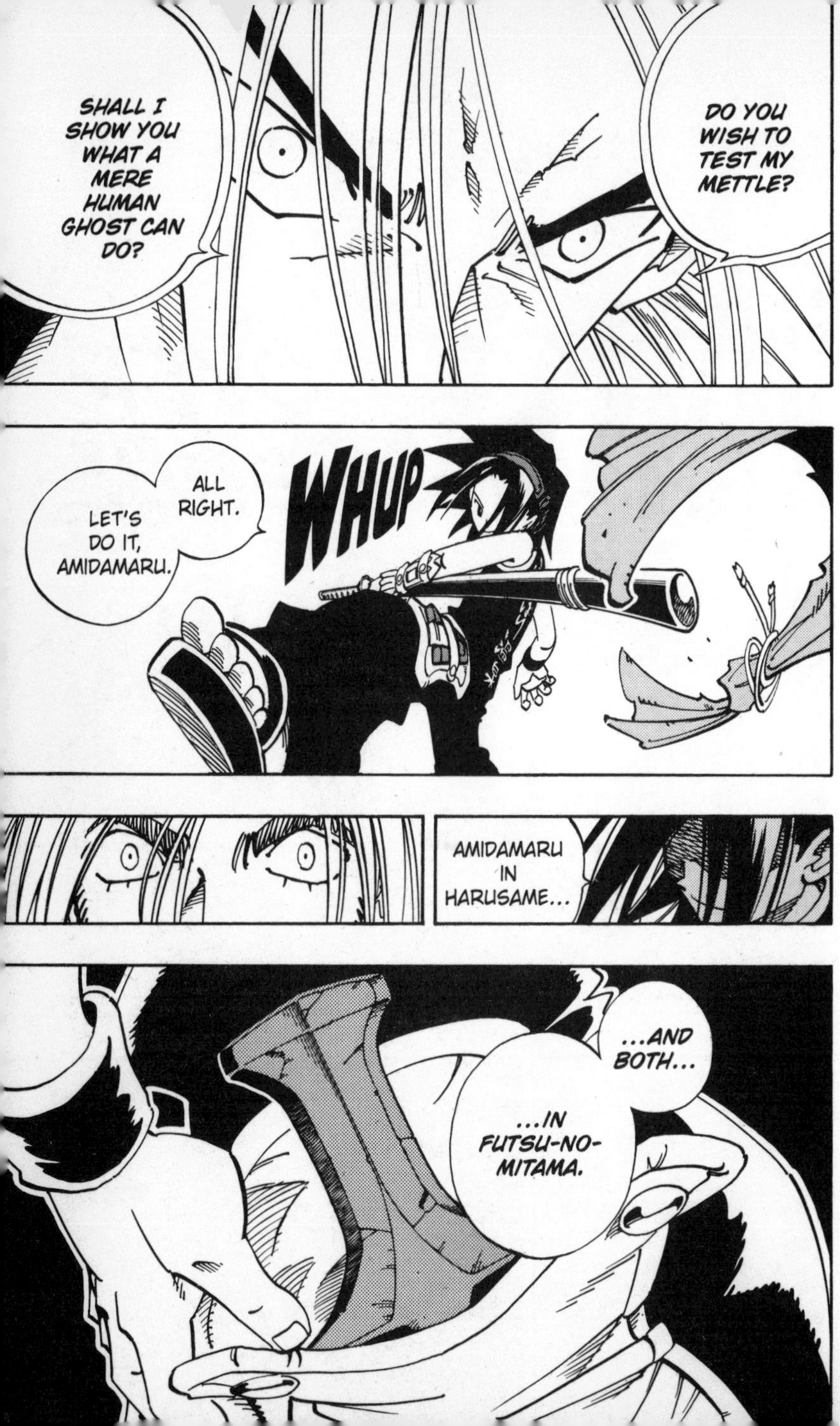
DO YOU WISH TO TEST MY METTLE?
SHALL I SHOW YOU WHAT A MERE HUMAN GHOST CAN DO?
WHUP
ALL RIGHT.
LET'S DO IT, AMIDAMARU.
AMIDAMARU IN HARUSAME...
...AND BOTH...
...IN FUTSU-NO-MITAMA.

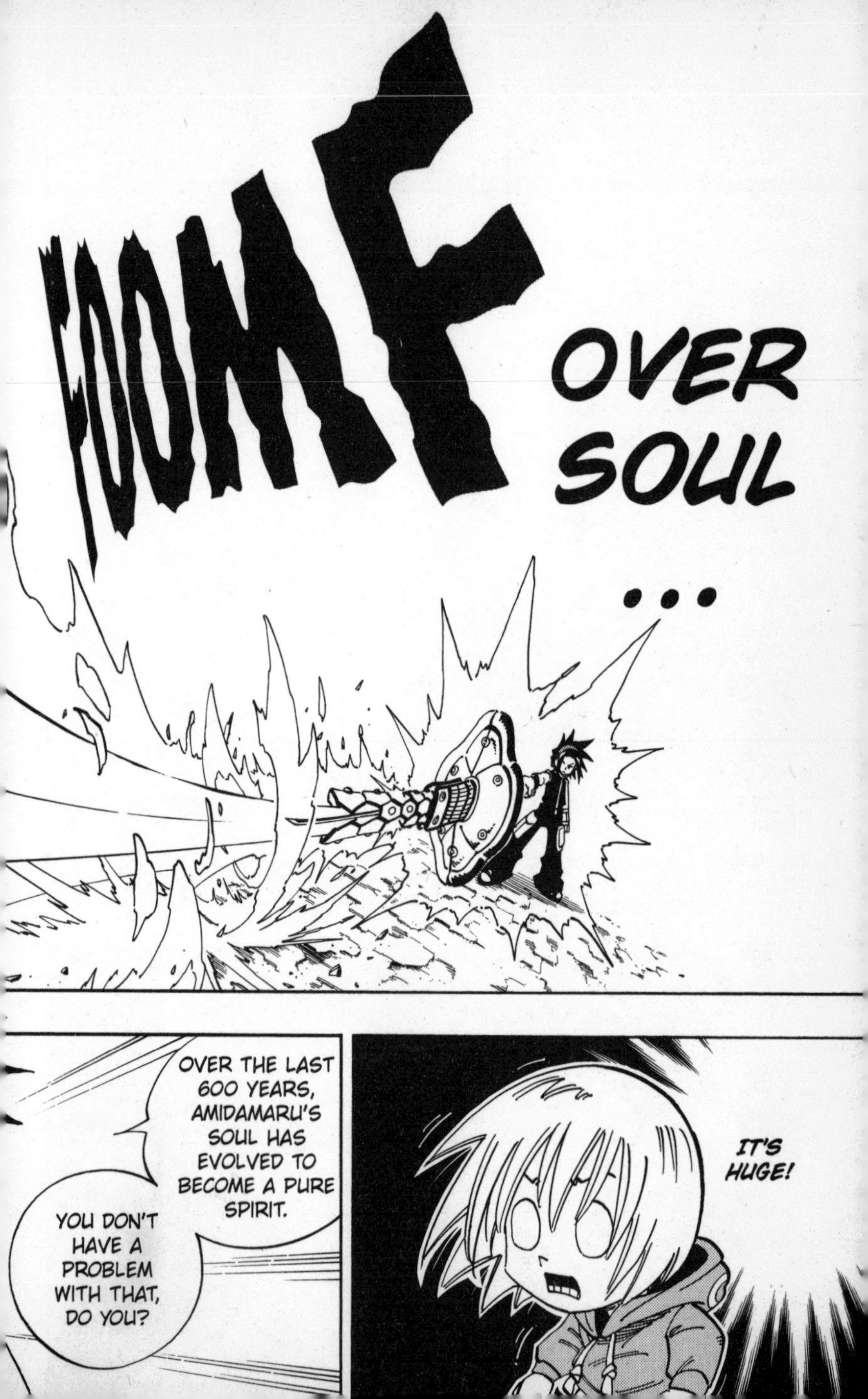
FOOMF
OVER SOUL
...
IT'S HUGE!
OVER THE LAST 600 YEARS, AMIDAMARU'S SOUL HAS EVOLVED TO BECOME A PURE SPIRIT.
YOU DON'T HAVE A PROBLEM WITH THAT, DO YOU?

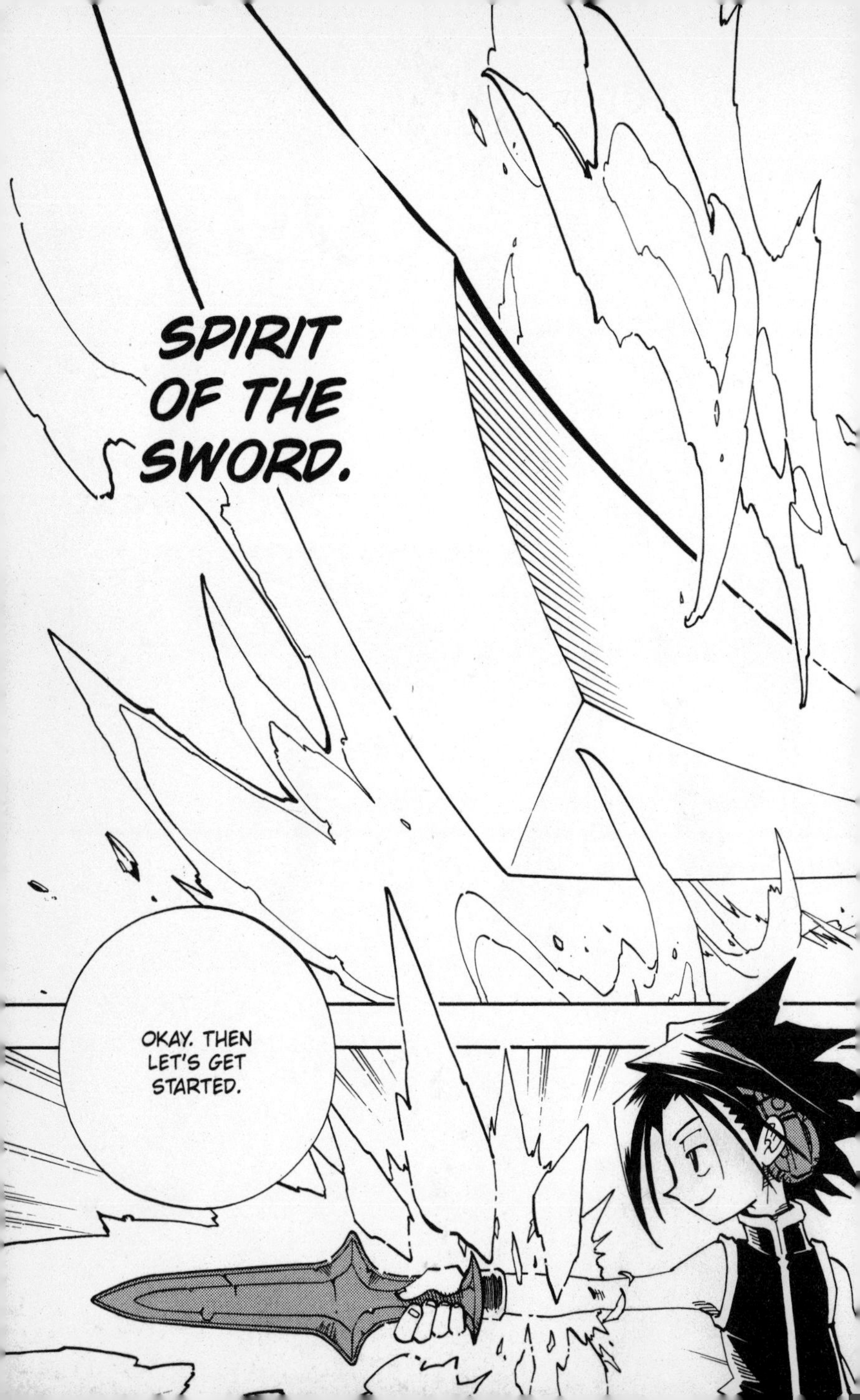
SPIRIT OF THE SWORD.
OKAY. THEN LET'S GET STARTED.

SHAMAN KING CHARACTER FILE No.72

ゾリャー

ZRIA

2001
(JULY)

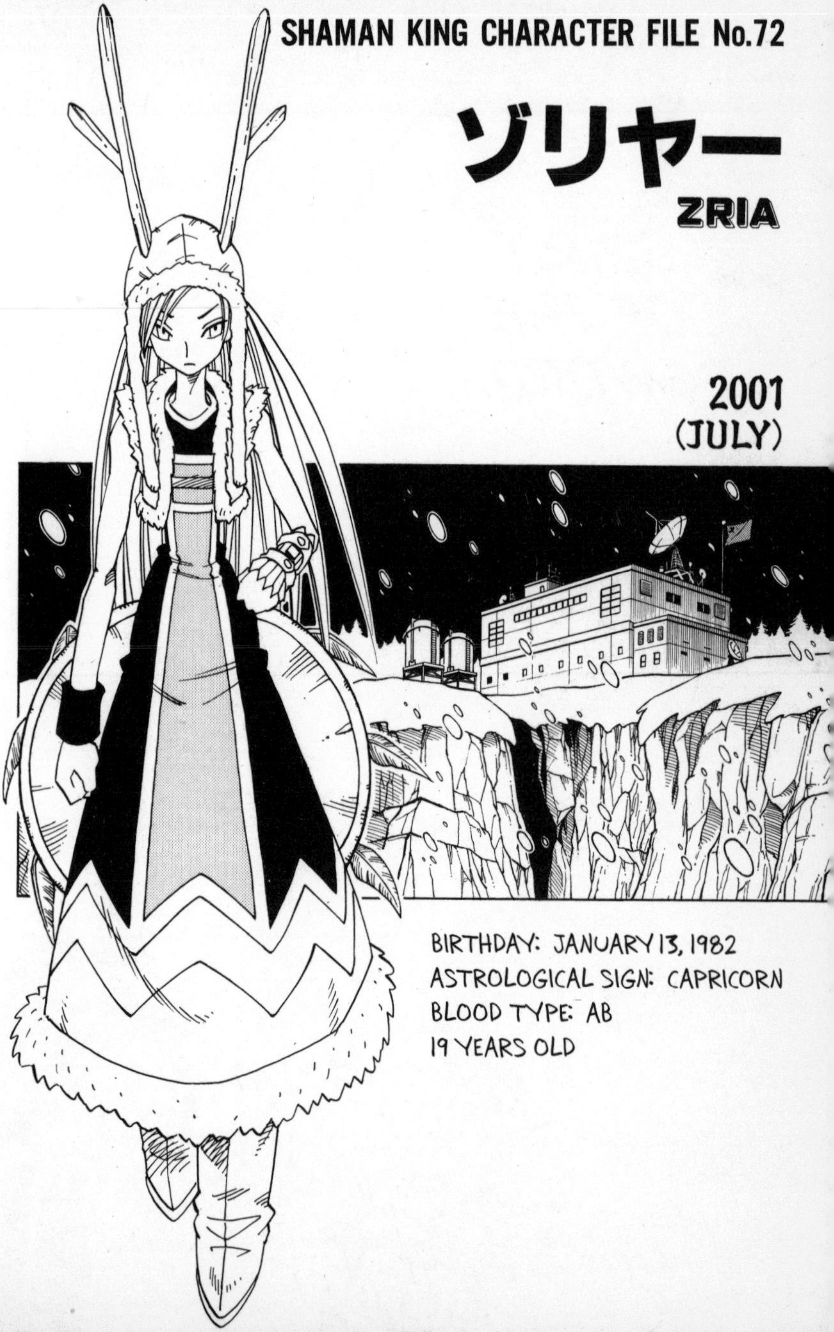

BIRTHDAY: JANUARY 13, 1982
ASTROLOGICAL SIGN: CAPRICORN
BLOOD TYPE: AB
19 YEARS OLD

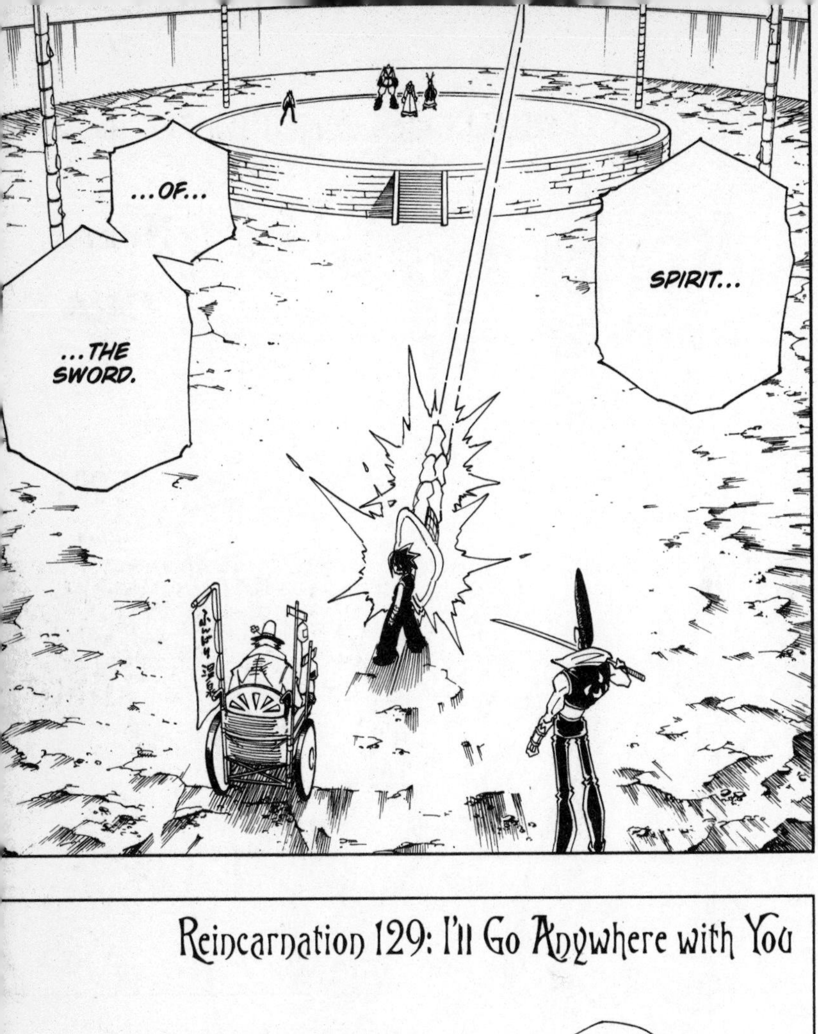
SPIRIT...
...OF...
...THE SWORD.

Reincarnation 129: I'll Go Anywhere with You

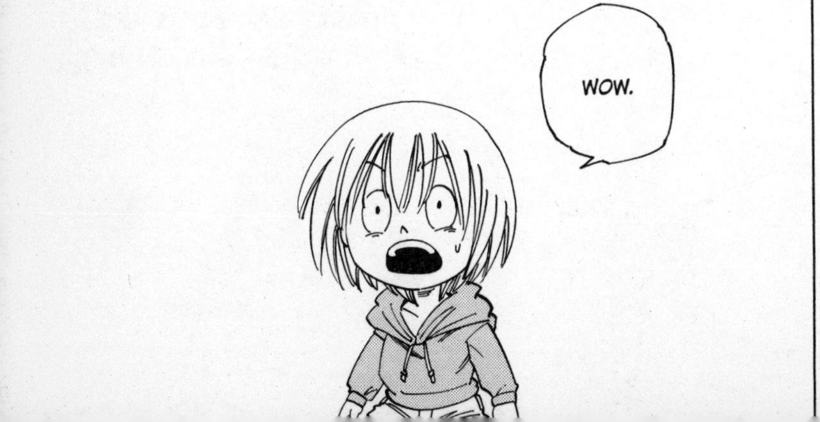
WOW.

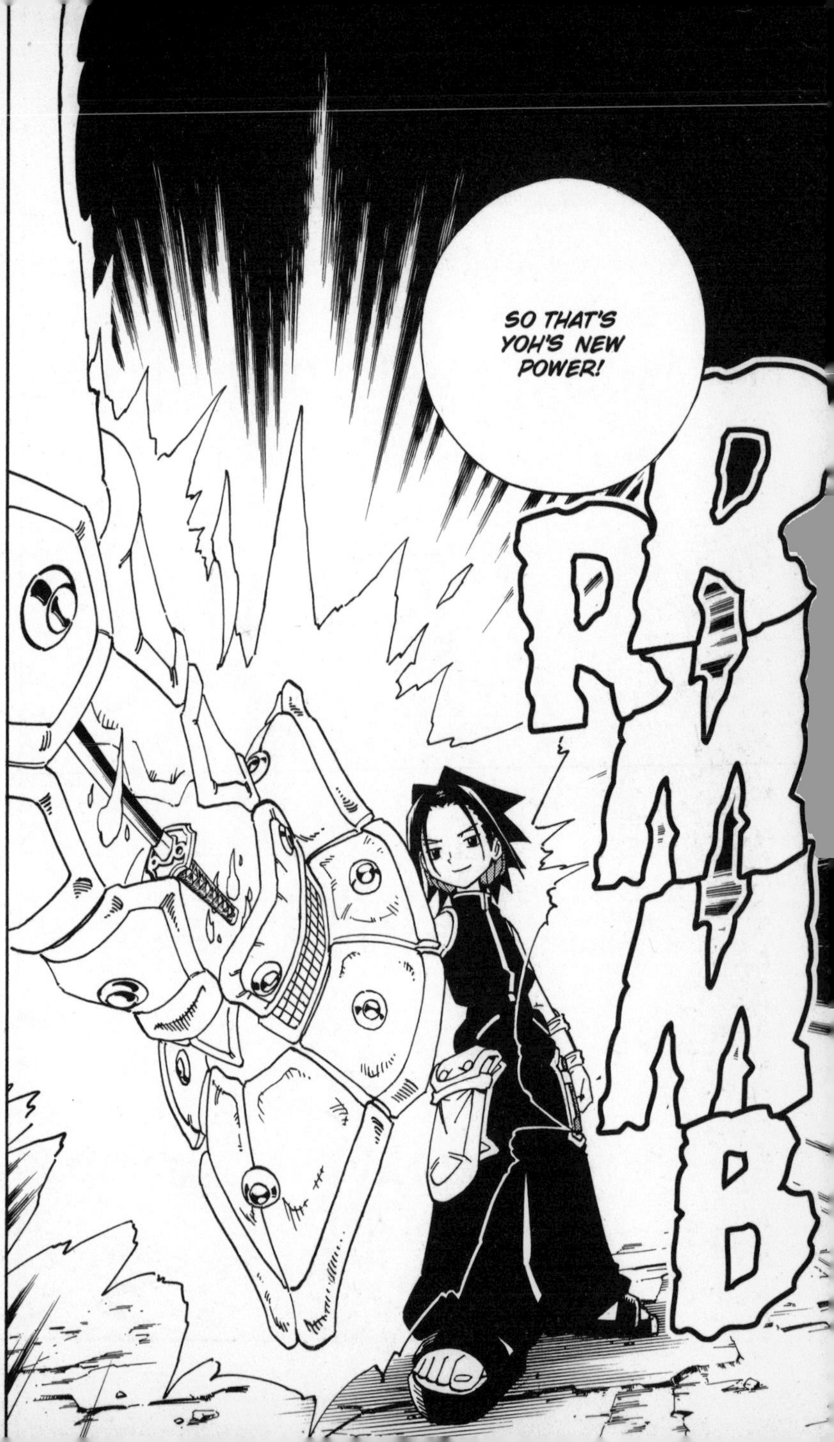
SO THAT'S YOH'S NEW POWER!

Reincarnation 129:

I'll Go Anywhere with You

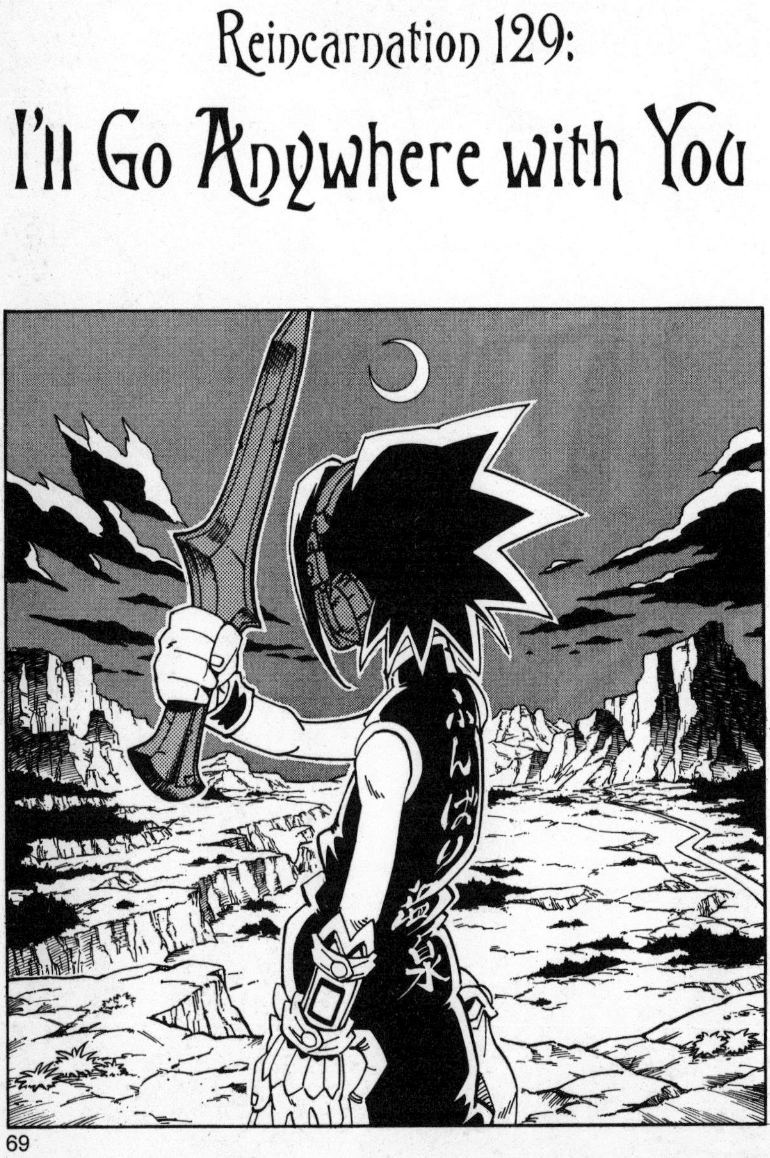
ふんばり温泉

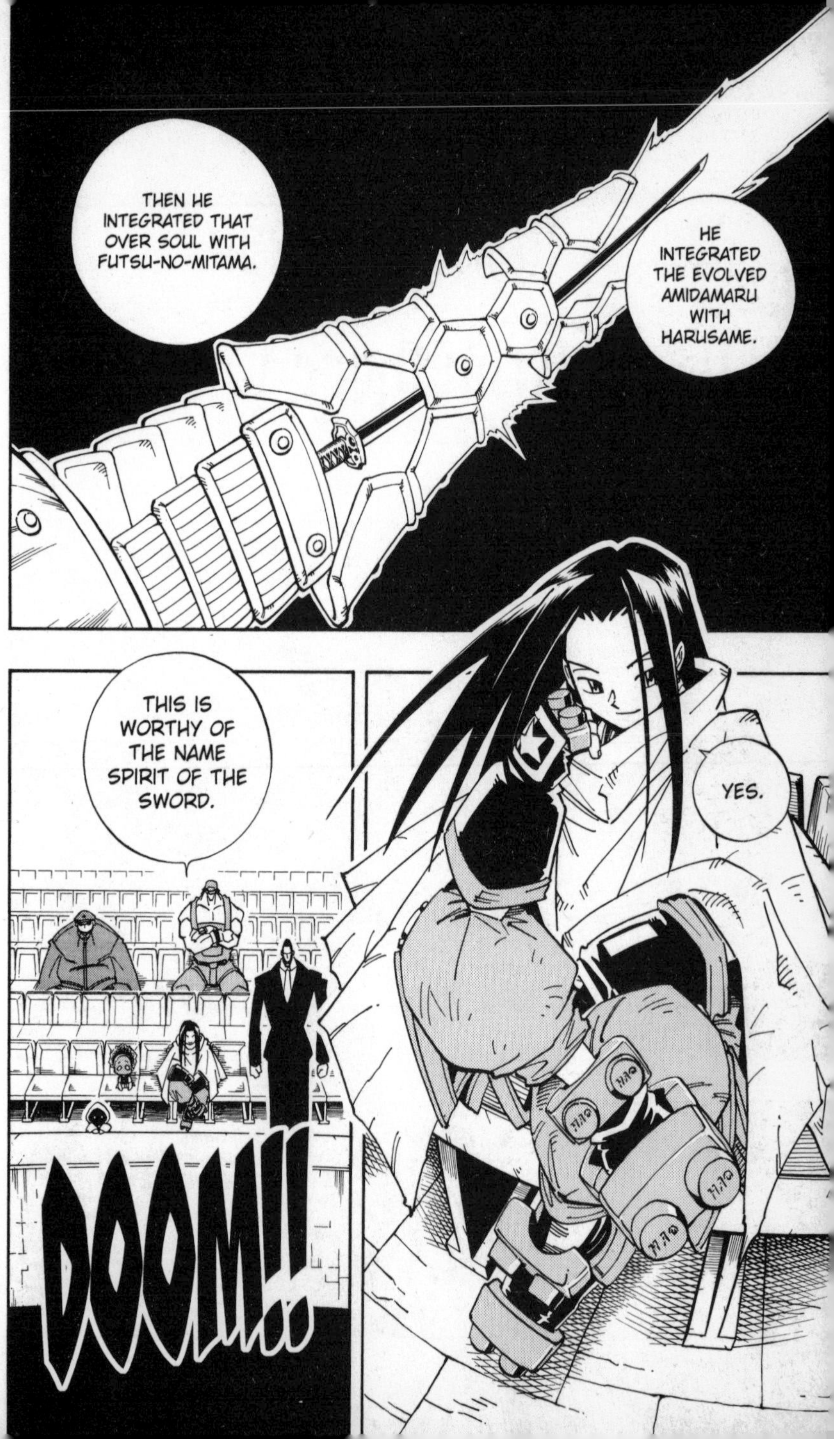
HE INTEGRATED THE EVOLVED AMIDAMARU WITH HARUSAME.
THEN HE INTEGRATED THAT OVER SOUL WITH FUTSU-NO-MITAMA.
YES.
THIS IS WORTHY OF THE NAME SPIRIT OF THE SWORD.
DOOM!!

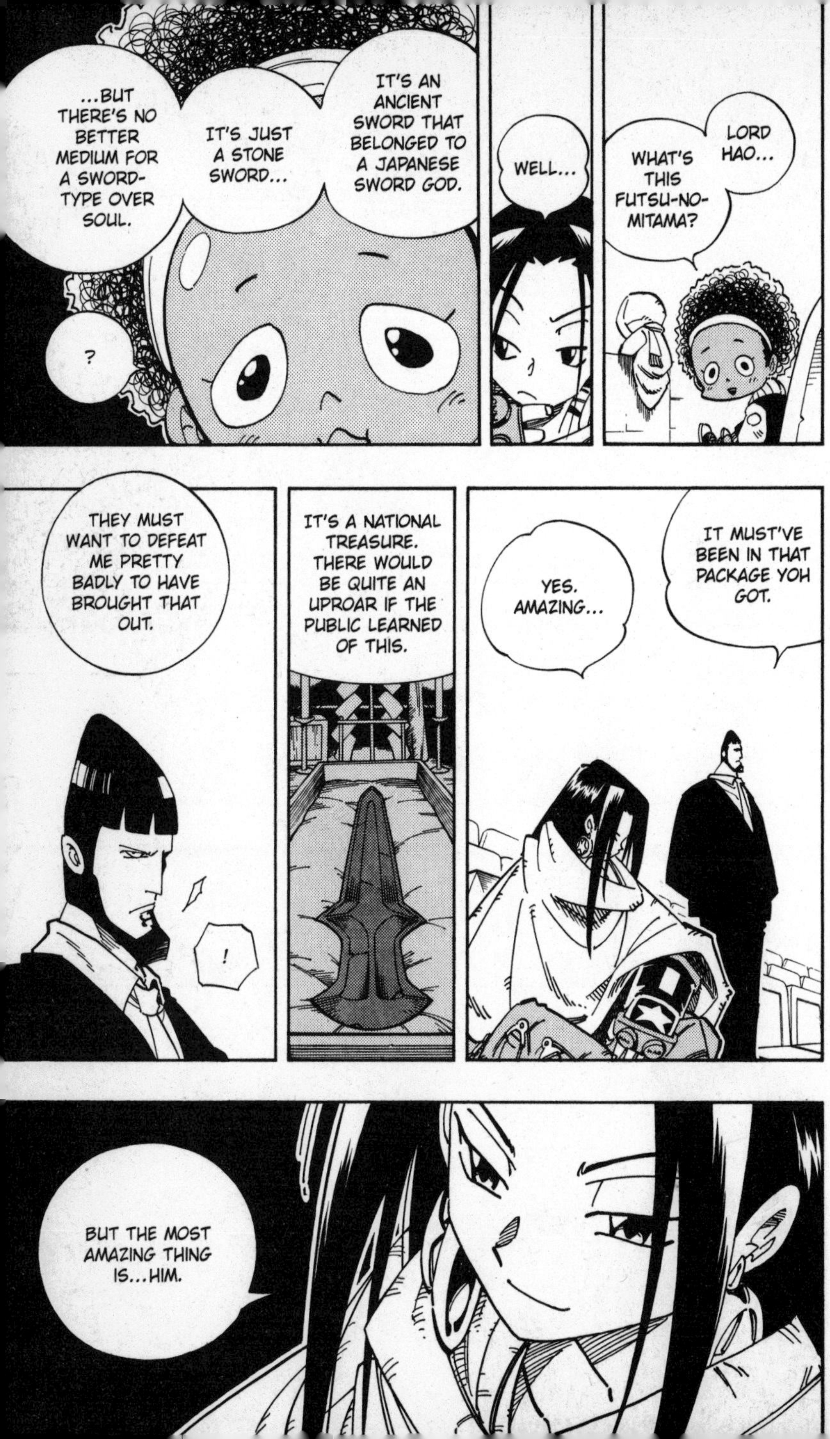
LORD HAO...
WHAT'S THIS FUTSU-NO-MITAMA?
WELL...
IT'S AN ANCIENT SWORD THAT BELONGED TO A JAPANESE SWORD GOD.
IT'S JUST A STONE SWORD...
...BUT THERE'S NO BETTER MEDIUM FOR A SWORD-TYPE OVER SOUL.
?
IT MUST'VE BEEN IN THAT PACKAGE YOH GOT.
YES. AMAZING...
IT'S A NATIONAL TREASURE. THERE WOULD BE QUITE AN UPROAR IF THE PUBLIC LEARNED OF THIS.
THEY MUST WANT TO DEFEAT ME PRETTY BADLY TO HAVE BROUGHT THAT OUT.
!
BUT THE MOST AMAZING THING IS...HIM.

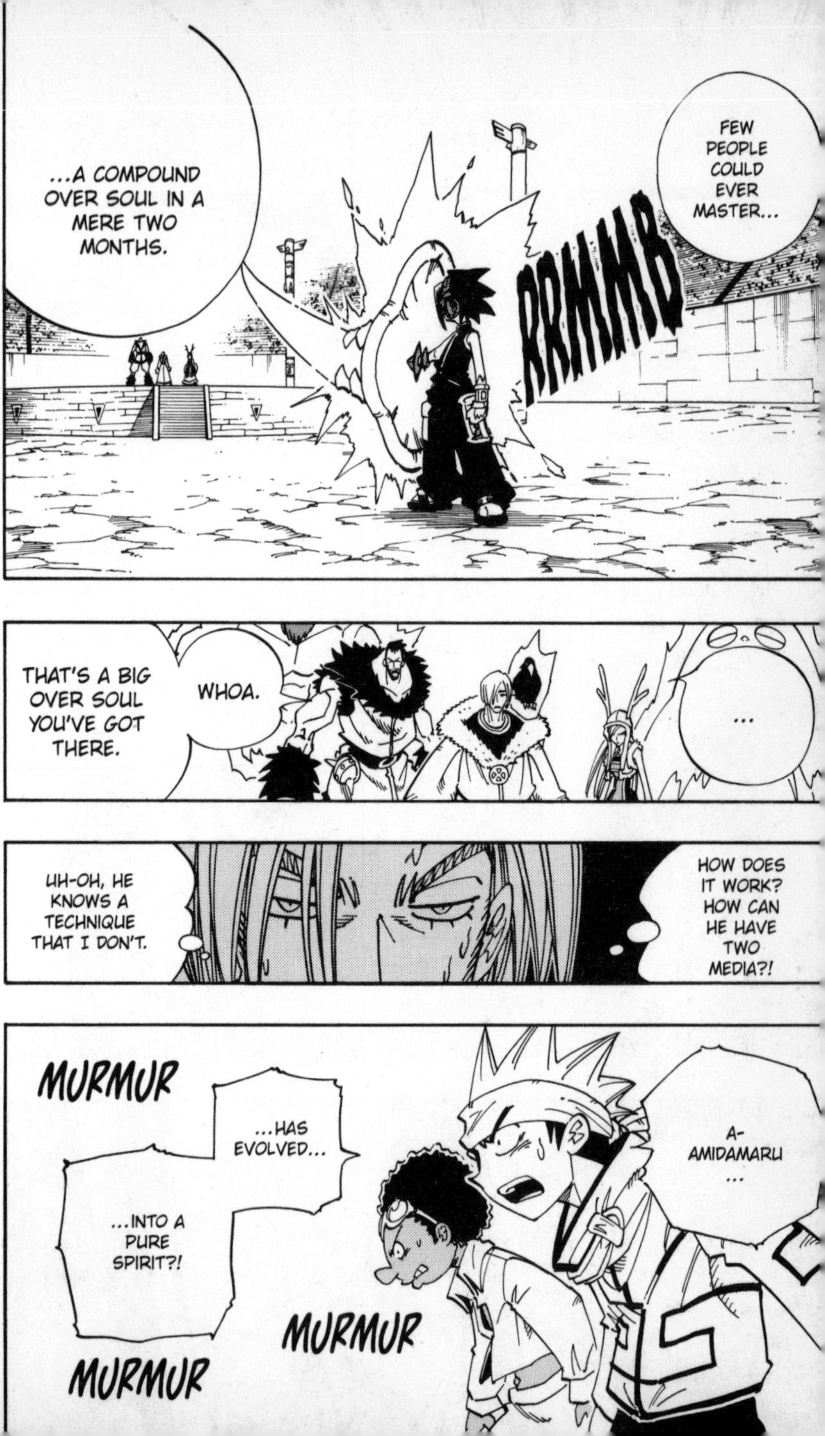
FEW PEOPLE COULD EVER MASTER...
RRMMB
...A COMPOUND OVER SOUL IN A MERE TWO MONTHS.
...
WHOA.
THAT'S A BIG OVER SOUL YOU'VE GOT THERE.
HOW DOES IT WORK? HOW CAN HE HAVE TWO MEDIA?!
UH-OH, HE KNOWS A TECHNIQUE THAT I DON'T.
A- AMIDAMARU ...
...HAS EVOLVED...
...INTO A PURE SPIRIT?!
MURMUR
MURMUR
MURMUR

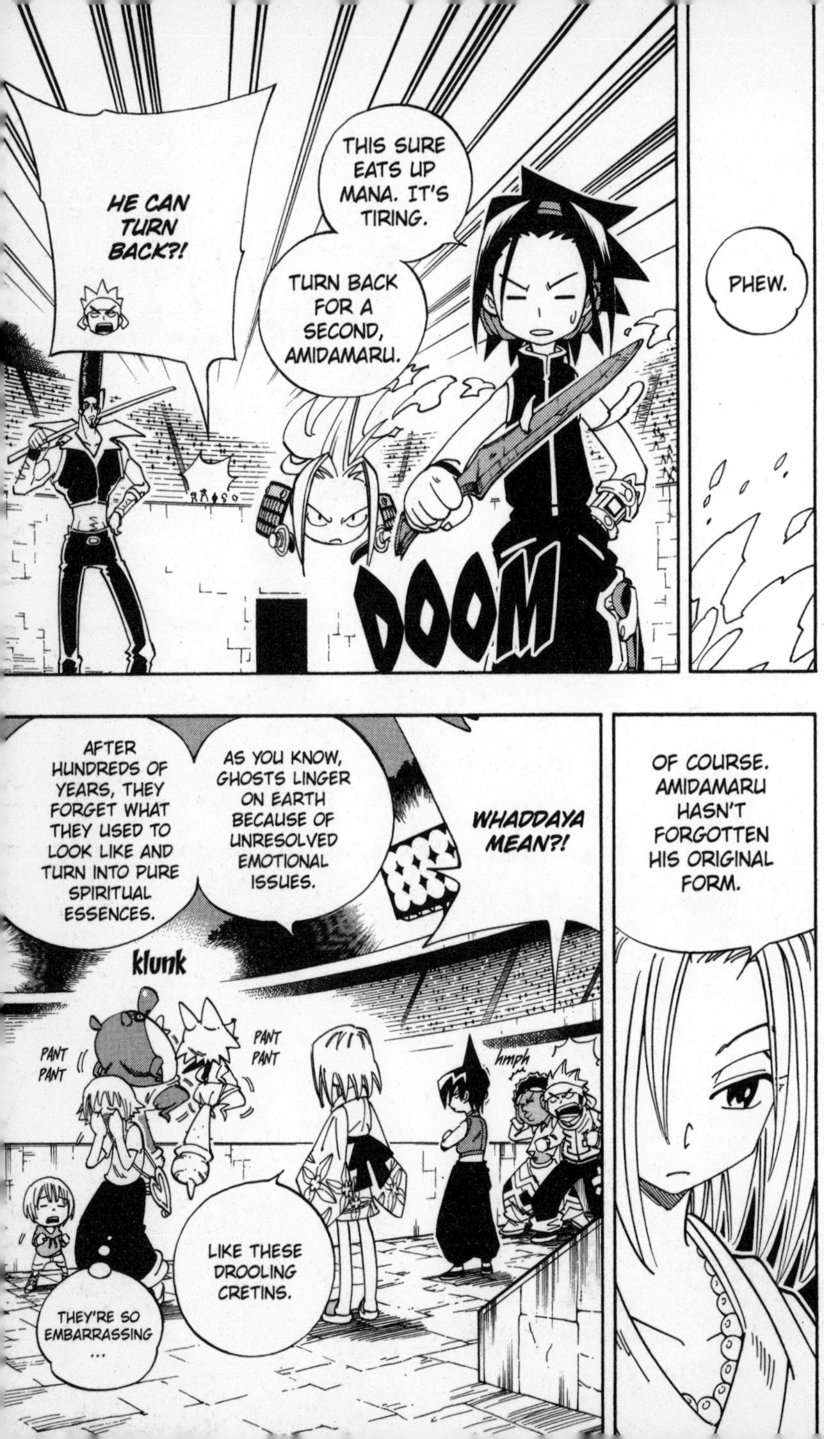
PHEW.
THIS SURE EATS UP MANA. IT'S TIRING.
TURN BACK FOR A SECOND, AMIDAMARU.
HE CAN TURN BACK?!
DOOM
OF COURSE. AMIDAMARU HASN'T FORGOTTEN HIS ORIGINAL FORM.
WHADDAYA MEAN?!
AS YOU KNOW, GHOSTS LINGER ON EARTH BECAUSE OF UNRESOLVED EMOTIONAL ISSUES.
AFTER HUNDREDS OF YEARS, THEY FORGET WHAT THEY USED TO LOOK LIKE AND TURN INTO PURE SPIRITUAL ESSENCES.
klunk
hmph
PANT PANT
PANT PANT
LIKE THESE DROOLING CRETINS.
THEY'RE SO EMBARRASSING ...

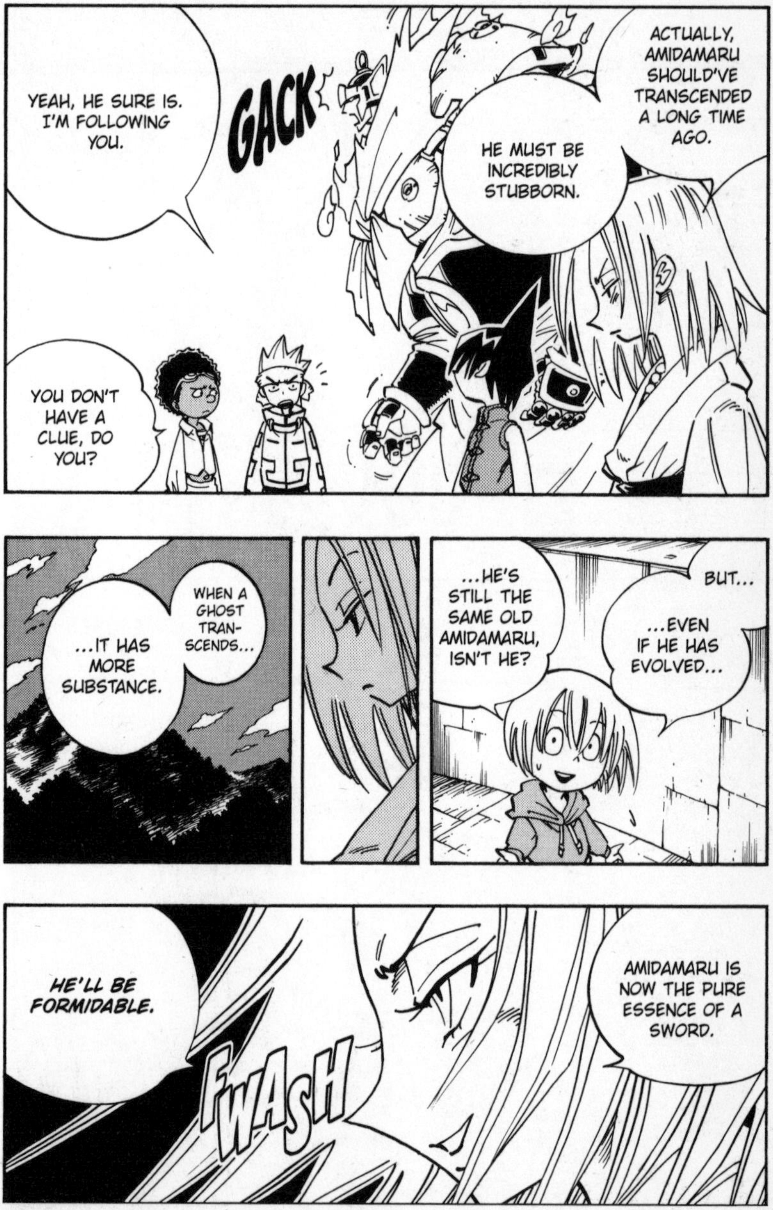
ACTUALLY, AMIDAMARU SHOULD'VE TRANSCENDED A LONG TIME AGO.
HE MUST BE INCREDIBLY STUBBORN.
GACK
YEAH, HE SURE IS. I'M FOLLOWING YOU.
YOU DON'T HAVE A CLUE, DO YOU?
BUT...
...EVEN IF HE HAS EVOLVED...
...HE'S STILL THE SAME OLD AMIDAMARU, ISN'T HE?
WHEN A GHOST TRAN-SCENDS...
...IT HAS MORE SUBSTANCE.
AMIDAMARU IS NOW THE PURE ESSENCE OF A SWORD.
FWASH
HE'LL BE FORMIDABLE.

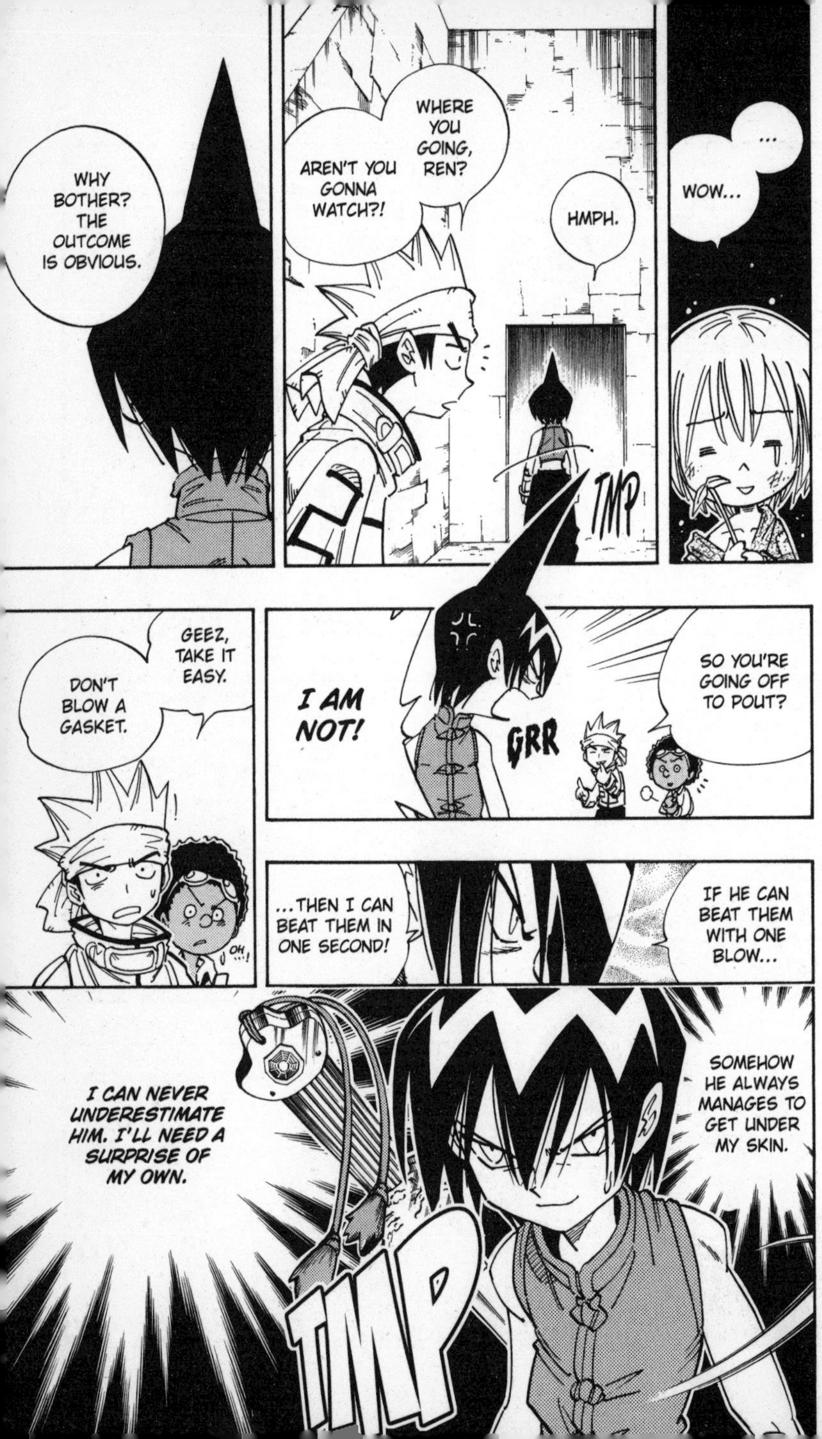
...
WOW...
WHERE YOU GOING, REN?
AREN'T YOU GONNA WATCH?!
HMPH.
TMP
WHY BOTHER? THE OUTCOME IS OBVIOUS.
SO YOU'RE GOING OFF TO POUT?
GRR
I AM NOT!
IF HE CAN BEAT THEM WITH ONE BLOW...
...THEN I CAN BEAT THEM IN ONE SECOND!
GEEZ, TAKE IT EASY.
DON'T BLOW A GASKET.
OH...!
SOMEHOW HE ALWAYS MANAGES TO GET UNDER MY SKIN.
I CAN NEVER UNDERESTIMATE HIM. I'LL NEED A SURPRISE OF MY OWN.
TMP

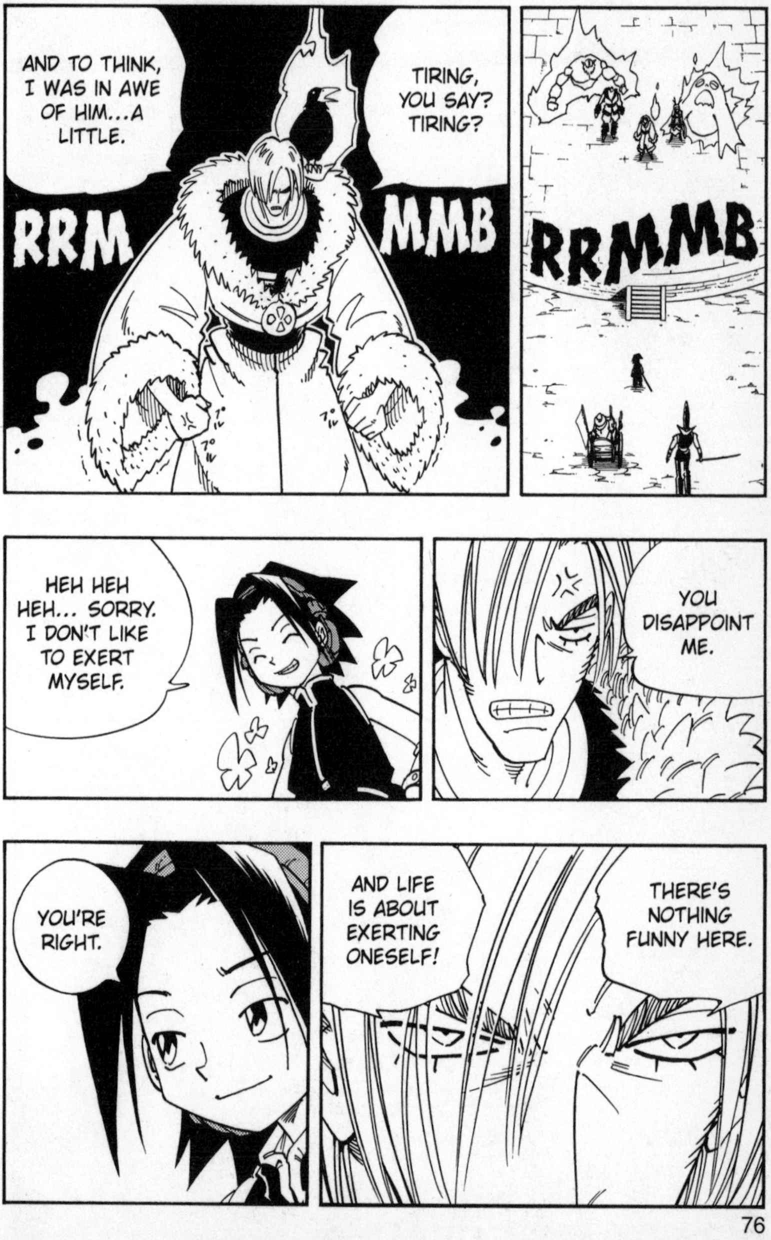
RRMMB
TIRING, YOU SAY? TIRING?
AND TO THINK, I WAS IN AWE OF HIM...A LITTLE.
RRM MMB
YOU DISAPPOINT ME.
HEH HEH HEH... SORRY. I DON'T LIKE TO EXERT MYSELF.
THERE'S NOTHING FUNNY HERE.
AND LIFE IS ABOUT EXERTING ONESELF!
YOU'RE RIGHT.

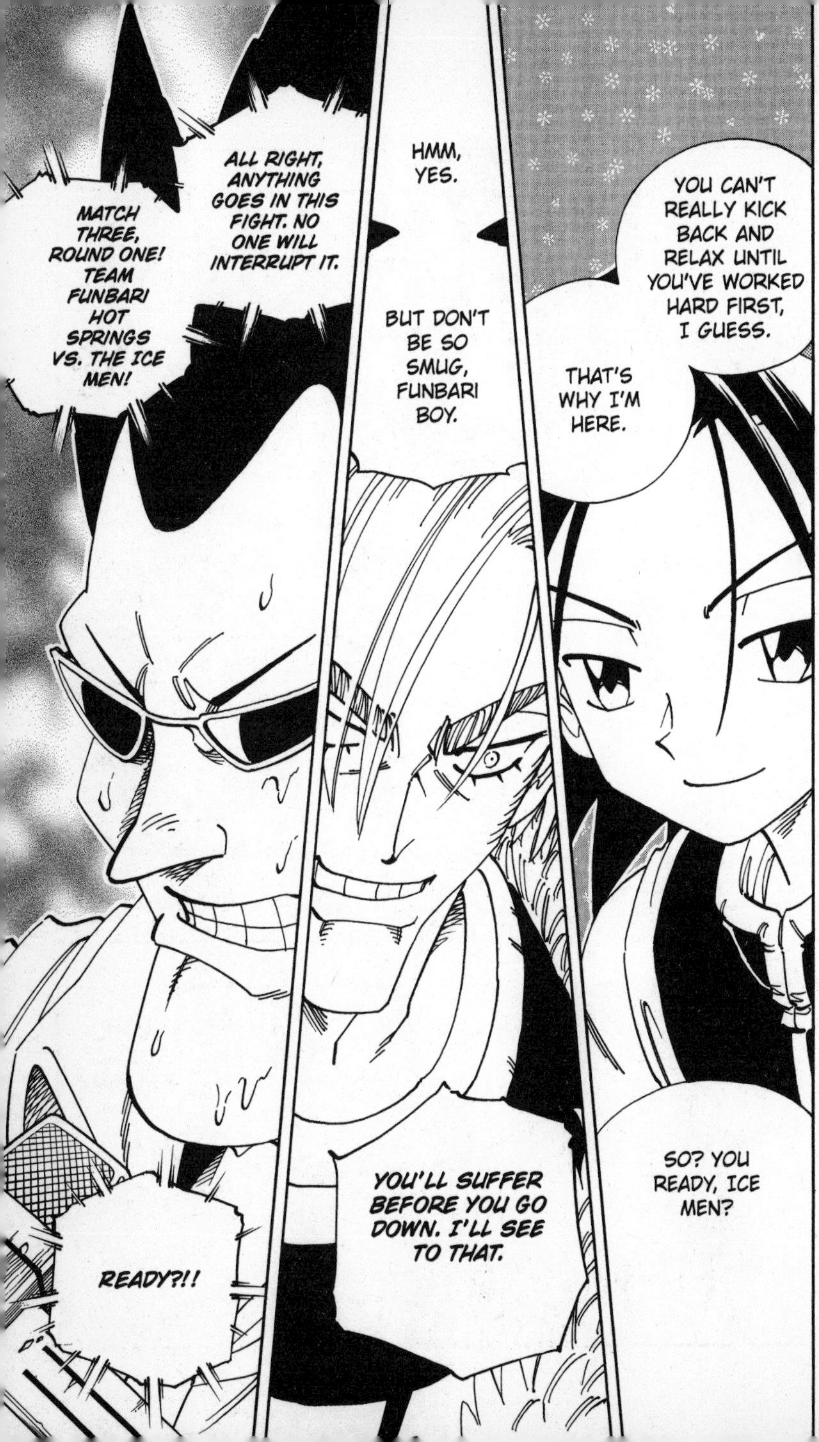

YOU CAN'T REALLY KICK BACK AND RELAX UNTIL YOU'VE WORKED HARD FIRST, I GUESS.
THAT'S WHY I'M HERE.
SO? YOU READY, ICE MEN?
HMM, YES.
BUT DON'T BE SO SMUG, FUNBARI BOY.
YOU'LL SUFFER BEFORE YOU GO DOWN. I'LL SEE TO THAT.
ALL RIGHT, ANYTHING GOES IN THIS FIGHT. NO ONE WILL INTERRUPT IT.
MATCH THREE, ROUND ONE! TEAM FUNBARI HOT SPRINGS VS. THE ICE MEN!
READY?!!

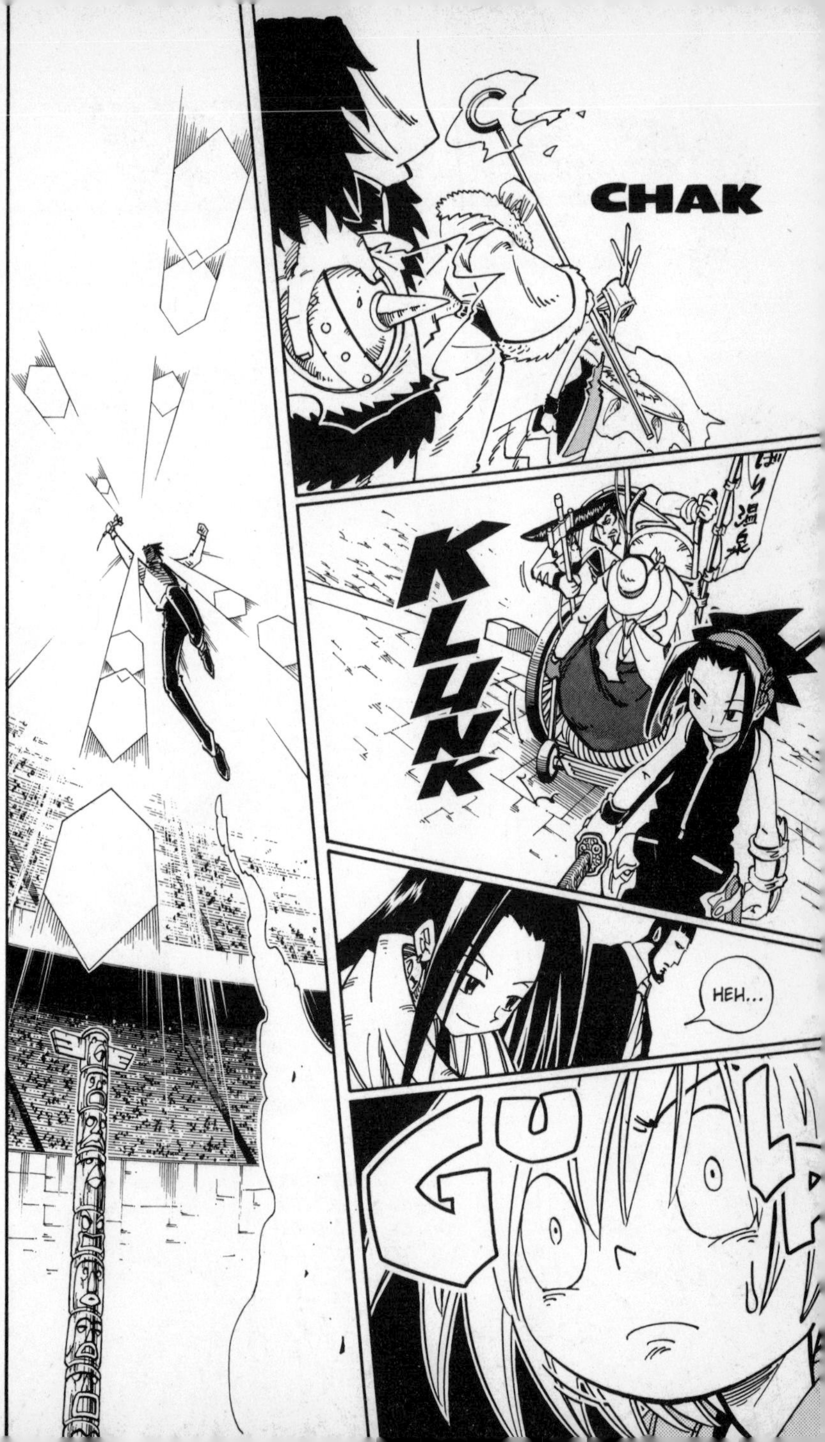
CHAK
KLUNK
HEH...

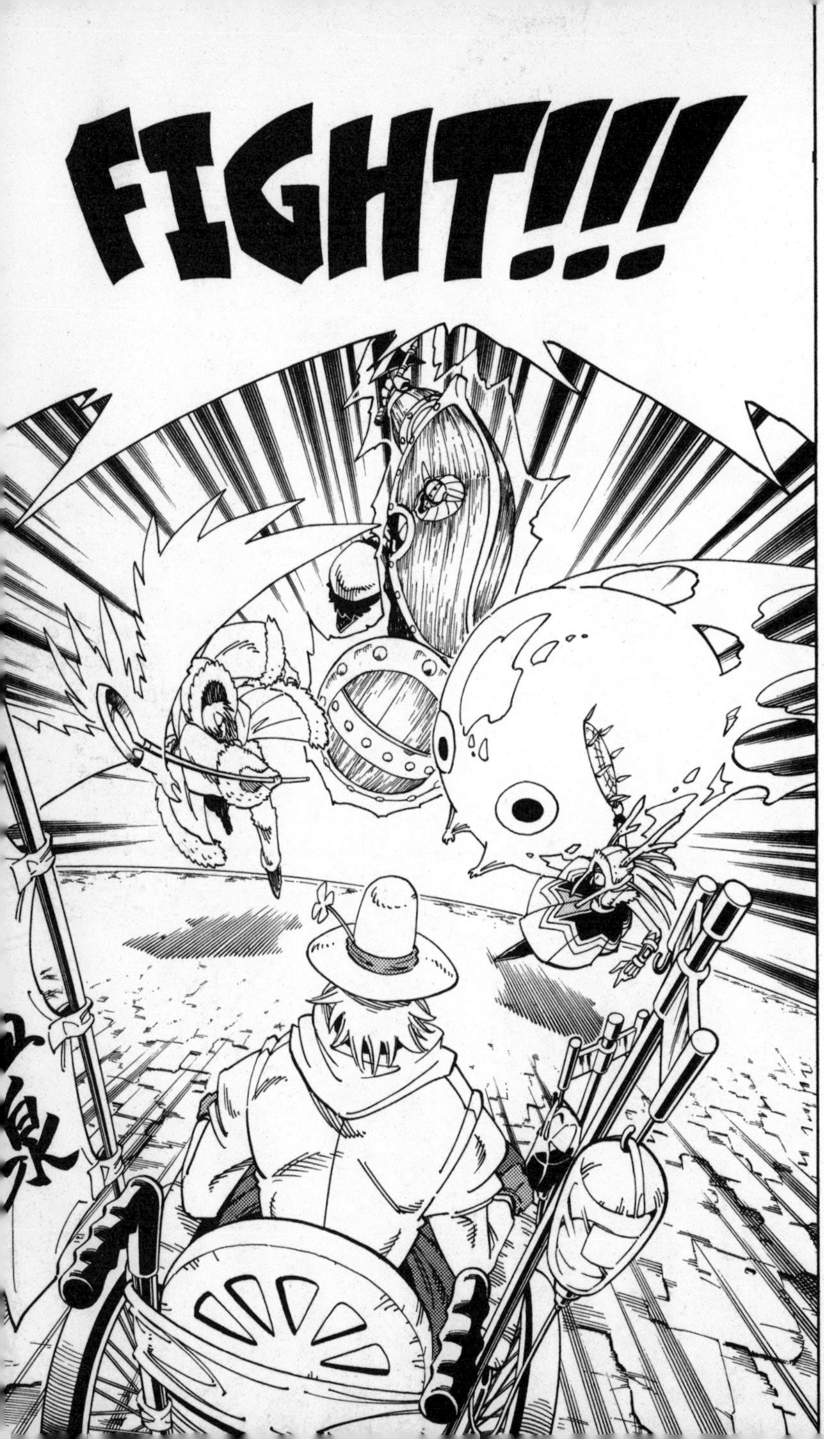
FIGHT!!!

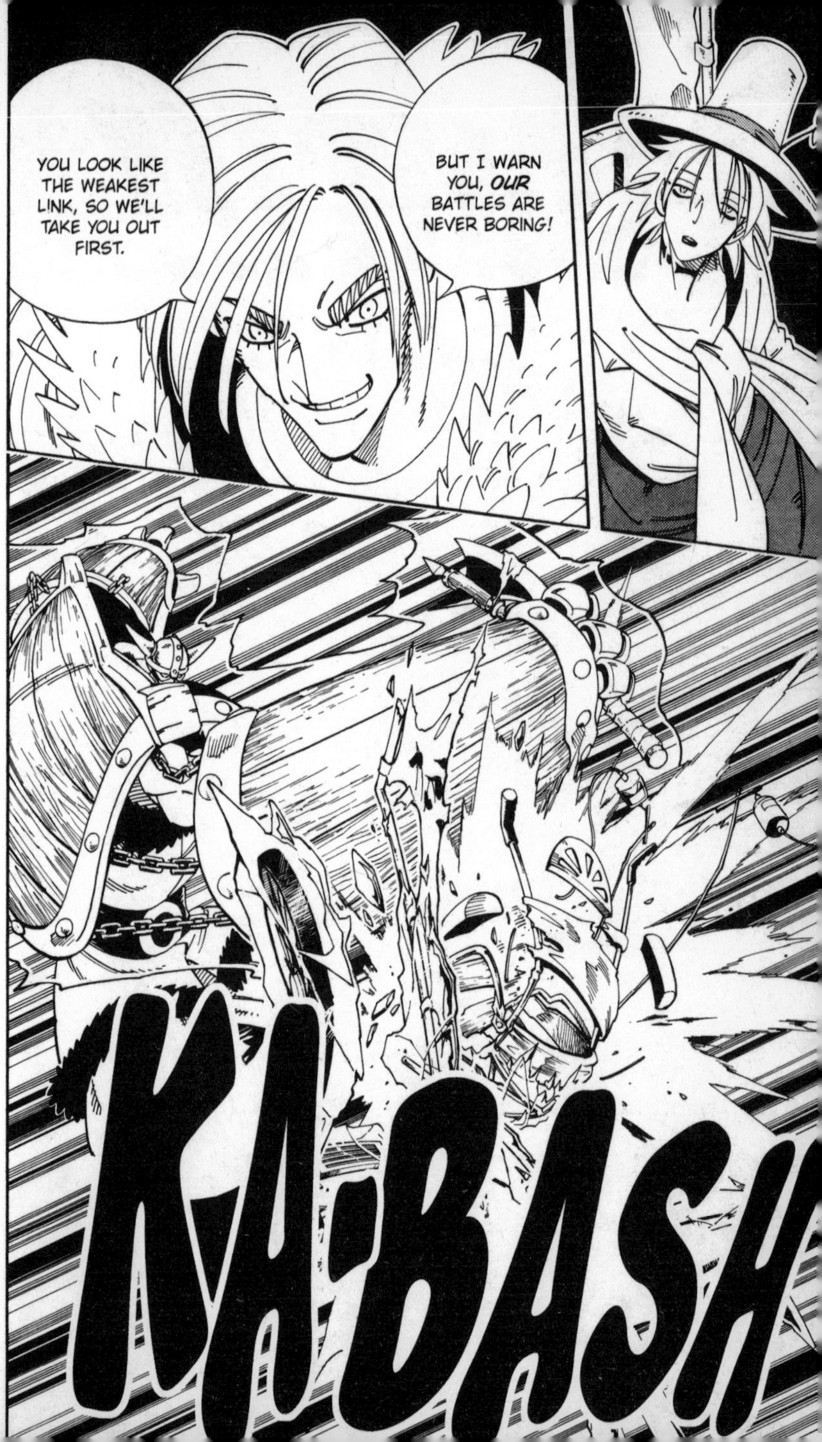
YOU LOOK LIKE THE WEAKEST LINK, SO WE'LL TAKE YOU OUT FIRST.
BUT I WARN YOU, *OUR* BATTLES ARE NEVER BORING!
KA-BASH

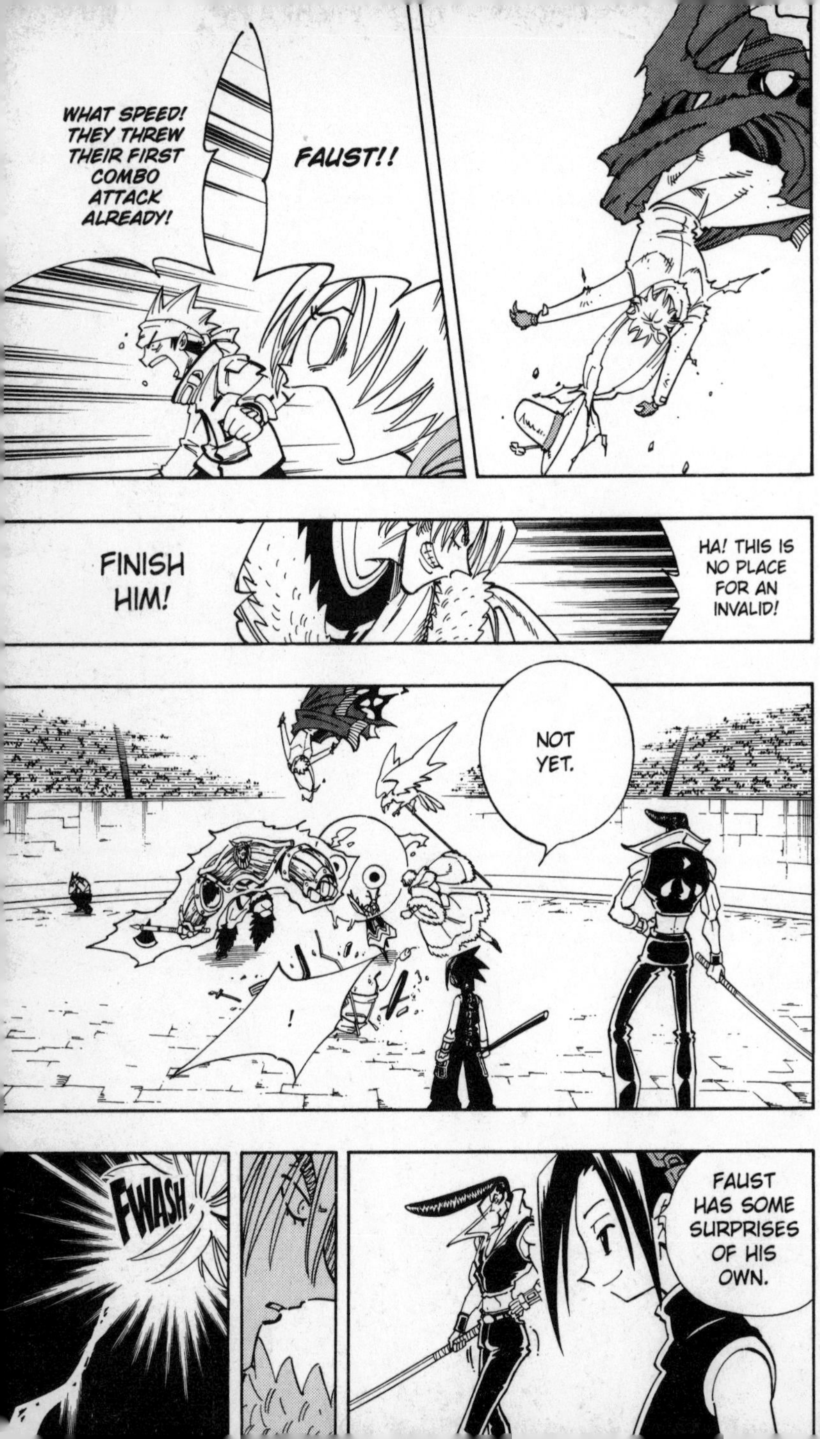
FAUST!!
WHAT SPEED! THEY THREW THEIR FIRST COMBO ATTACK ALREADY!
HA! THIS IS NO PLACE FOR AN INVALID!
FINISH HIM!
NOT YET.
!
FAUST HAS SOME SURPRISES OF HIS OWN.
FWASH

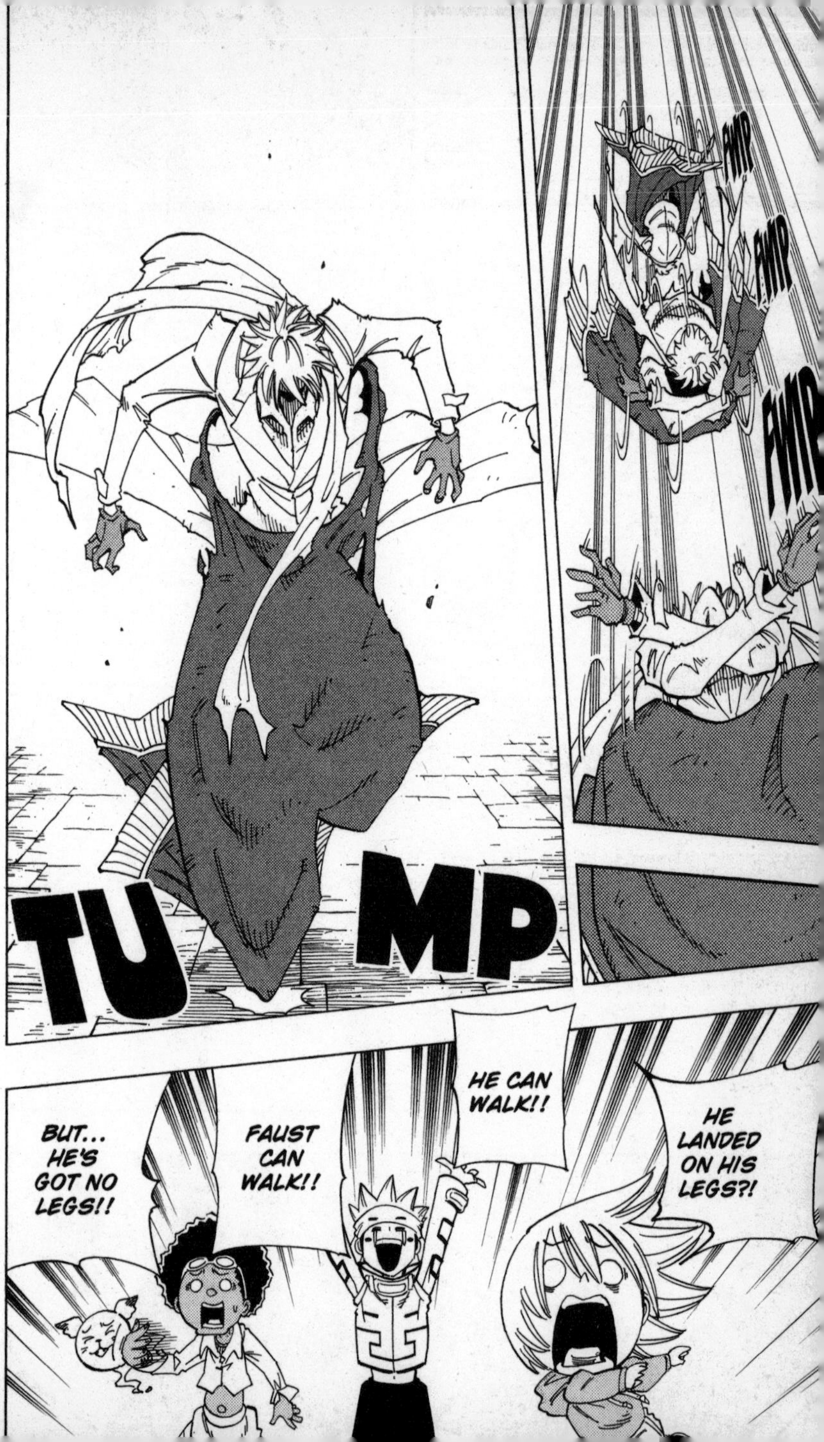
FWIP
FWIP
FWIP
TUMP
HE LANDED ON HIS LEGS?!
HE CAN WALK!!
FAUST CAN WALK!!
BUT... HE'S GOT NO LEGS!!

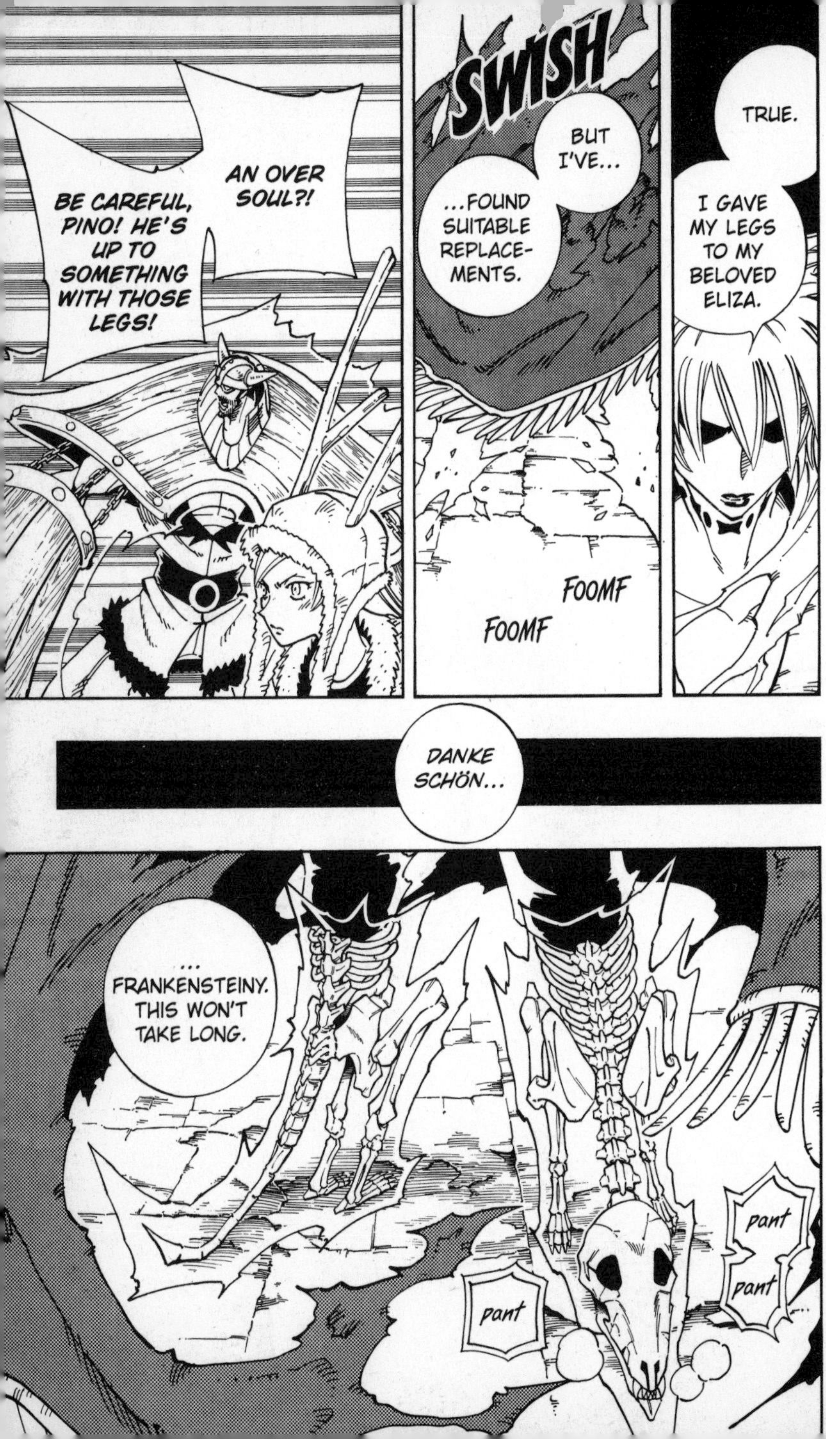
TRUE.
I GAVE MY LEGS TO MY BELOVED ELIZA.
SWISH
BUT I'VE...
...FOUND SUITABLE REPLACE-MENTS.
FOOMF
FOOMF
AN OVER SOUL?!
BE CAREFUL, PINO! HE'S UP TO SOMETHING WITH THOSE LEGS!
DANKE SCHÖN...
...FRANKENSTEINY. THIS WON'T TAKE LONG.
pant
pant
pant

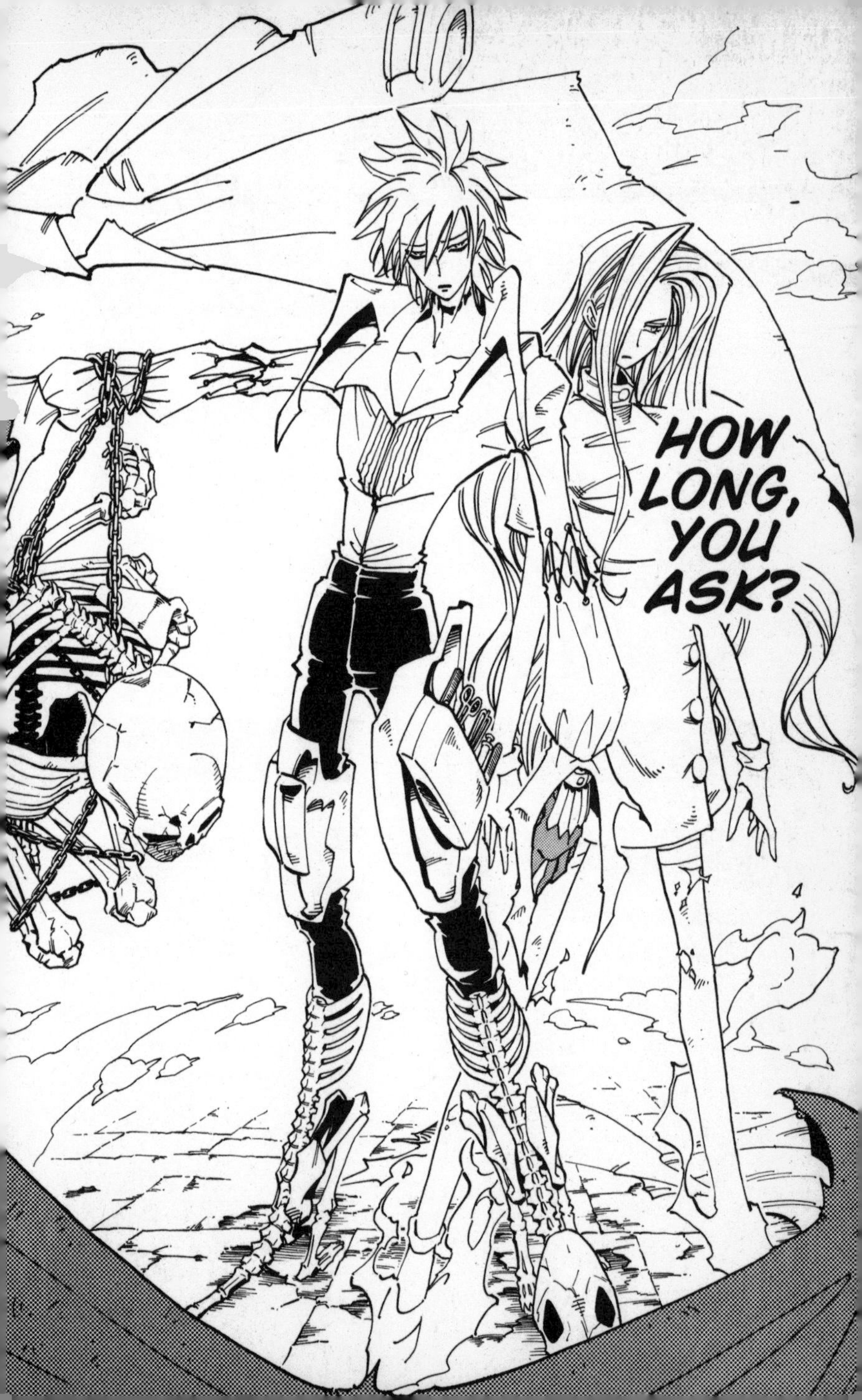
HOW LONG, YOU ASK?

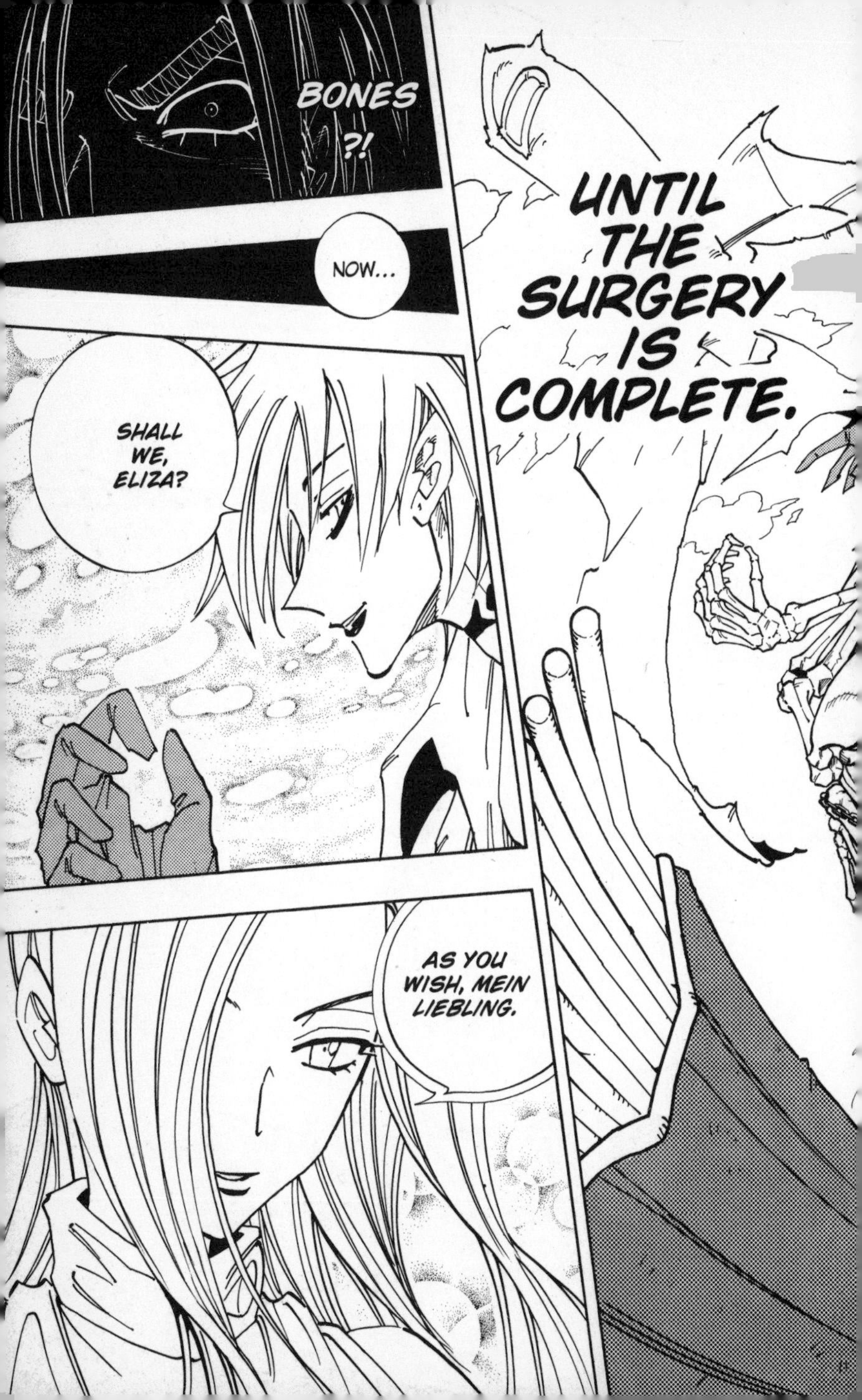
UNTIL THE SURGERY IS COMPLETE.
BONES ?!
NOW...
SHALL WE, ELIZA?
AS YOU WISH, MEIN LIEBLING.

SHAMAN KING CHARACTER FILE No.73

2001
(JULY)

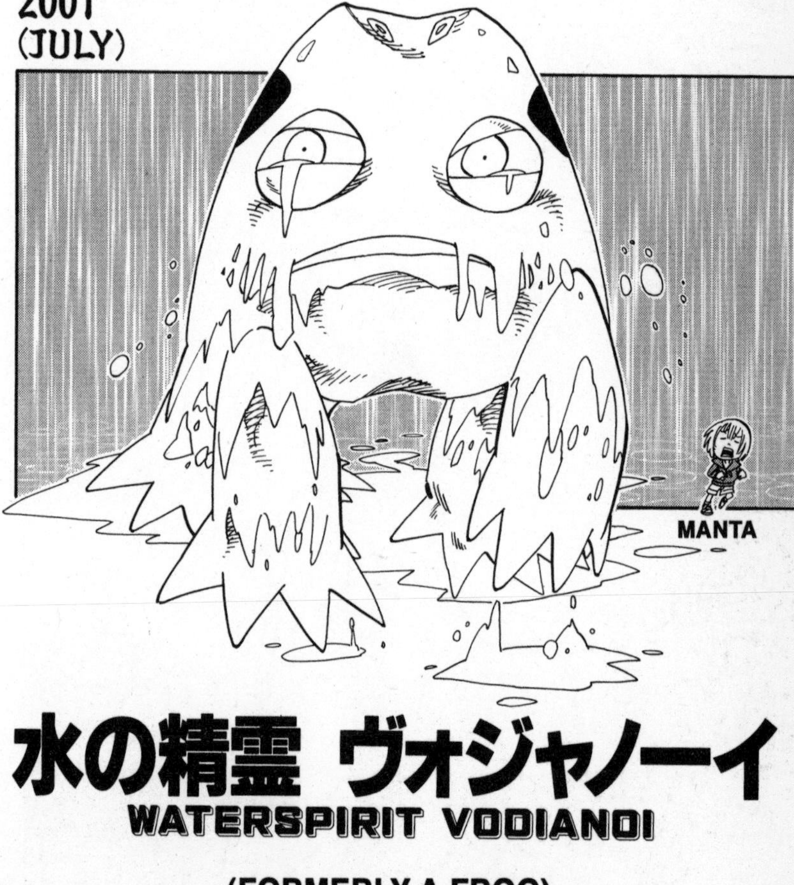
MANTA

水の精霊 ヴォジャノーイ
WATERSPIRIT VODIANOI

(FORMERLY A FROG)

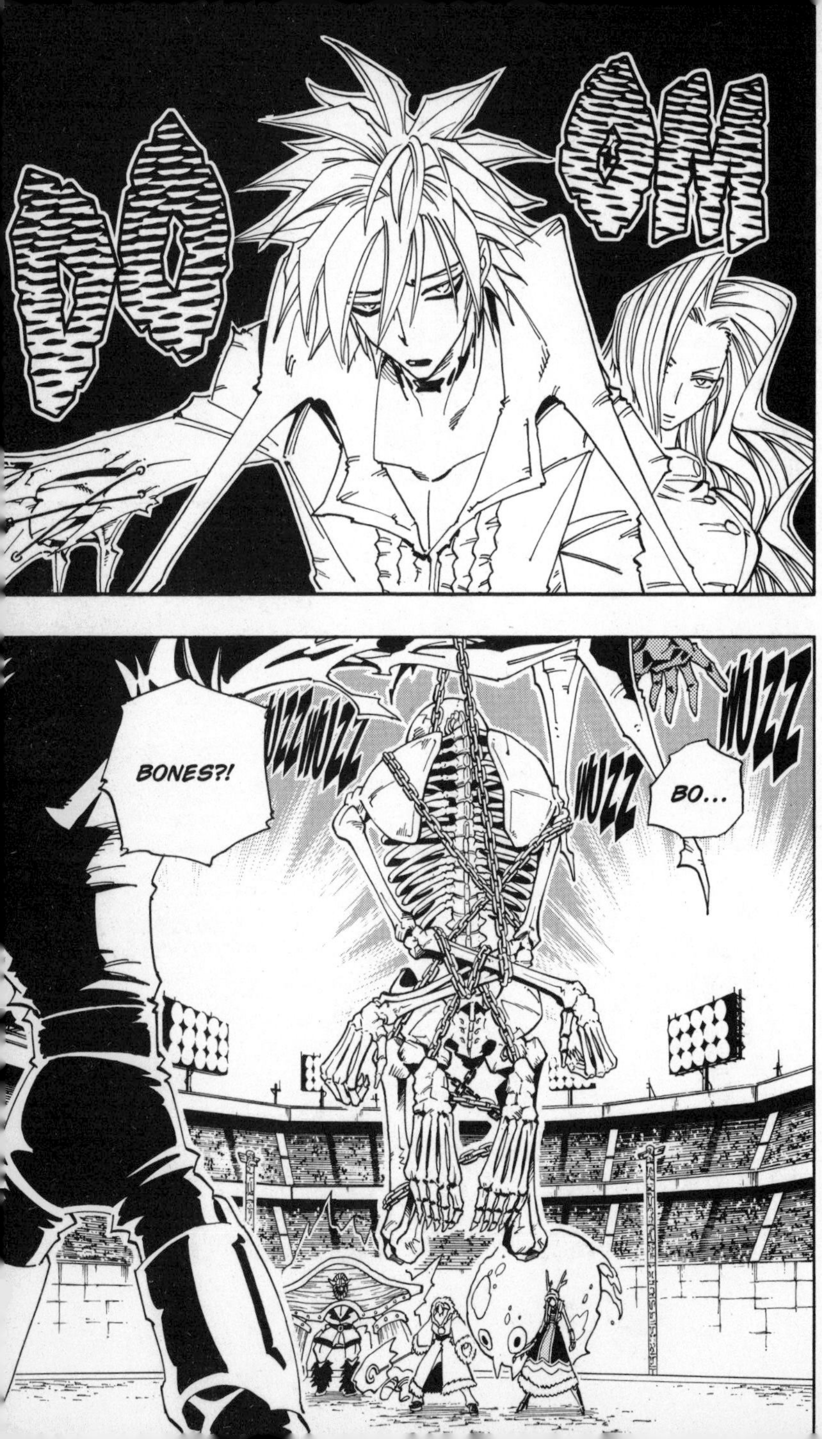
DOOM
WUZZ
WUZZ
BO...
WUZZWUZZ
BONES?!

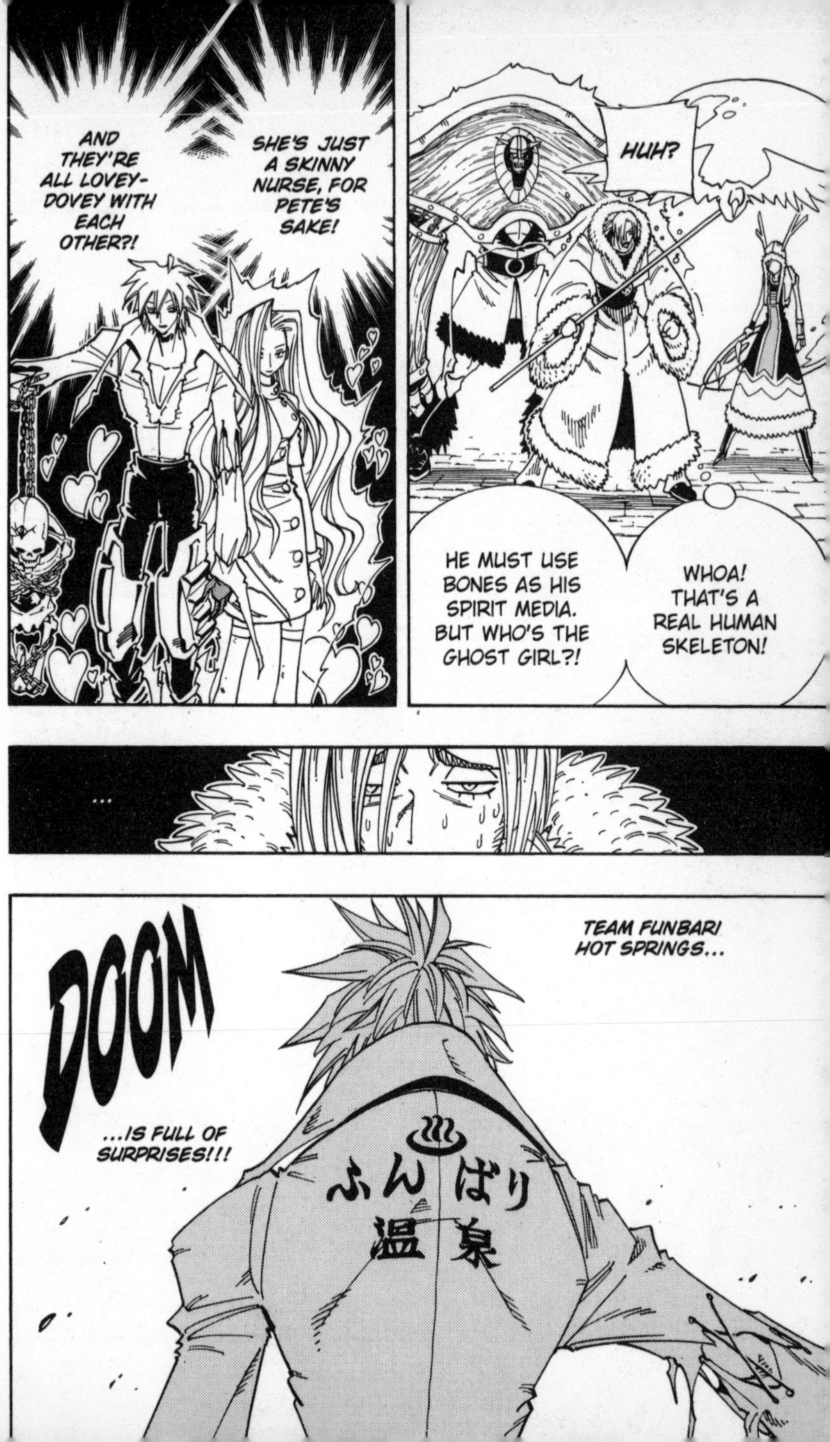
HUH?
WHOA! THAT'S A REAL HUMAN SKELETON!
HE MUST USE BONES AS HIS SPIRIT MEDIA. BUT WHO'S THE GHOST GIRL?!
SHE'S JUST A SKINNY NURSE, FOR PETE'S SAKE!
AND THEY'RE ALL LOVEY-DOVEY WITH EACH OTHER?!
...
TEAM FUNBARI HOT SPRINGS...
DOOM
...IS FULL OF SURPRISES!!!
ふんばり温泉

Reincarnation 130:

Faust's Album

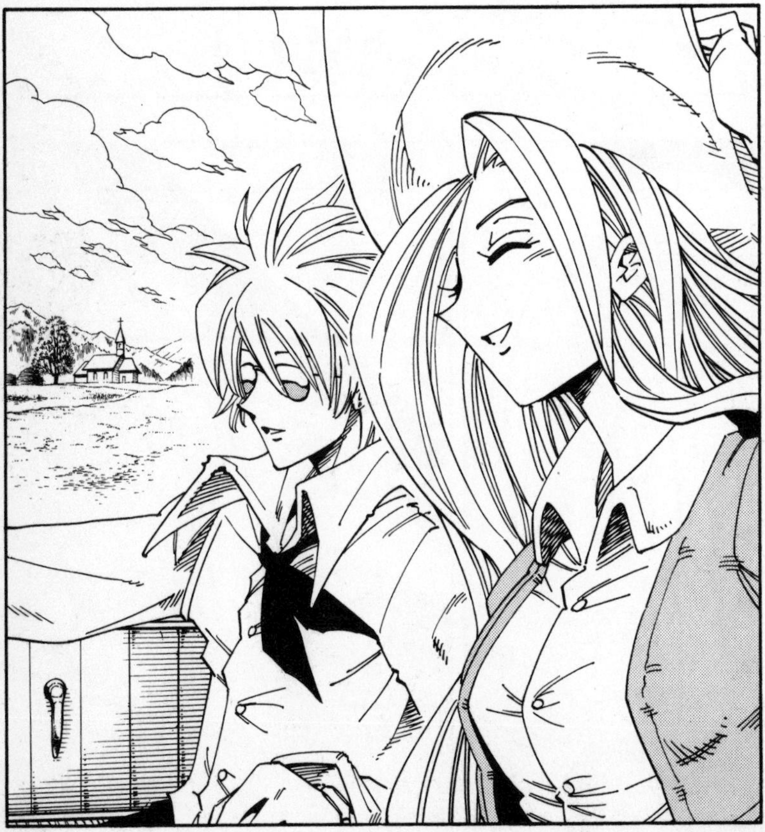

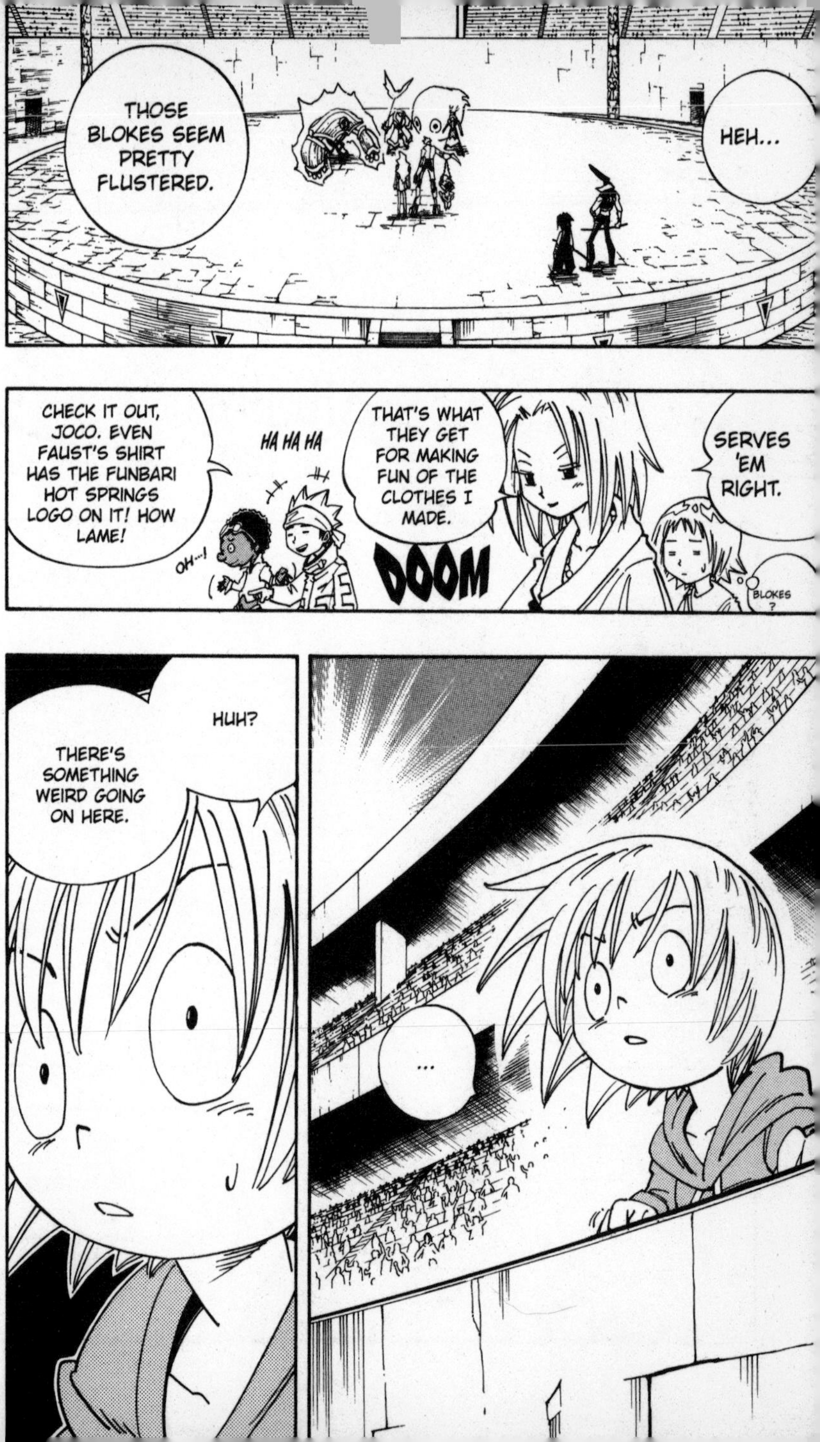
HEH...
THOSE BLOKES SEEM PRETTY FLUSTERED.
SERVES 'EM RIGHT.
BLOKES?
THAT'S WHAT THEY GET FOR MAKING FUN OF THE CLOTHES I MADE.
DOOM
HA HA HA
CHECK IT OUT, JOCO. EVEN FAUST'S SHIRT HAS THE FUNBARI HOT SPRINGS LOGO ON IT! HOW LAME!
OH...!
...
HUH?
THERE'S SOMETHING WEIRD GOING ON HERE.

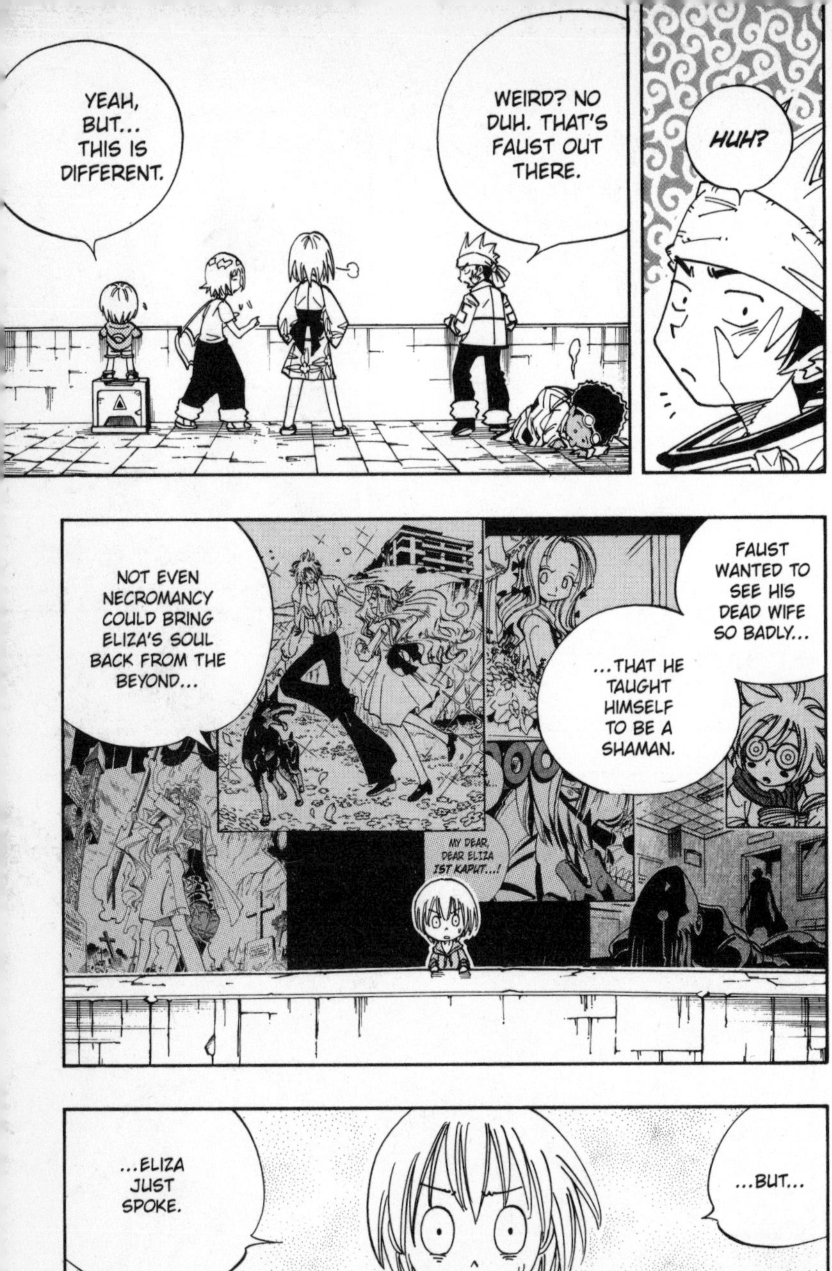
HUH?
WEIRD? NO DUH. THAT'S FAUST OUT THERE.
YEAH, BUT... THIS IS DIFFERENT.
FAUST WANTED TO SEE HIS DEAD WIFE SO BADLY...
...THAT HE TAUGHT HIMSELF TO BE A SHAMAN.
NOT EVEN NECROMANCY COULD BRING ELIZA'S SOUL BACK FROM THE BEYOND...
MY DEAR, DEAR ELIZA IST KAPUT...!
...BUT...
...ELIZA JUST SPOKE.

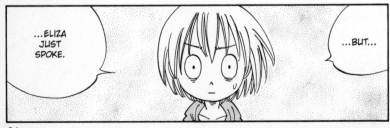

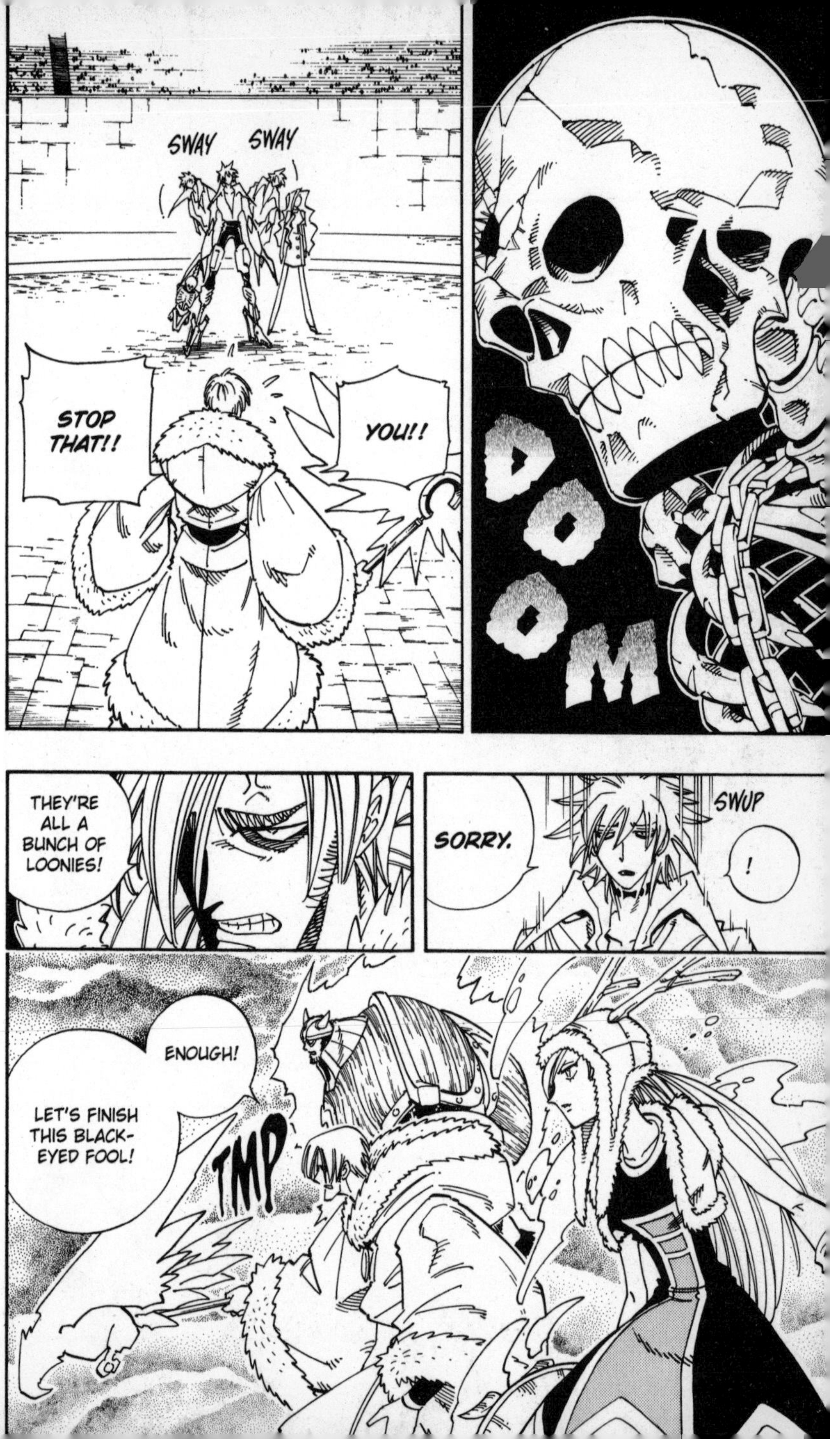
DOOM
SWAY SWAY
YOU!!
STOP THAT!!
SWUP
!
SORRY.
THEY'RE ALL A BUNCH OF LOONIES!
ENOUGH!
LET'S FINISH THIS BLACK-EYED FOOL!
TMP

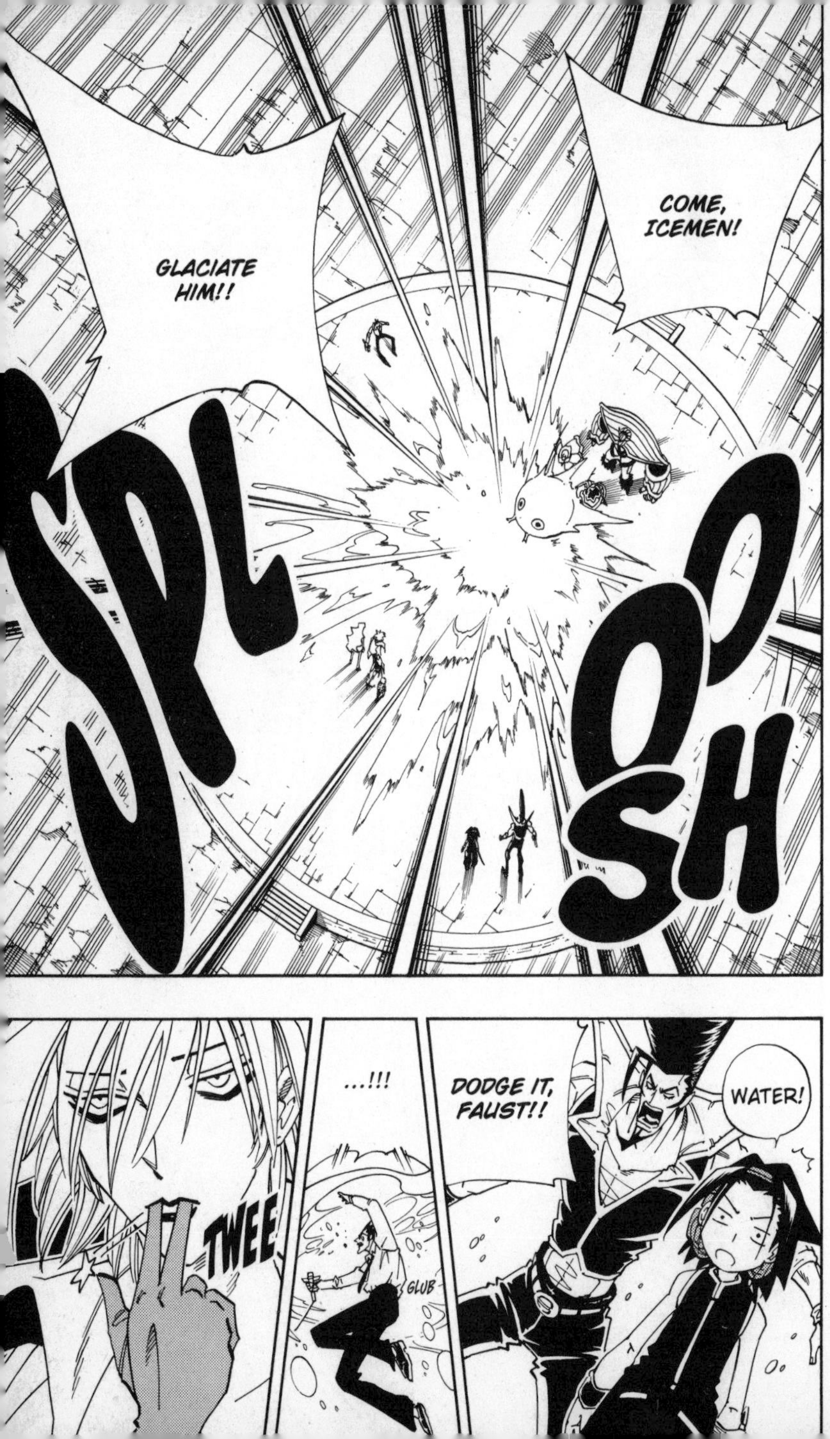
COME, ICEMEN!
GLACIATE HIM!!
SPLOOSH
WATER!
DODGE IT, FAUST!!
GLUB
...!!!
TWEE

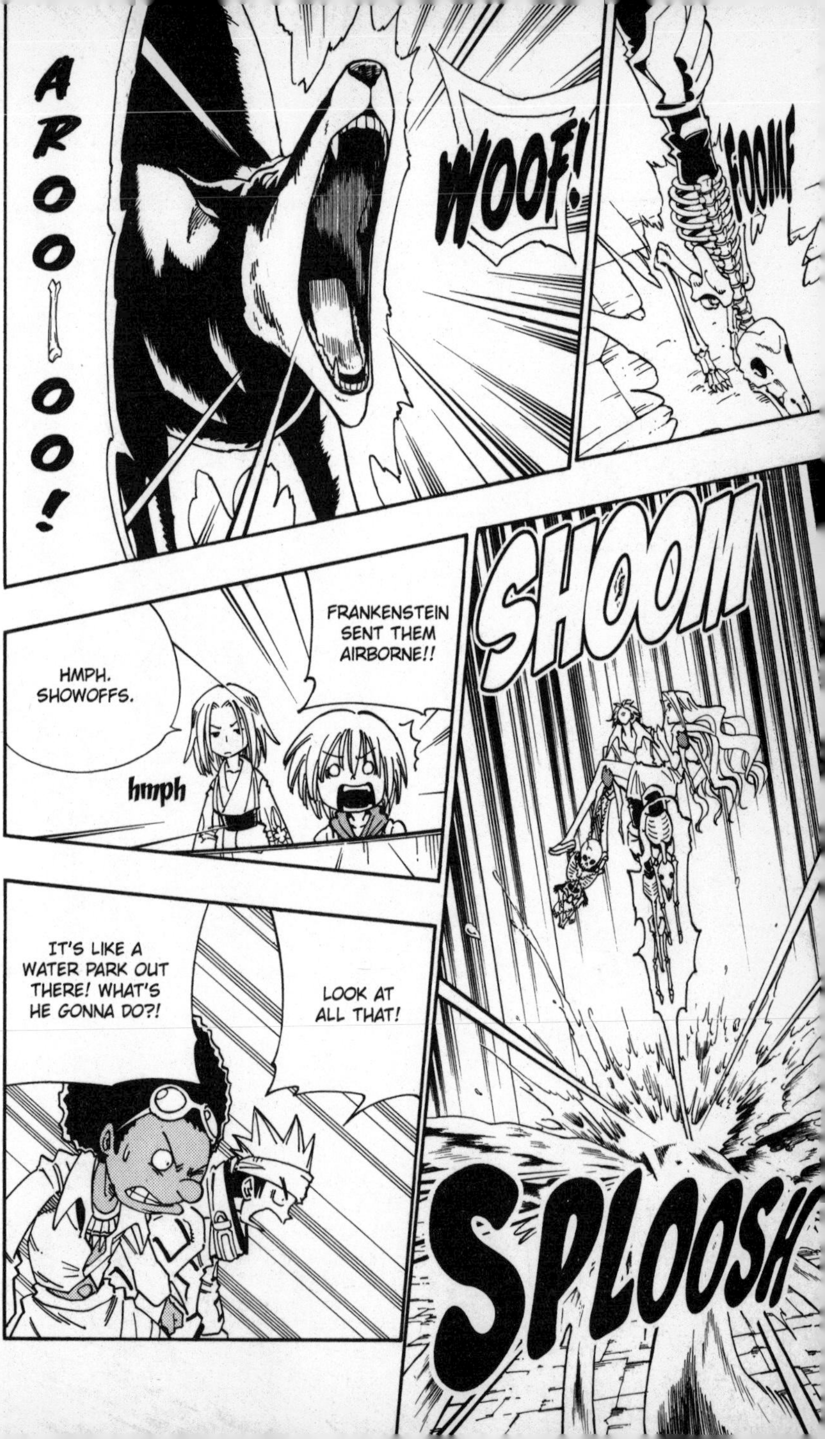
FOOMF
WOOF!
AROOO—OOO!
SHOOM
FRANKENSTEIN SENT THEM AIRBORNE!!
HMPH. SHOWOFFS.
hmph
SPLOOSH
LOOK AT ALL THAT!
IT'S LIKE A WATER PARK OUT THERE! WHAT'S HE GONNA DO?!

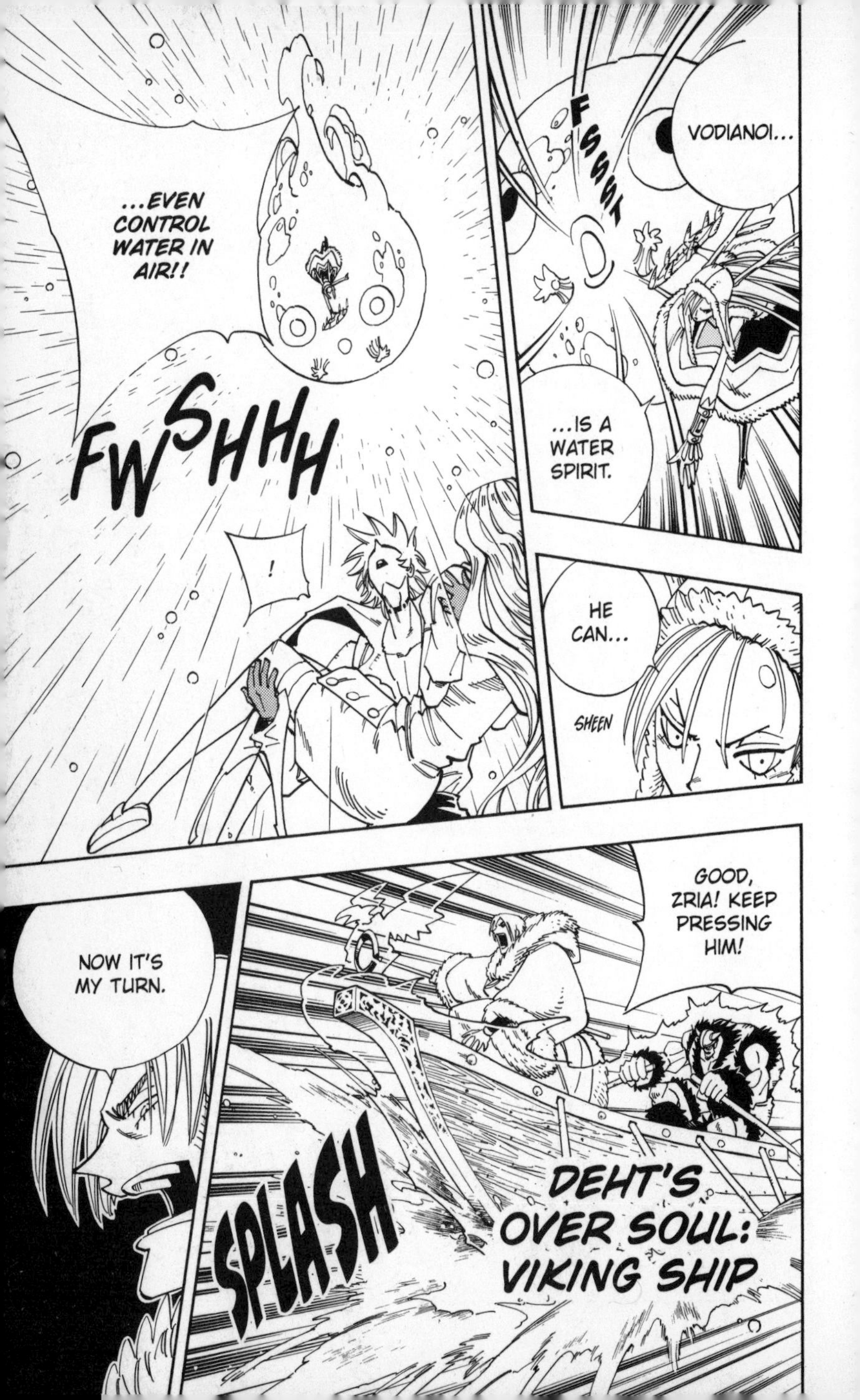
VODIANOI...
FSSST
...IS A WATER SPIRIT.
HE CAN...
SHEEN
...EVEN CONTROL WATER IN AIR!!
FWSHHH
!
GOOD, ZRIA! KEEP PRESSING HIM!
DEHT'S OVER SOUL: VIKING SHIP
SPLASH
NOW IT'S MY TURN.

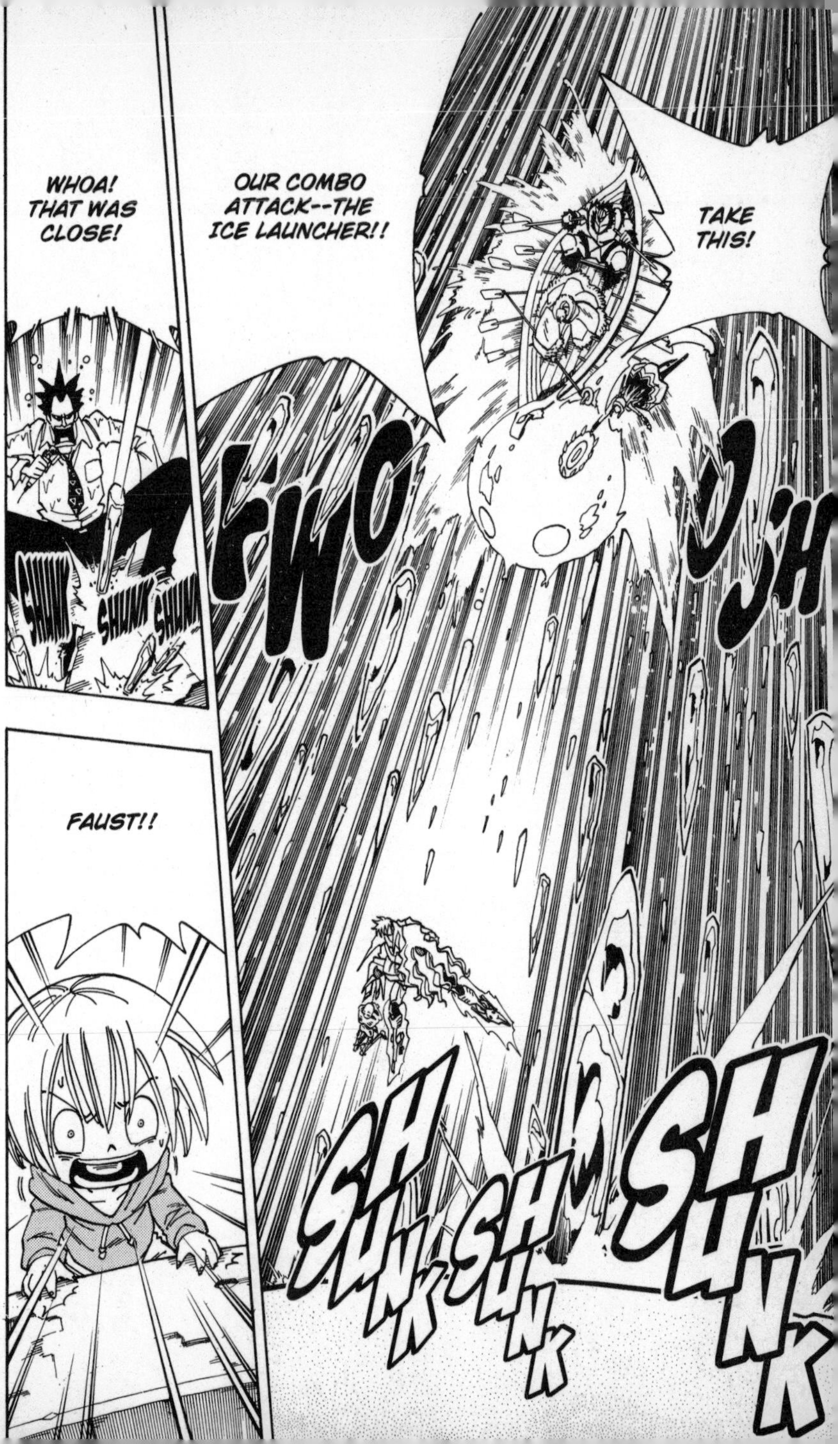
TAKE THIS!
OUR COMBO ATTACK--THE ICE LAUNCHER!!
FWOOSH
SHUNK SHUNK SHUNK
WHOA! THAT WAS CLOSE!
SHUNK SHUNK SHUNK
FAUST!!

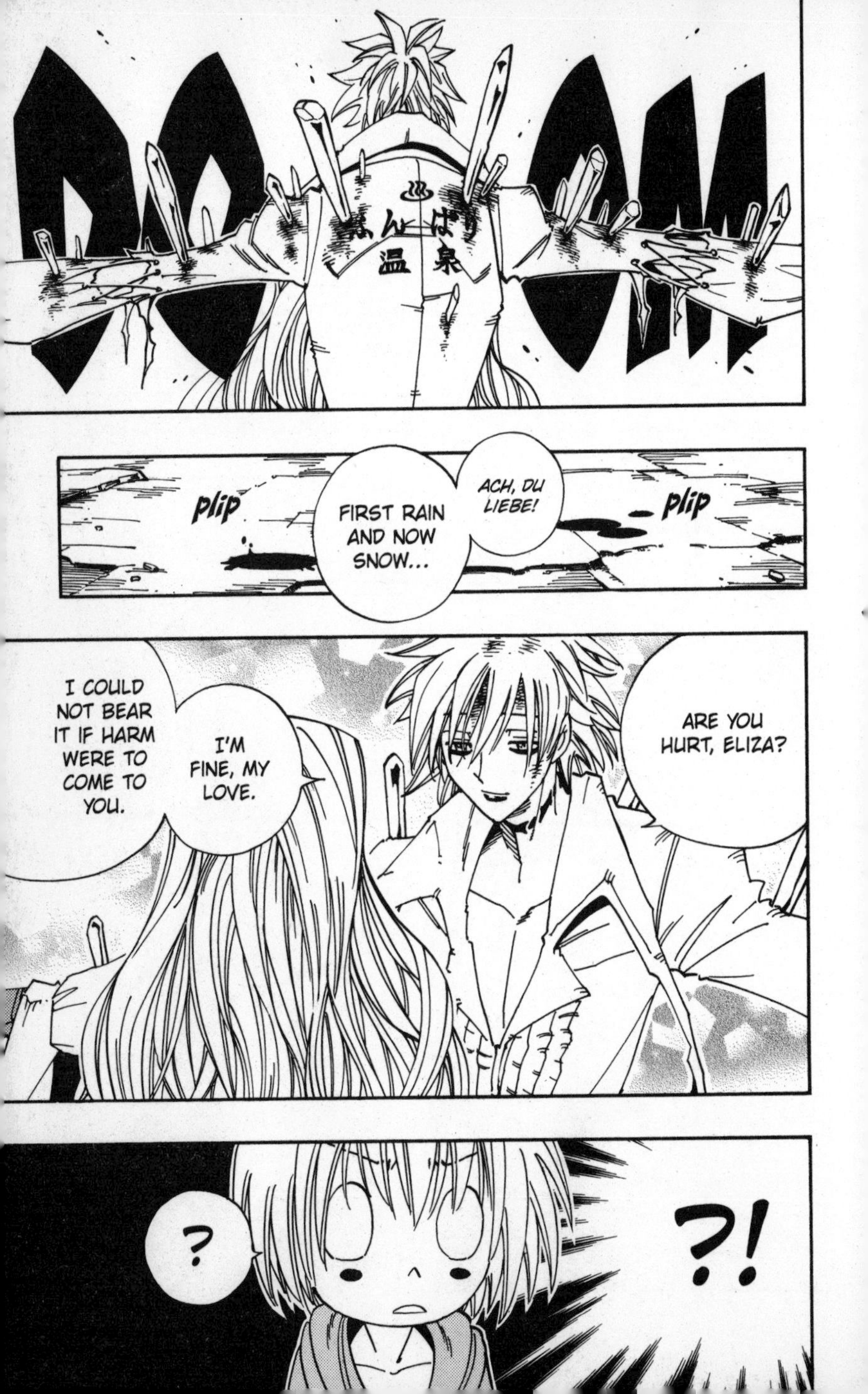
DOOM!
温泉
plip
ACH, DU LIEBE!
FIRST RAIN AND NOW SNOW...
plip
ARE YOU HURT, ELIZA?
I'M FINE, MY LOVE.
I COULD NOT BEAR IT IF HARM WERE TO COME TO YOU.
?!
?

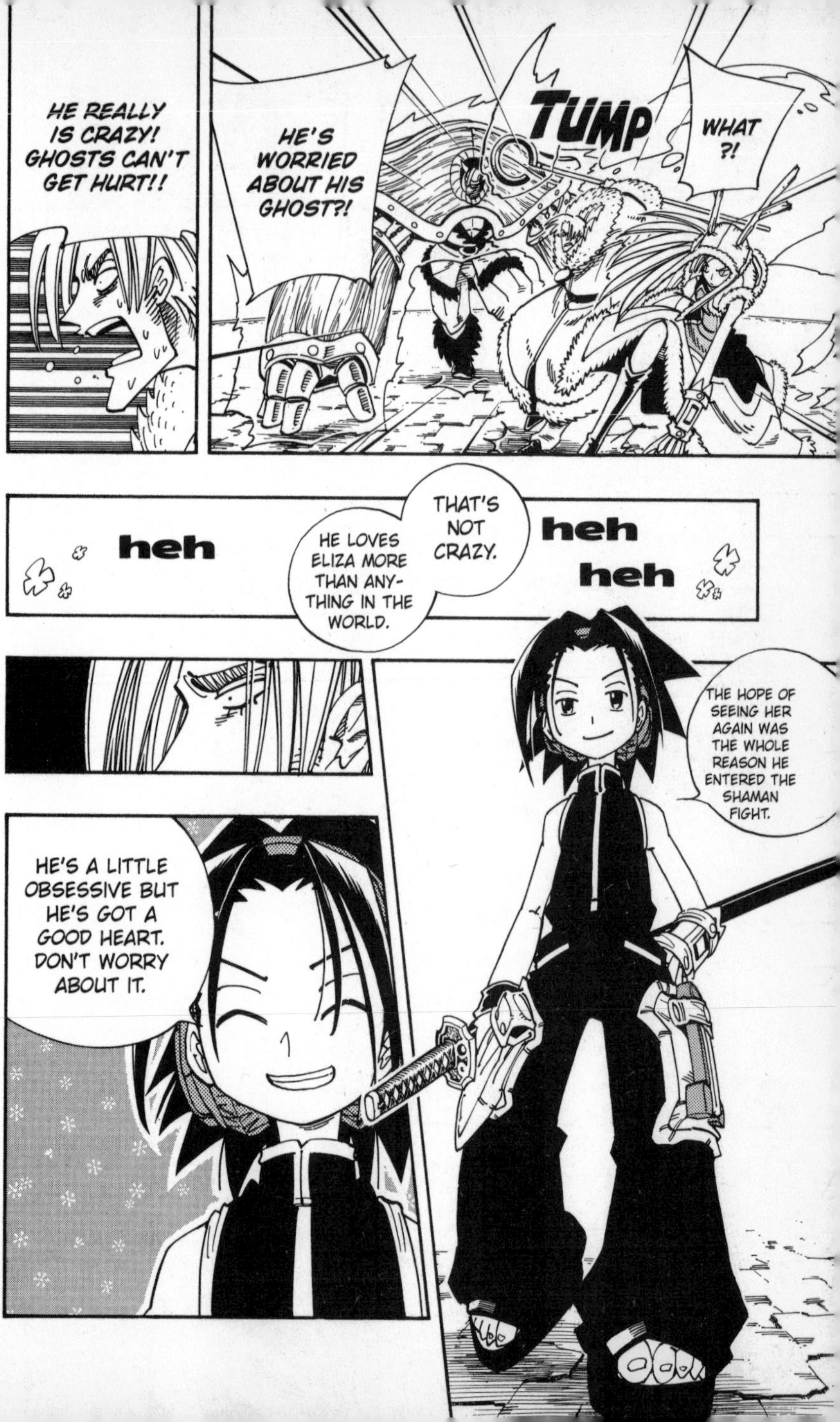
TUMP
WHAT ?!
HE'S WORRIED ABOUT HIS GHOST?!
HE REALLY IS CRAZY! GHOSTS CAN'T GET HURT!!
heh heh
THAT'S NOT CRAZY.
HE LOVES ELIZA MORE THAN ANY-THING IN THE WORLD.
heh
THE HOPE OF SEEING HER AGAIN WAS THE WHOLE REASON HE ENTERED THE SHAMAN FIGHT.
HE'S A LITTLE OBSESSIVE BUT HE'S GOT A GOOD HEART. DON'T WORRY ABOUT IT.

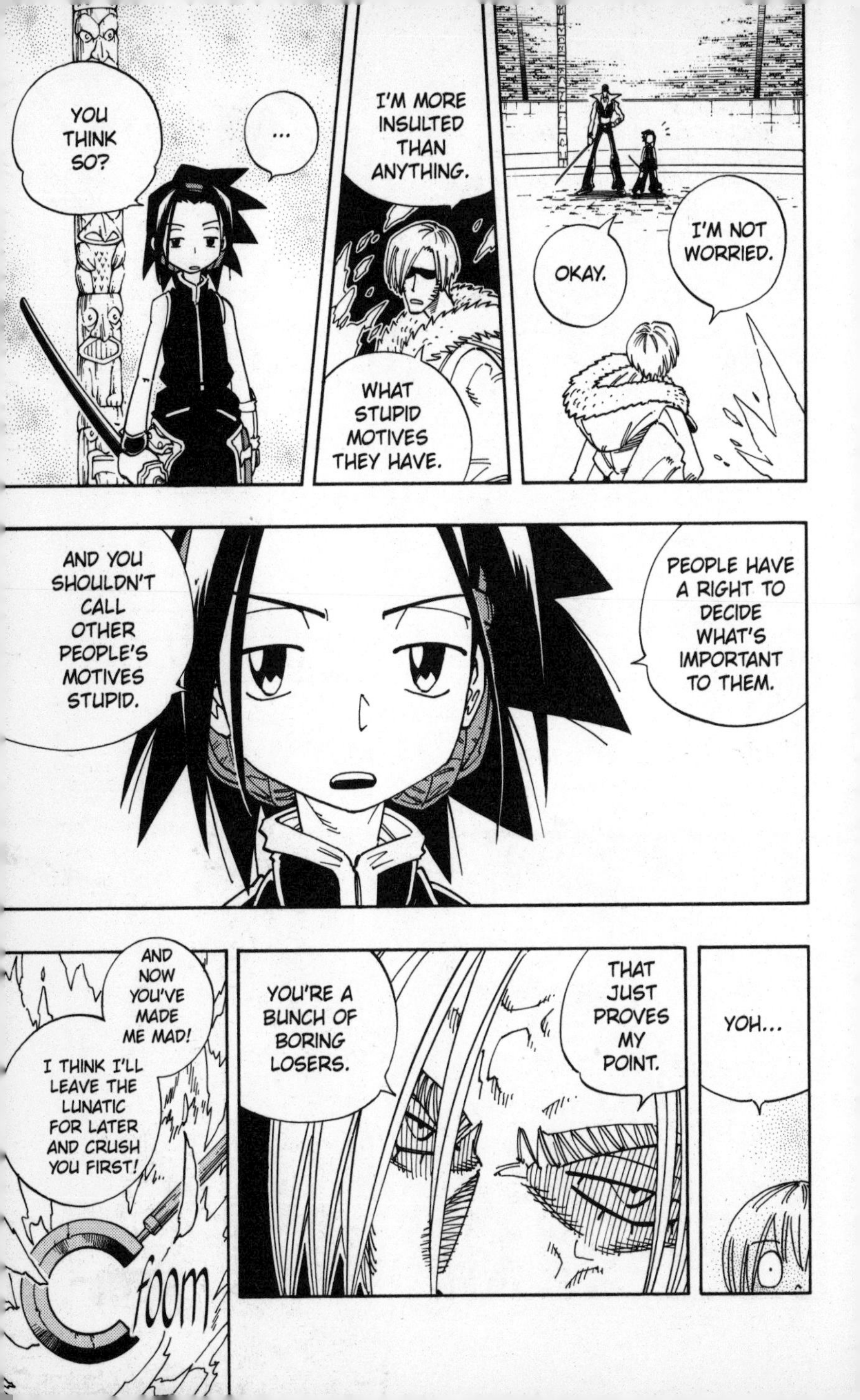
I'M NOT WORRIED.
OKAY.
I'M MORE INSULTED THAN ANYTHING.
WHAT STUPID MOTIVES THEY HAVE.
...
YOU THINK SO?
PEOPLE HAVE A RIGHT TO DECIDE WHAT'S IMPORTANT TO THEM.
AND YOU SHOULDN'T CALL OTHER PEOPLE'S MOTIVES STUPID.
YOH...
THAT JUST PROVES MY POINT.
YOU'RE A BUNCH OF BORING LOSERS.
AND NOW YOU'VE MADE ME MAD!
I THINK I'LL LEAVE THE LUNATIC FOR LATER AND CRUSH YOU FIRST!
foom

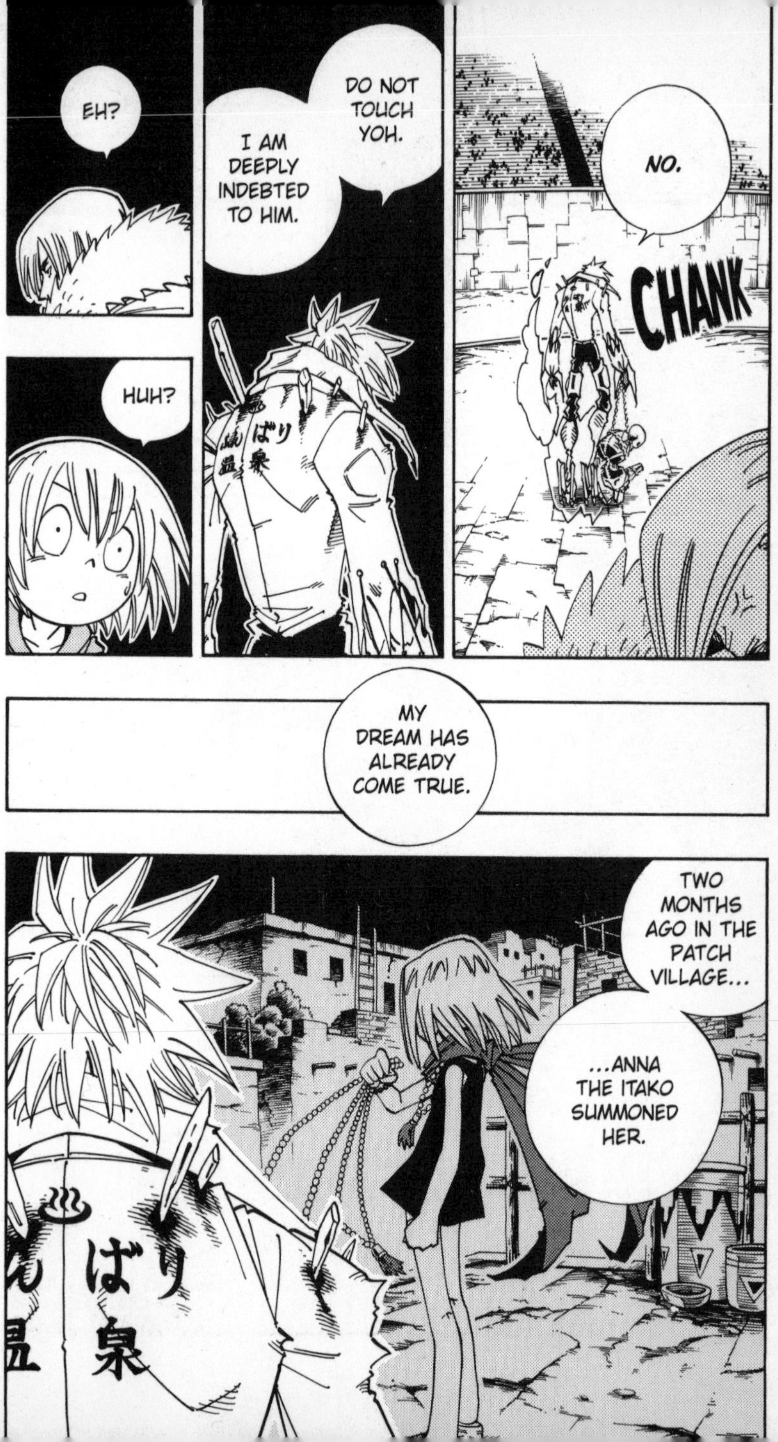
NO.
CHANK
DO NOT TOUCH YOH.
I AM DEEPLY INDEBTED TO HIM.
EH?
HUH?
MY DREAM HAS ALREADY COME TRUE.
TWO MONTHS AGO IN THE PATCH VILLAGE...
...ANNA THE ITAKO SUMMONED HER.

READ THIS WAY

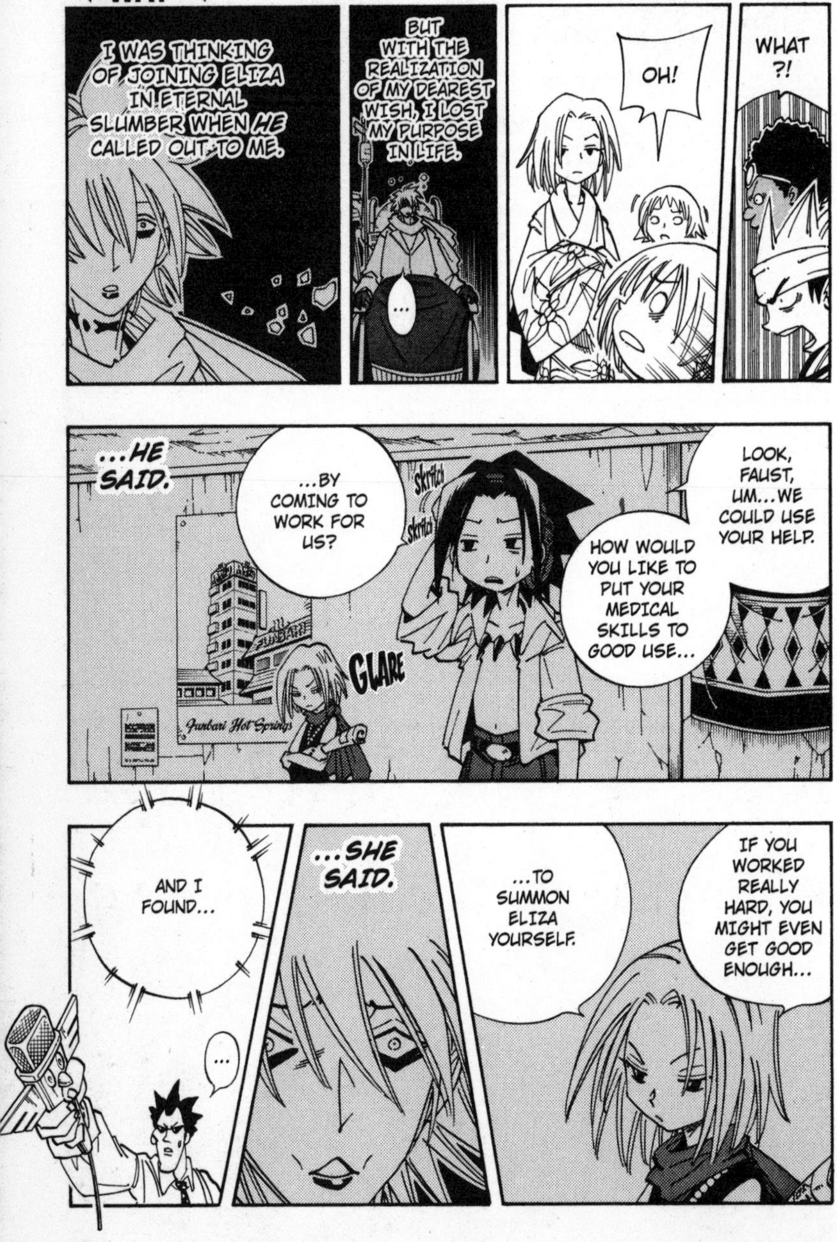
WHAT ?!
OH!
BUT WITH THE REALIZATION OF MY DEAREST WISH, I LOST MY PURPOSE IN LIFE.
...
I WAS THINKING OF JOINING ELIZA IN ETERNAL SLUMBER WHEN HE CALLED OUT TO ME.
LOOK, FAUST, UM...WE COULD USE YOUR HELP.
HOW WOULD YOU LIKE TO PUT YOUR MEDICAL SKILLS TO GOOD USE...
...BY COMING TO WORK FOR US?
skritch
skritch
GLARE
Funbari Hot Springs
...HE SAID.
IF YOU WORKED REALLY HARD, YOU MIGHT EVEN GET GOOD ENOUGH...
...TO SUMMON ELIZA YOURSELF.
...SHE SAID.
AND I FOUND...
...

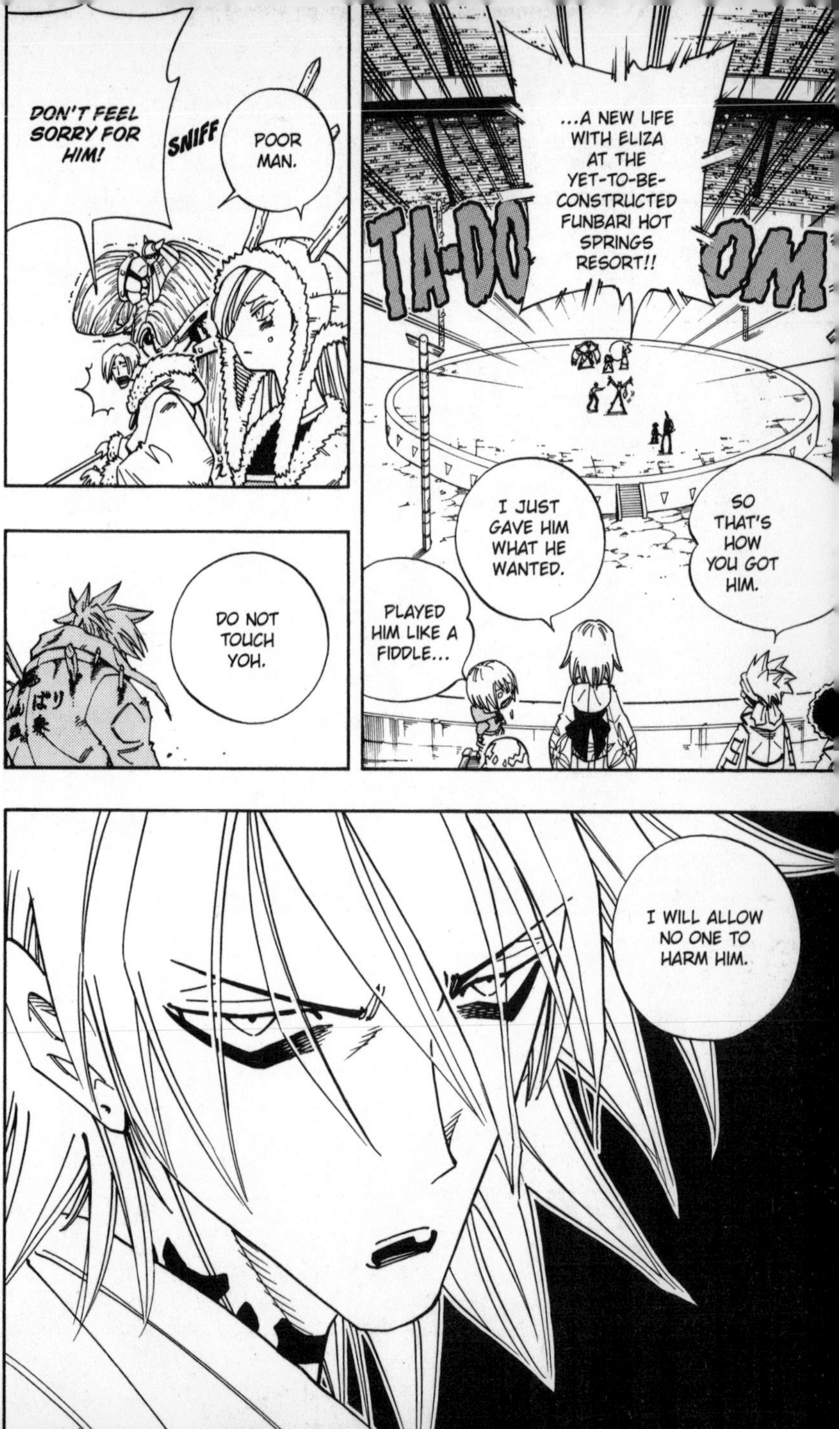
...A NEW LIFE WITH ELIZA AT THE YET-TO-BE-CONSTRUCTED FUNBARI HOT SPRINGS RESORT!!
TA-DOOM
SO THAT'S HOW YOU GOT HIM.
I JUST GAVE HIM WHAT HE WANTED.
PLAYED HIM LIKE A FIDDLE...
POOR MAN.
SNIFF
DON'T FEEL SORRY FOR HIM!
DO NOT TOUCH YOH.
I WILL ALLOW NO ONE TO HARM HIM.

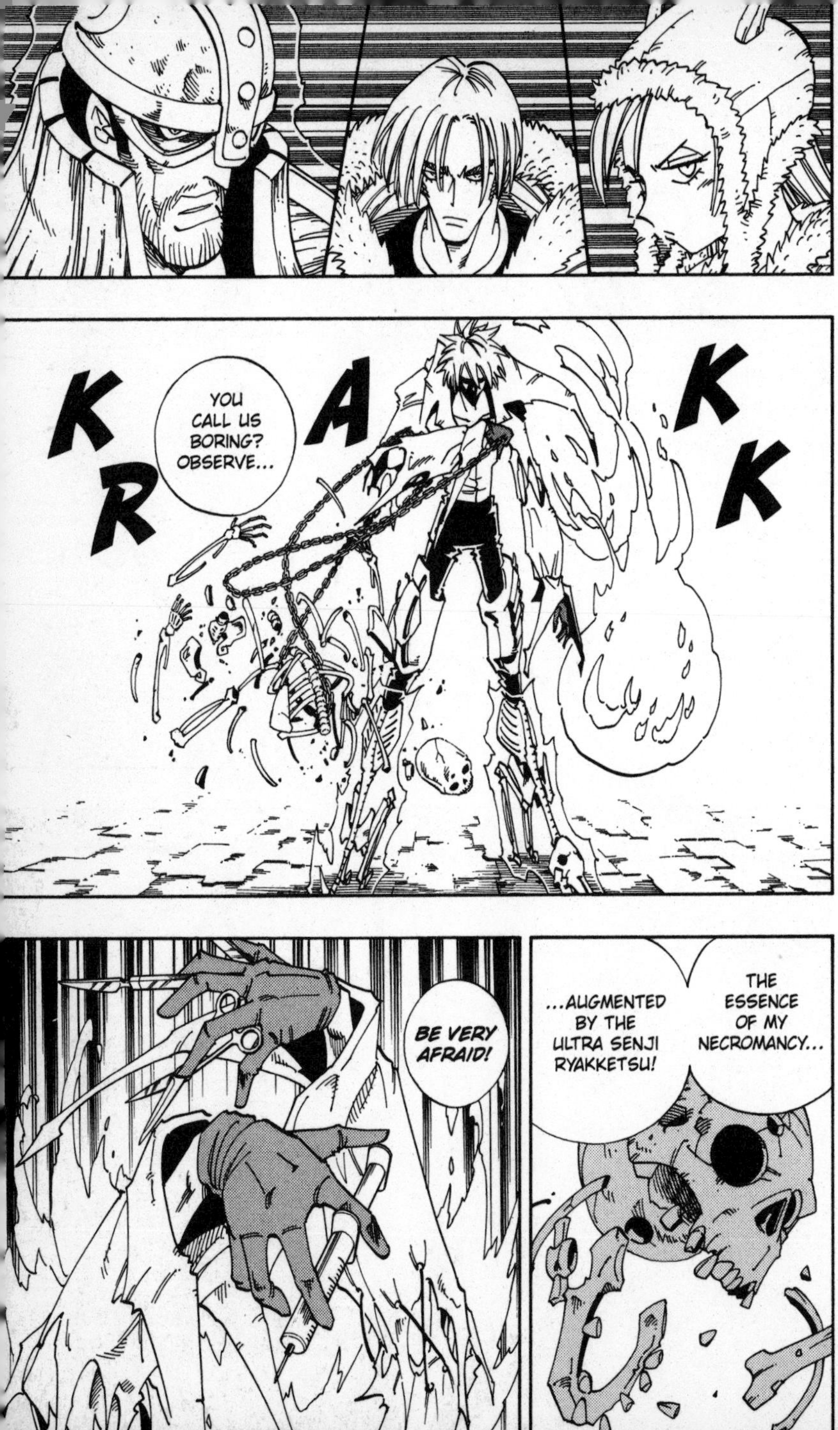
YOU CALL US BORING? OBSERVE...
KRAKK
THE ESSENCE OF MY NECROMANCY...
...AUGMENTED BY THE ULTRA SENJI RYAKKETSU!
BE VERY AFRAID!

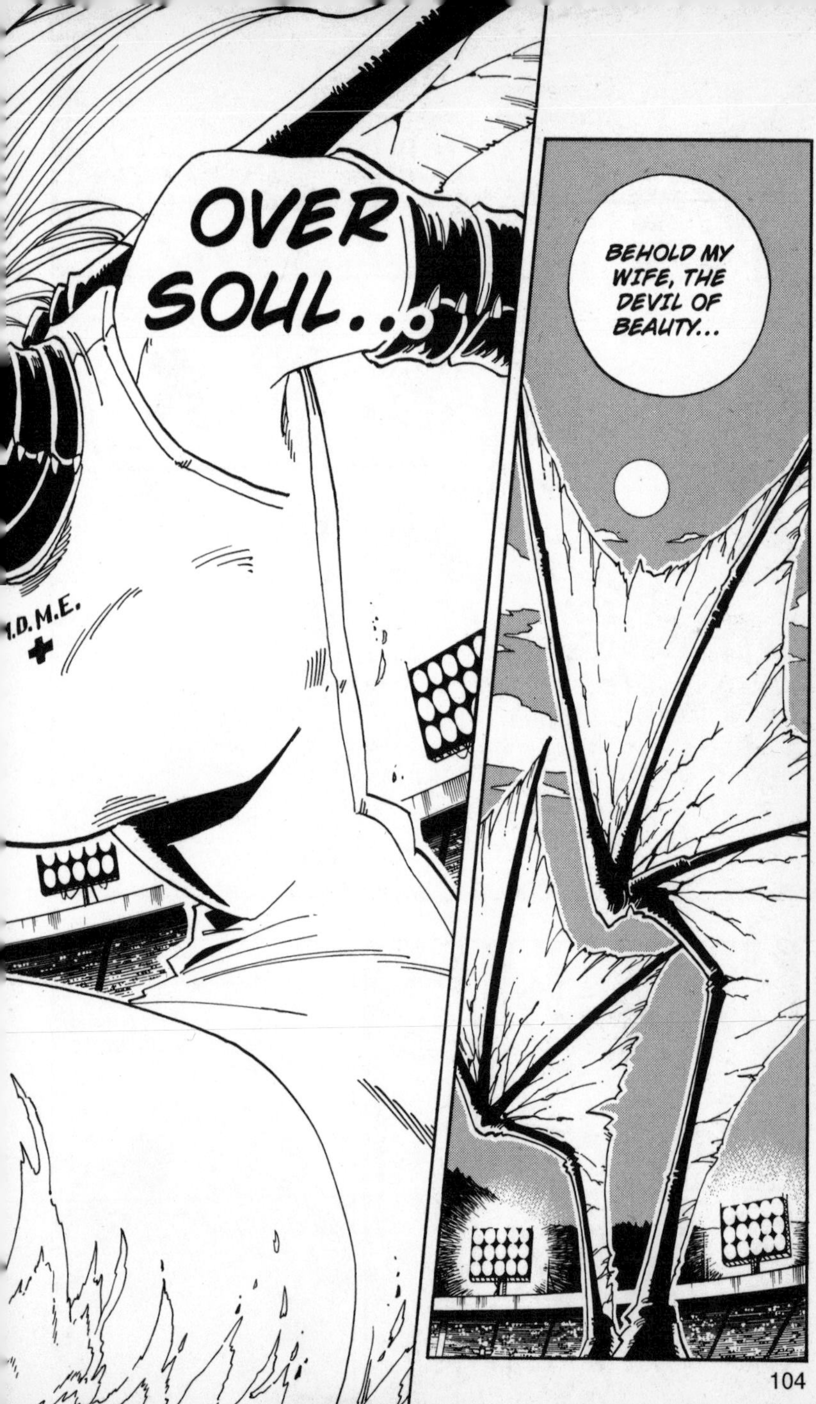
BEHOLD MY WIFE, THE DEVIL OF BEAUTY...
OVER SOUL...

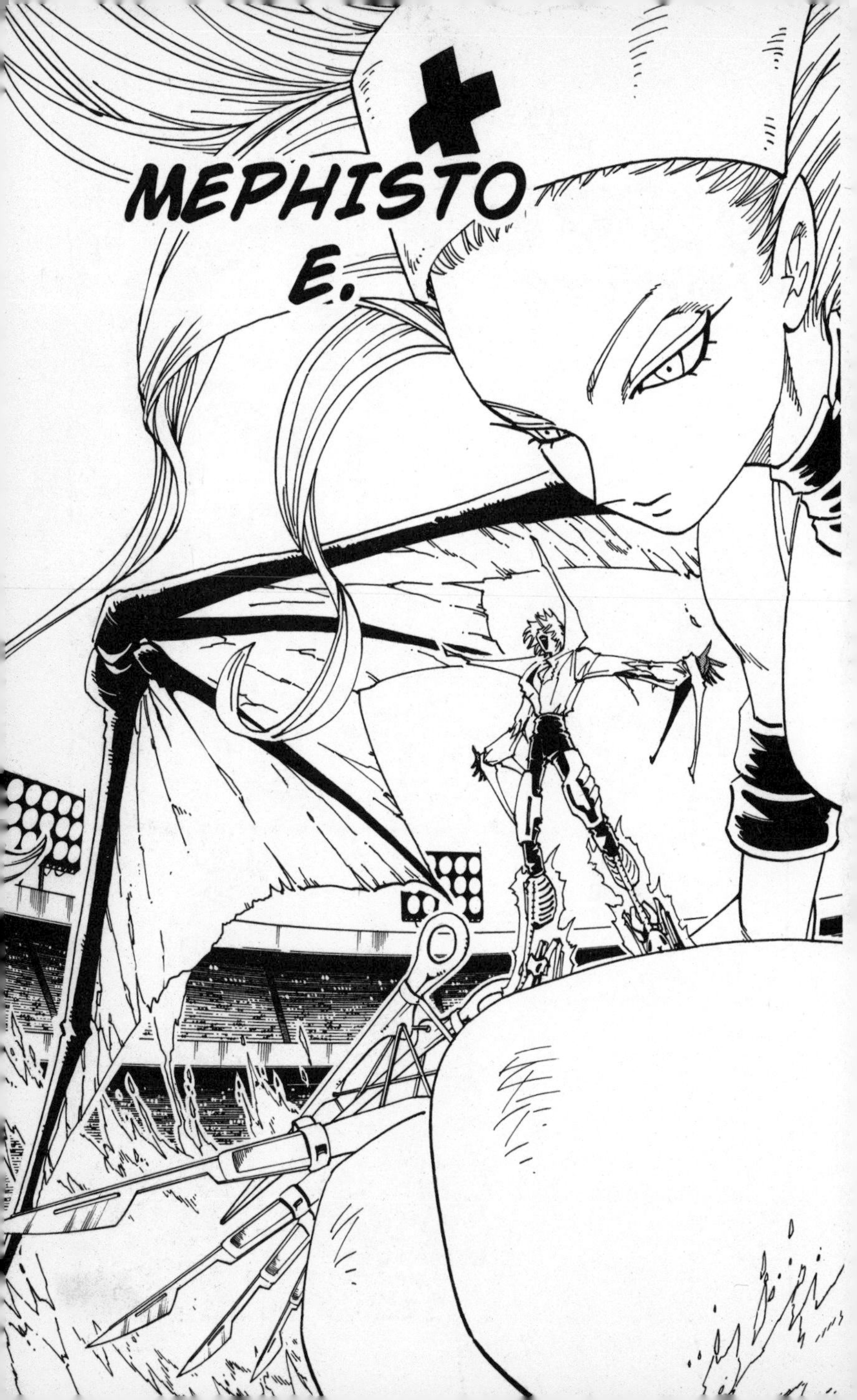
MEPHISTO
E.

SHAMAN KING CHARACTER FILE No.74

カジマヒデ
CARDIMAHIDE

2001
(JULY)

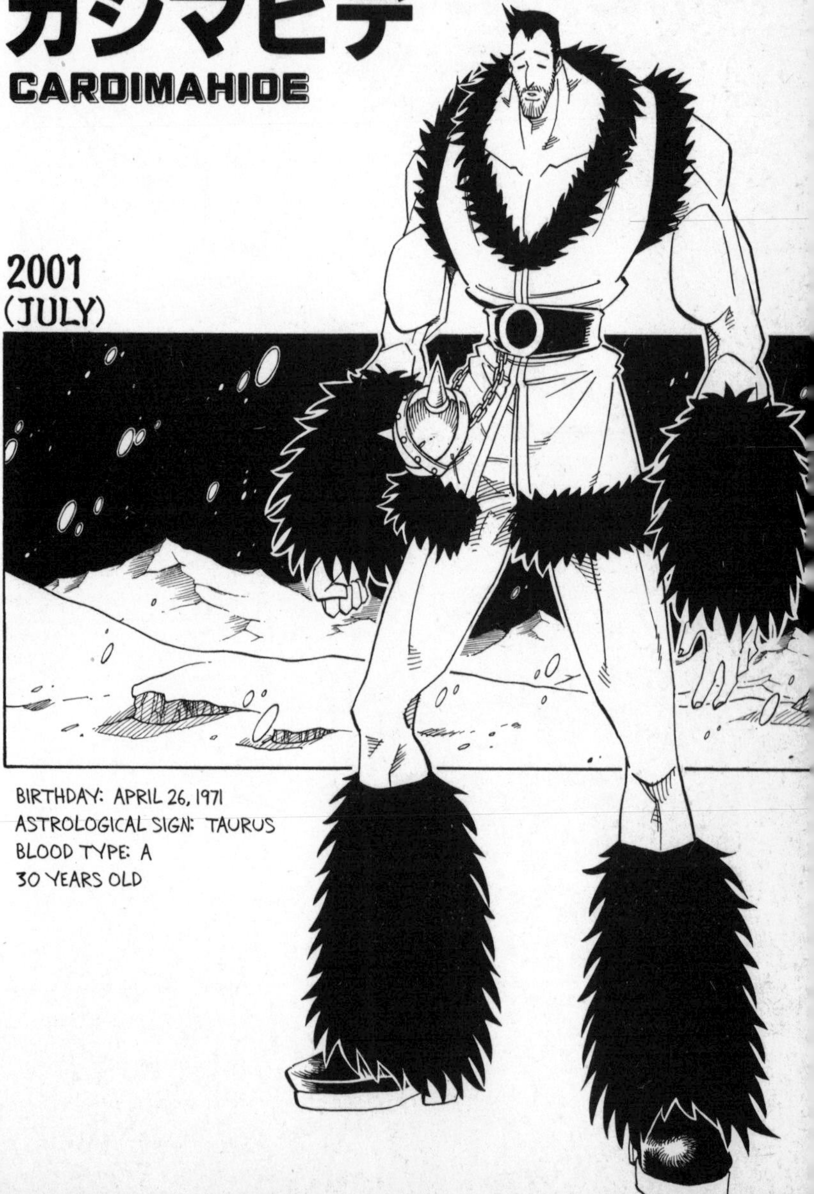

BIRTHDAY: APRIL 26, 1971
ASTROLOGICAL SIGN: TAURUS
BLOOD TYPE: A
30 YEARS OLD

Reincarnation 131: Bedeviled

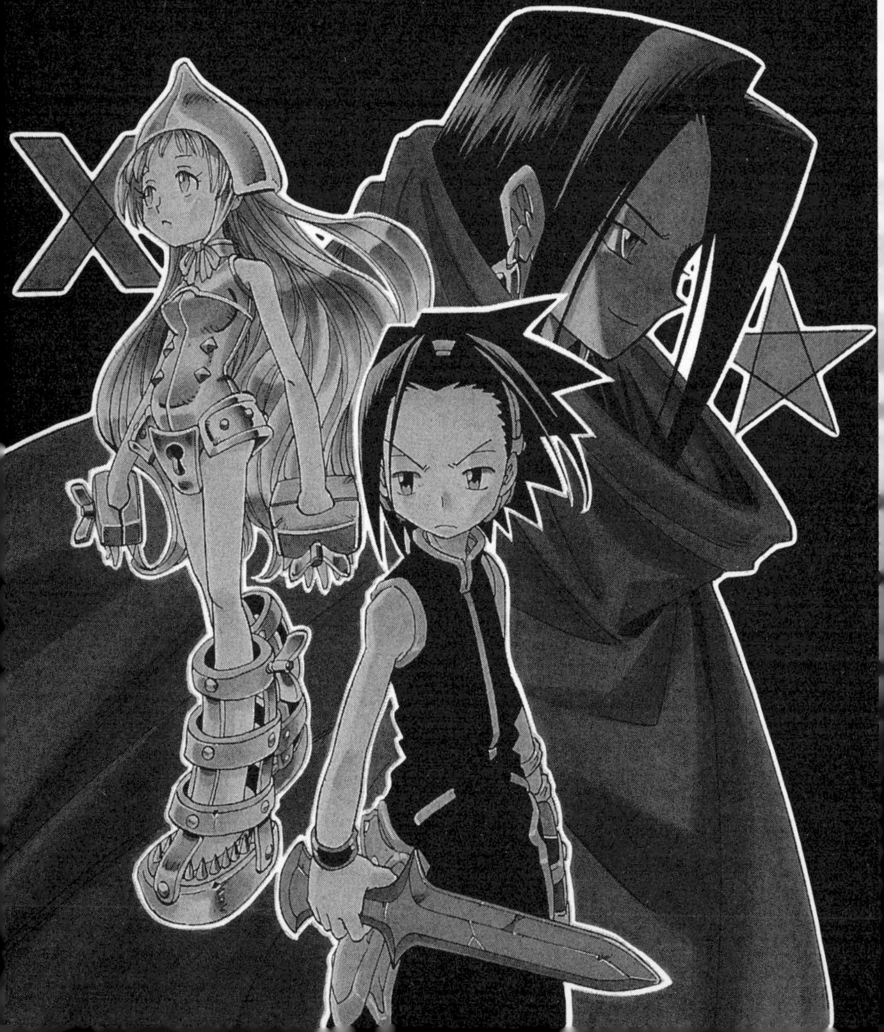

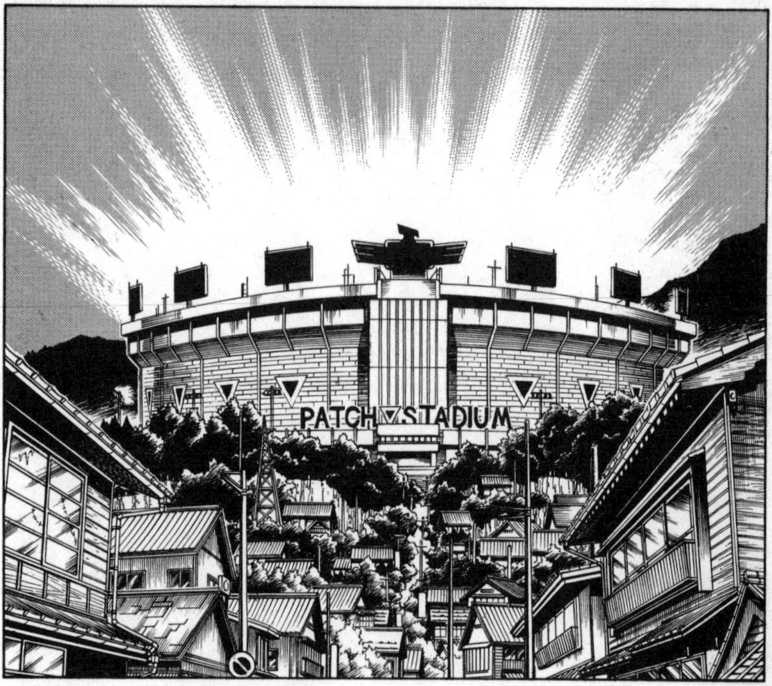
PATCH STADIUM

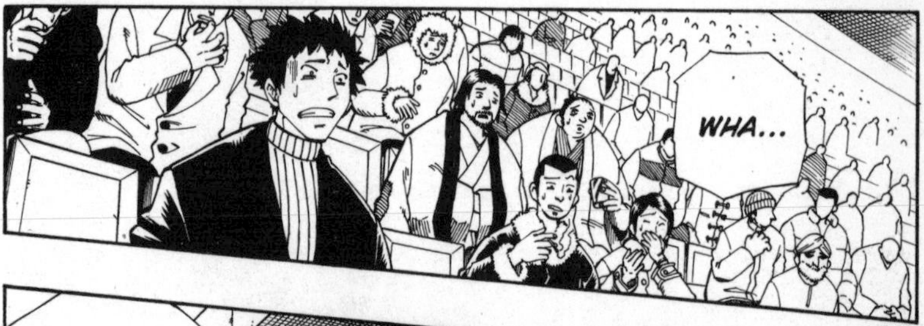
WHA...

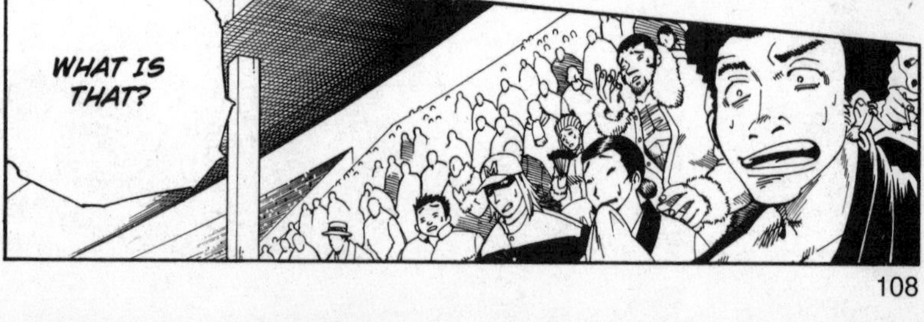
WHAT IS THAT?

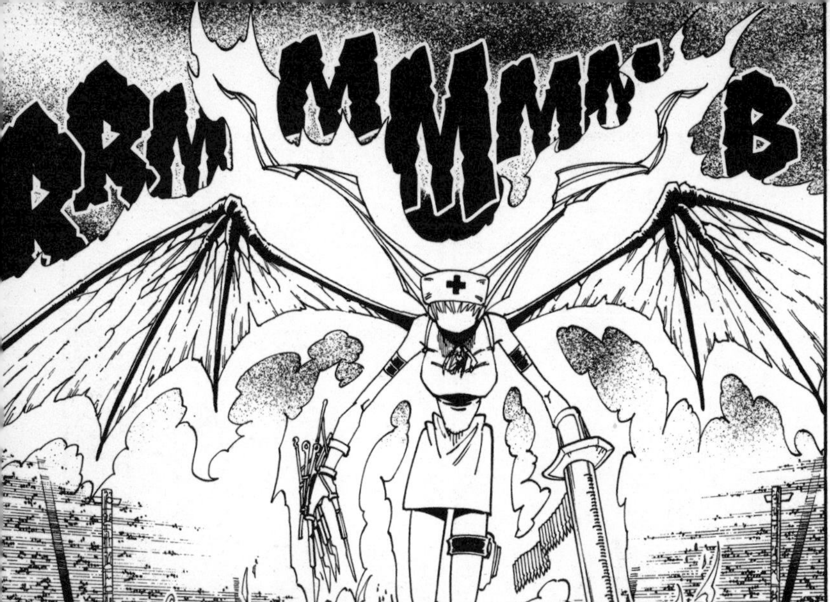
BRMMMMMB
HIS GHOST'S A GIANT!
THOSE BAT-LIKE WINGS!! THAT NIMBUS OF WITCH-FIRE!!
SHE LOOKS LIKE...

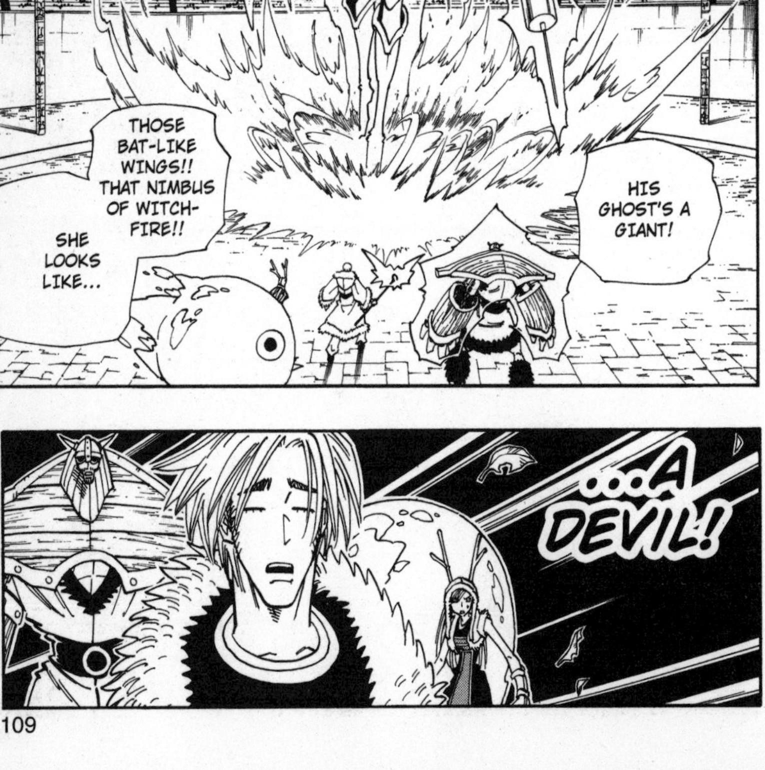
...A DEVIL!

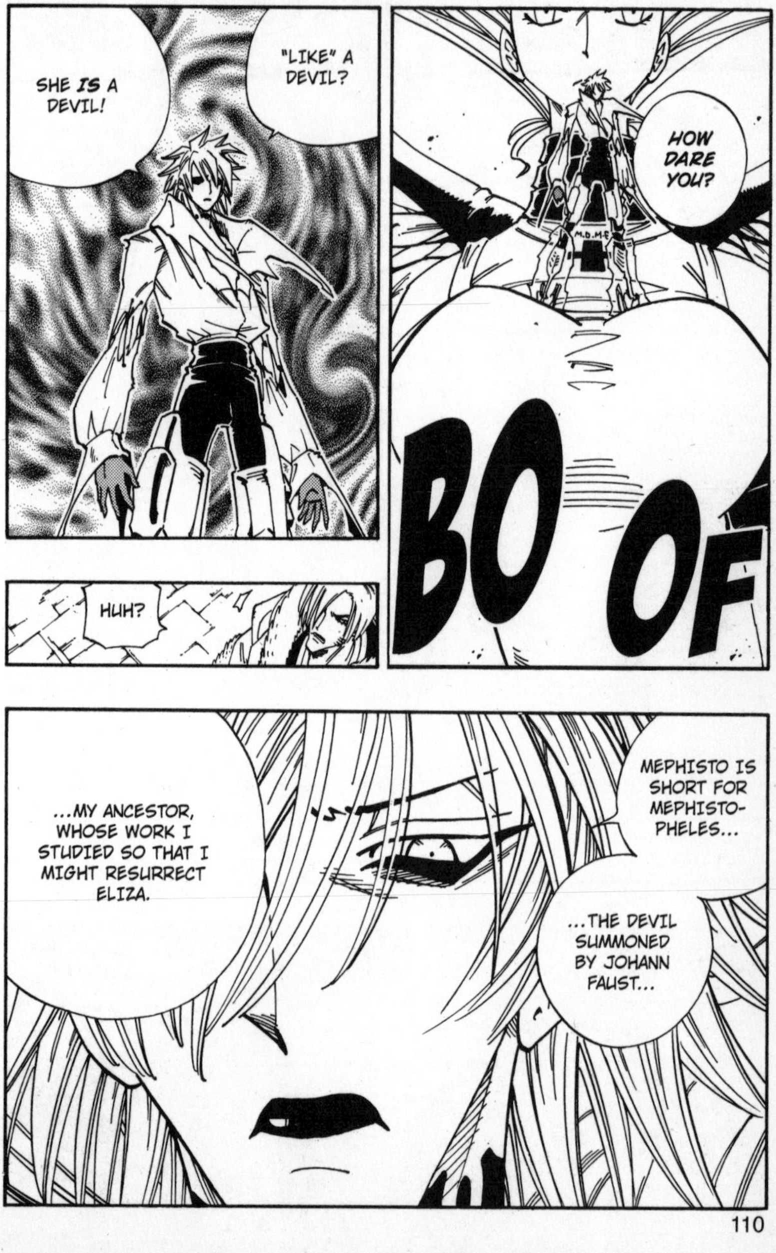
HOW DARE YOU?
BOOF
"LIKE" A DEVIL?
SHE *IS* A DEVIL!
HUH?
MEPHISTO IS SHORT FOR MEPHISTO-PHELES...
...THE DEVIL SUMMONED BY JOHANN FAUST...
...MY ANCESTOR, WHOSE WORK I STUDIED SO THAT I MIGHT RESURRECT ELIZA.

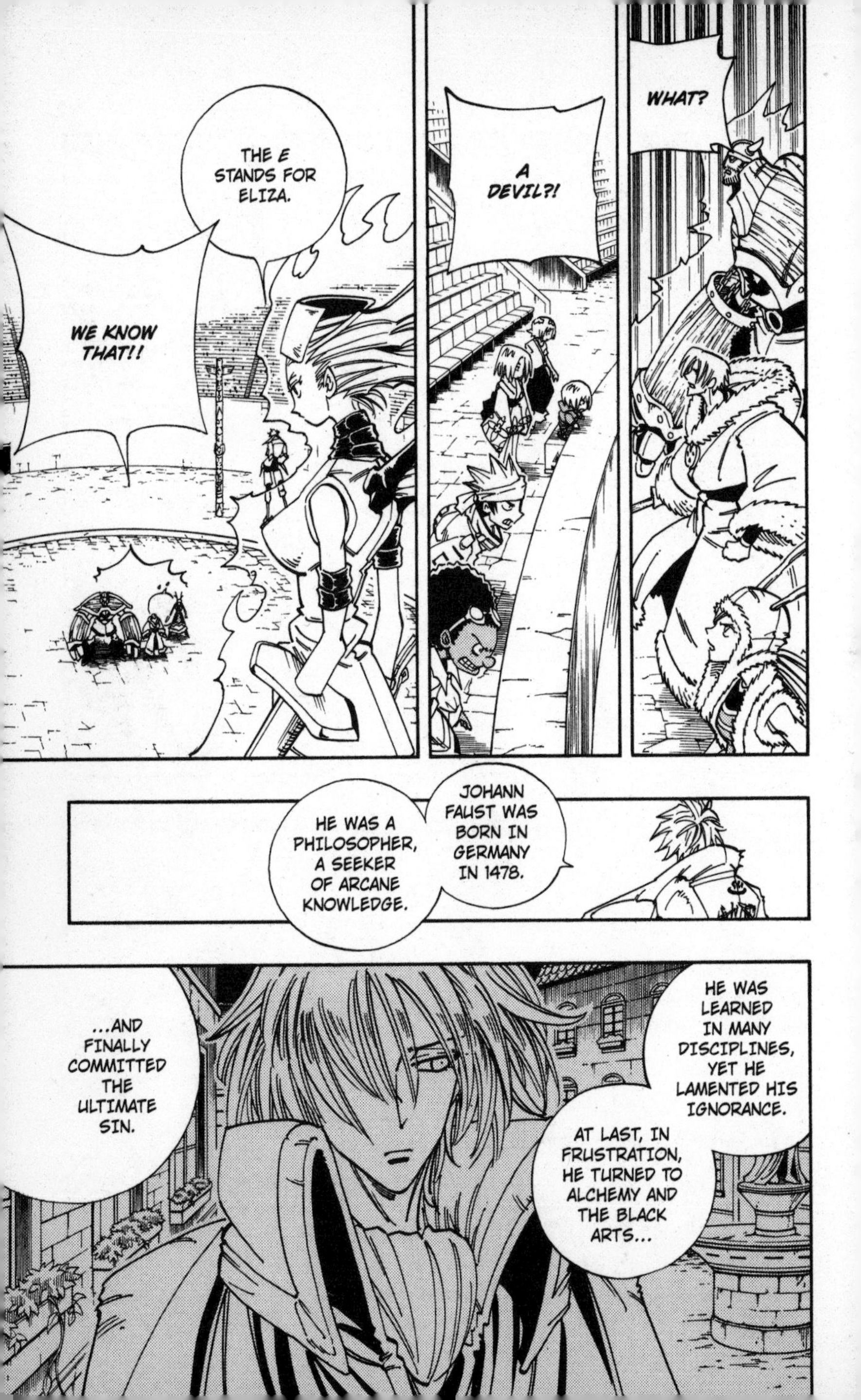
WHAT?
A DEVIL?!
THE E STANDS FOR ELIZA.
WE KNOW THAT!!
JOHANN FAUST WAS BORN IN GERMANY IN 1478.
HE WAS A PHILOSOPHER, A SEEKER OF ARCANE KNOWLEDGE.
HE WAS LEARNED IN MANY DISCIPLINES, YET HE LAMENTED HIS IGNORANCE.
AT LAST, IN FRUSTRATION, HE TURNED TO ALCHEMY AND THE BLACK ARTS...
...AND FINALLY COMMITTED THE ULTIMATE SIN.

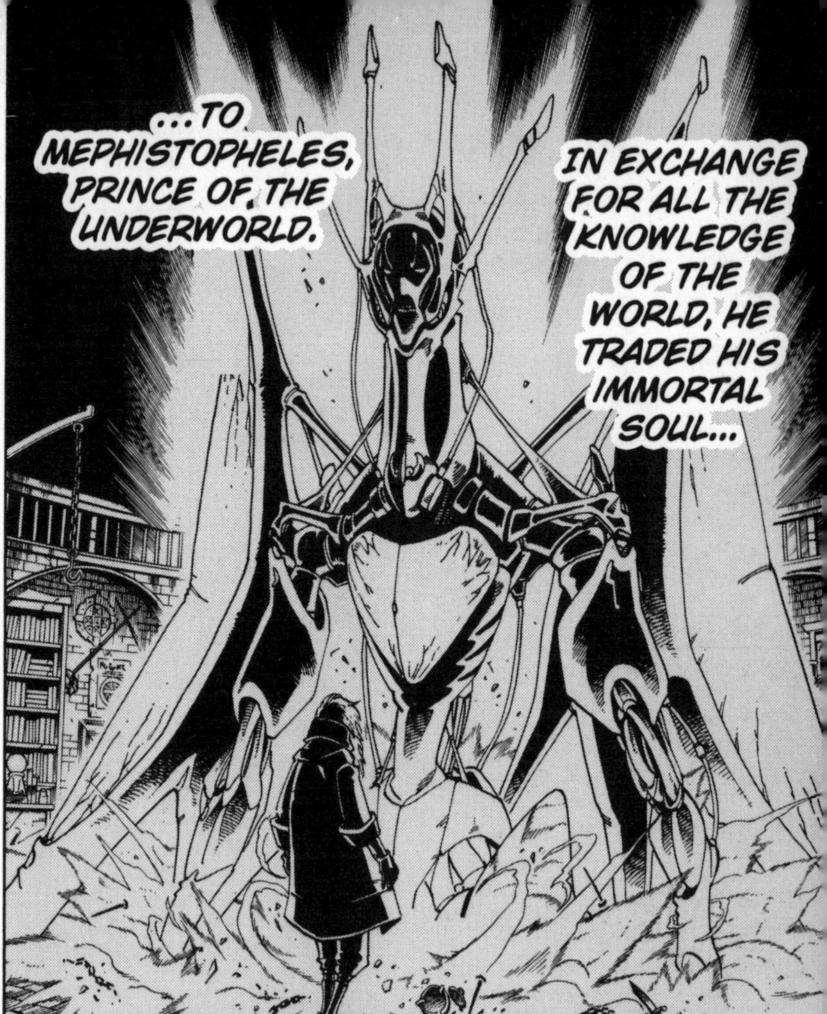
IN EXCHANGE FOR ALL THE KNOWLEDGE OF THE WORLD, HE TRADED HIS IMMORTAL SOUL...
...TO MEPHISTOPHELES, PRINCE OF THE UNDERWORLD.

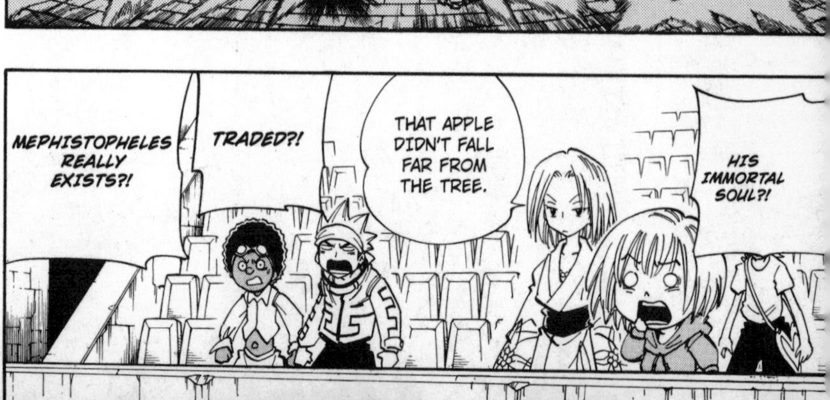
HIS IMMORTAL SOUL?!
THAT APPLE DIDN'T FALL FAR FROM THE TREE.
TRADED?!
MEPHISTOPHELES REALLY EXISTS?!

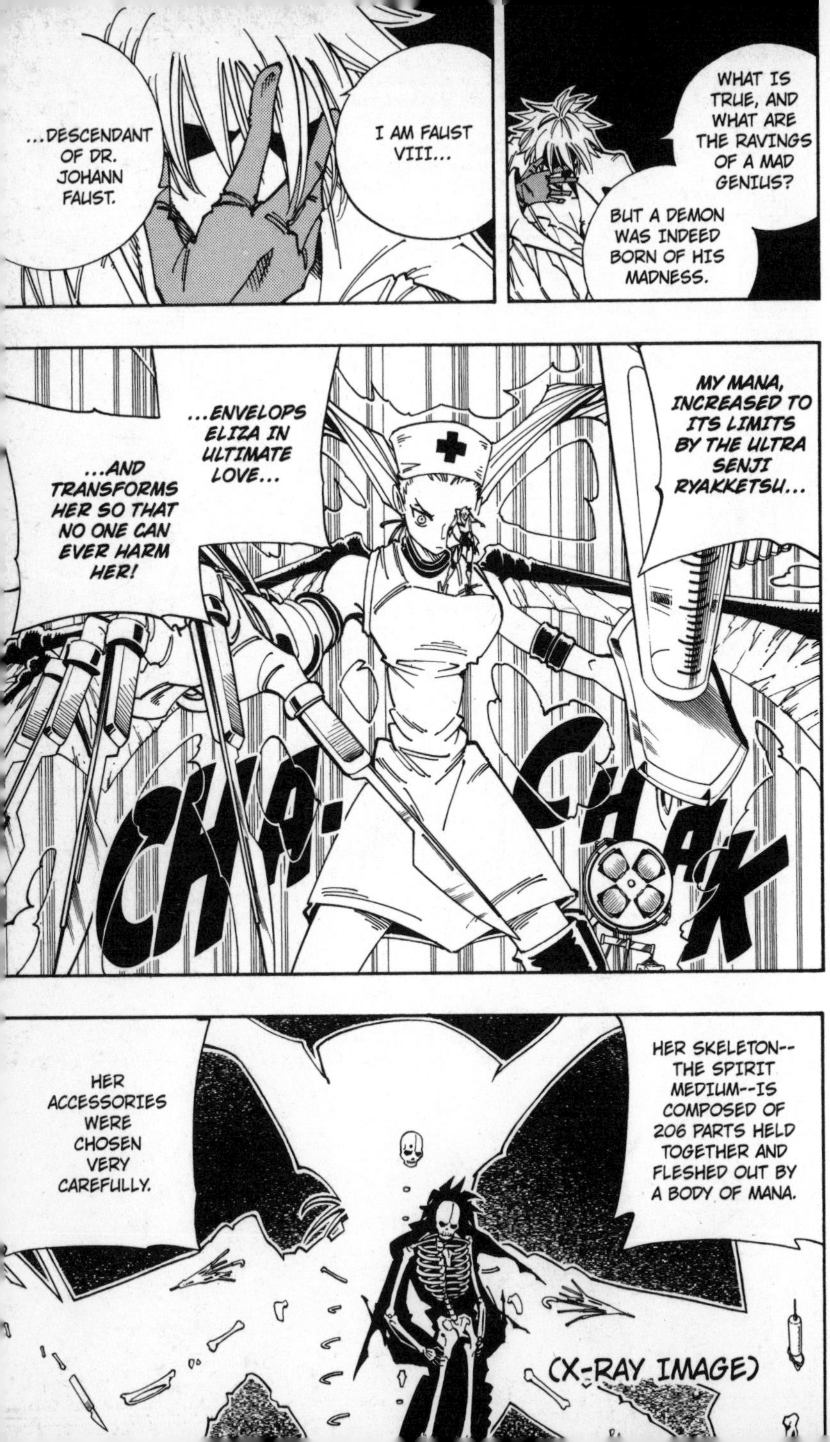
WHAT IS TRUE, AND WHAT ARE THE RAVINGS OF A MAD GENIUS?
BUT A DEMON WAS INDEED BORN OF HIS MADNESS.
I AM FAUST VIII...
...DESCENDANT OF DR. JOHANN FAUST.
MY MANA, INCREASED TO ITS LIMITS BY THE ULTRA SENJI RYAKKETSU...
...ENVELOPS ELIZA IN ULTIMATE LOVE...
...AND TRANSFORMS HER SO THAT NO ONE CAN EVER HARM HER!
CHA-
CHAK
HER SKELETON--THE SPIRIT MEDIUM--IS COMPOSED OF 206 PARTS HELD TOGETHER AND FLESHED OUT BY A BODY OF MANA.
HER ACCESSORIES WERE CHOSEN VERY CAREFULLY.
(X-RAY IMAGE)

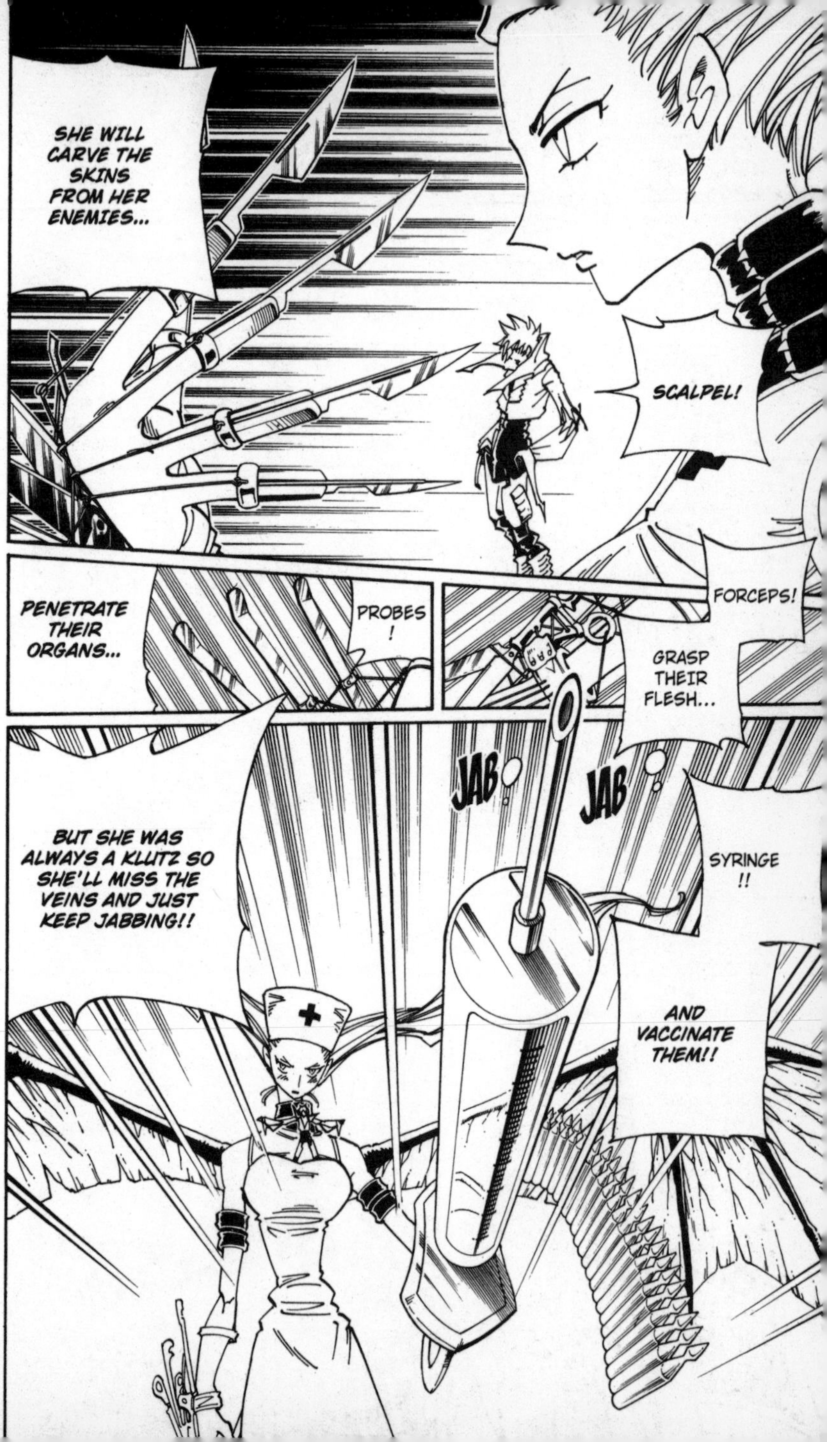
SCALPEL!
SHE WILL CARVE THE SKINS FROM HER ENEMIES...
FORCEPS!
GRASP THEIR FLESH...
PROBES!
PENETRATE THEIR ORGANS...
JAB
JAB
SYRINGE!!
AND VACCINATE THEM!!
BUT SHE WAS ALWAYS A KLUTZ SO SHE'LL MISS THE VEINS AND JUST KEEP JABBING!!

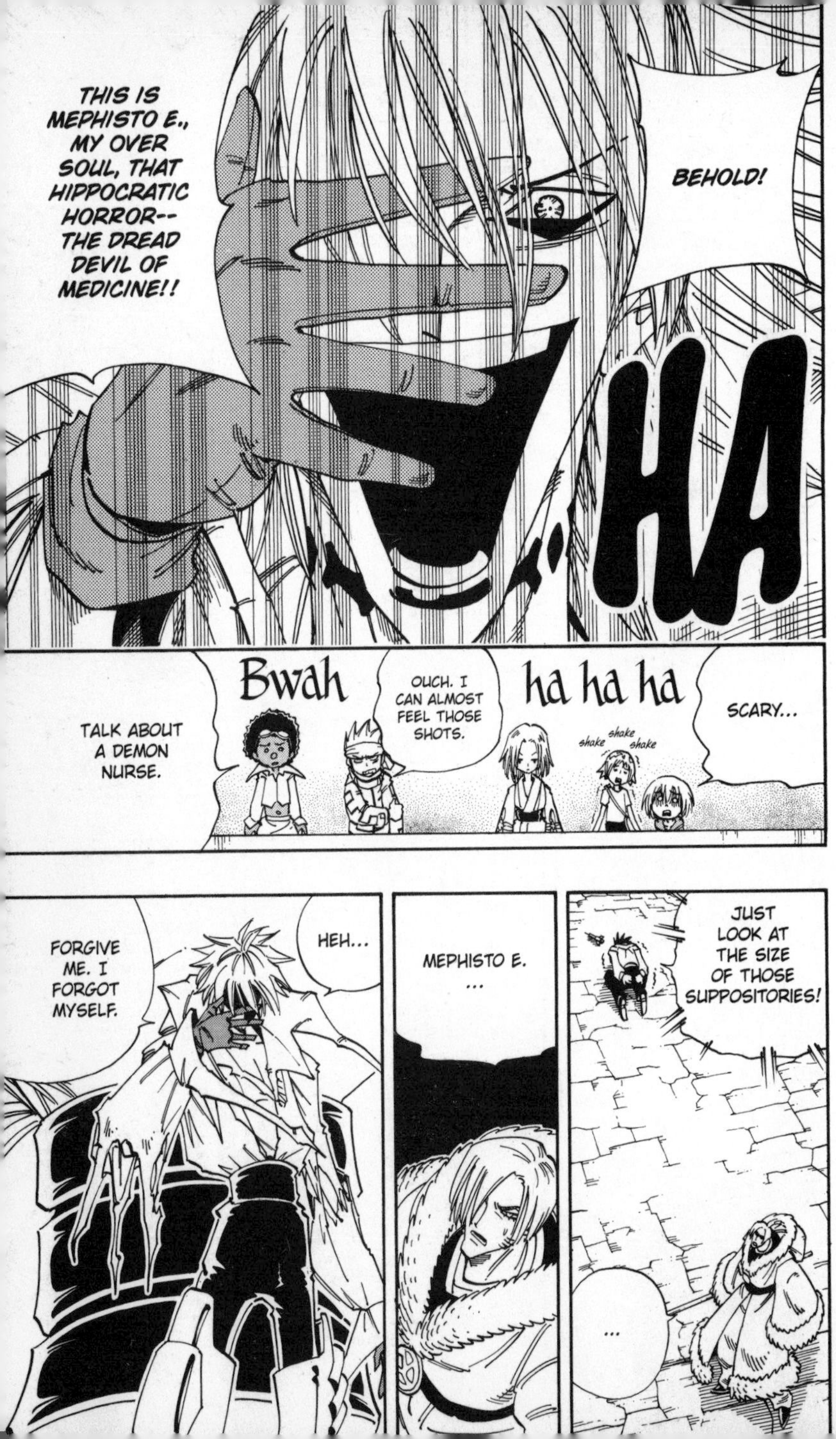
BEHOLD!
THIS IS MEPHISTO E., MY OVER SOUL, THAT HIPPOCRATIC HORROR-- THE DREAD DEVIL OF MEDICINE!!
HA
SCARY...
shake shake shake
ha ha ha
OUCH. I CAN ALMOST FEEL THOSE SHOTS.
Bwah
TALK ABOUT A DEMON NURSE.
JUST LOOK AT THE SIZE OF THOSE SUPPOSITORIES!
...
MEPHISTO E. ...
HEH...
FORGIVE ME. I FORGOT MYSELF.

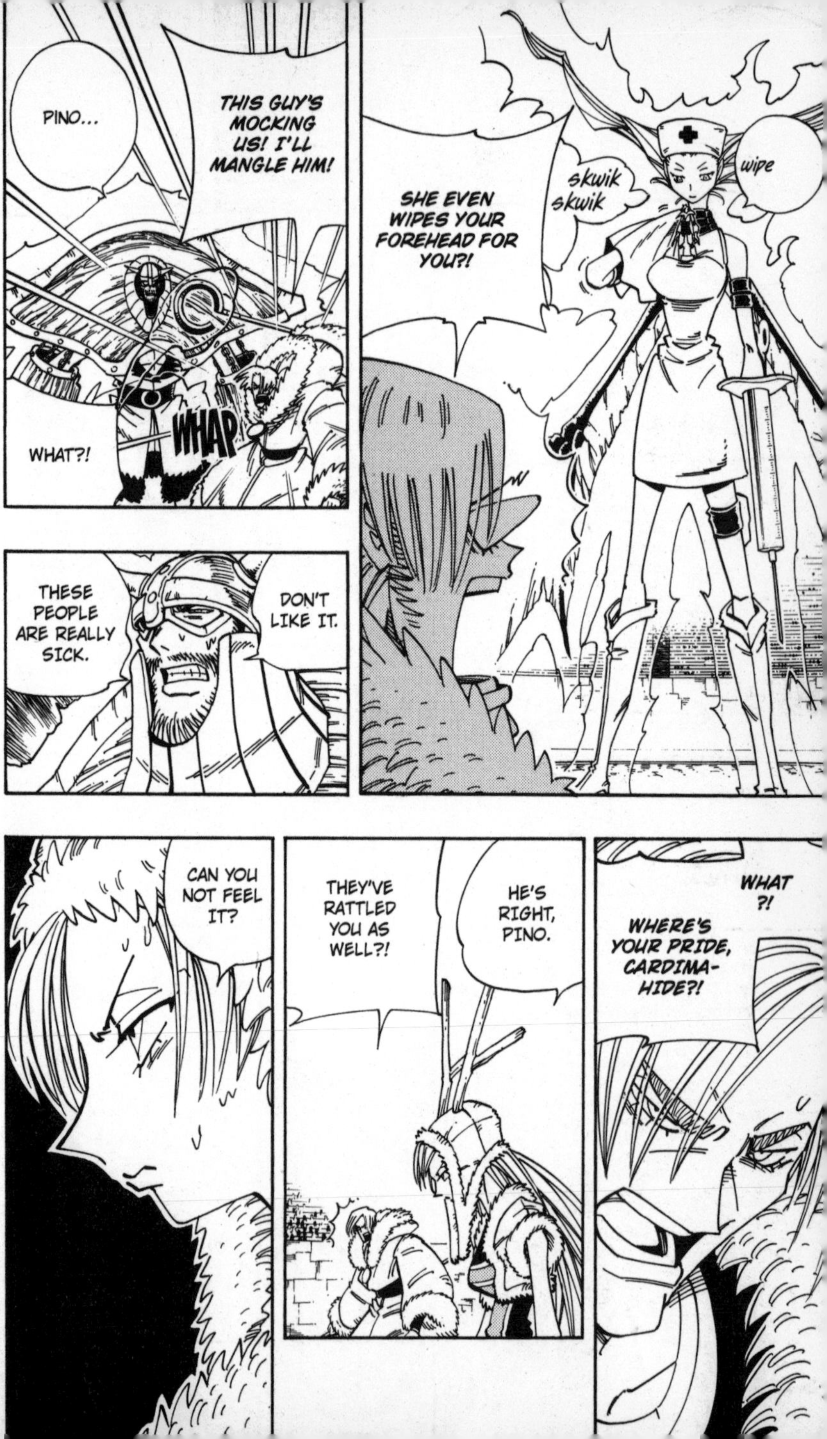
wipe
skwik skwik
SHE EVEN WIPES YOUR FOREHEAD FOR YOU?!
THIS GUY'S MOCKING US! I'LL MANGLE HIM!
PINO...
WHAP
WHAT?!
DON'T LIKE IT.
THESE PEOPLE ARE REALLY SICK.
WHAT ?!
WHERE'S YOUR PRIDE, CARDIMA-HIDE?!
HE'S RIGHT, PINO.
THEY'VE RATTLED YOU AS WELL?!
CAN YOU NOT FEEL IT?

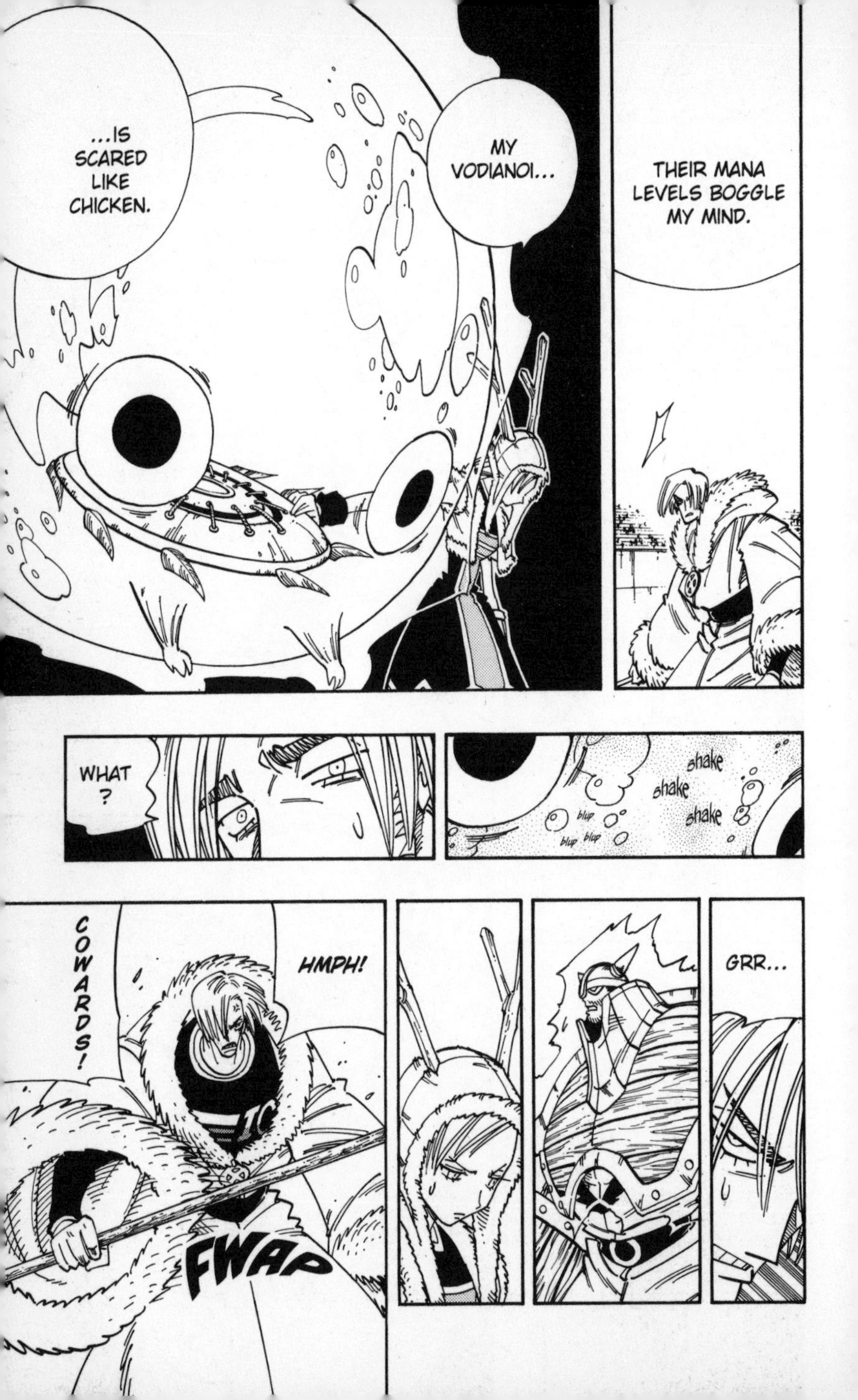
THEIR MANA LEVELS BOGGLE MY MIND.
MY VODIANOI...
...IS SCARED LIKE CHICKEN.
shake shake shake
blup blup blup
WHAT?
GRR...
HMPH!
COWARDS!
FWAP

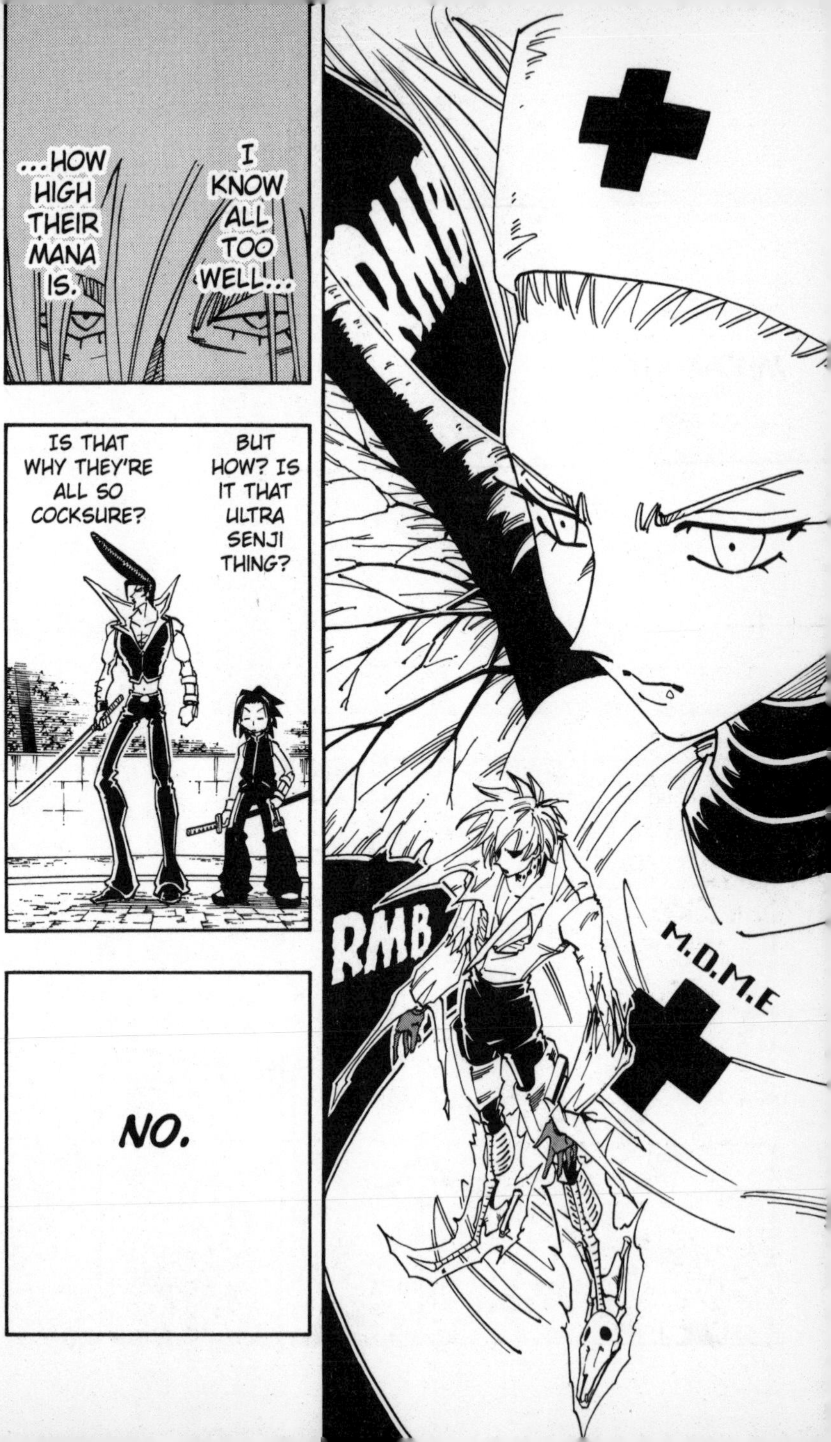
RMB
RMB
M.D.M.E
I KNOW ALL TOO WELL...
...HOW HIGH THEIR MANA IS.
BUT HOW? IS IT THAT ULTRA SENJI THING?
IS THAT WHY THEY'RE ALL SO COCKSURE?
NO.

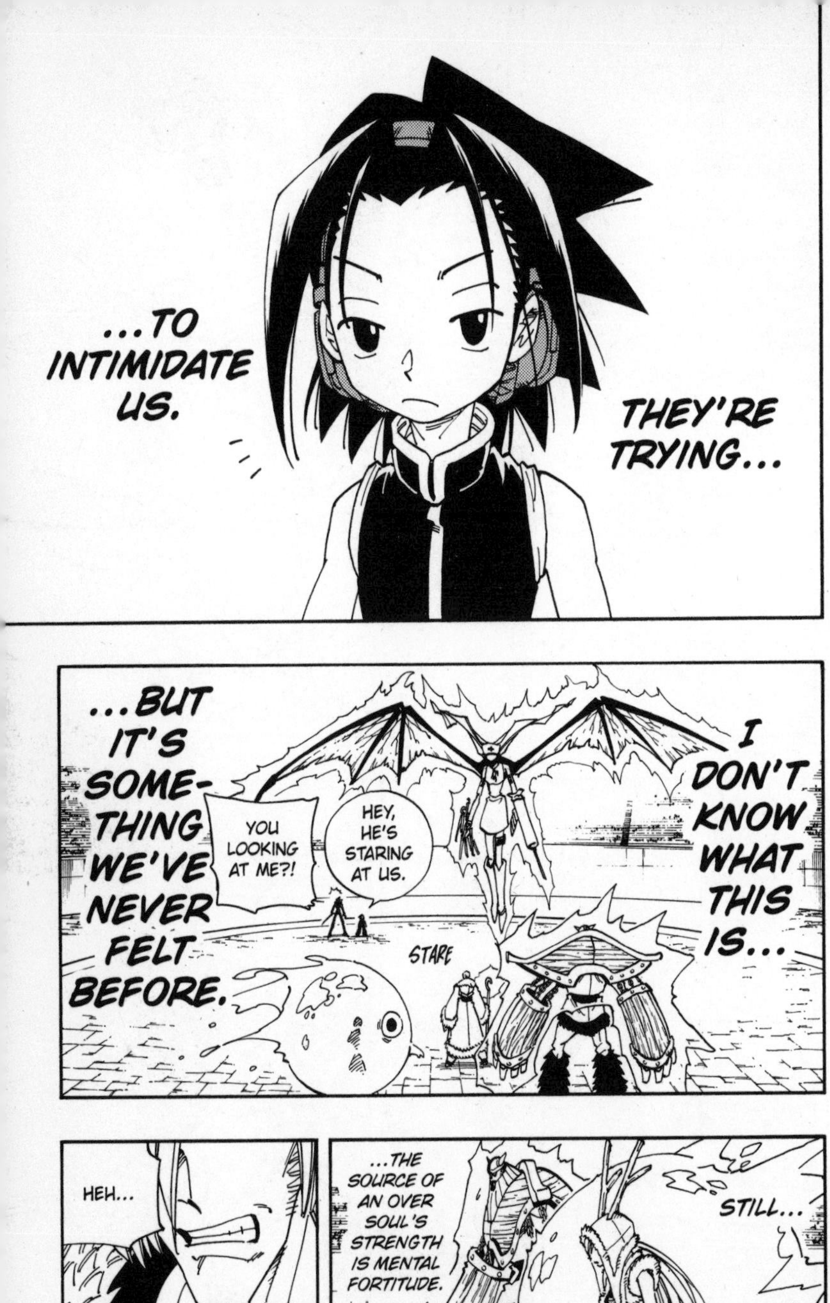
THEY'RE TRYING...
...TO INTIMIDATE US.
I DON'T KNOW WHAT THIS IS...
...BUT IT'S SOME-THING WE'VE NEVER FELT BEFORE.
HEY, HE'S STARING AT US.
YOU LOOKING AT ME?!
STARE
STILL...
...THE SOURCE OF AN OVER SOUL'S STRENGTH IS MENTAL FORTITUDE.
HEH...

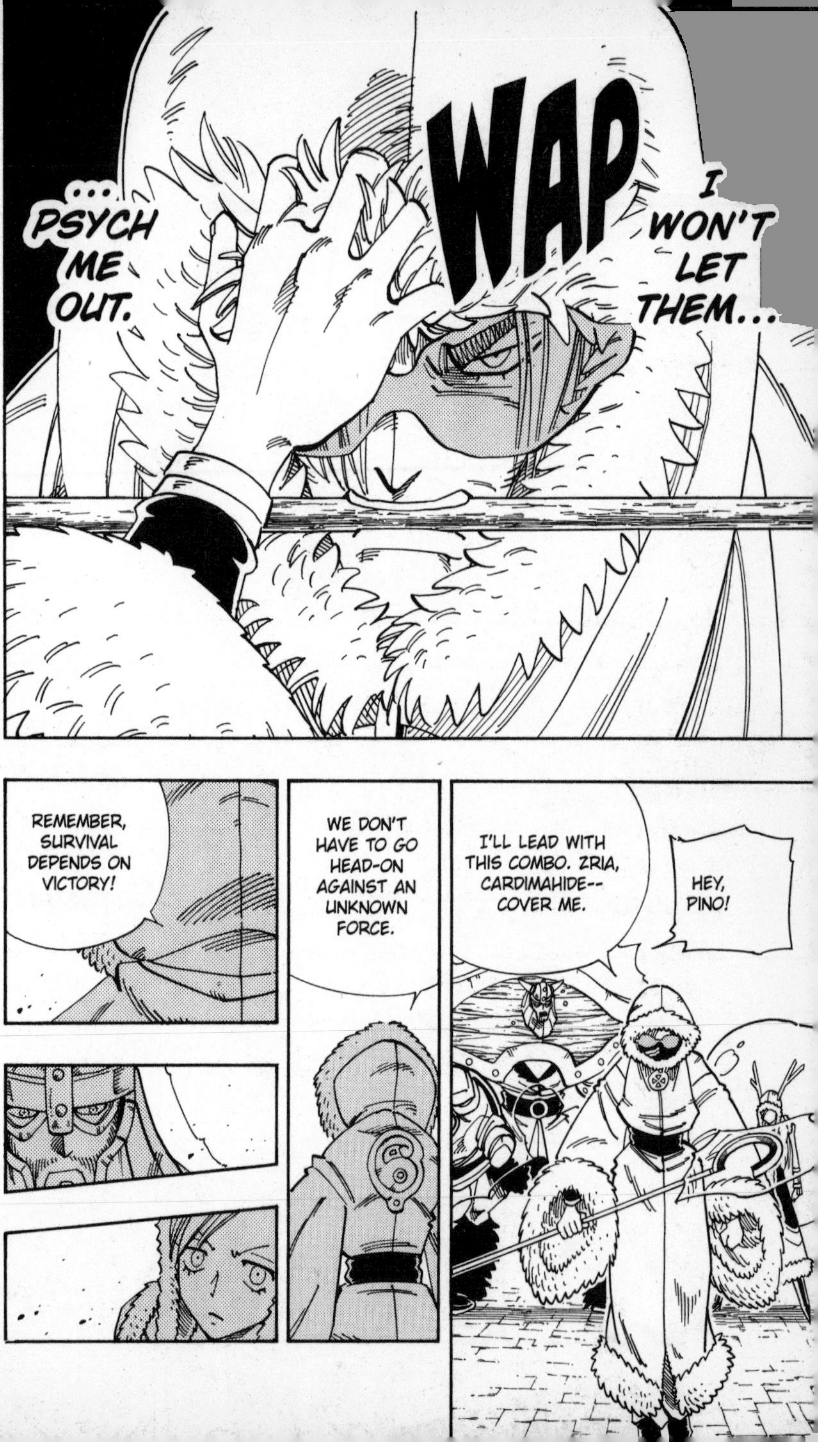
I WON'T LET THEM...
WAP
...PSYCH ME OUT.
HEY, PINO!
I'LL LEAD WITH THIS COMBO. ZRIA, CARDIMAHIDE--COVER ME.
WE DON'T HAVE TO GO HEAD-ON AGAINST AN UNKNOWN FORCE.
REMEMBER, SURVIVAL DEPENDS ON VICTORY!

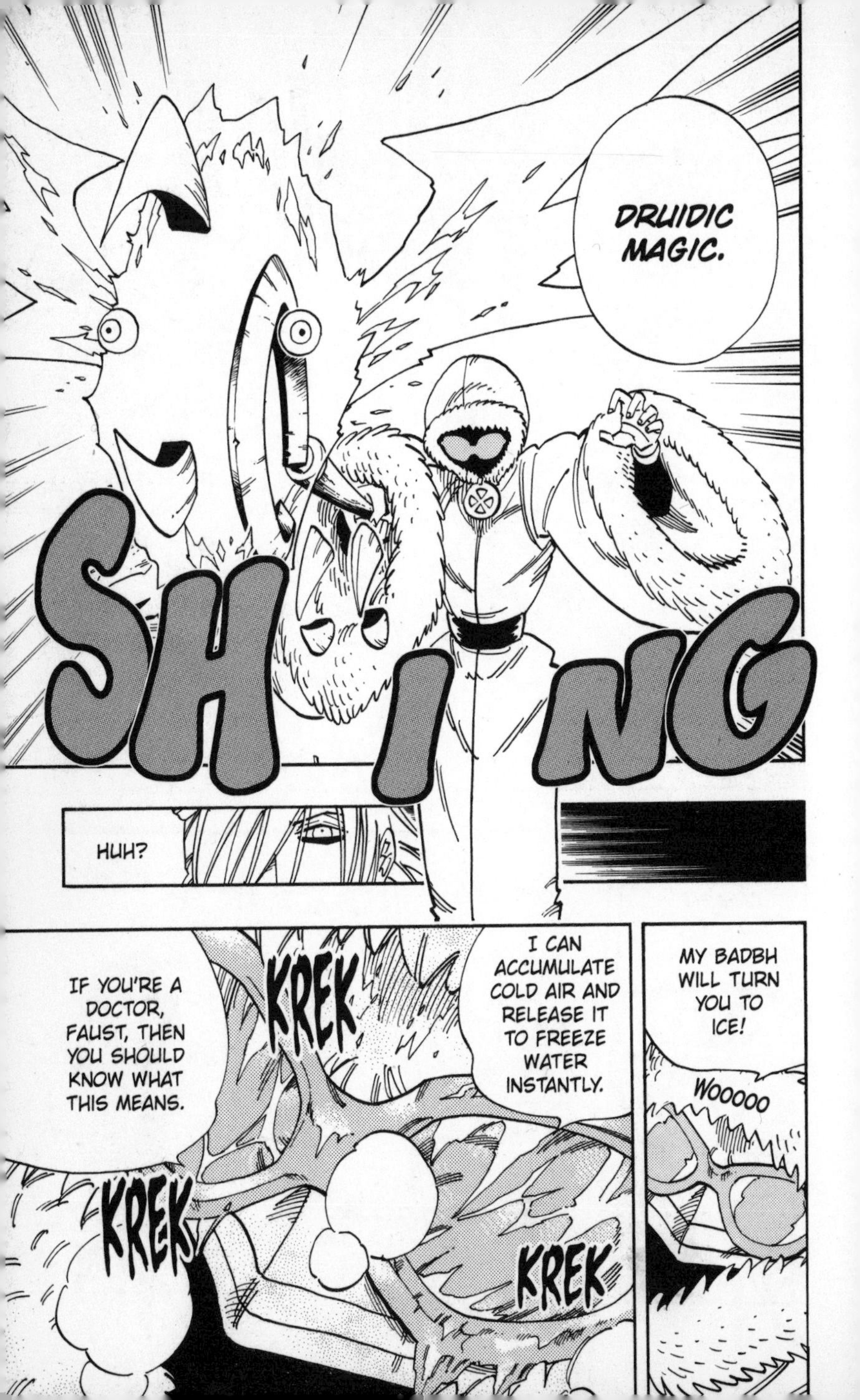
DRUIDIC MAGIC.
SHING
HUH?
MY BADBH WILL TURN YOU TO ICE!
WOOOOO
I CAN ACCUMULATE COLD AIR AND RELEASE IT TO FREEZE WATER INSTANTLY.
KREK
IF YOU'RE A DOCTOR, FAUST, THEN YOU SHOULD KNOW WHAT THIS MEANS.
KREK
KREK

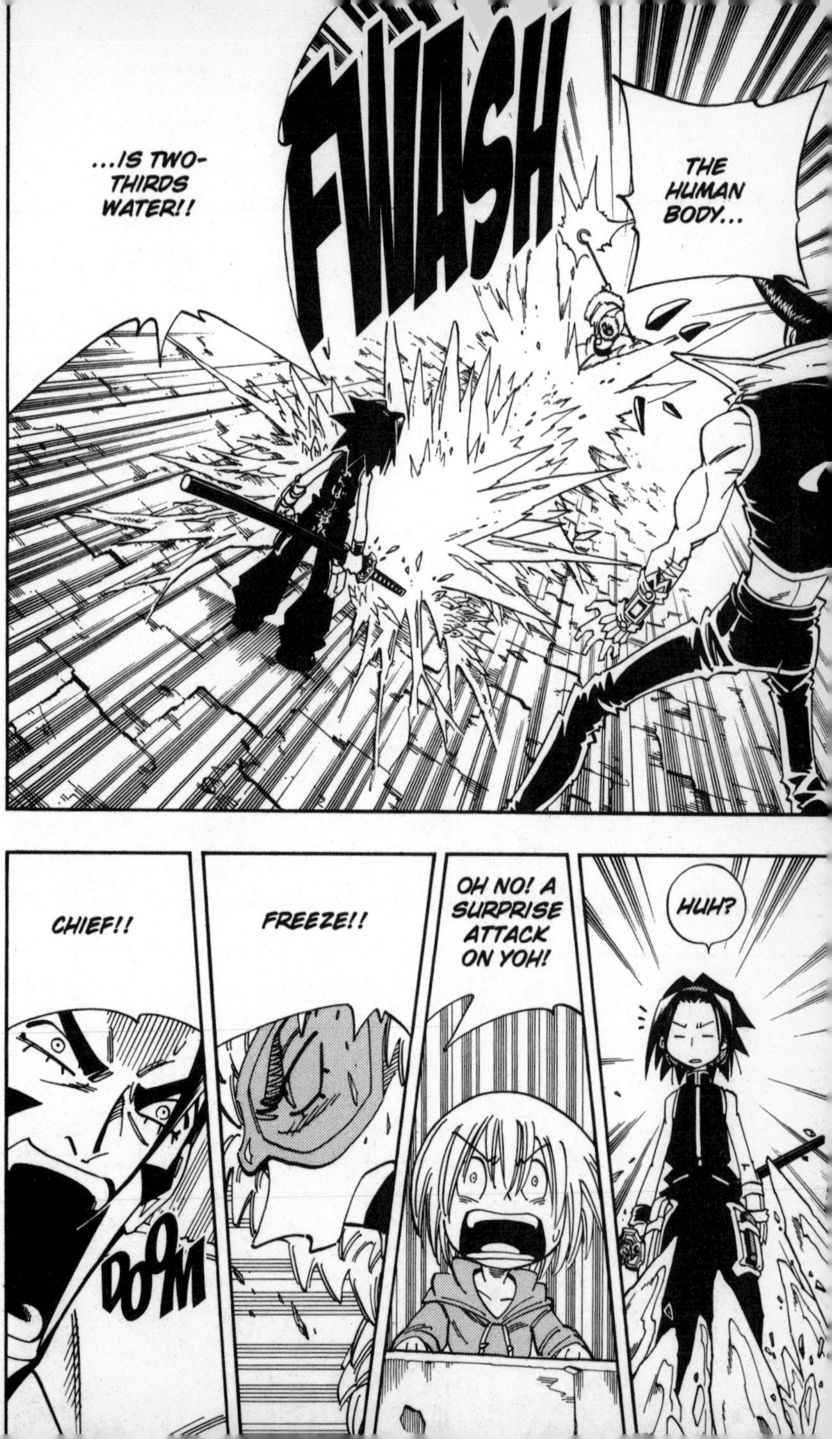
THE HUMAN BODY...
FWASH
...IS TWO-THIRDS WATER!!
HUH?
OH NO! A SURPRISE ATTACK ON YOH!
FREEZE!!
CHIEF!!
DOOM

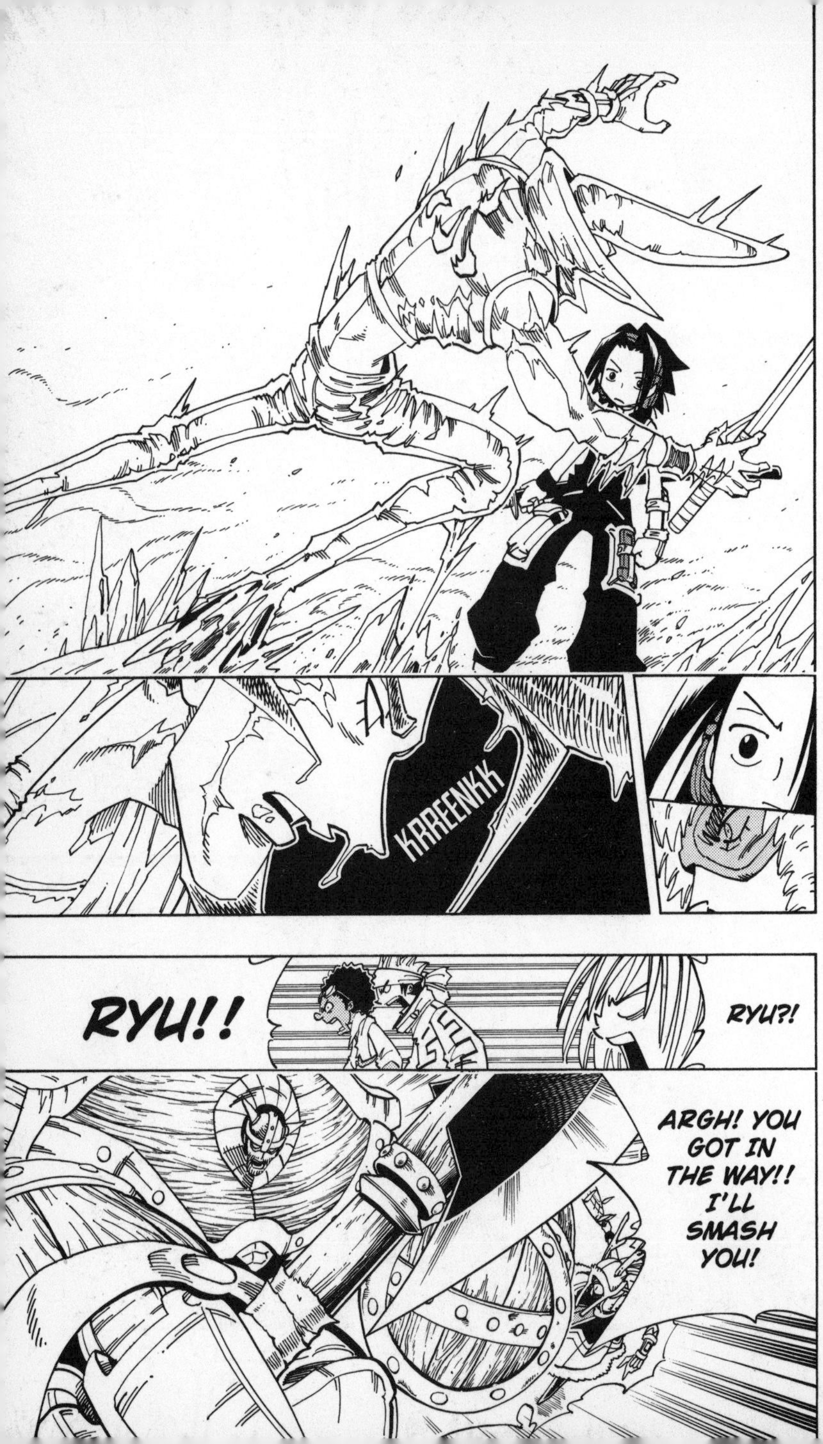
KRREENKK
RYU?!
RYU!!
ARGH! YOU GOT IN THE WAY!! I'LL SMASH YOU!

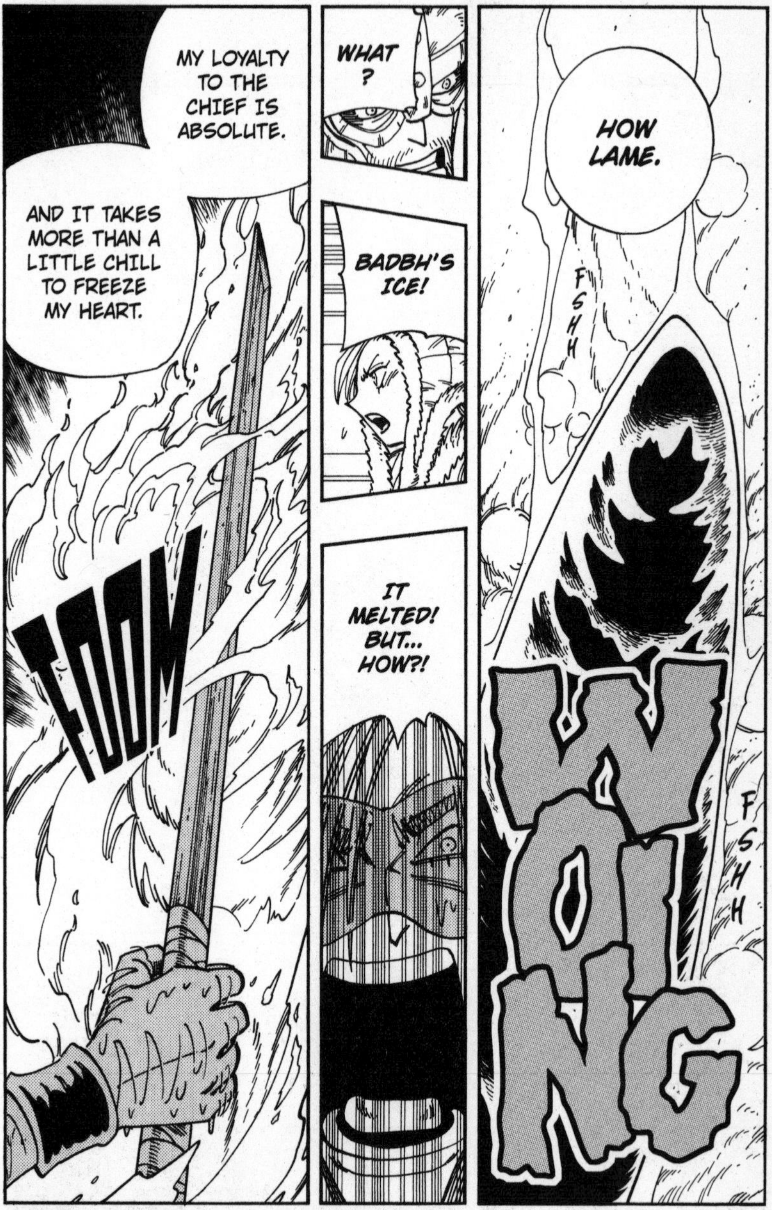
HOW LAME.
FSHH
WOING
FSHH
WHAT?
BADBH'S ICE!
IT MELTED! BUT... HOW?!
MY LOYALTY TO THE CHIEF IS ABSOLUTE.
AND IT TAKES MORE THAN A LITTLE CHILL TO FREEZE MY HEART.
FOOM

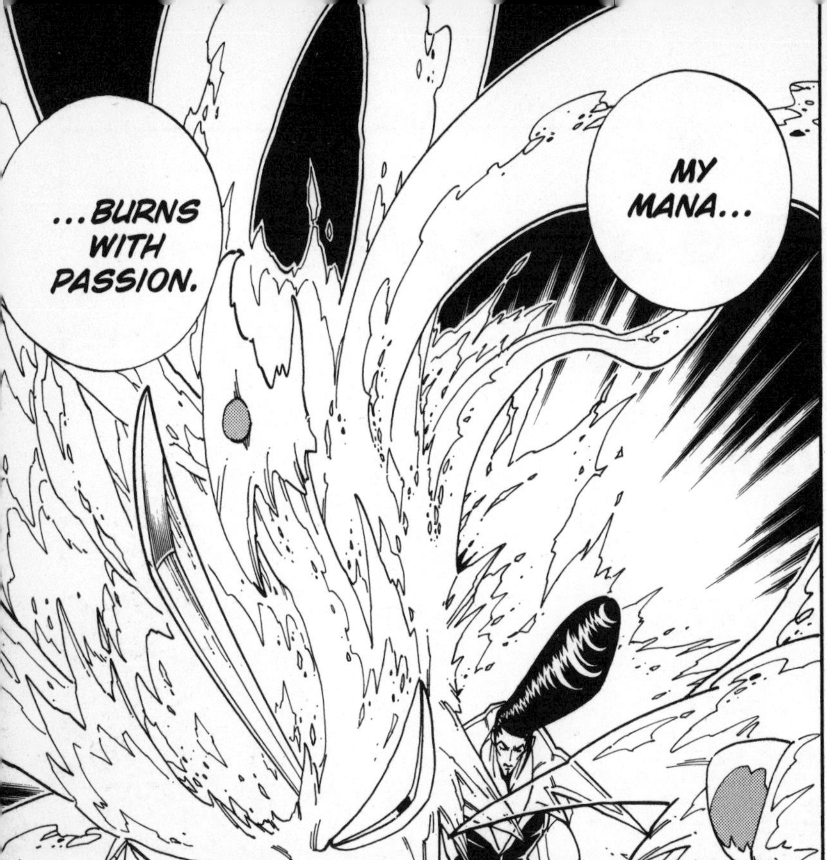
MY MANA...
...BURNS WITH PASSION.

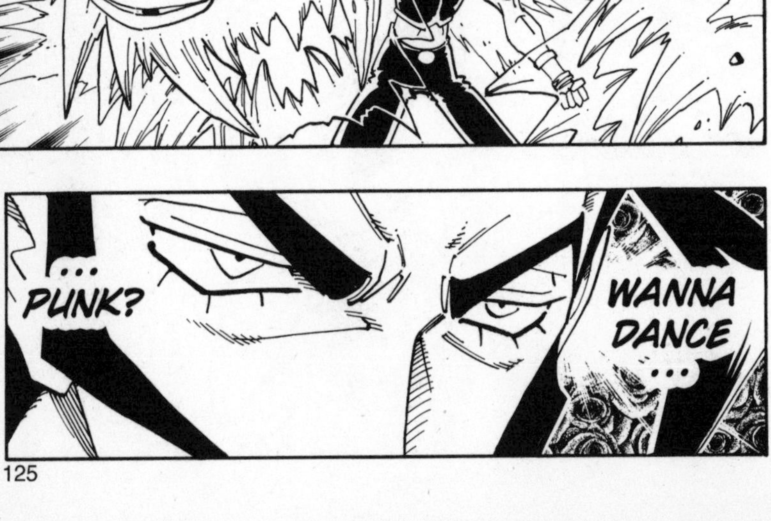
WANNA DANCE ...
...PUNK?

SHAMAN KING CHARACTER FILE No.75

ヴァイキング デヒト

DEHT THE VIKING

2001
(JULY)

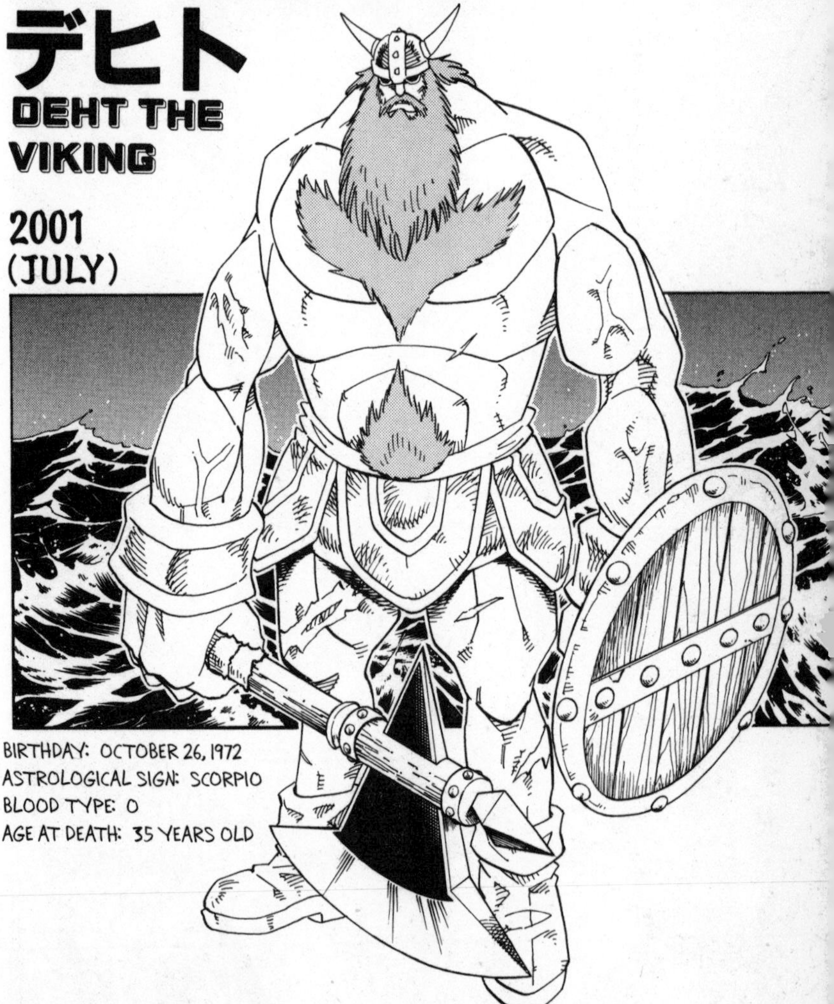

BIRTHDAY: OCTOBER 26, 1972
ASTROLOGICAL SIGN: SCORPIO
BLOOD TYPE: O
AGE AT DEATH: 35 YEARS OLD

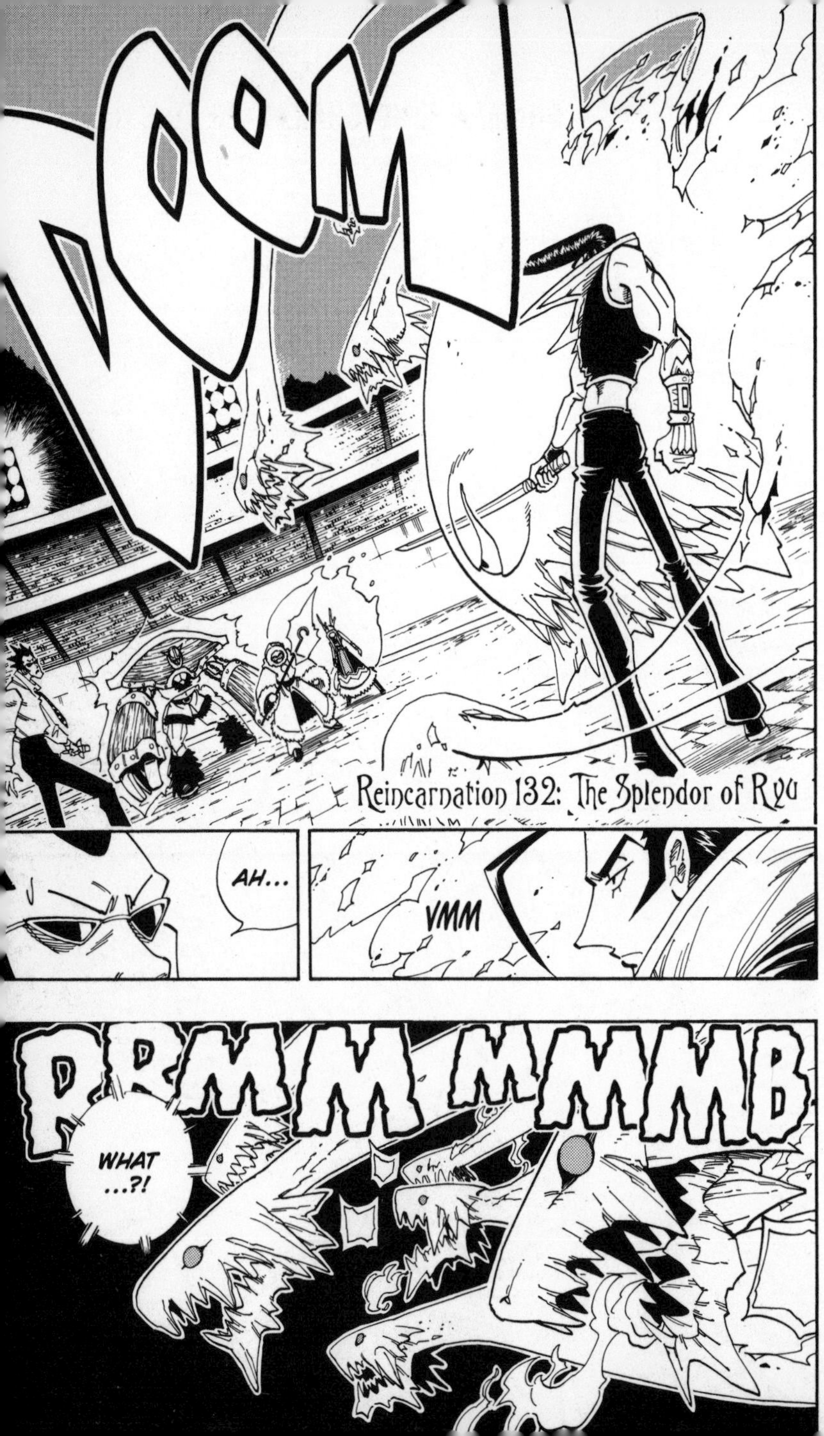
DOOM
Reincarnation 132: The Splendor of Ryu
VMM
AH...
RMM MMMB
WHAT ...?!

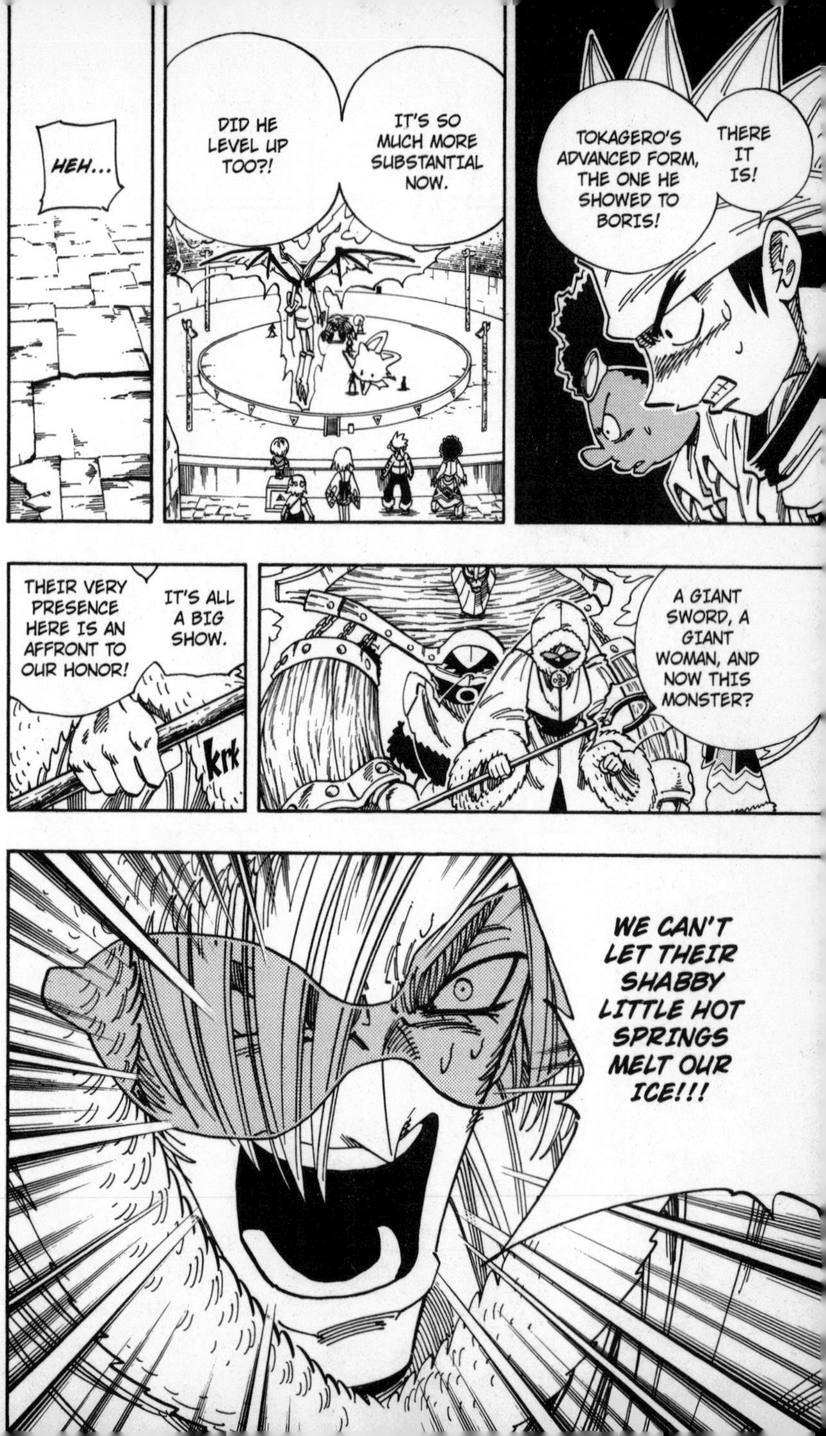
THERE IT IS!
TOKAGERO'S ADVANCED FORM, THE ONE HE SHOWED TO BORIS!
IT'S SO MUCH MORE SUBSTANTIAL NOW.
DID HE LEVEL UP TOO?!
HEH...
A GIANT SWORD, A GIANT WOMAN, AND NOW THIS MONSTER?
IT'S ALL A BIG SHOW.
THEIR VERY PRESENCE HERE IS AN AFFRONT TO OUR HONOR!
krk
WE CAN'T LET THEIR SHABBY LITTLE HOT SPRINGS MELT OUR ICE!!!

Reincarnation 132:

The Splendor of Ryu

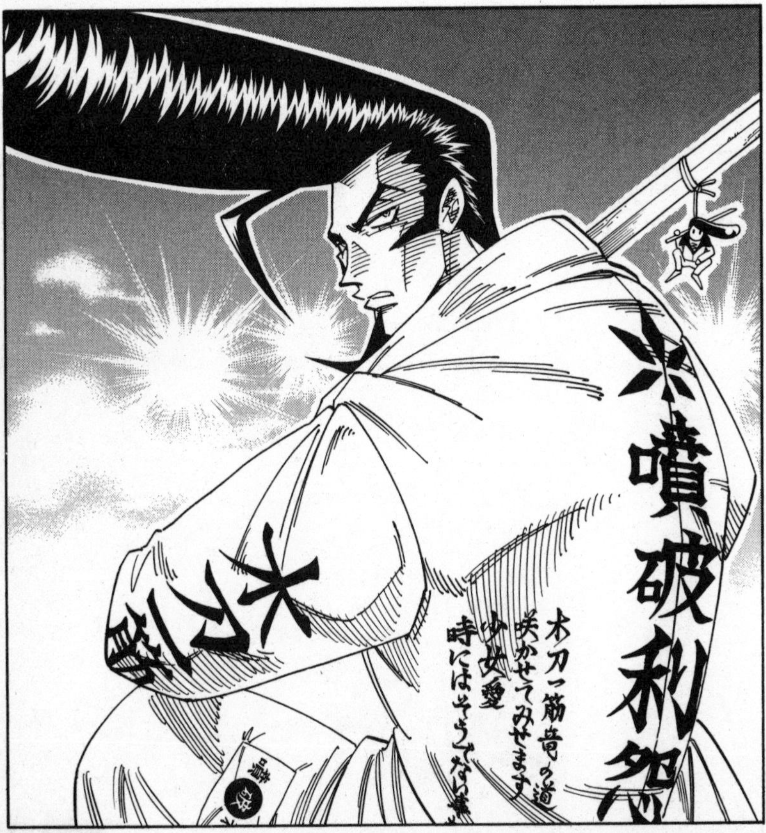
噴破利
木刀一筋竜の道
咲かせてみせます
少女愛

BACK: FUNBARI
BOTTOM: MY LIFE IS DEVOTED TO THE WOODEN SWORD. I WILL MAKE LOVE HAPPEN, THOUGH IT MAY NOT TAKE THE FORM I WISH FOR.
SLEEVE: MY LIFE IS DEVOTED TO THE WOODEN SWORD.
LEG: FUNBARI

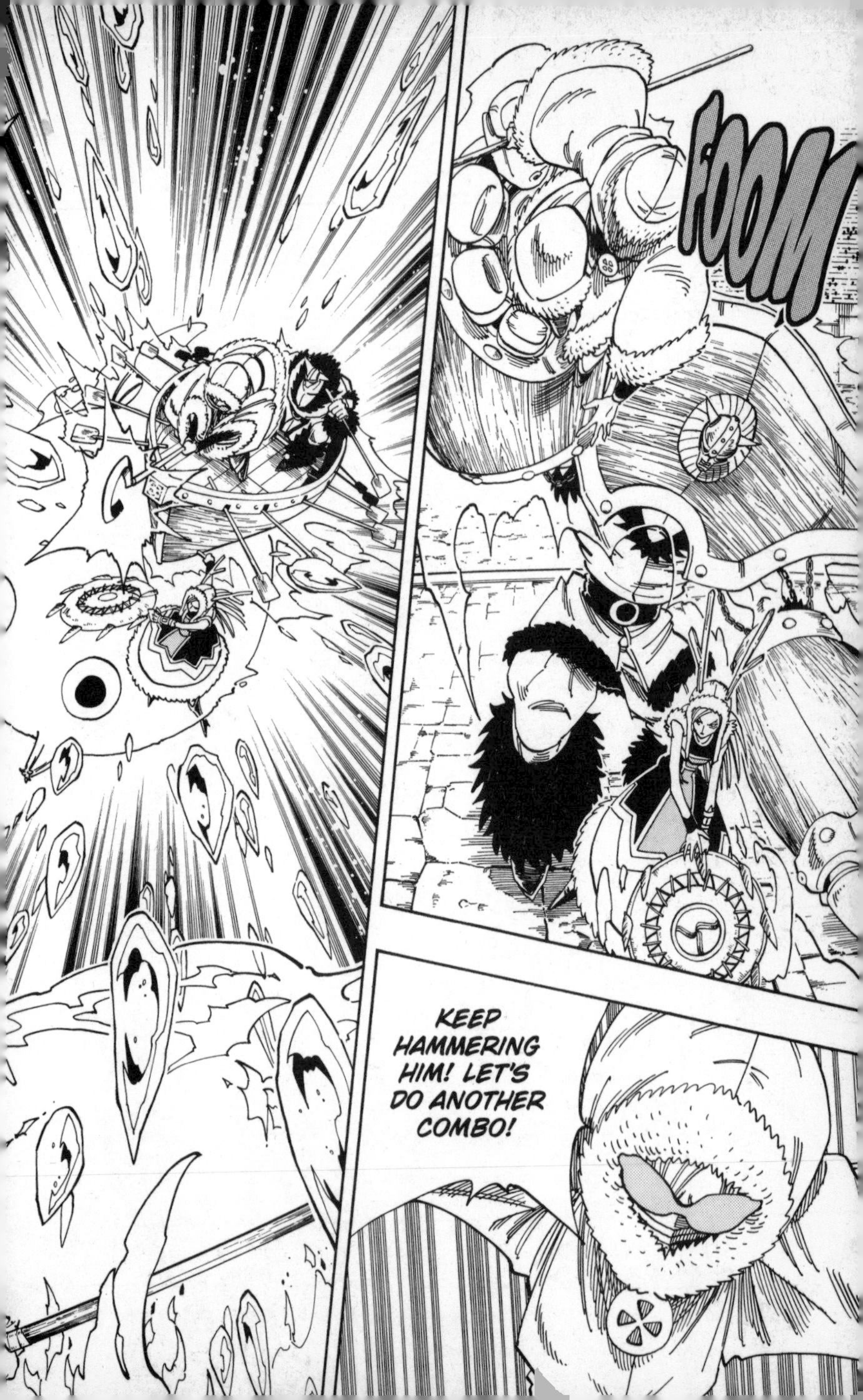
FOOM
KEEP HAMMERING HIM! LET'S DO ANOTHER COMBO!

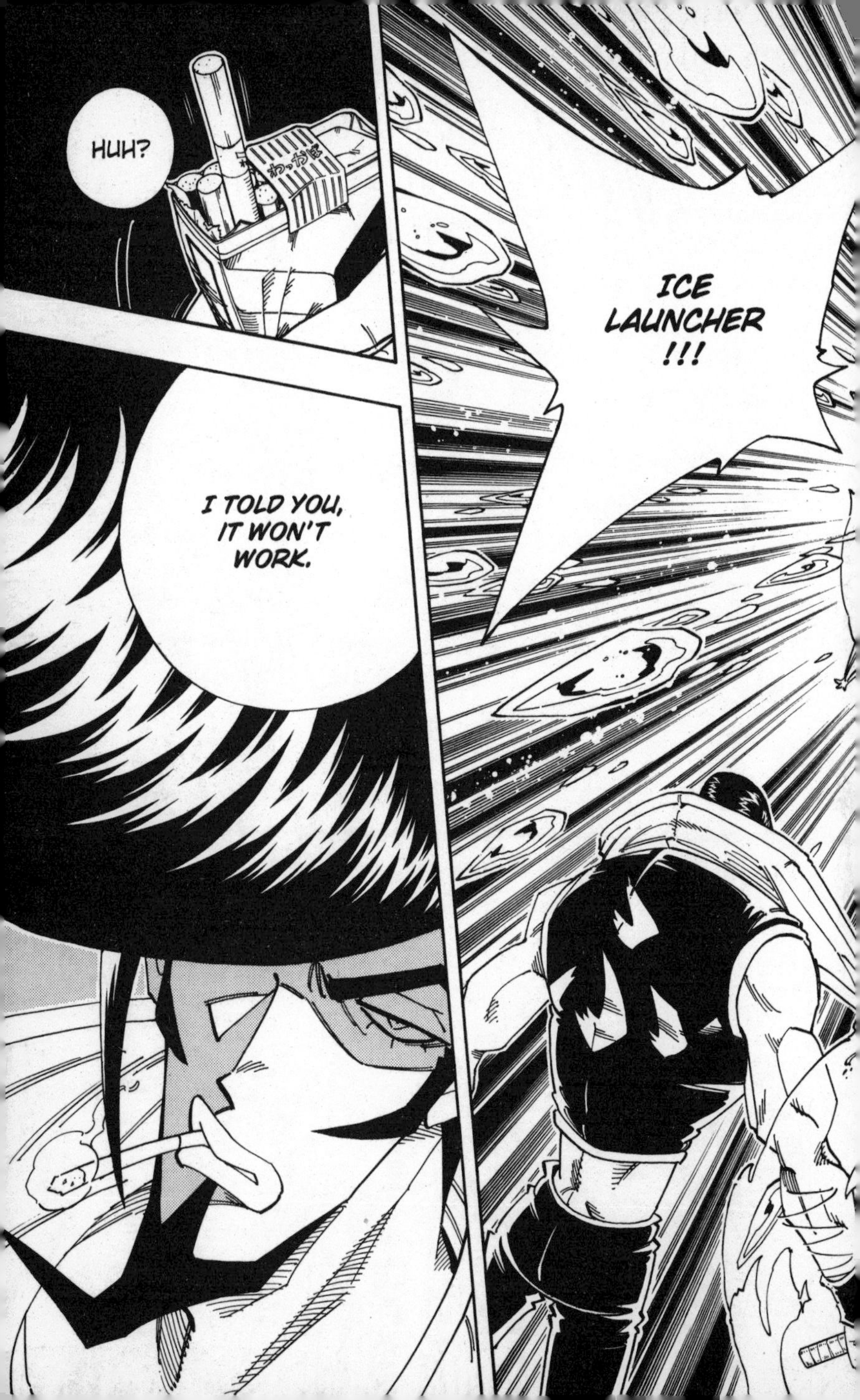
ICE LAUNCHER !!!
HUH?
I TOLD YOU, IT WON'T WORK.

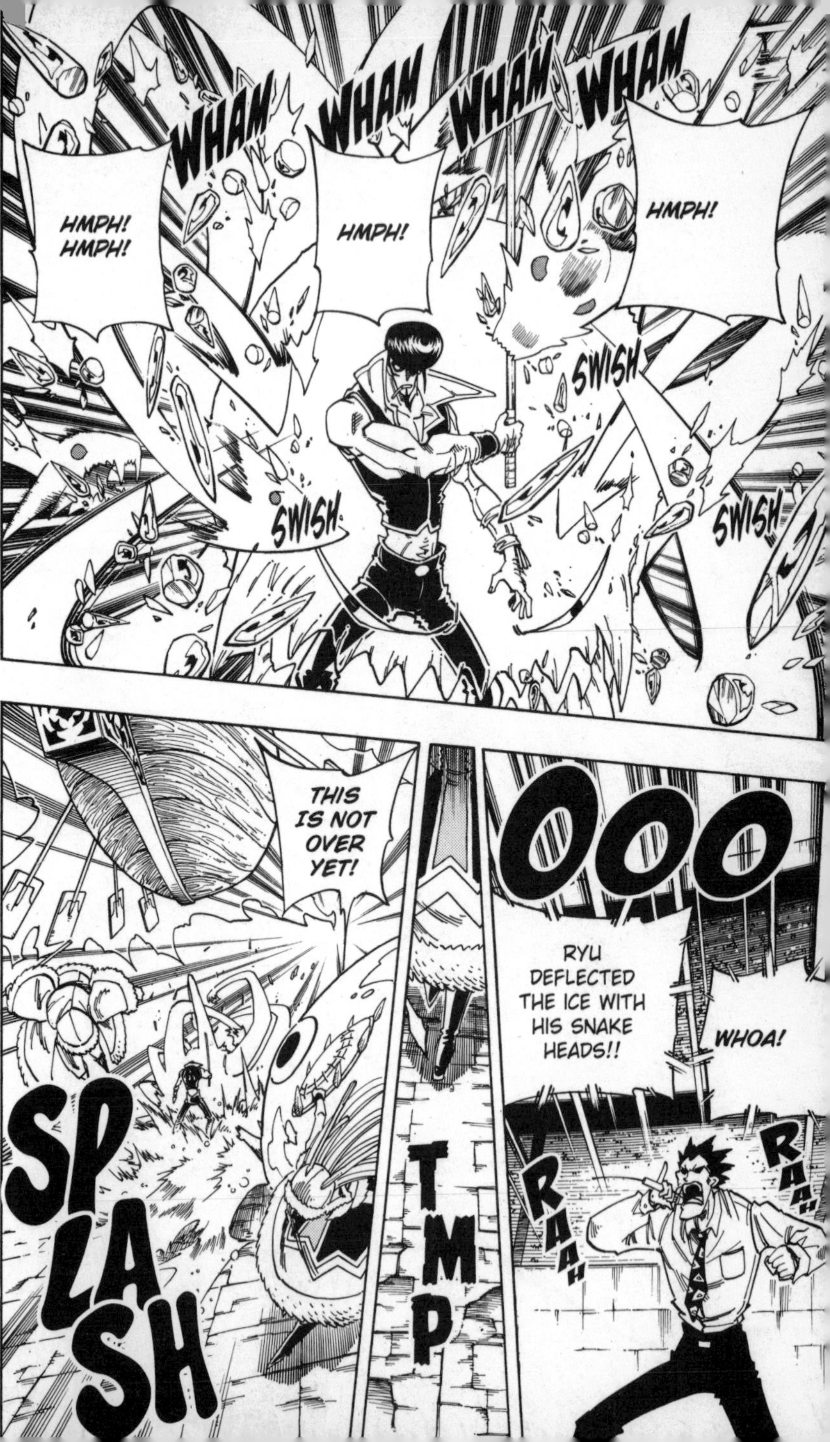

WHAM
WHAM
WHAM
WHAM
HMPH!
HMPH!
HMPH! HMPH!
SWISH
SWISH
SWISH
OOO
RYU DEFLECTED THE ICE WITH HIS SNAKE HEADS!!
WHOA!
RAAH
RAAH
TMP
THIS IS NOT OVER YET!
SPLASH

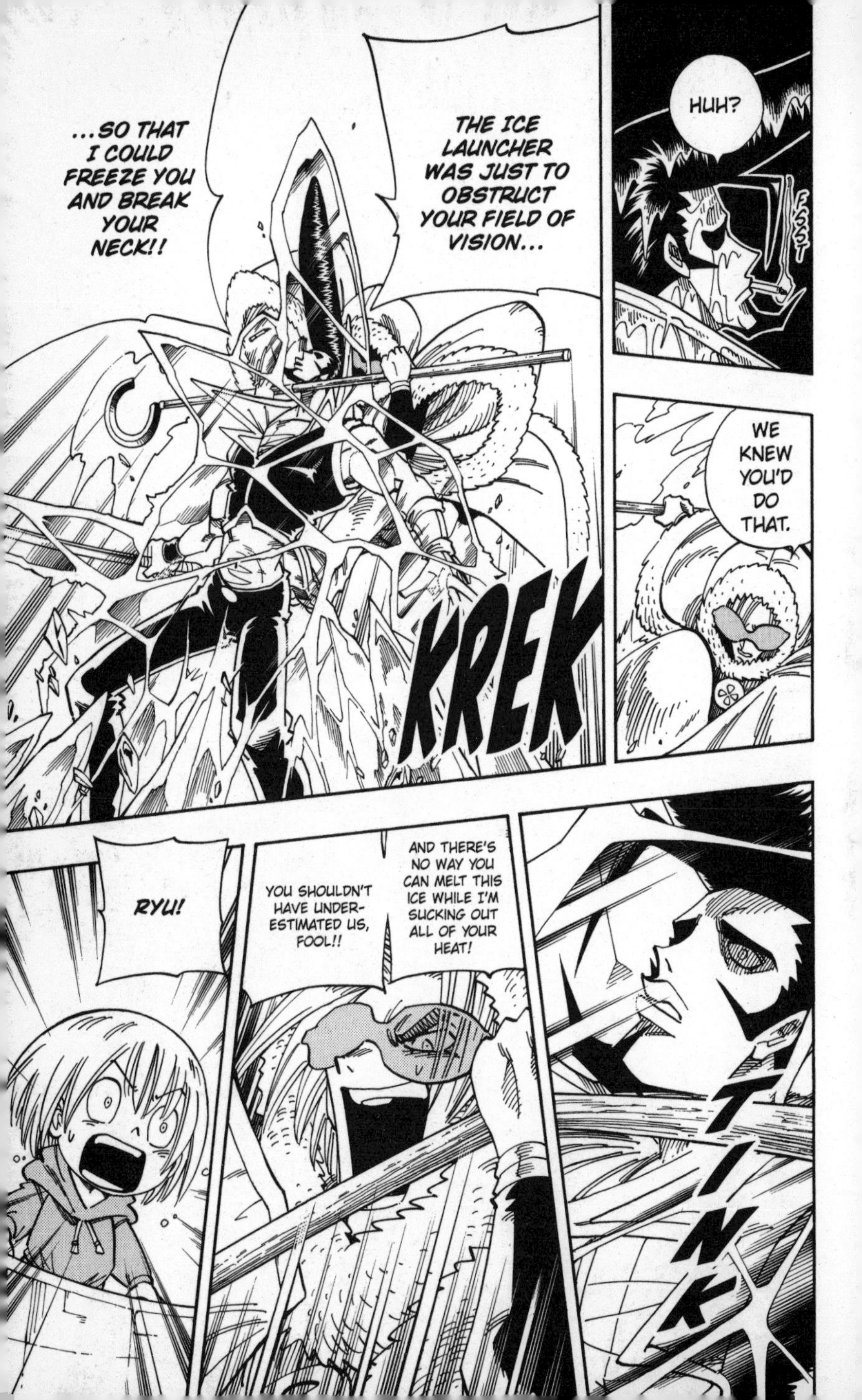
HUH?
FSST
WE KNEW YOU'D DO THAT.
THE ICE LAUNCHER WAS JUST TO OBSTRUCT YOUR FIELD OF VISION...
...SO THAT I COULD FREEZE YOU AND BREAK YOUR NECK!!
KREK
TINK
AND THERE'S NO WAY YOU CAN MELT THIS ICE WHILE I'M SUCKING OUT ALL OF YOUR HEAT!
YOU SHOULDN'T HAVE UNDER-ESTIMATED US, FOOL!!
RYU!

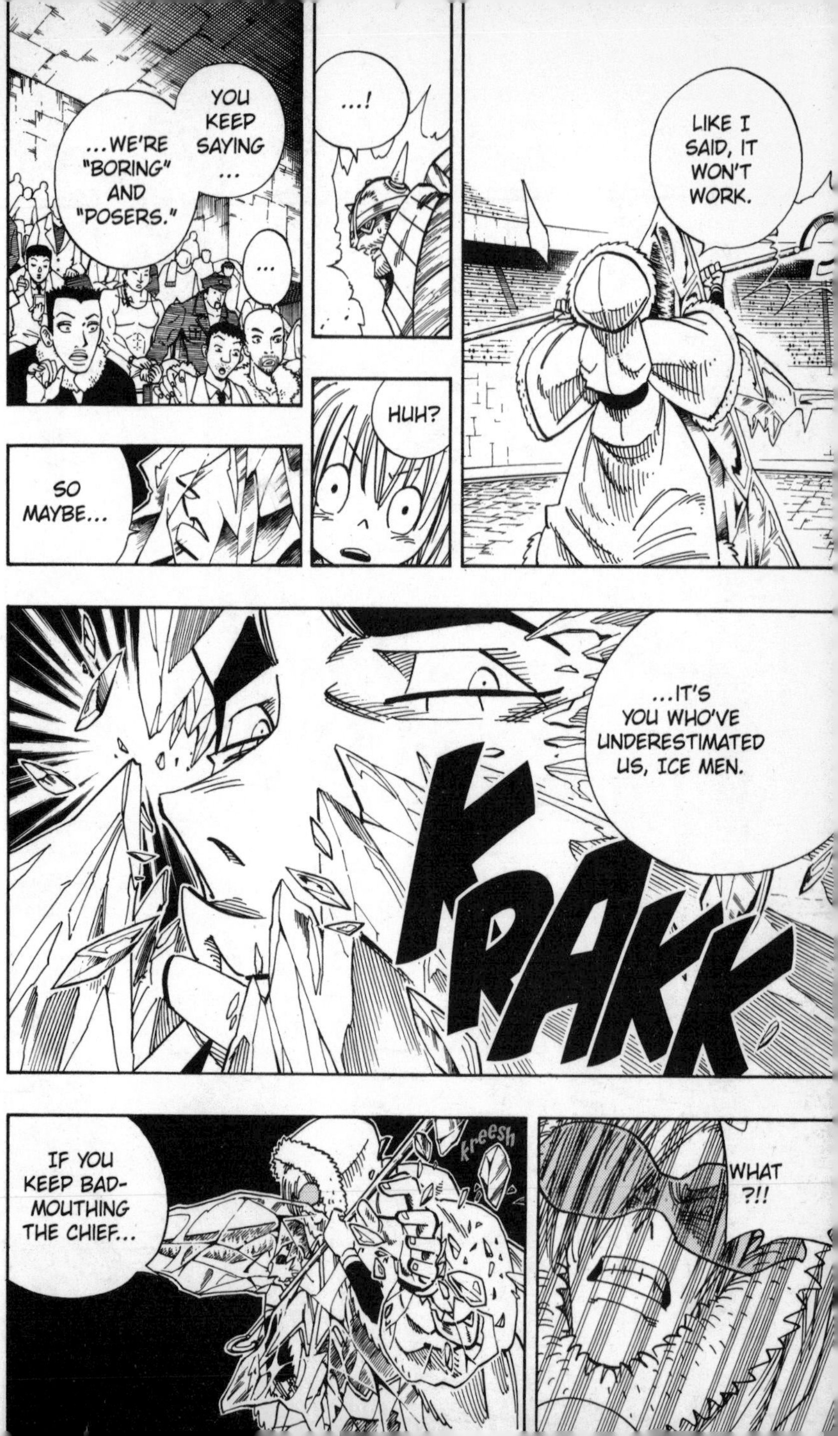
LIKE I SAID, IT WON'T WORK.
...!
YOU KEEP SAYING...
...WE'RE "BORING" AND "POSERS."
...
HUH?
SO MAYBE...
...IT'S YOU WHO'VE UNDERESTIMATED US, ICE MEN.
KRAKK
WHAT ?!!
kreesh
IF YOU KEEP BAD-MOUTHING THE CHIEF...

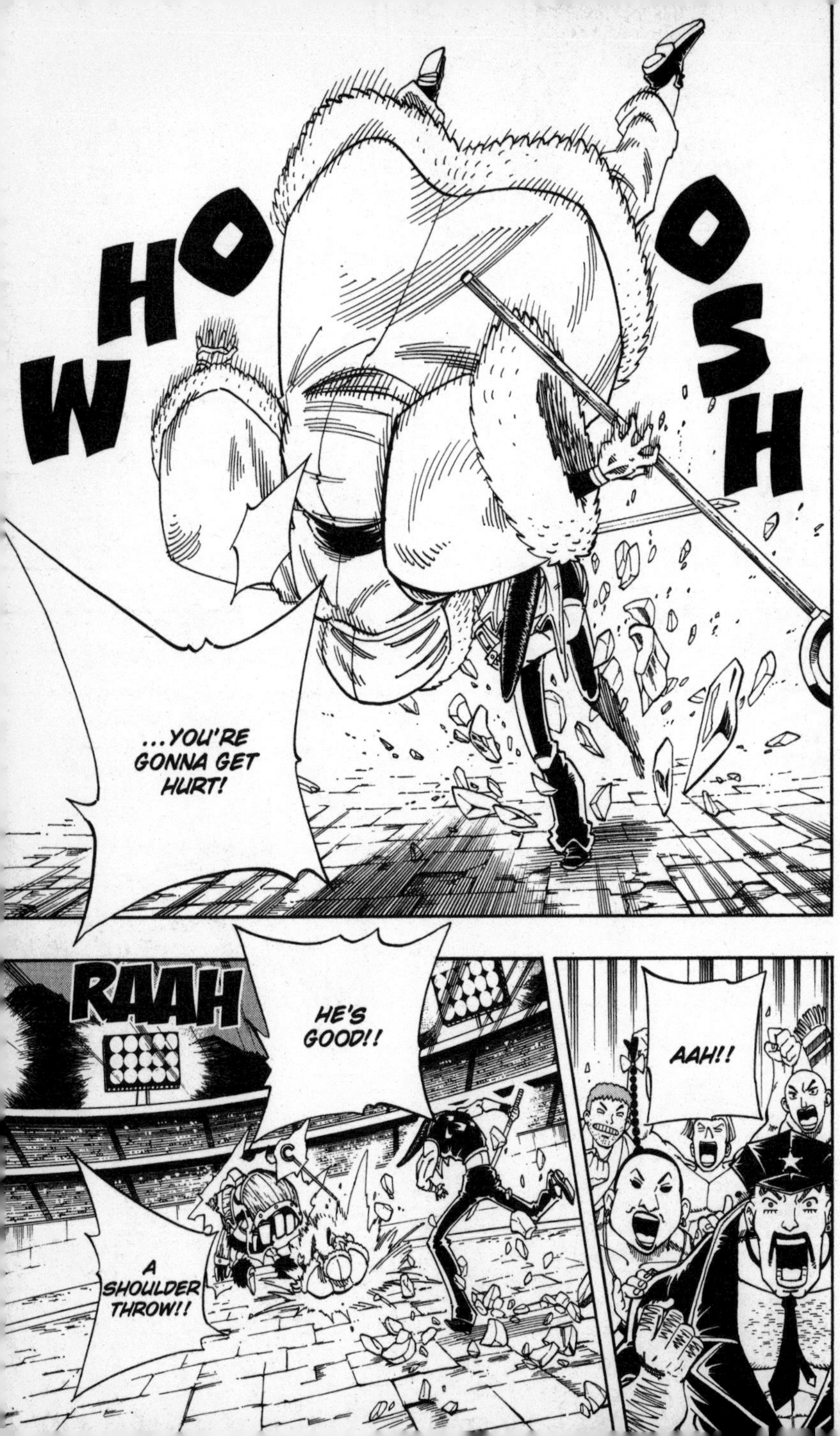
WHOOSH
...YOU'RE GONNA GET HURT!
AAH!!
HE'S GOOD!!
RAAH
A SHOULDER THROW!!

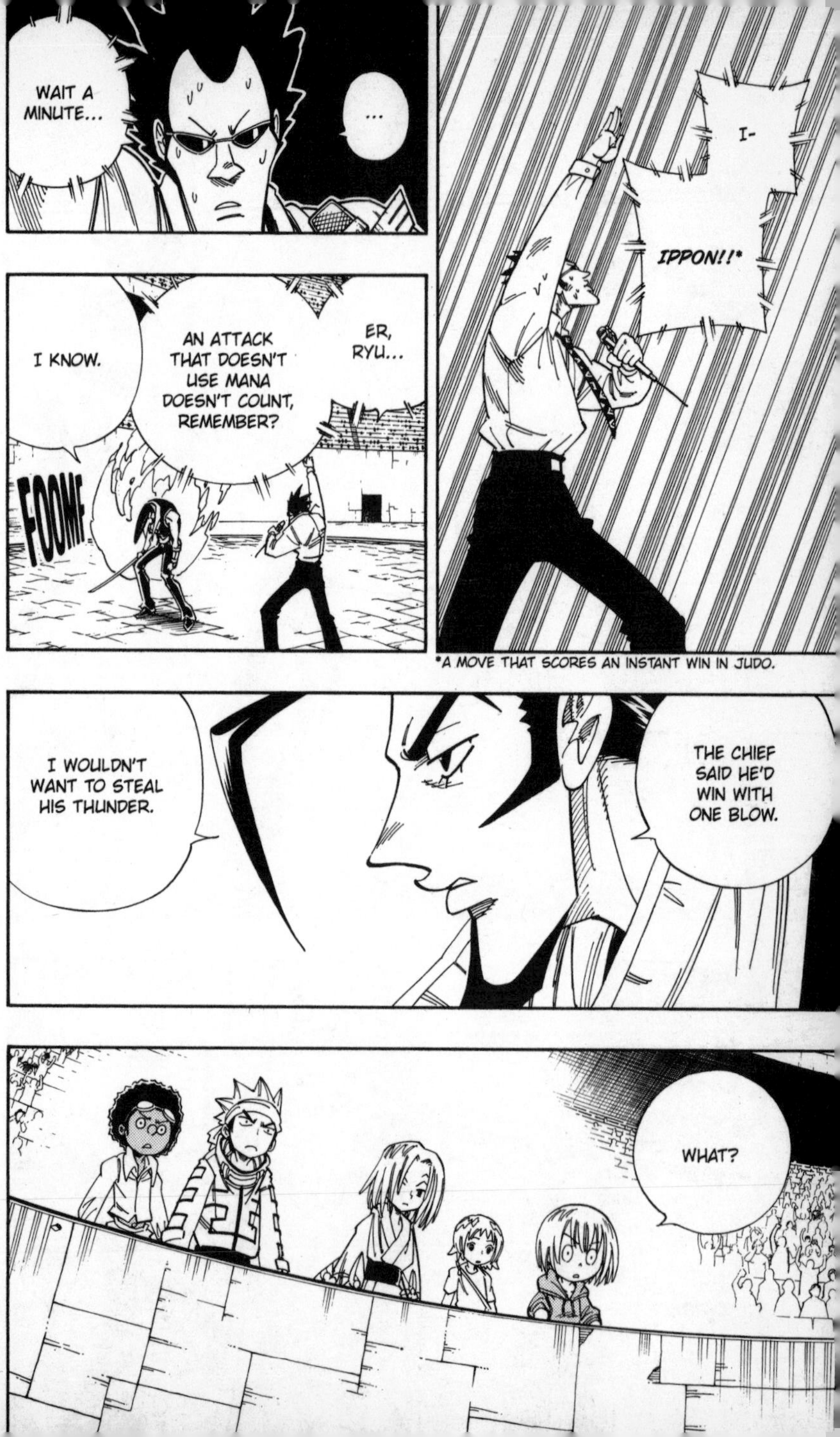
I-
IPPON!!*
...
WAIT A MINUTE...
ER, RYU...
AN ATTACK THAT DOESN'T USE MANA DOESN'T COUNT, REMEMBER?
I KNOW.
FOOMF
THE CHIEF SAID HE'D WIN WITH ONE BLOW.
I WOULDN'T WANT TO STEAL HIS THUNDER.
WHAT?
*A MOVE THAT SCORES AN INSTANT WIN IN JUDO.

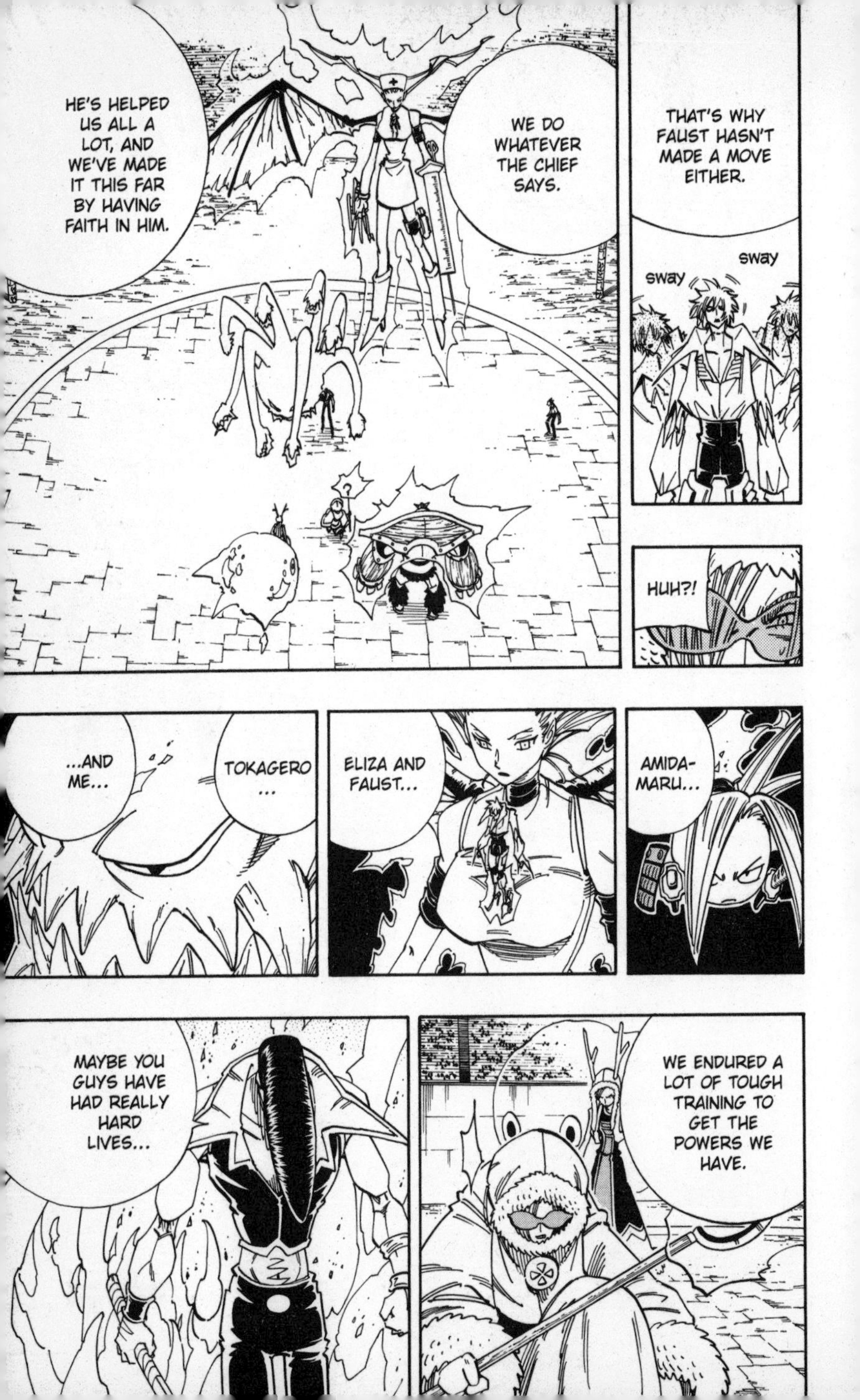
THAT'S WHY FAUST HASN'T MADE A MOVE EITHER.
sway
sway
HUH?!
WE DO WHATEVER THE CHIEF SAYS.
HE'S HELPED US ALL A LOT, AND WE'VE MADE IT THIS FAR BY HAVING FAITH IN HIM.
AMIDA-MARU...
ELIZA AND FAUST...
TOKAGERO ...
...AND ME...
WE ENDURED A LOT OF TOUGH TRAINING TO GET THE POWERS WE HAVE.
MAYBE YOU GUYS HAVE HAD REALLY HARD LIVES...

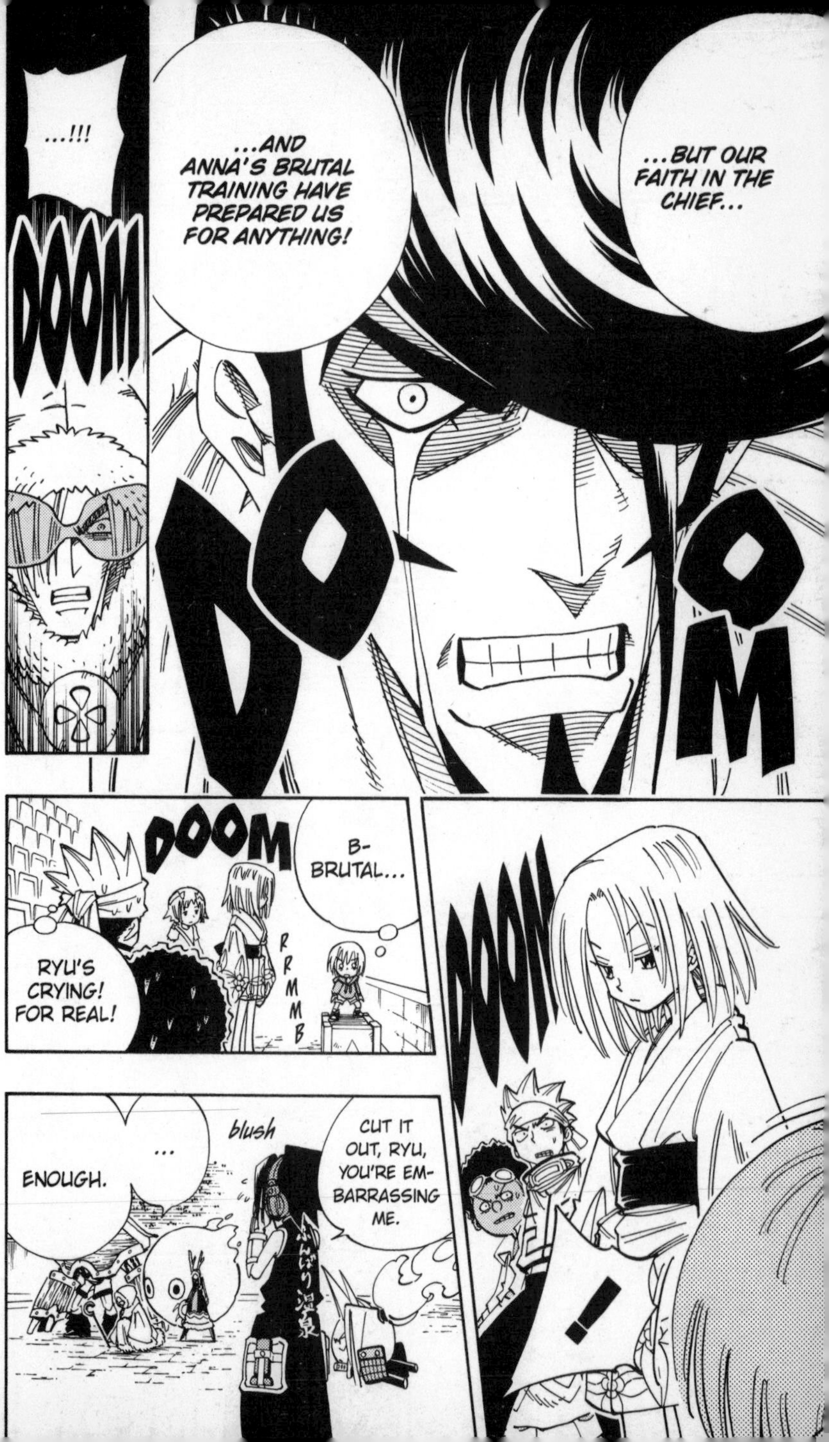
...BUT OUR FAITH IN THE CHIEF...
...AND ANNA'S BRUTAL TRAINING HAVE PREPARED US FOR ANYTHING!
DOOM
...!!!
DOOM
DOOM
!
B- BRUTAL...
DOOM
RRMMB
RYU'S CRYING! FOR REAL!
CUT IT OUT, RYU, YOU'RE EM-BARRASSING ME.
blush
ふんばり温泉
...
ENOUGH.

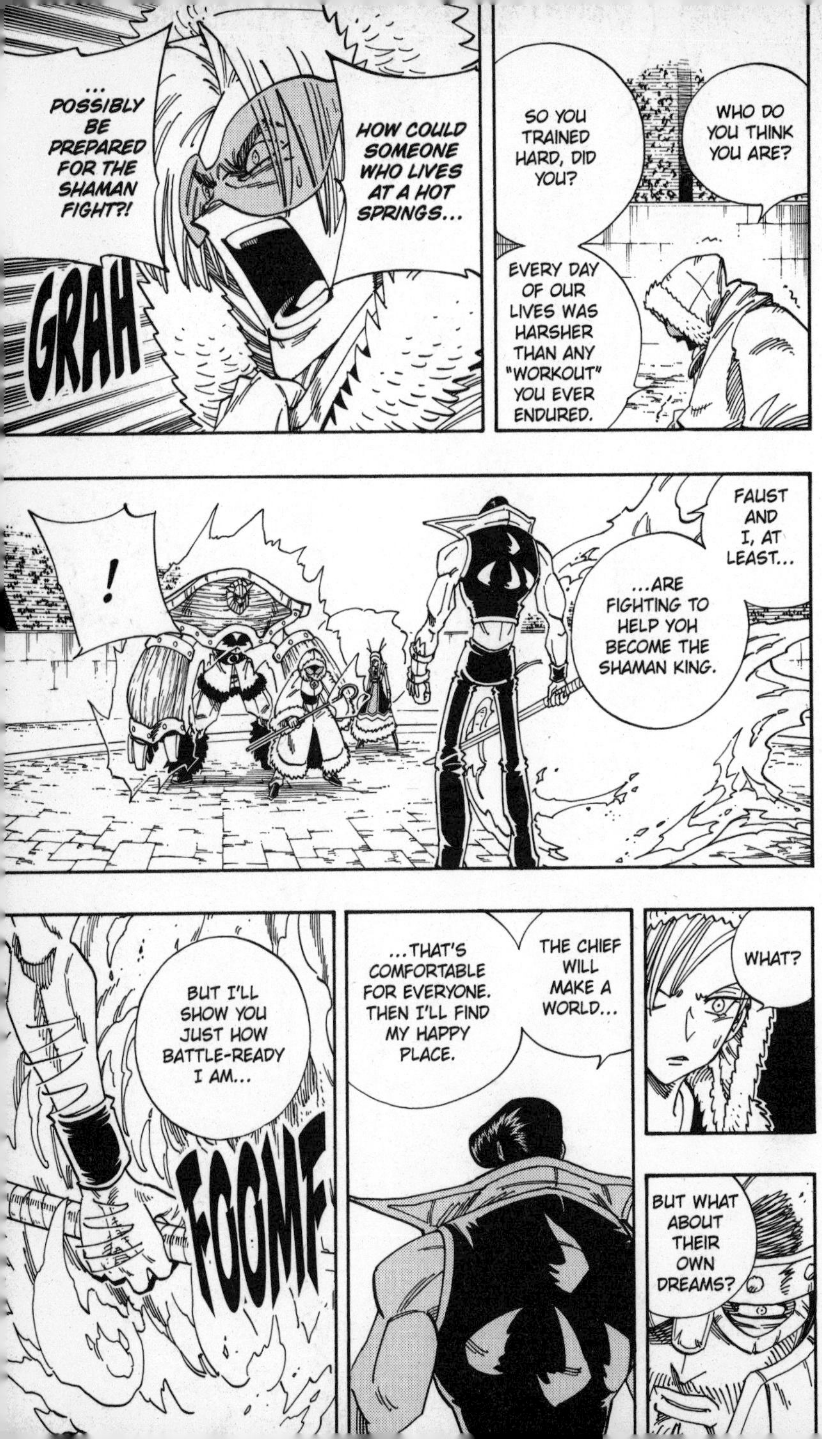
WHO DO YOU THINK YOU ARE?
SO YOU TRAINED HARD, DID YOU?
EVERY DAY OF OUR LIVES WAS HARSHER THAN ANY "WORKOUT" YOU EVER ENDURED.
HOW COULD SOMEONE WHO LIVES AT A HOT SPRINGS...
...POSSIBLY BE PREPARED FOR THE SHAMAN FIGHT?!
GRAH
FAUST AND I, AT LEAST...
...ARE FIGHTING TO HELP YOH BECOME THE SHAMAN KING.
!
WHAT?
BUT WHAT ABOUT THEIR OWN DREAMS?
THE CHIEF WILL MAKE A WORLD...
...THAT'S COMFORTABLE FOR EVERYONE. THEN I'LL FIND MY HAPPY PLACE.
BUT I'LL SHOW YOU JUST HOW BATTLE-READY I AM...
FOOMF

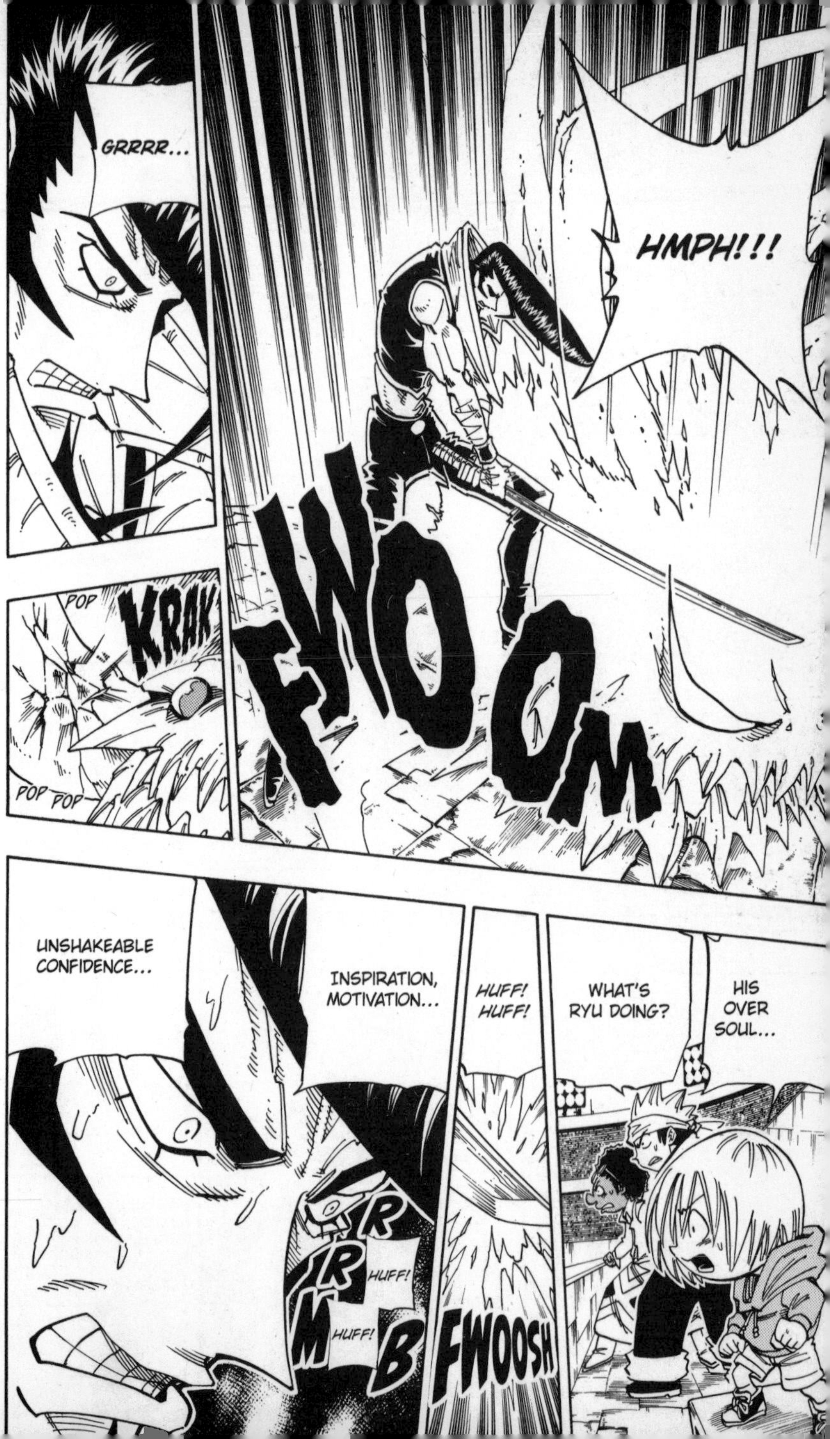
HMPH!!!
FWOOM
GRRRR...
POP
KRAK
POP POP
HIS OVER SOUL...
WHAT'S RYU DOING?
HUFF! HUFF!
FWOOSH
INSPIRATION, MOTIVATION...
RRRMB
HUFF!
HUFF!
UNSHAKEABLE CONFIDENCE...

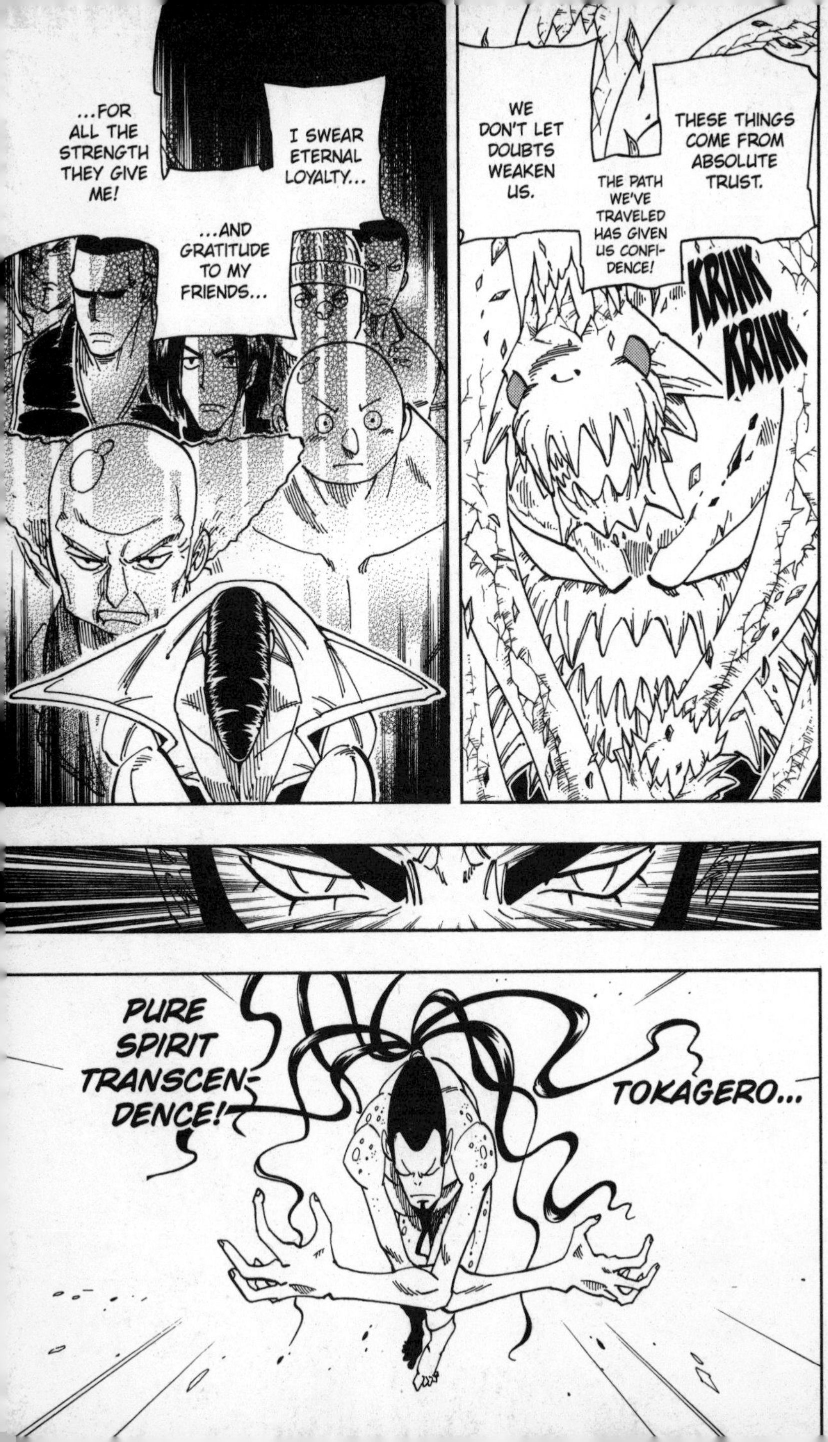

THESE THINGS COME FROM ABSOLUTE TRUST.
WE DON'T LET DOUBTS WEAKEN US.
THE PATH WE'VE TRAVELED HAS GIVEN US CONFI-DENCE!
KRINK KRINK
I SWEAR ETERNAL LOYALTY...
...AND GRATITUDE TO MY FRIENDS...
...FOR ALL THE STRENGTH THEY GIVE ME!
TOKAGERO...
PURE SPIRIT TRANSCEN-DENCE!

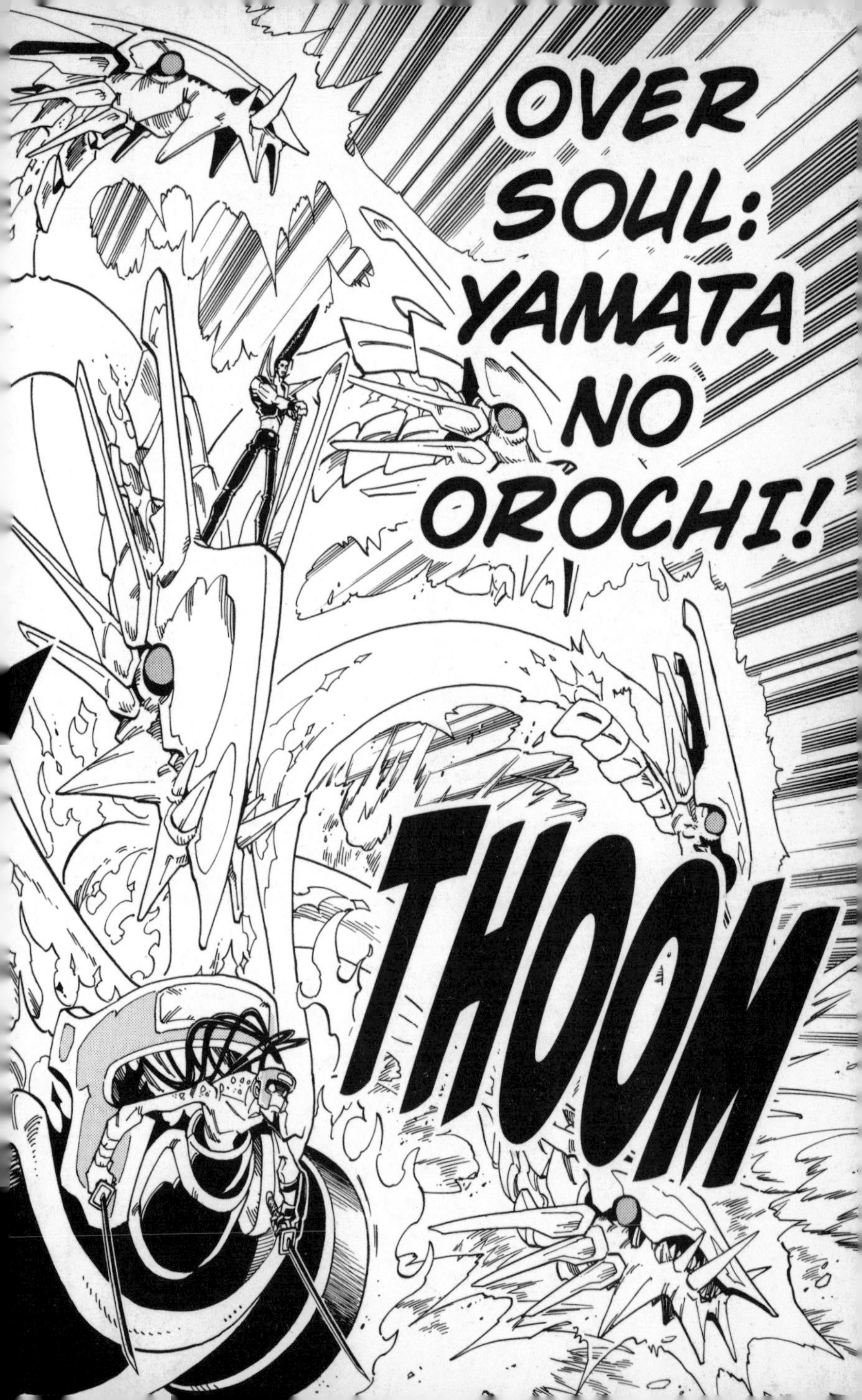
OVER SOUL: YAMATA NO OROCHI!
THOOM

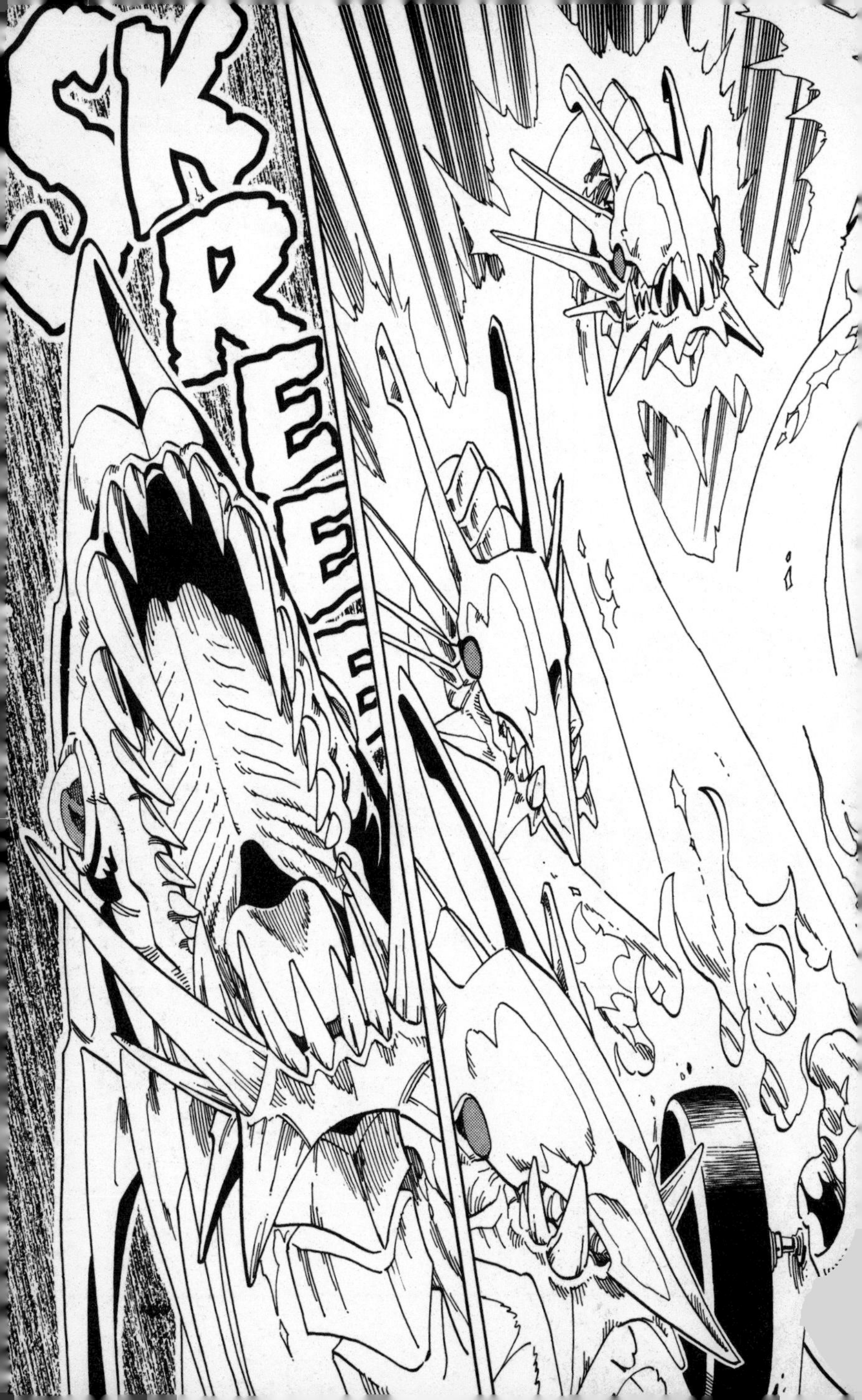
SKREEE

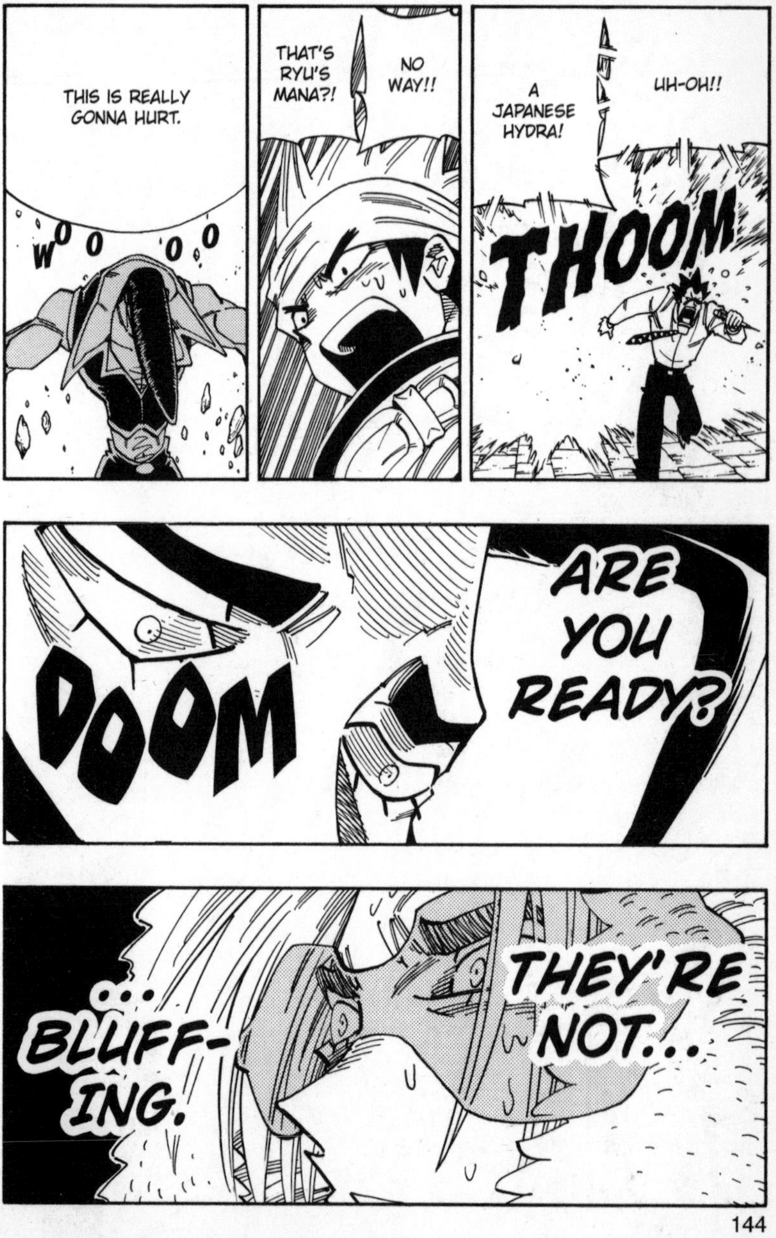
UH-OH!!
A JAPANESE HYDRA!
THOOM
NO WAY!!
THAT'S RYU'S MANA?!
THIS IS REALLY GONNA HURT.
WOOOO
ARE YOU READY?
DOOM
THEY'RE NOT...
...BLUFF-ING.

Shaman King

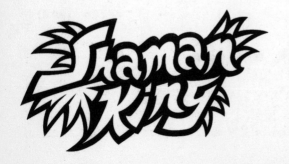

SHAMAN KING CHARACTER FILE No.76

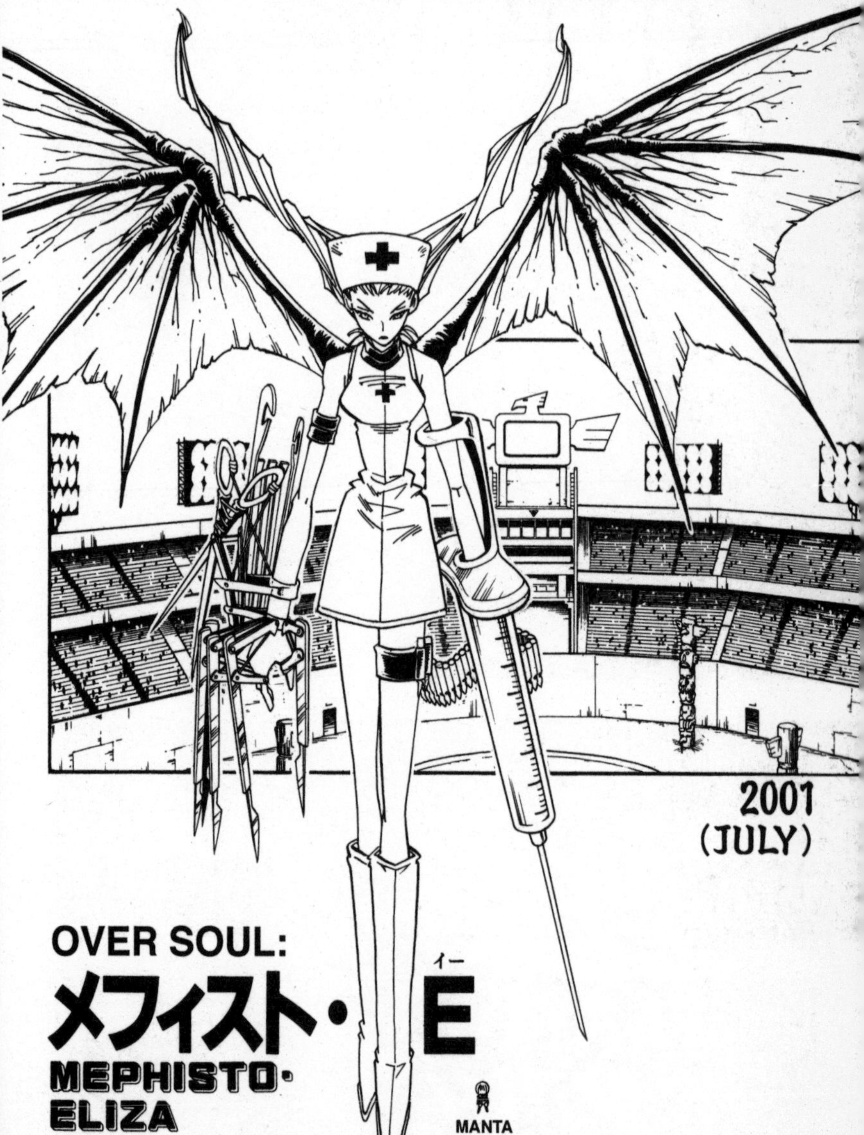

2001
(JULY)

OVER SOUL:
メフィスト・E(イー)
MEPHISTO-ELIZA

MANTA

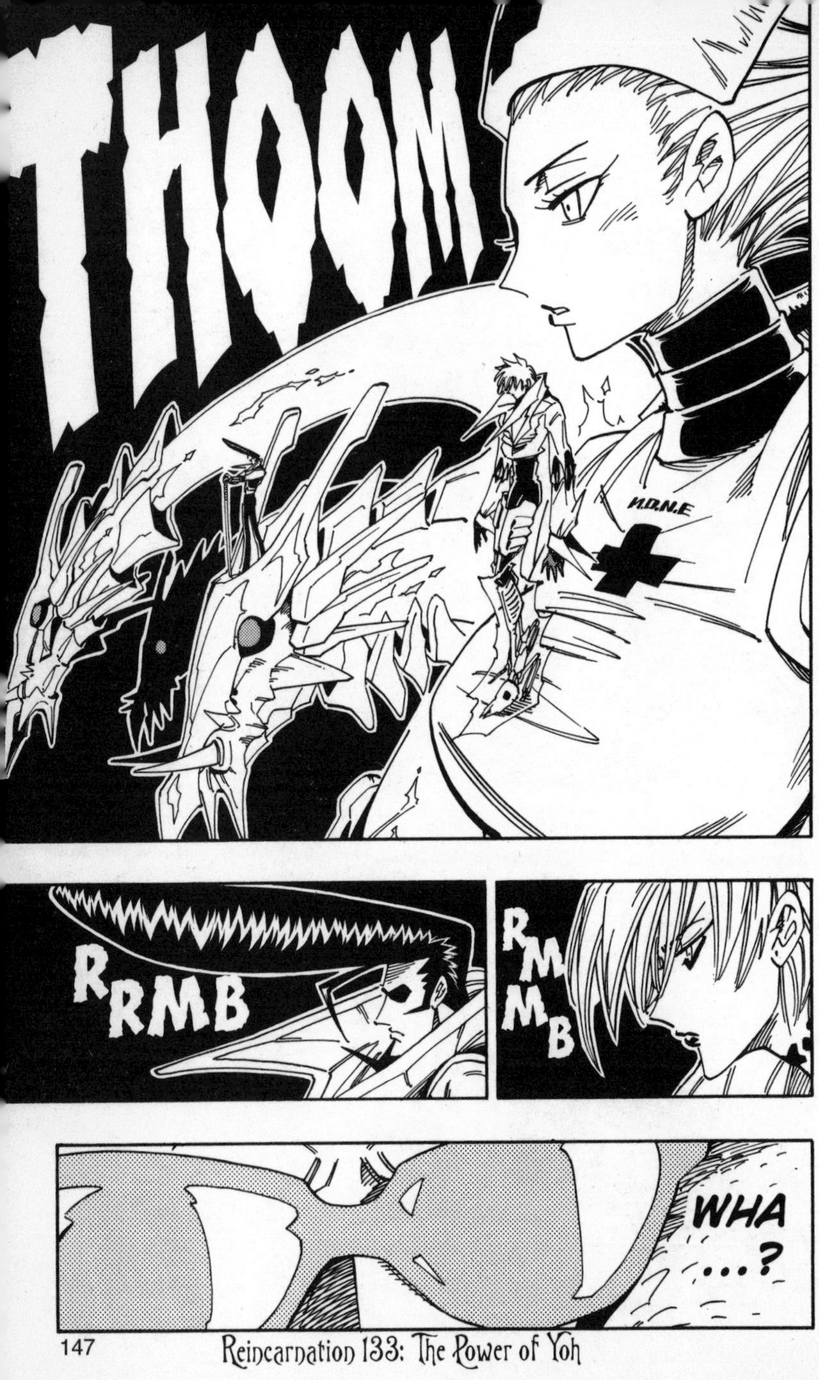
THOOM
N.O.N.E
RMMB
RRMB
WHA ...?

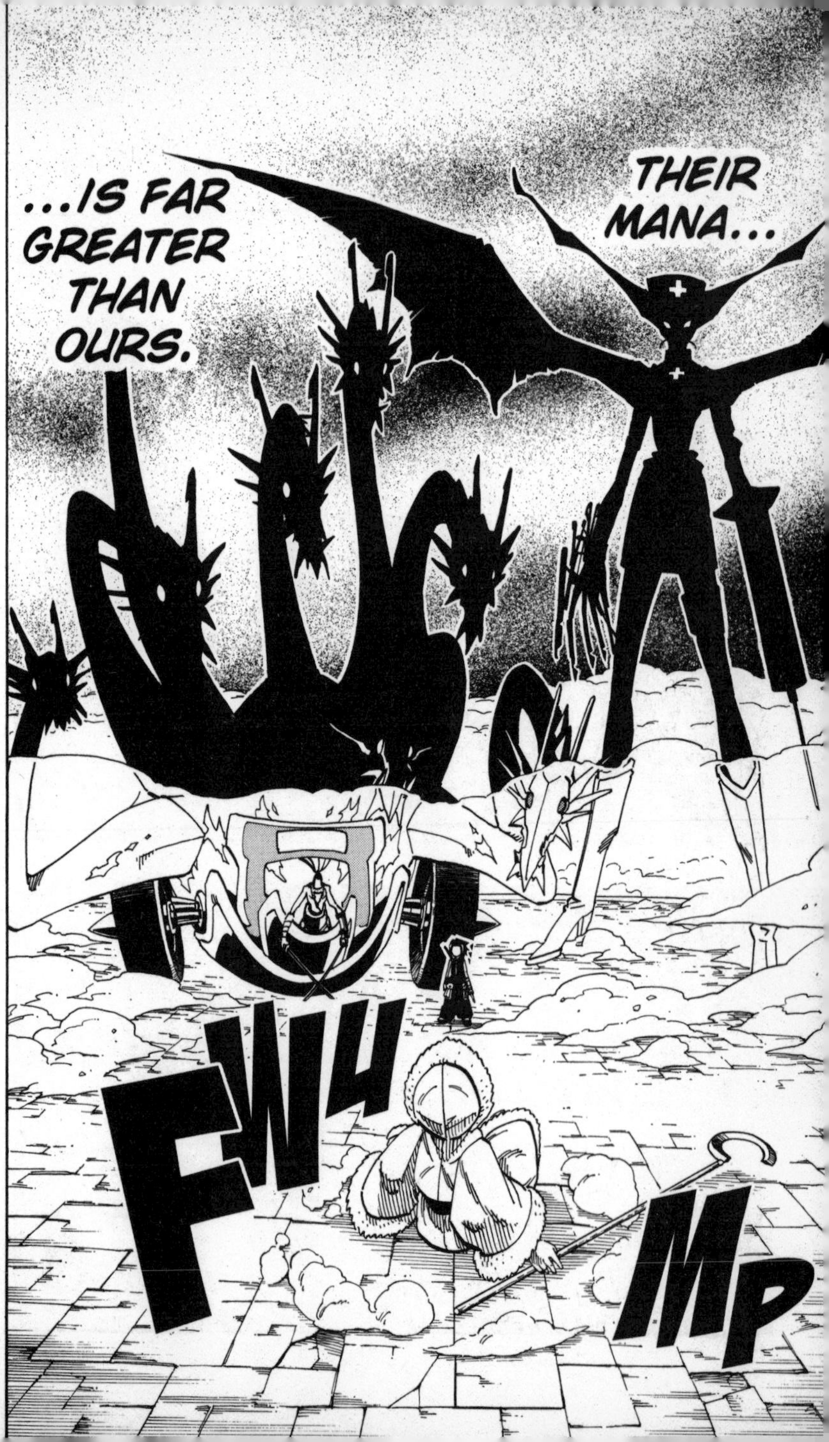
THEIR MANA...
...IS FAR GREATER THAN OURS.
FWUMP

Reincarnation 133:
The Power of Yoh

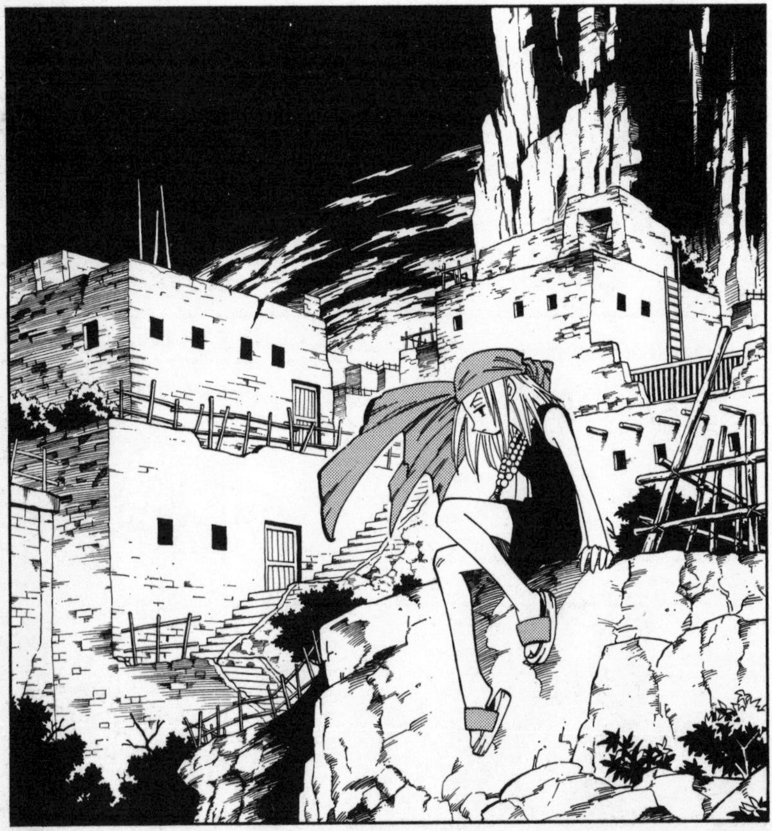

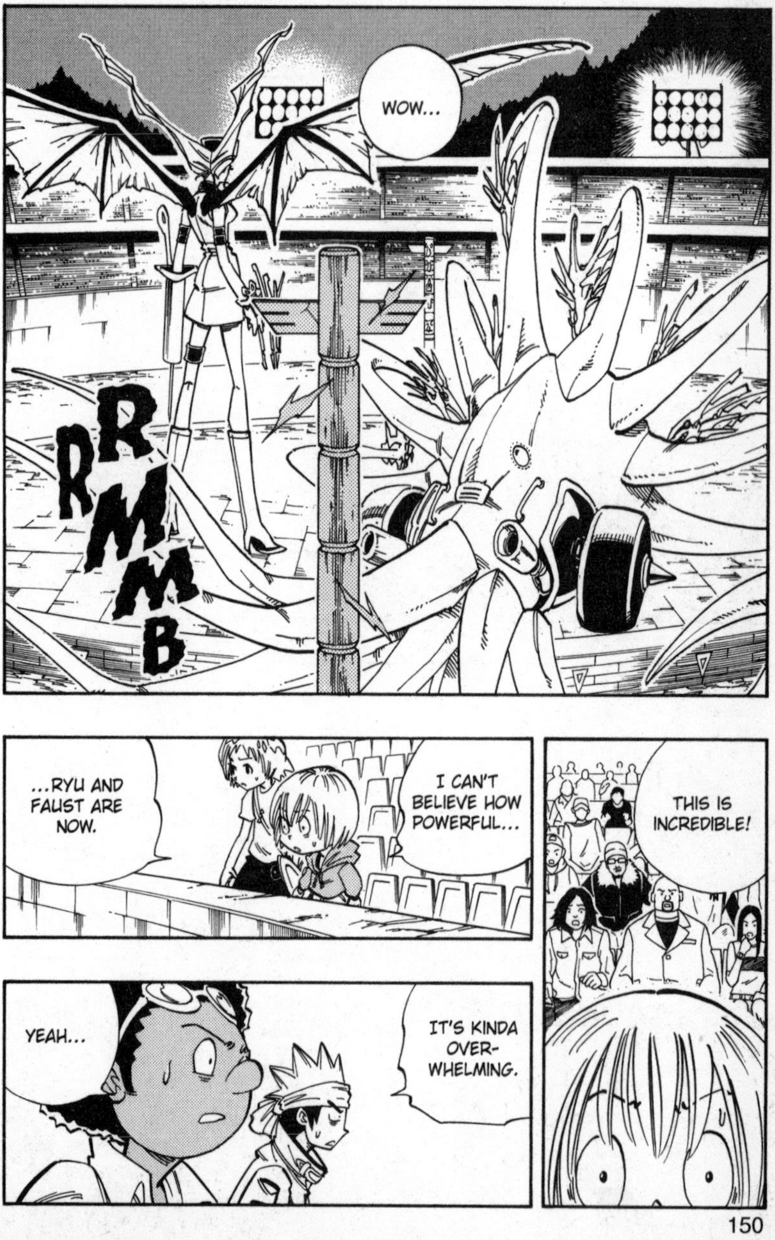
WOW...
RRMMB
THIS IS INCREDIBLE!
I CAN'T BELIEVE HOW POWERFUL...
...RYU AND FAUST ARE NOW.
IT'S KINDA OVER-WHELMING.
YEAH...

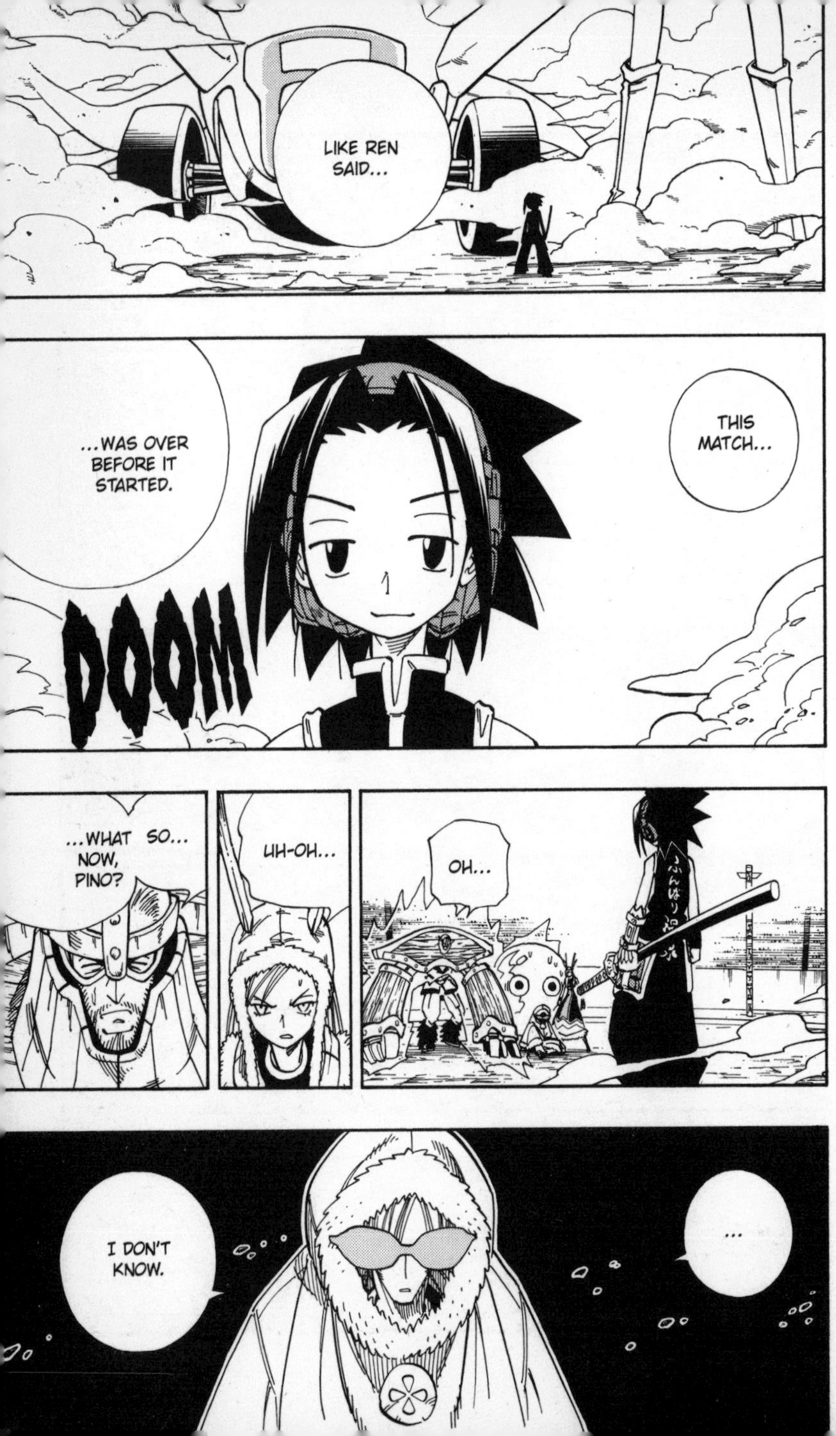
LIKE REN SAID...
THIS MATCH...
...WAS OVER BEFORE IT STARTED.
DOOM
OH...
UH-OH...
SO...
...WHAT NOW, PINO?
...
I DON'T KNOW.

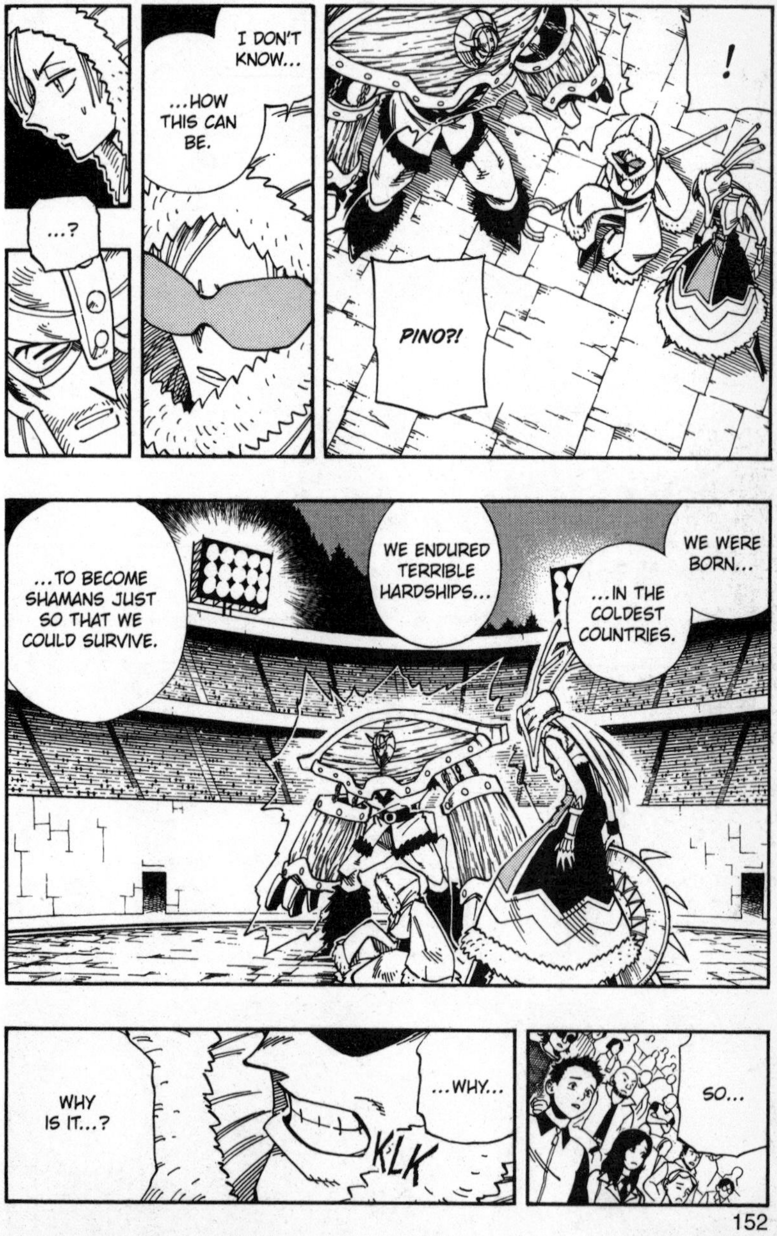
!
PINO?!
I DON'T KNOW...
...HOW THIS CAN BE.
...?
WE WERE BORN...
...IN THE COLDEST COUNTRIES.
WE ENDURED TERRIBLE HARDSHIPS...
...TO BECOME SHAMANS JUST SO THAT WE COULD SURVIVE.
SO...
...WHY...
KLK
WHY IS IT...?

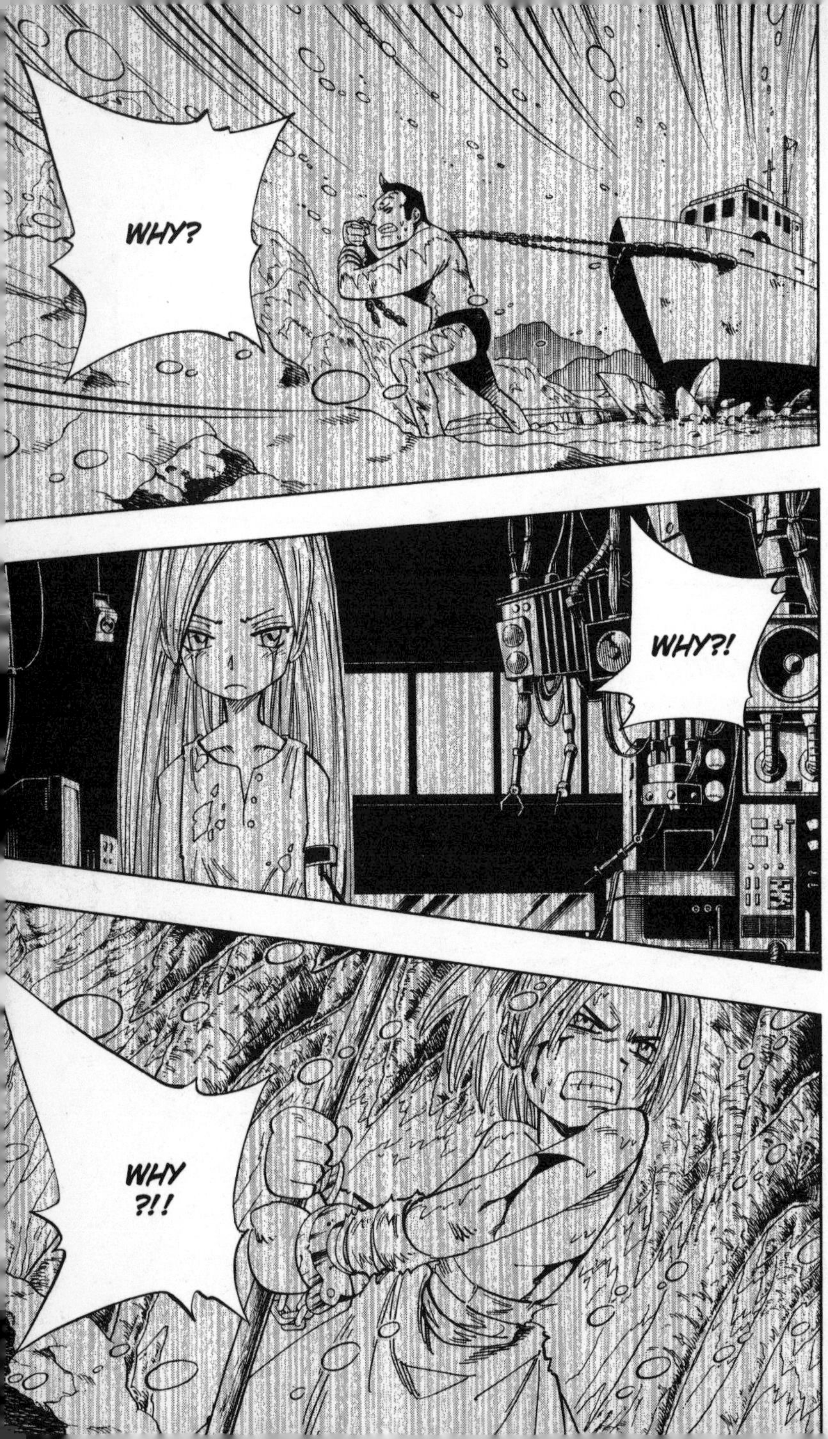
WHY?
WHY?!
WHY ?!!

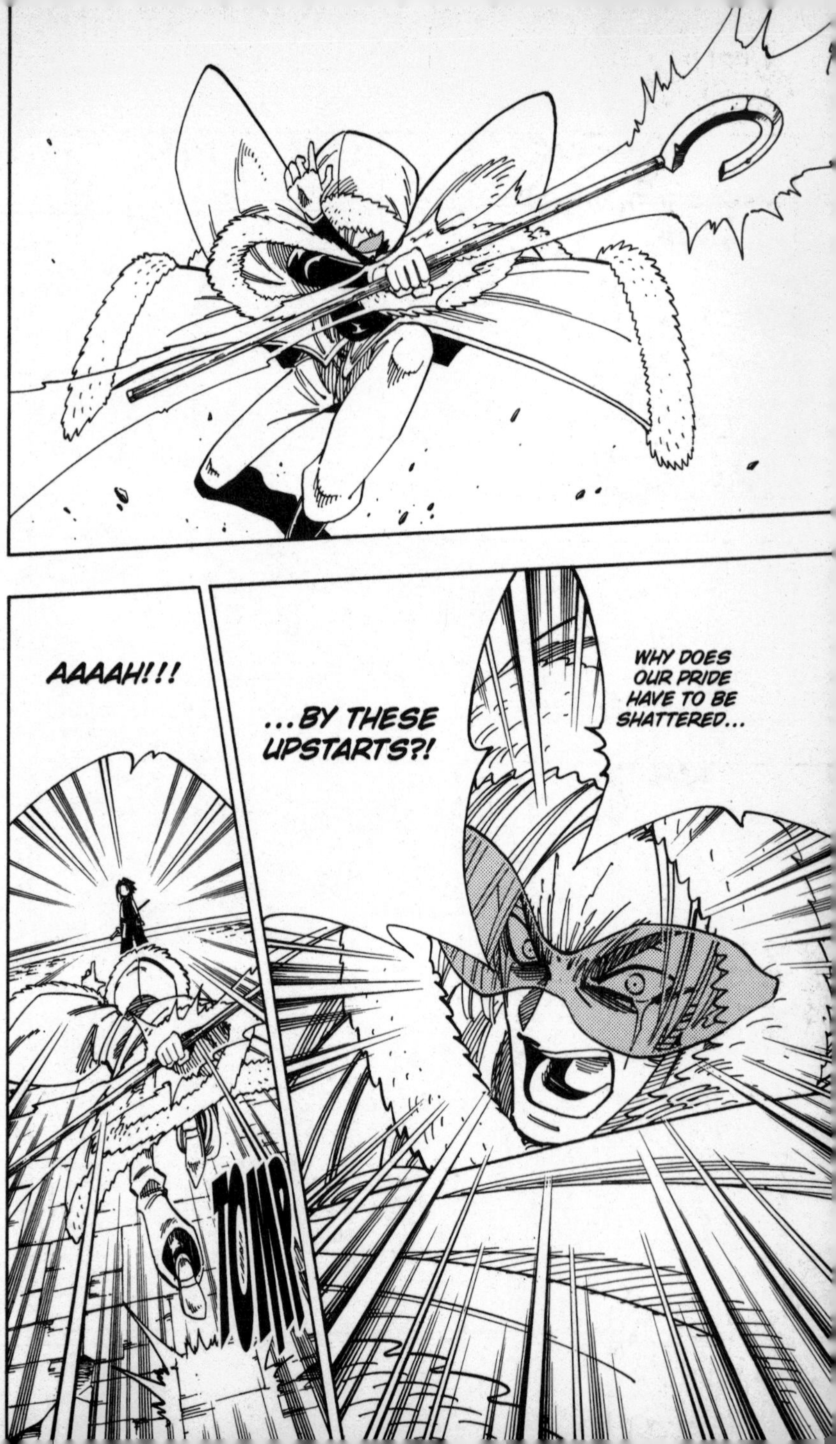
WHY DOES OUR PRIDE HAVE TO BE SHATTERED...
...BY THESE UPSTARTS?!
AAAAH!!!

READ THIS WAY

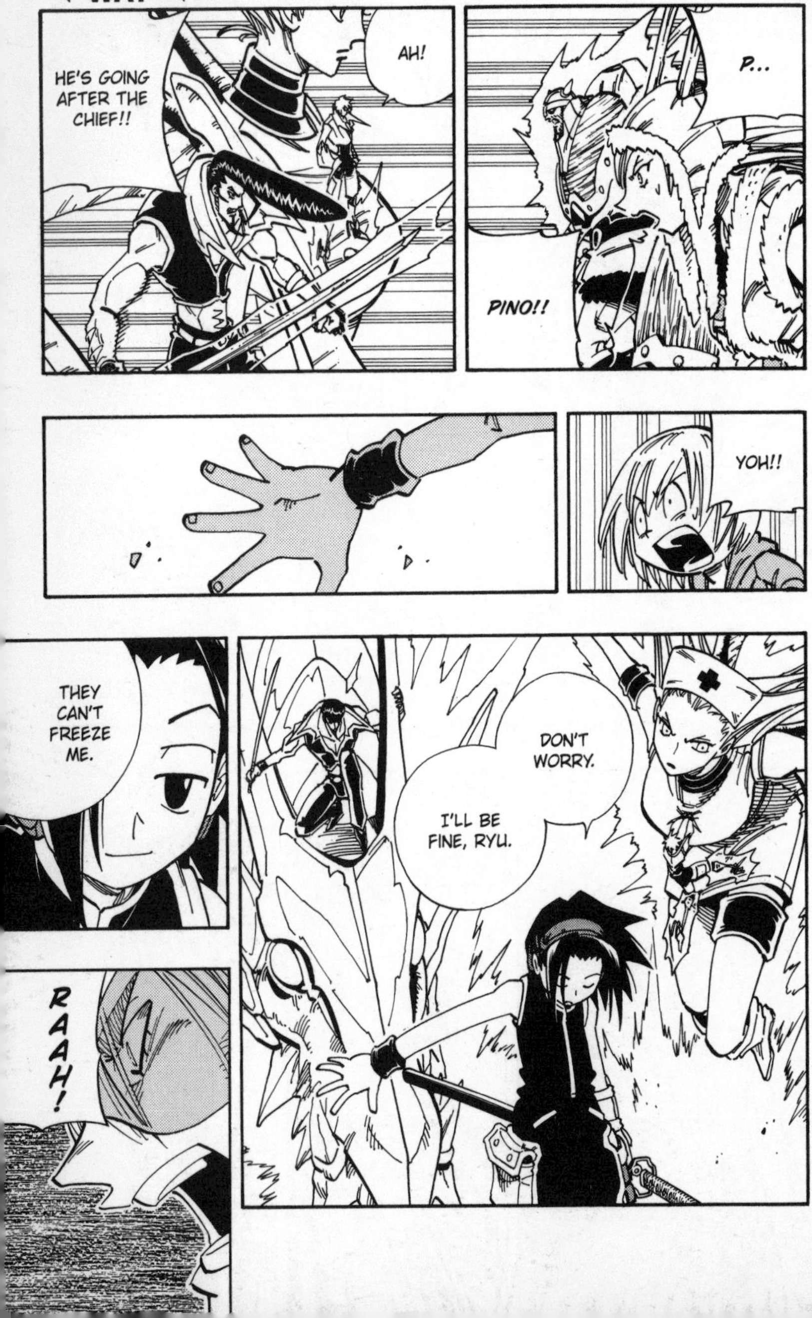
P...
PINO!!
AH!
HE'S GOING AFTER THE CHIEF!!
YOH!!
DON'T WORRY.
I'LL BE FINE, RYU.
THEY CAN'T FREEZE ME.
RAAH!

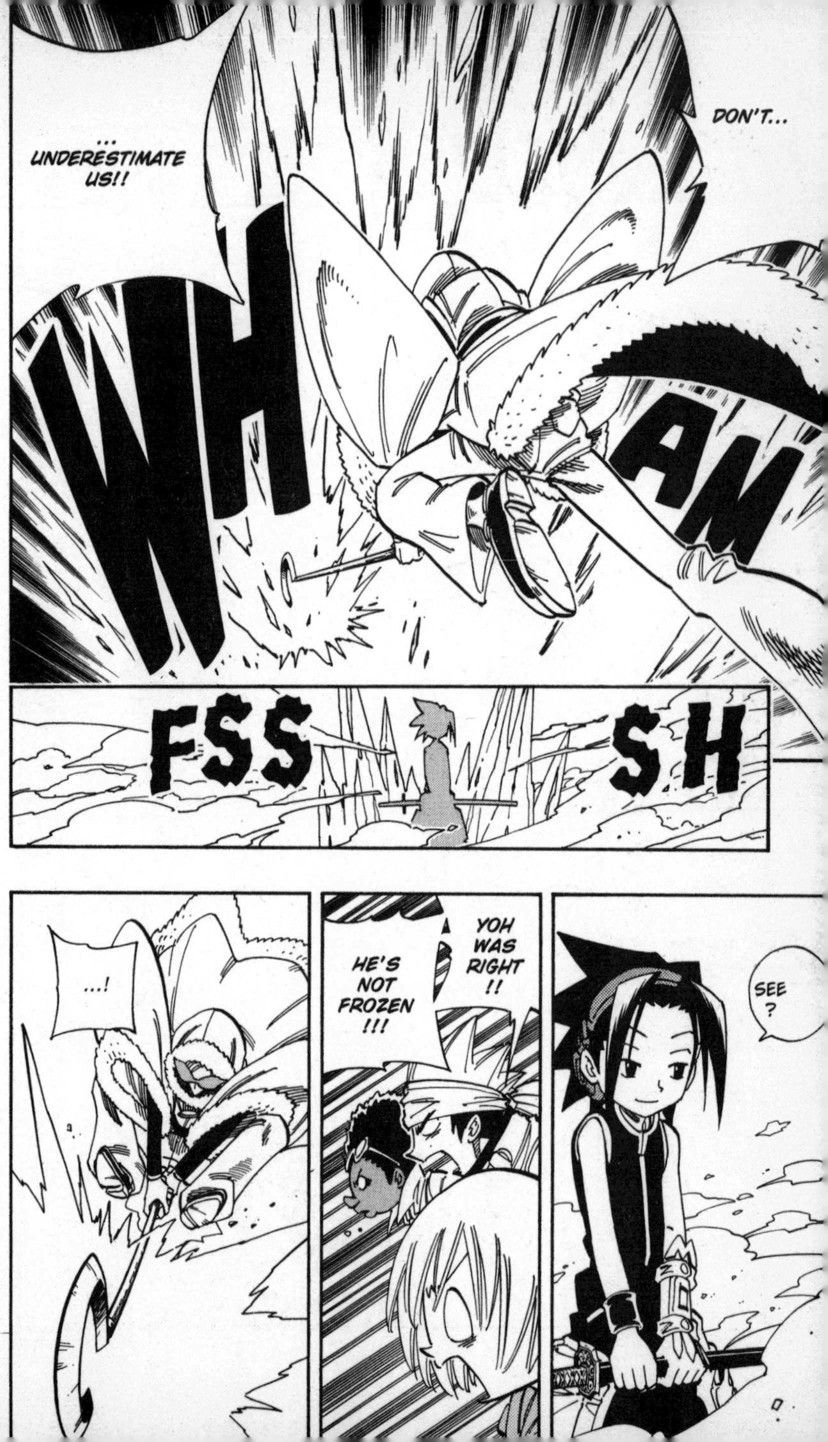
DON'T...
... UNDERESTIMATE US!!
WHAM
FSSSH
SEE ?
YOH WAS RIGHT !!
HE'S NOT FROZEN !!!
...!

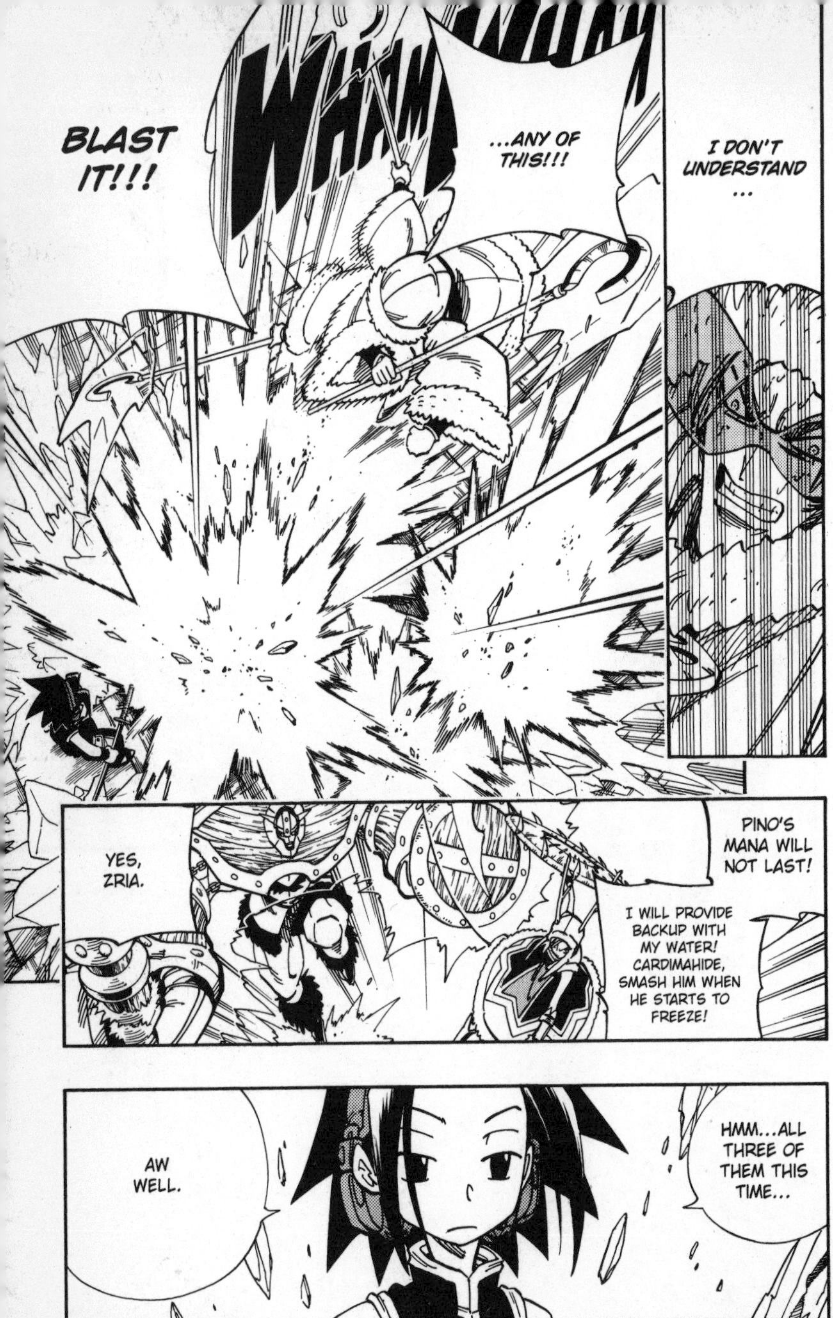

I DON'T UNDERSTAND ...
...ANY OF THIS!!!
WHAM
BLAST IT!!!
PINO'S MANA WILL NOT LAST!
I WILL PROVIDE BACKUP WITH MY WATER! CARDIMAHIDE, SMASH HIM WHEN HE STARTS TO FREEZE!
YES, ZRIA.
HMM...ALL THREE OF THEM THIS TIME...
AW WELL.

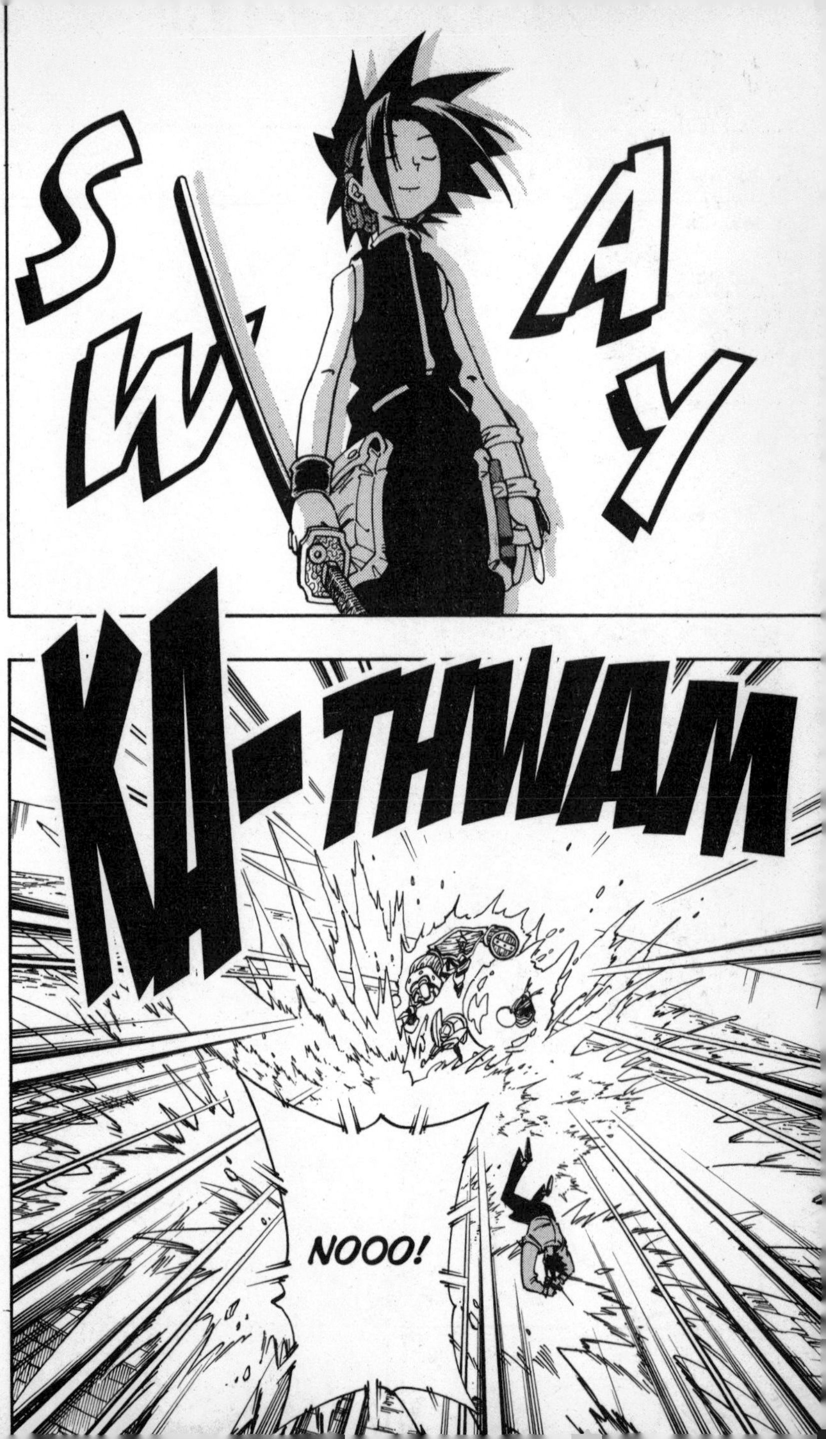
SWAY
KA-THWAM
NOOO!

READ THIS WAY

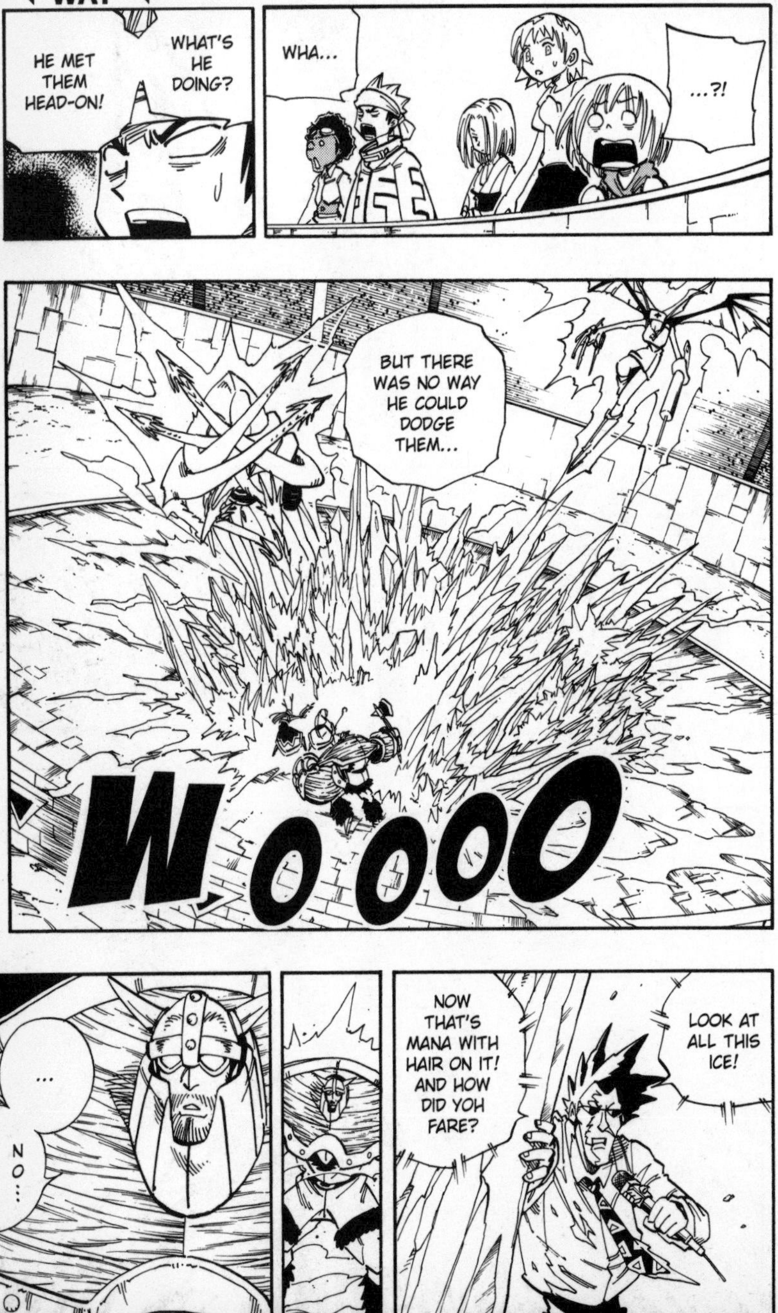

...?!
WHA...
WHAT'S HE DOING?
HE MET THEM HEAD-ON!
BUT THERE WAS NO WAY HE COULD DODGE THEM...
WOOOO
LOOK AT ALL THIS ICE!
NOW THAT'S MANA WITH HAIR ON IT! AND HOW DID YOH FARE?
...
NO...

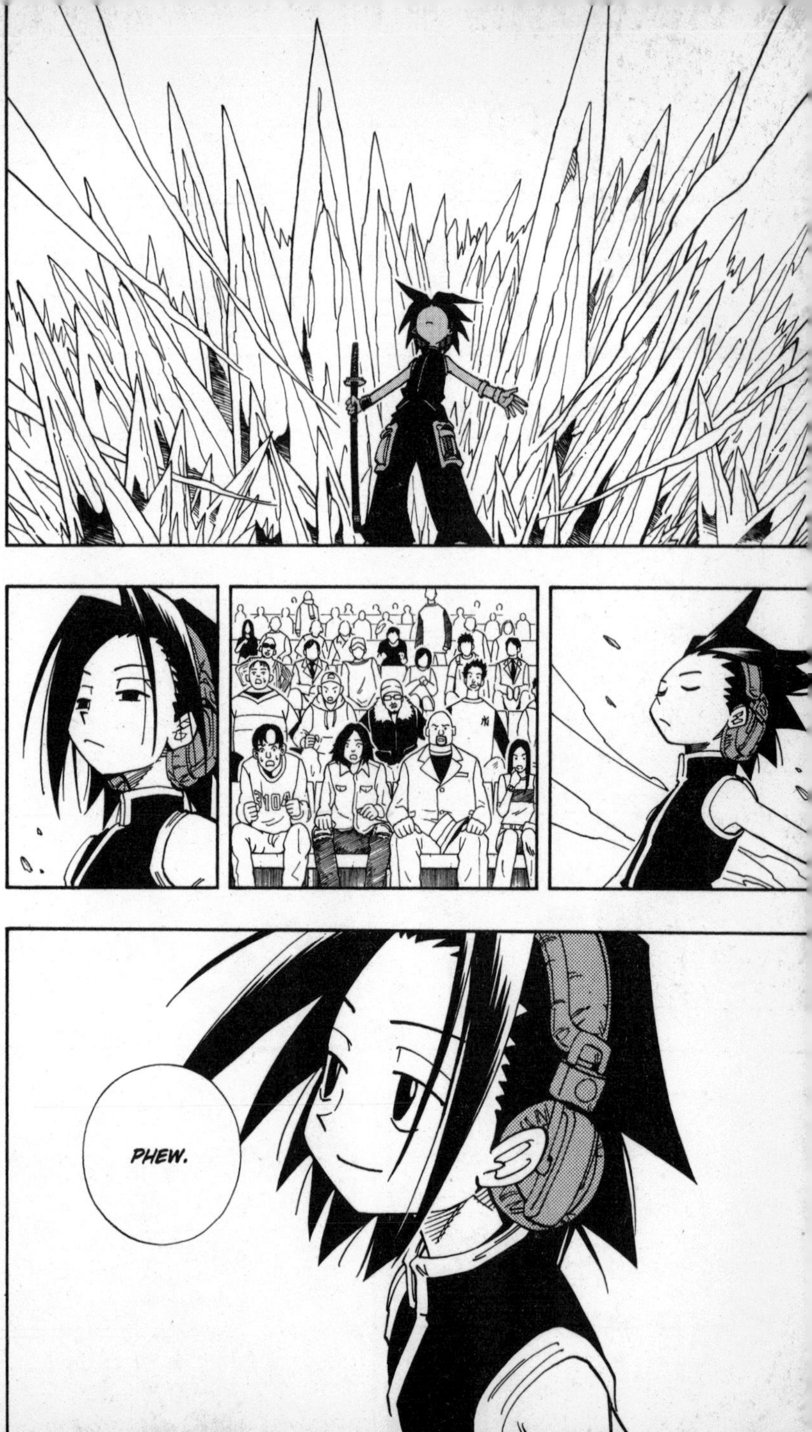
PHEW.

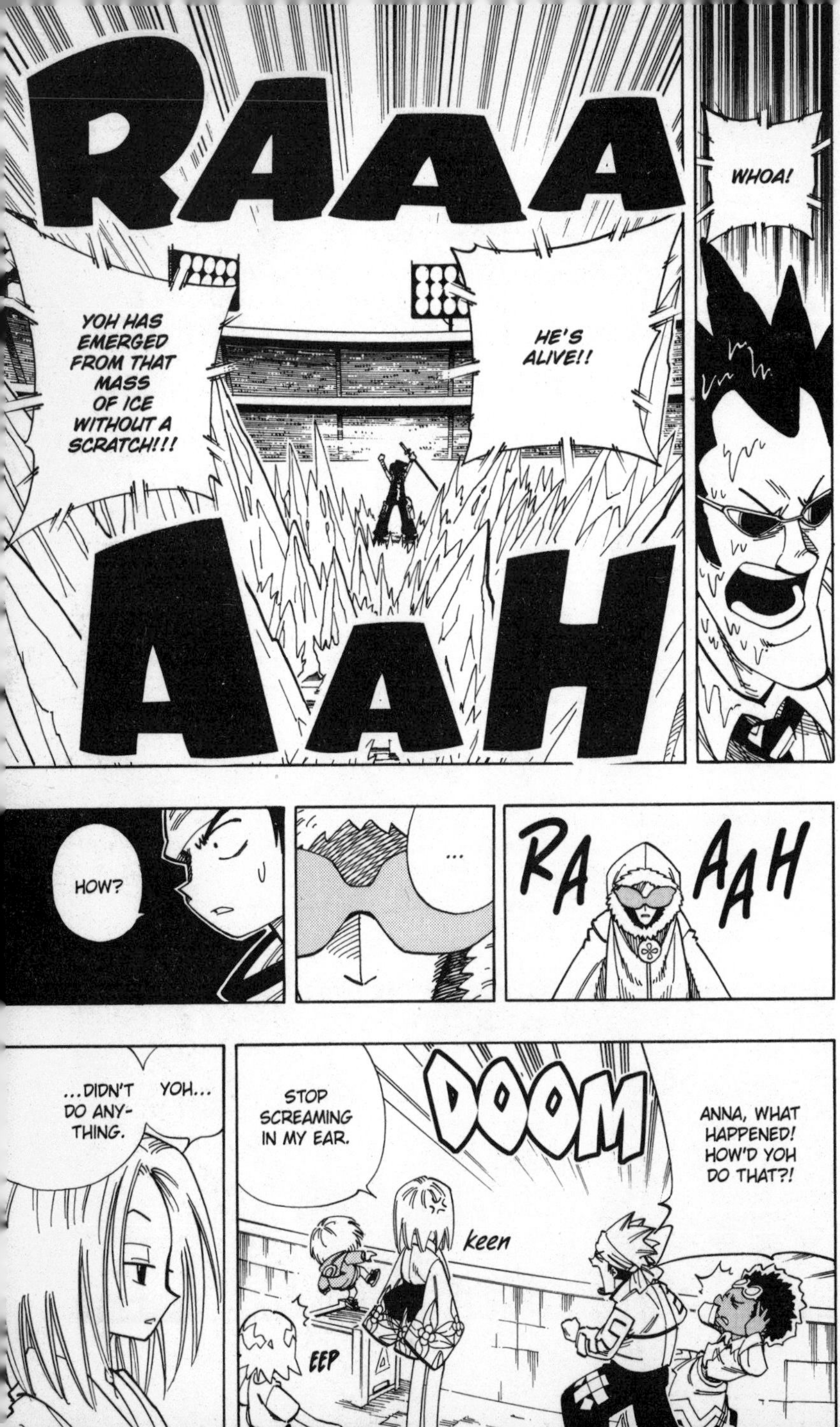

WHOA!
RAAAAAH
HE'S ALIVE!!
YOH HAS EMERGED FROM THAT MASS OF ICE WITHOUT A SCRATCH!!!
RAAAH
...
HOW?
ANNA, WHAT HAPPENED! HOW'D YOH DO THAT?!
DOOM
STOP SCREAMING IN MY EAR.
keen
EEP
YOH...
...DIDN'T DO ANY-THING.

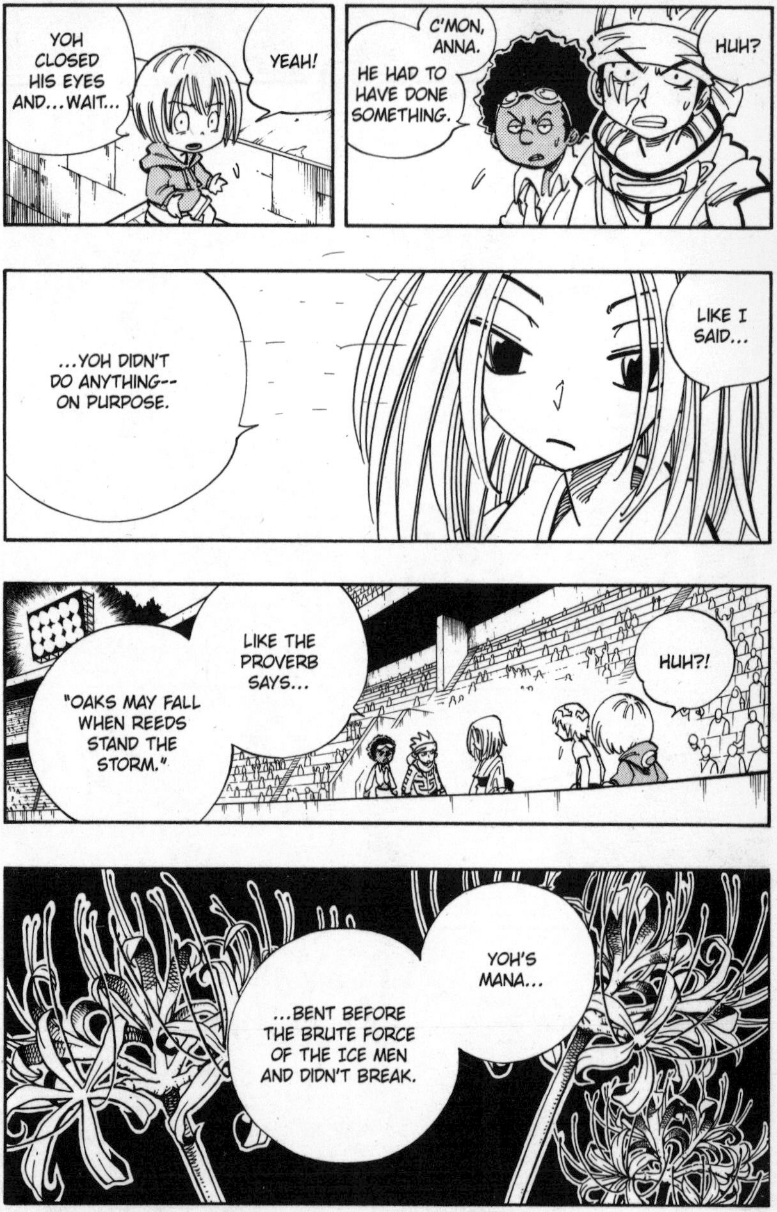

HUH?
C'MON, ANNA.
HE HAD TO HAVE DONE SOMETHING.
YEAH!
YOH CLOSED HIS EYES AND...WAIT...
LIKE I SAID...
...YOH DIDN'T DO ANYTHING--ON PURPOSE.
HUH?!
LIKE THE PROVERB SAYS...
"OAKS MAY FALL WHEN REEDS STAND THE STORM."
YOH'S MANA...
...BENT BEFORE THE BRUTE FORCE OF THE ICE MEN AND DIDN'T BREAK.

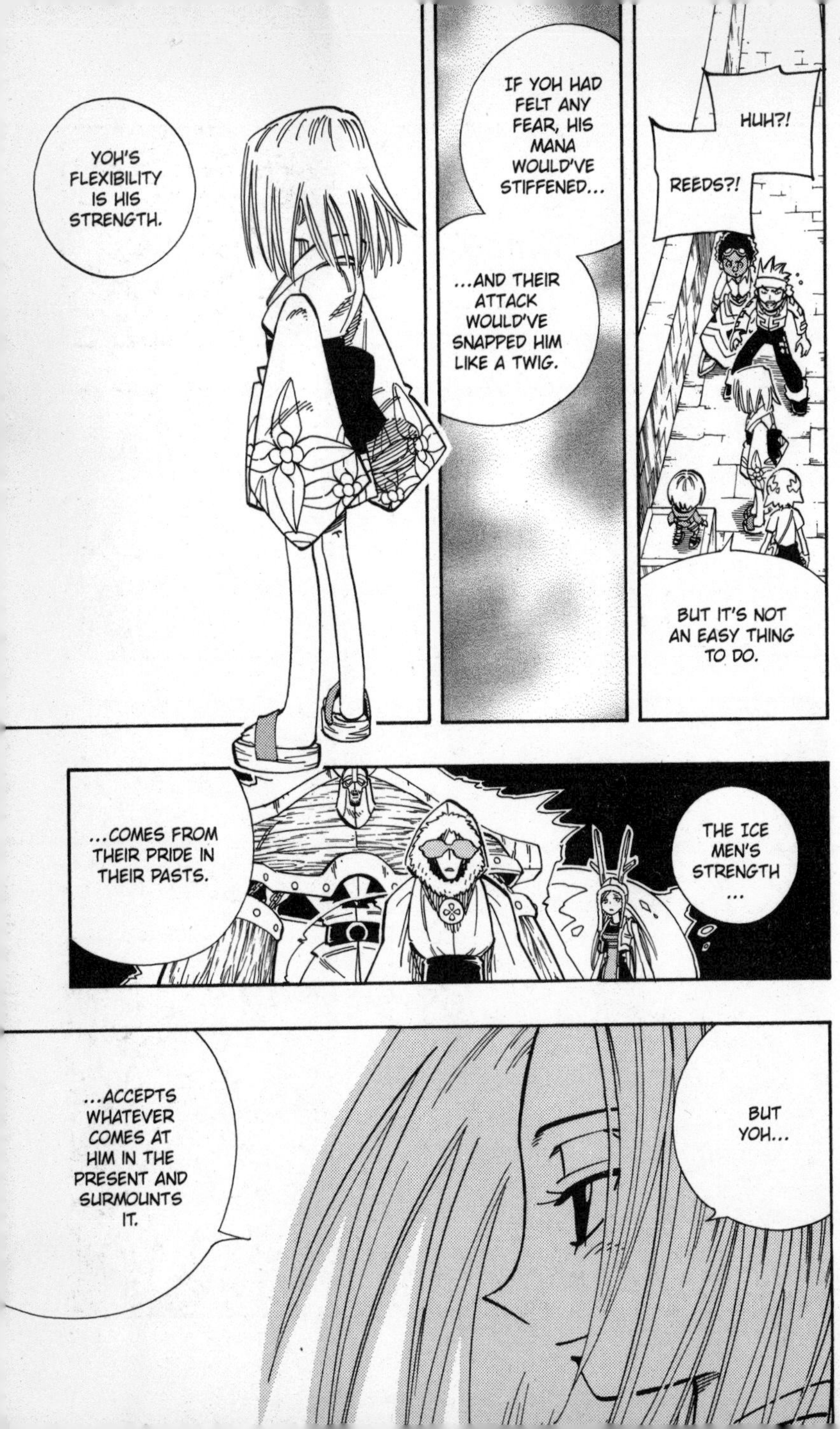
HUH?!
REEDS?!
BUT IT'S NOT AN EASY THING TO DO.
IF YOH HAD FELT ANY FEAR, HIS MANA WOULD'VE STIFFENED...
...AND THEIR ATTACK WOULD'VE SNAPPED HIM LIKE A TWIG.
YOH'S FLEXIBILITY IS HIS STRENGTH.
THE ICE MEN'S STRENGTH ...
...COMES FROM THEIR PRIDE IN THEIR PASTS.
BUT YOH...
...ACCEPTS WHATEVER COMES AT HIM IN THE PRESENT AND SURMOUNTS IT.

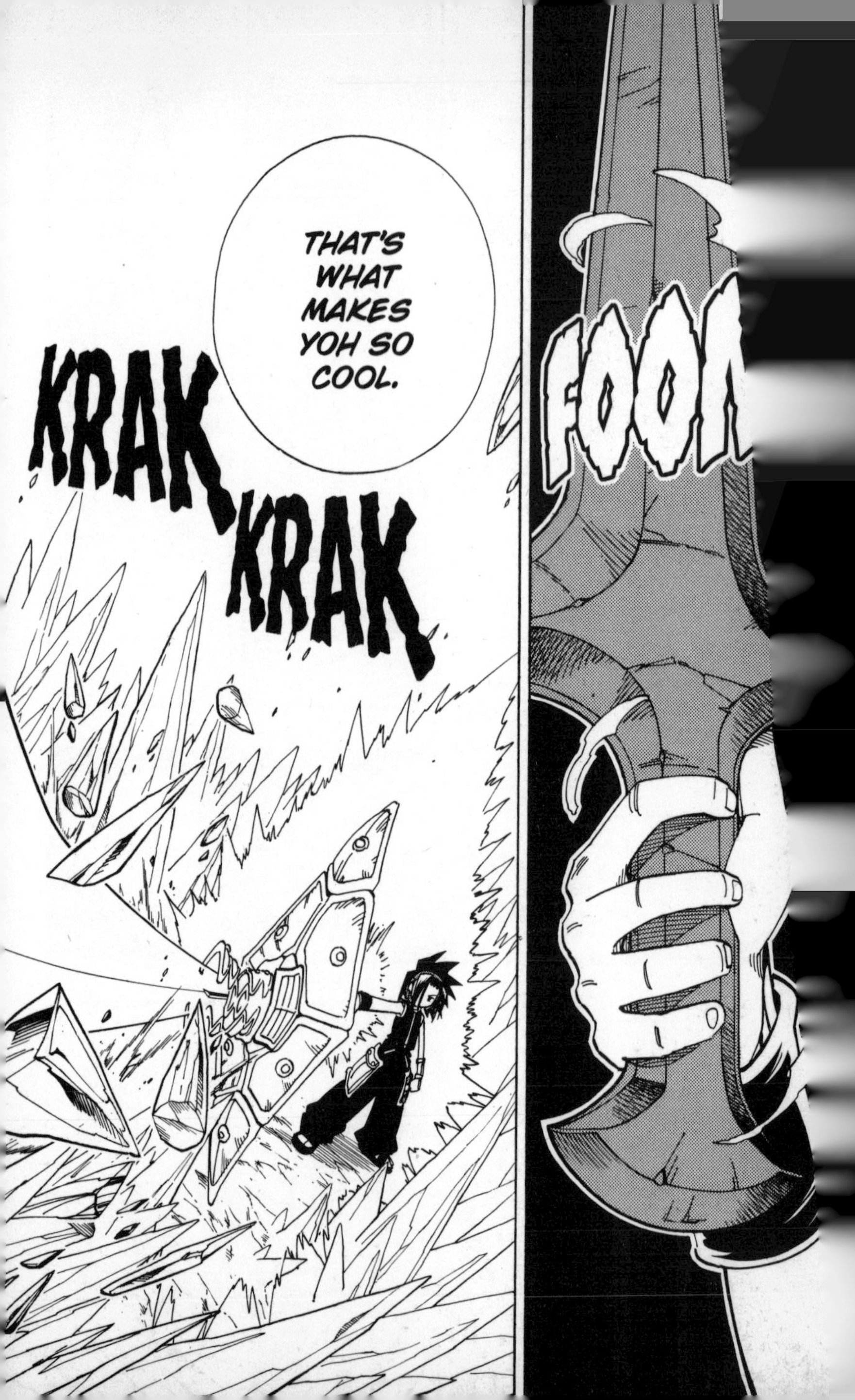
FOO
THAT'S WHAT MAKES YOH SO COOL.
KRAK
KRAK

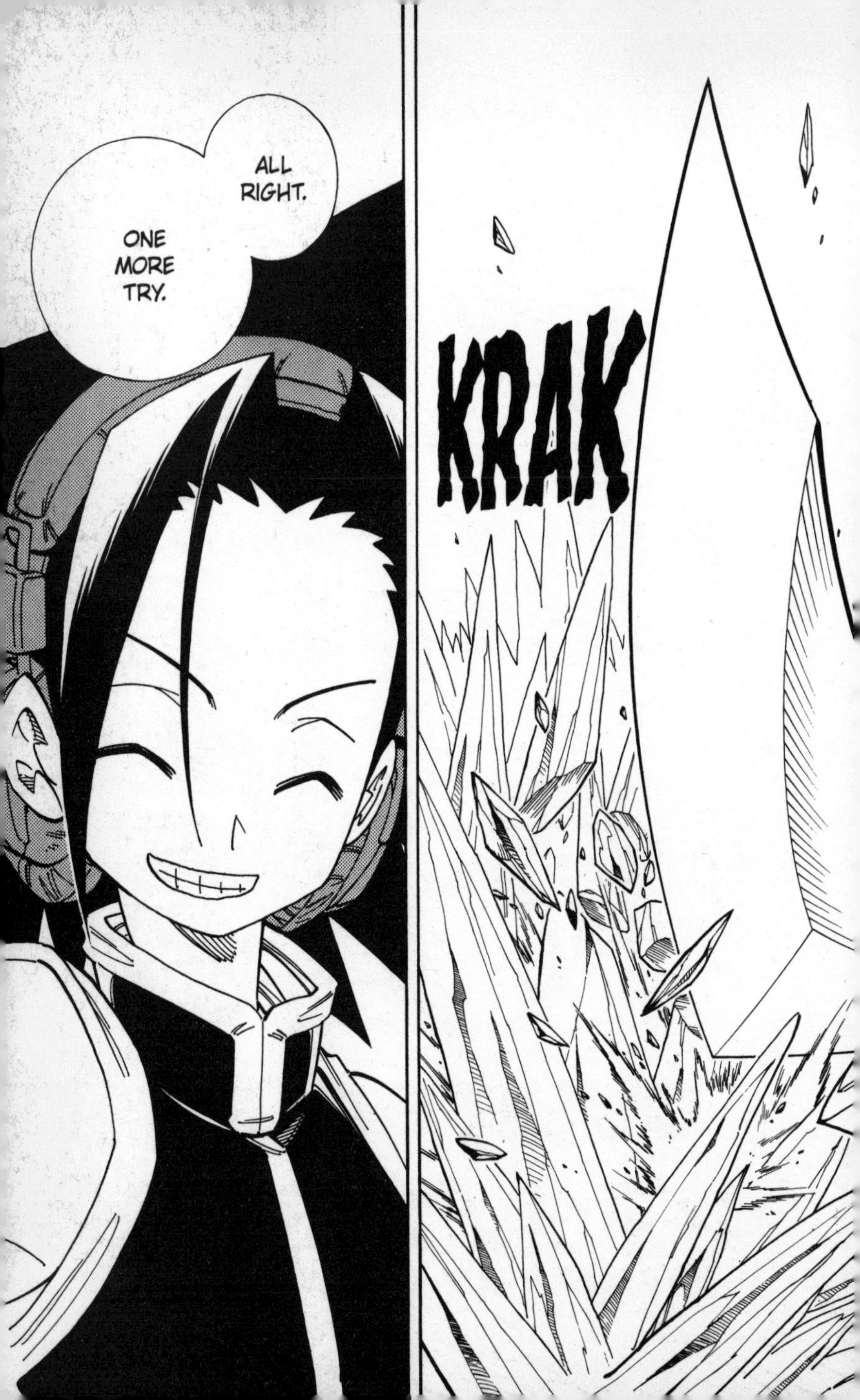
KRAK
ALL RIGHT.
ONE MORE TRY.

SHAMAN KING CHARACTER FILE No.77

2001
(JULY)

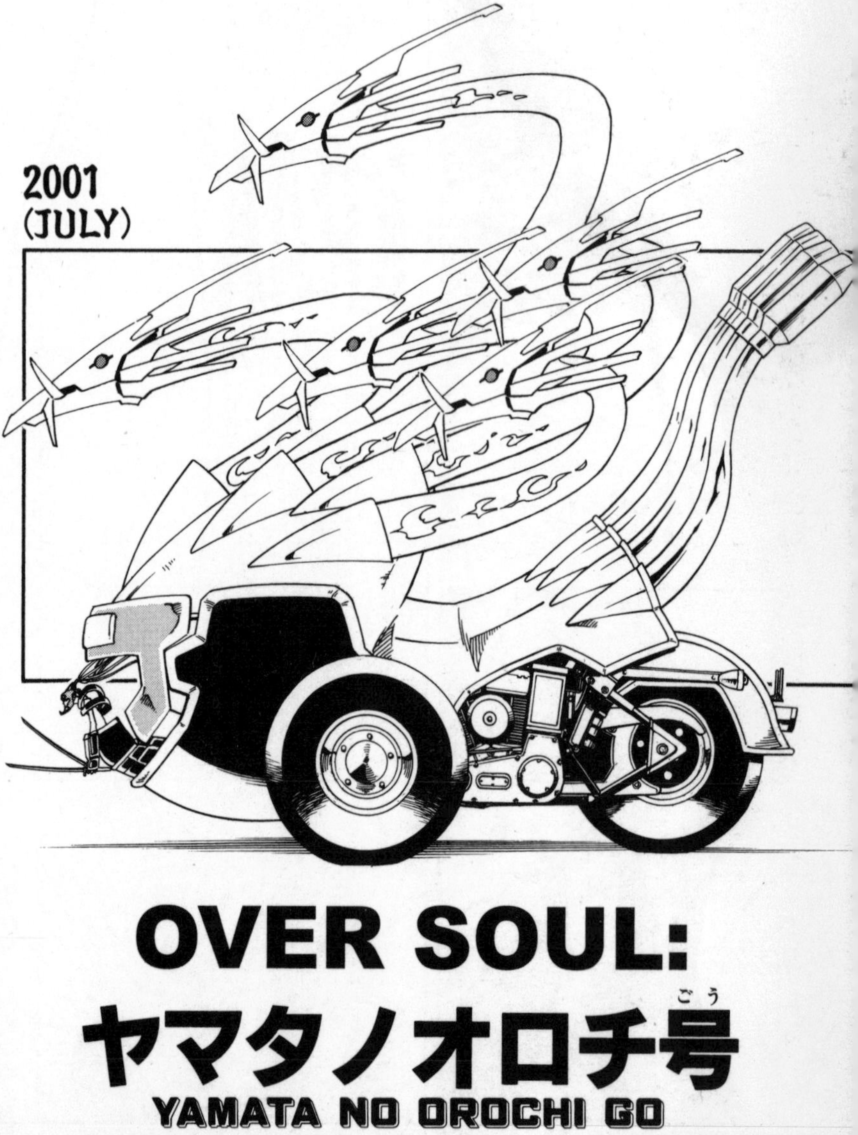

OVER SOUL:

ごう
ヤマタノオロチ号

YAMATA NO OROCHI GO

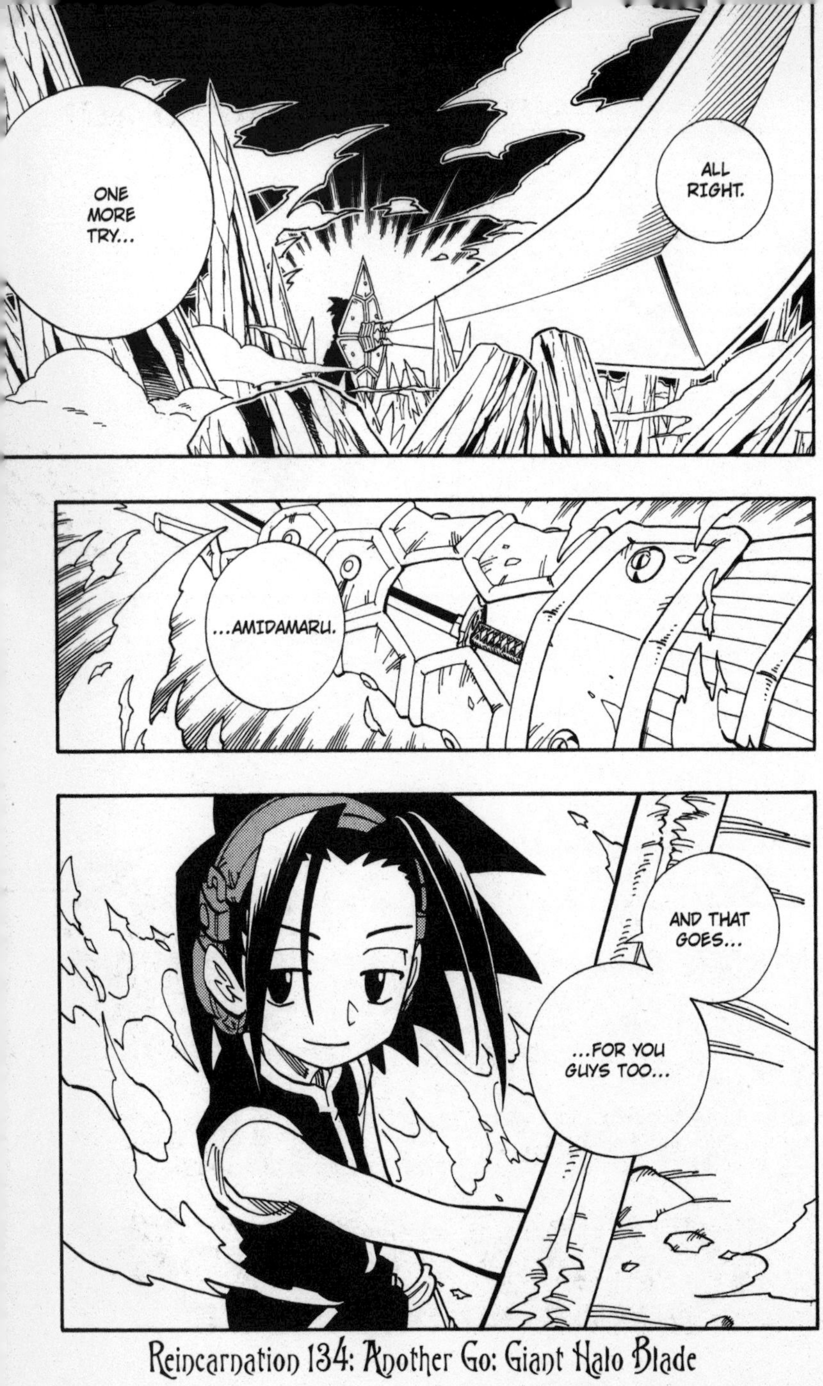
ALL RIGHT.
ONE MORE TRY...
...AMIDAMARU.
AND THAT GOES...
...FOR YOU GUYS TOO...

Reincarnation 134: Another Go: Giant Halo Blade

...ICE MEN.

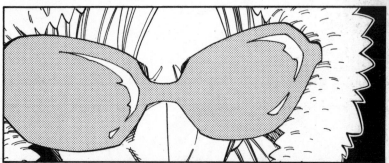

ONE
MORE TRY.

Reincarnation 134:
Another Go: Giant Halo Blade

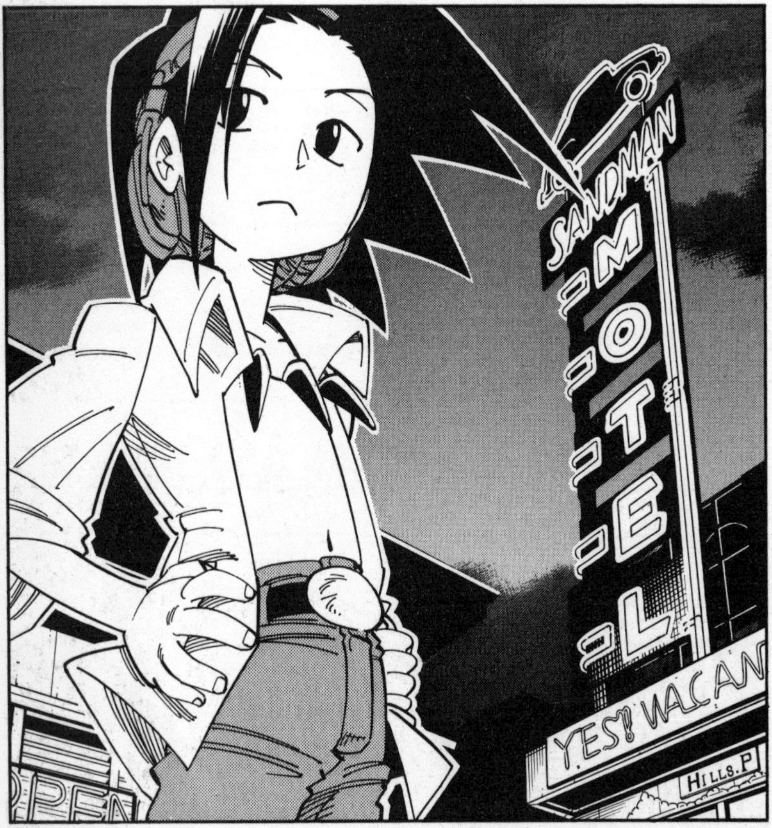
SANDMAN
MOTEL
YES! VACAN
HILLS.P
OPEN

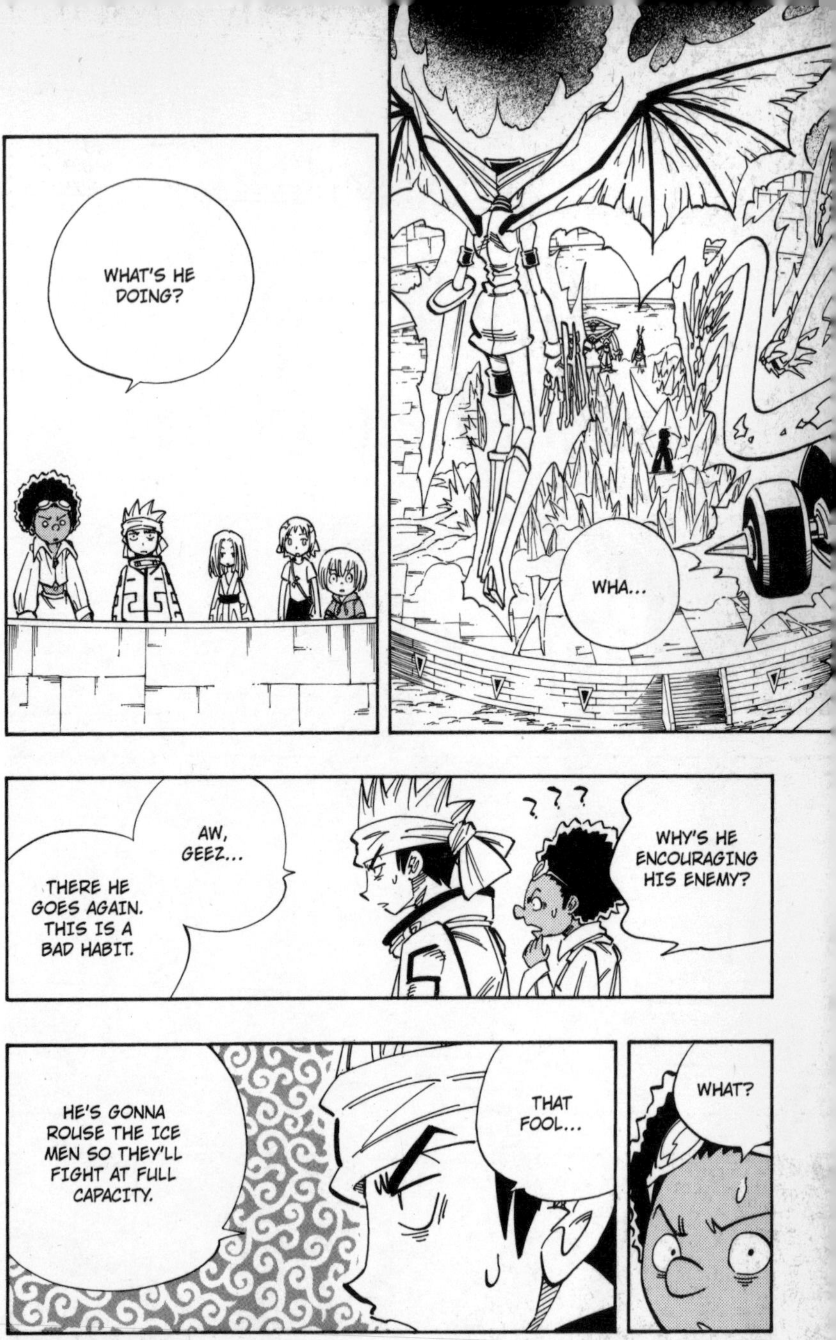
WHA...
WHAT'S HE DOING?
WHY'S HE ENCOURAGING HIS ENEMY?
???
AW, GEEZ...
THERE HE GOES AGAIN. THIS IS A BAD HABIT.
WHAT?
THAT FOOL...
HE'S GONNA ROUSE THE ICE MEN SO THEY'LL FIGHT AT FULL CAPACITY.

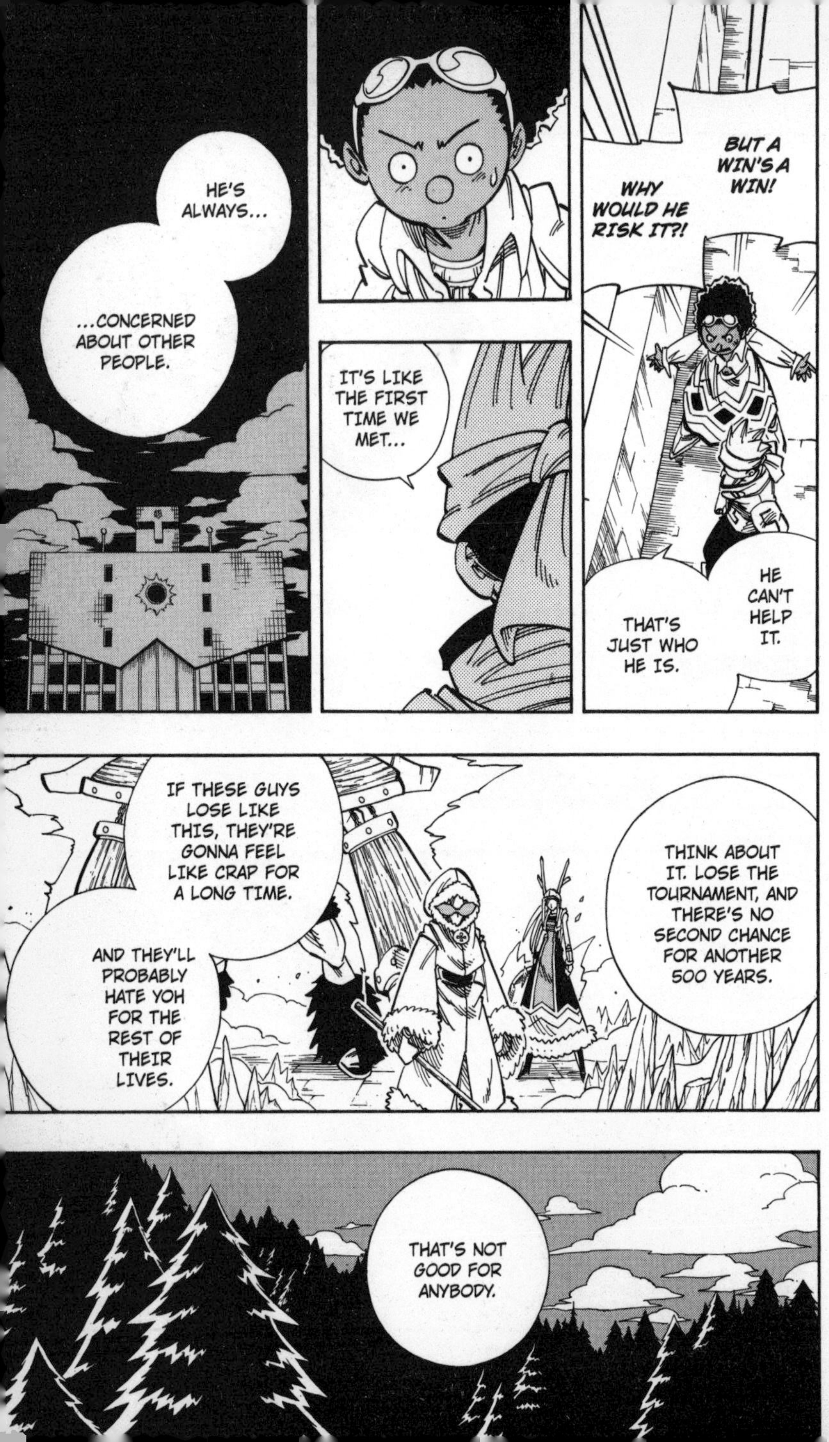
BUT A WIN'S A WIN!
WHY WOULD HE RISK IT?!
HE CAN'T HELP IT.
THAT'S JUST WHO HE IS.
IT'S LIKE THE FIRST TIME WE MET...
HE'S ALWAYS...
...CONCERNED ABOUT OTHER PEOPLE.
THINK ABOUT IT. LOSE THE TOURNAMENT, AND THERE'S NO SECOND CHANCE FOR ANOTHER 500 YEARS.
IF THESE GUYS LOSE LIKE THIS, THEY'RE GONNA FEEL LIKE CRAP FOR A LONG TIME.
AND THEY'LL PROBABLY HATE YOH FOR THE REST OF THEIR LIVES.
THAT'S NOT GOOD FOR ANYBODY.

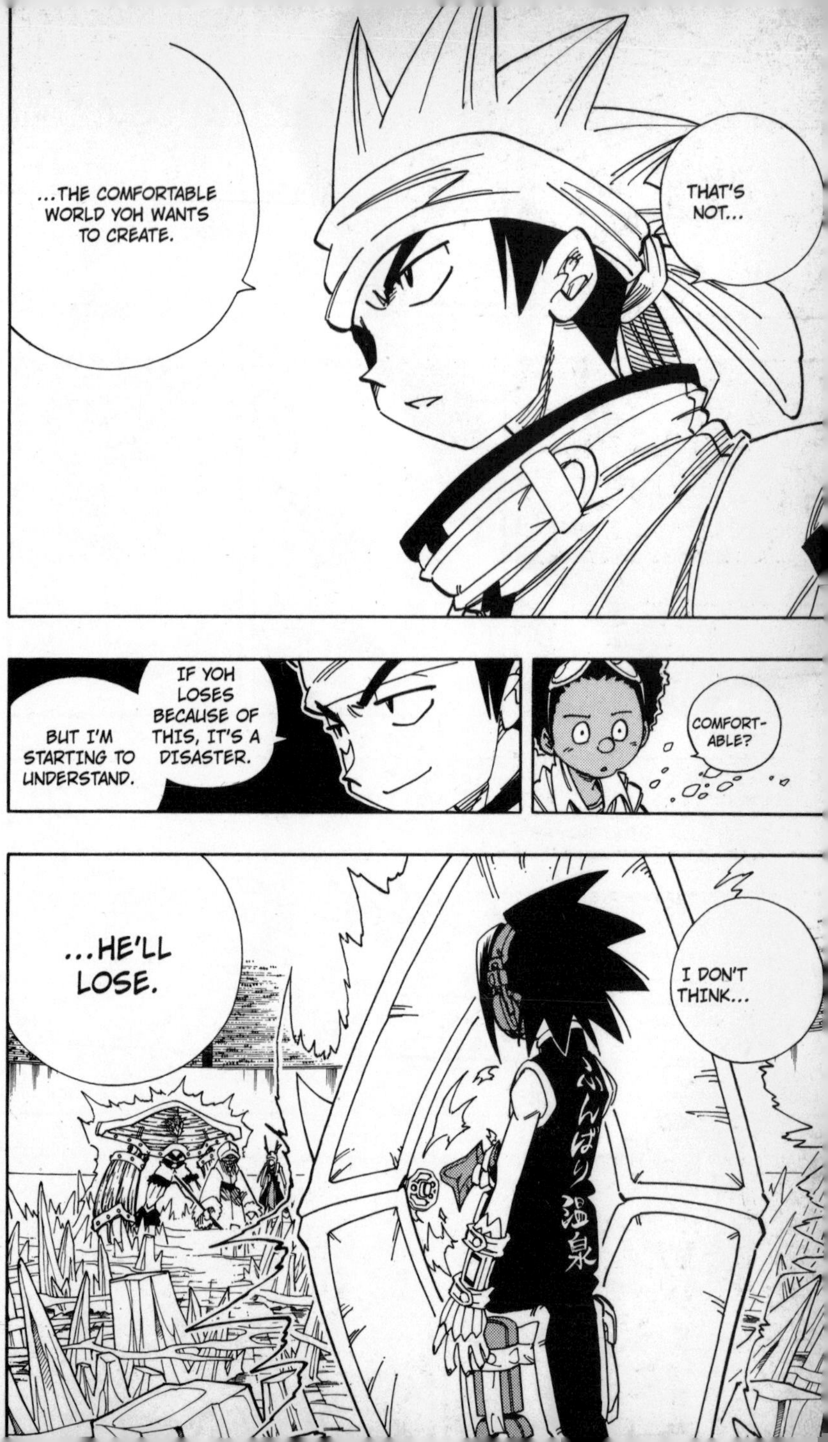
THAT'S NOT...
...THE COMFORTABLE WORLD YOH WANTS TO CREATE.
COMFORT-ABLE?
IF YOH LOSES BECAUSE OF THIS, IT'S A DISASTER.
BUT I'M STARTING TO UNDERSTAND.
I DON'T THINK...
ふんばり温泉
...HE'LL LOSE.

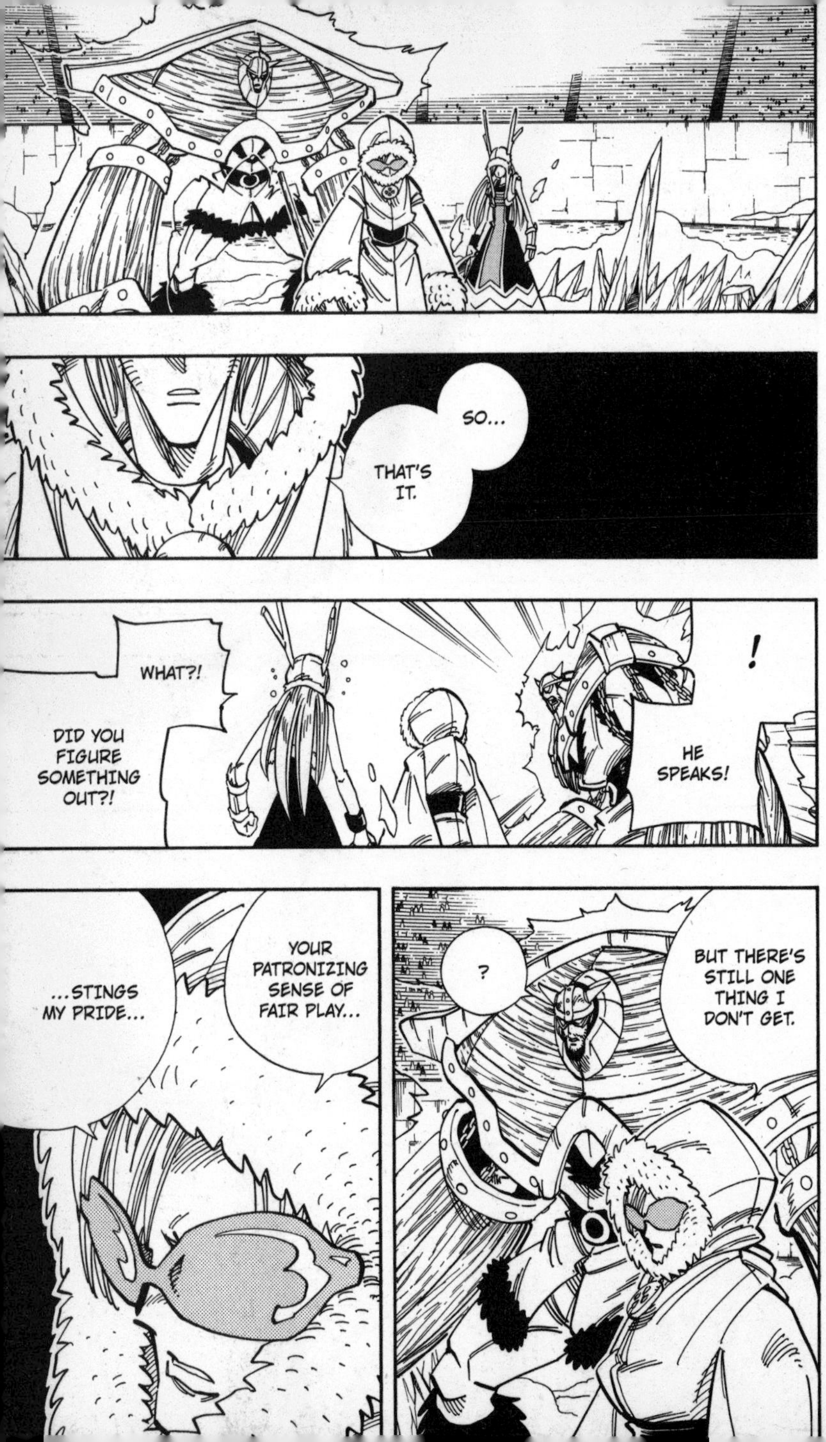
SO...
THAT'S IT.
!
HE SPEAKS!
WHAT?!
DID YOU FIGURE SOMETHING OUT?!
BUT THERE'S STILL ONE THING I DON'T GET.
?
YOUR PATRONIZING SENSE OF FAIR PLAY...
...STINGS MY PRIDE...

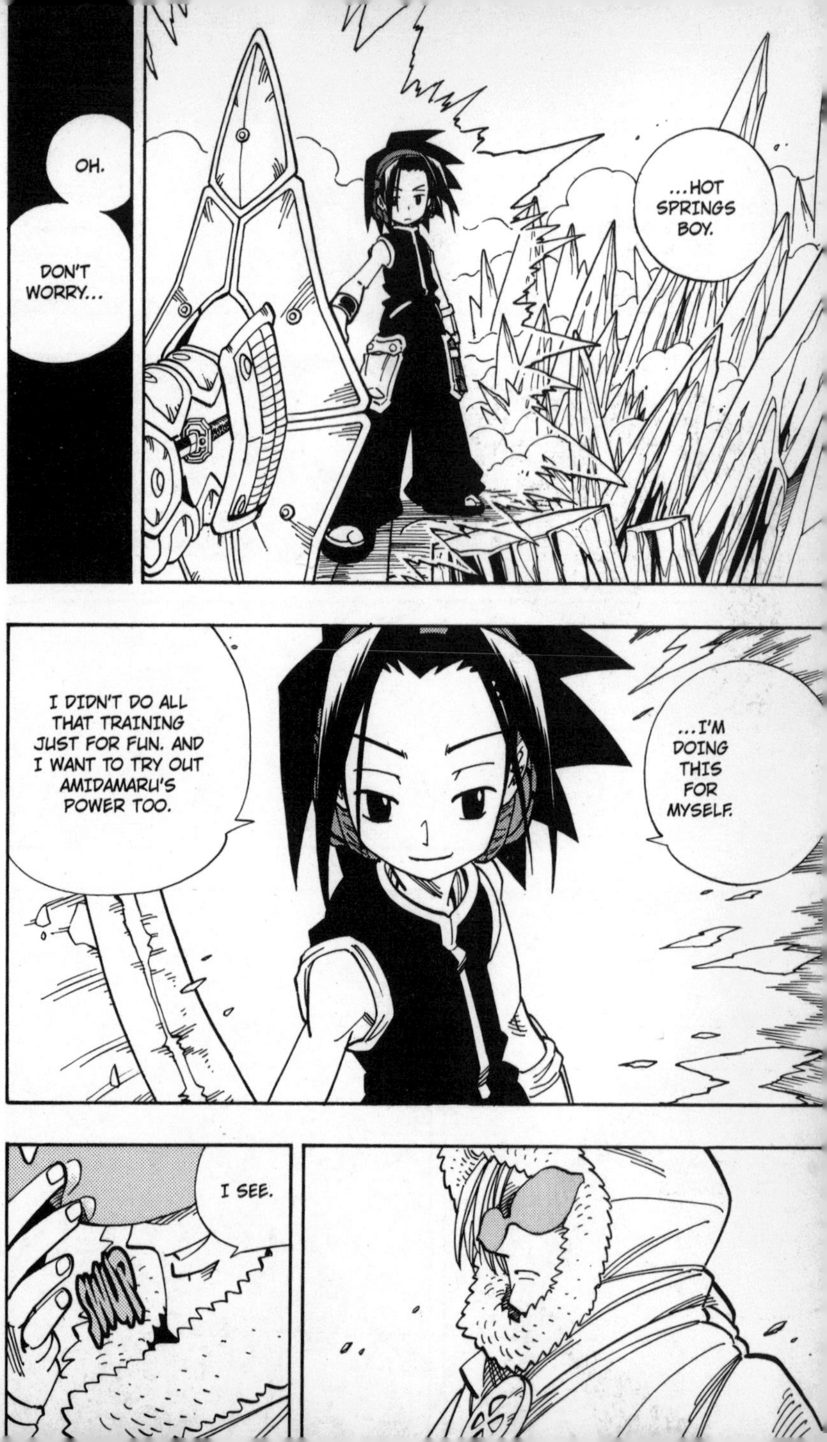
...HOT SPRINGS BOY.
OH.
DON'T WORRY...
...I'M DOING THIS FOR MYSELF.
I DIDN'T DO ALL THAT TRAINING JUST FOR FUN. AND I WANT TO TRY OUT AMIDAMARU'S POWER TOO.
I SEE.
SWIP

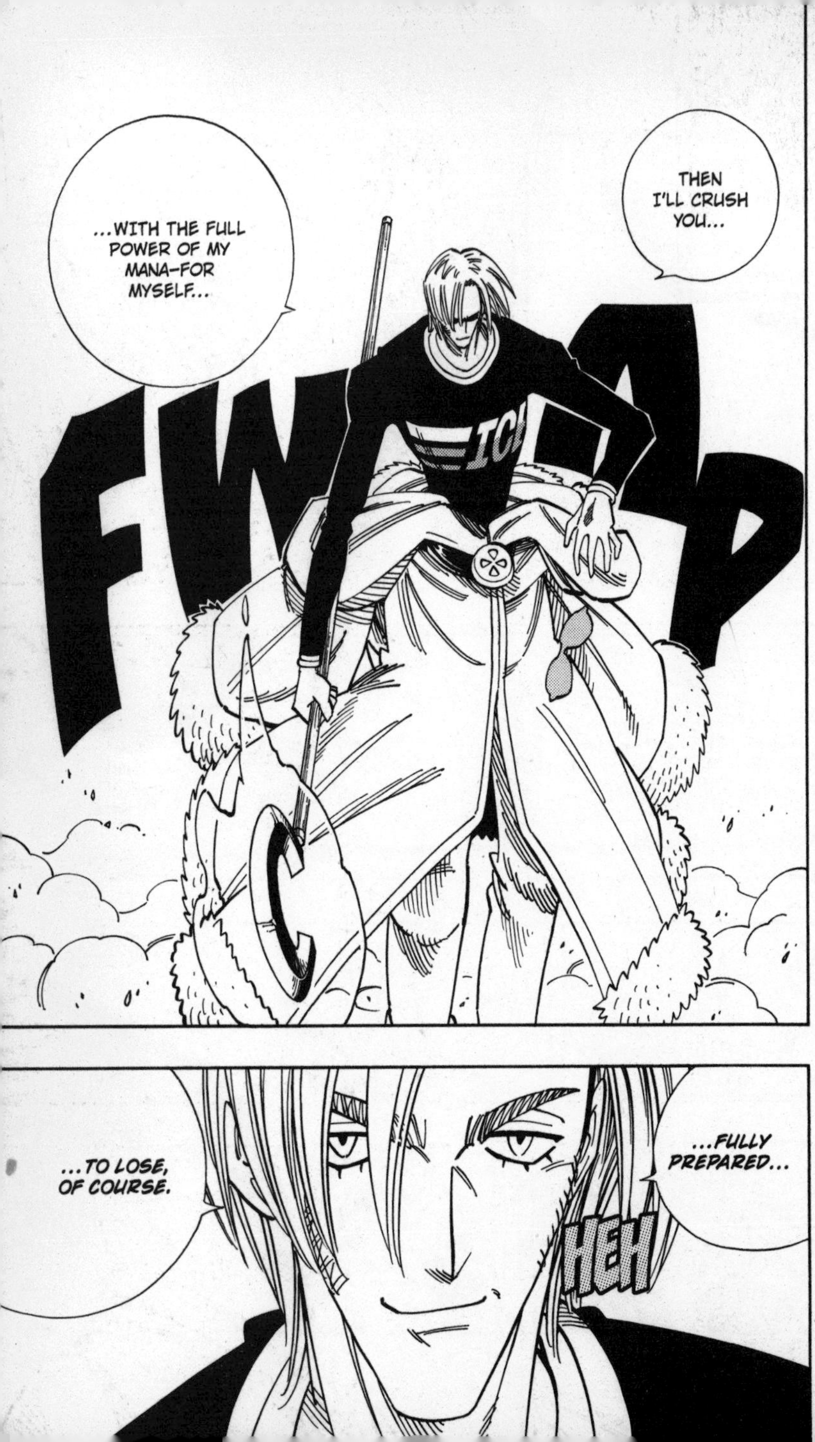
THEN I'LL CRUSH YOU...
...WITH THE FULL POWER OF MY MANA—FOR MYSELF...
FWAP
...FULLY PREPARED...
HEH
...TO LOSE, OF COURSE.

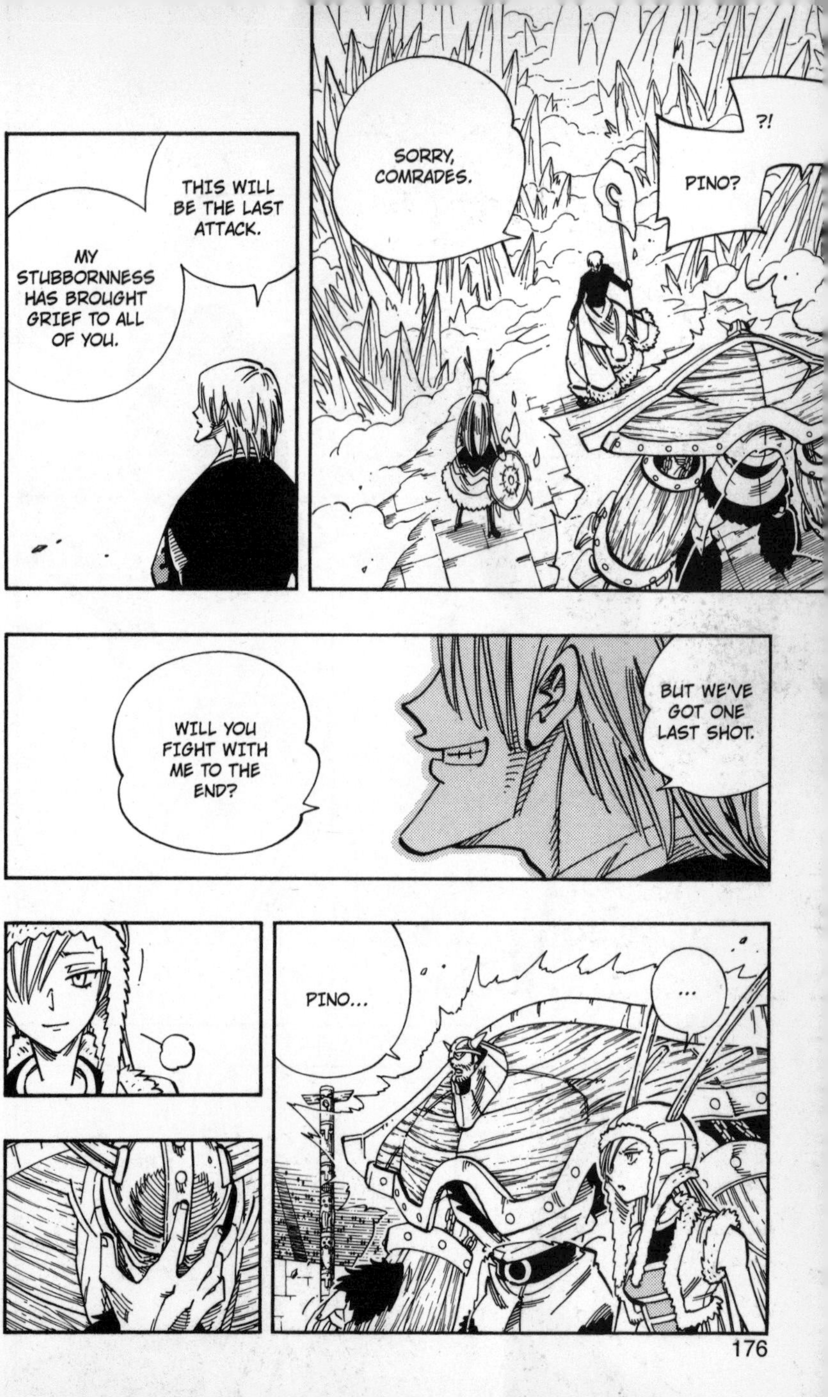
?!
PINO?
SORRY, COMRADES.
THIS WILL BE THE LAST ATTACK.
MY STUBBORNNESS HAS BROUGHT GRIEF TO ALL OF YOU.
BUT WE'VE GOT ONE LAST SHOT.
WILL YOU FIGHT WITH ME TO THE END?
...
PINO...
!

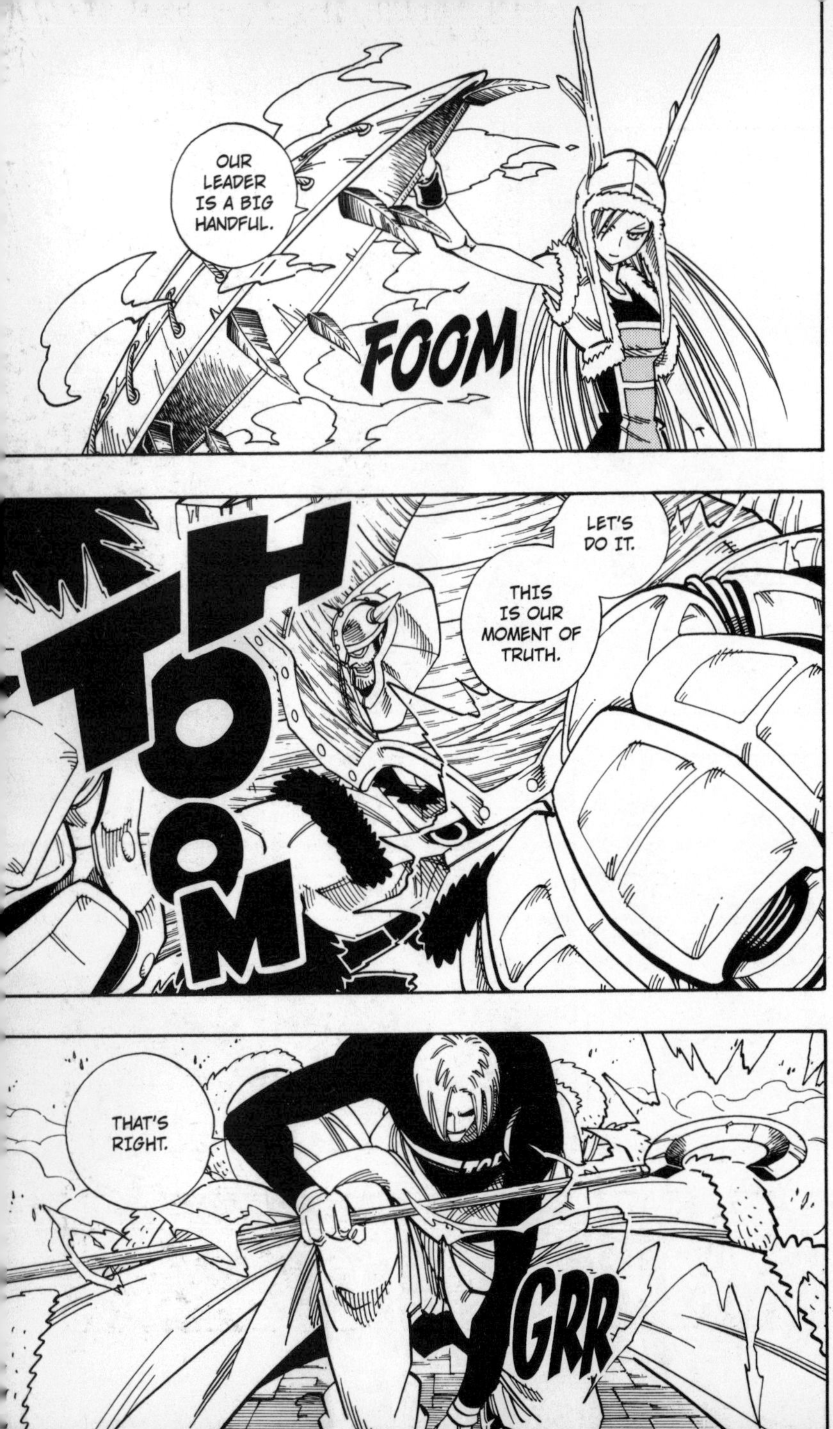
OUR LEADER IS A BIG HANDFUL.
FOOM
LET'S DO IT.
THIS IS OUR MOMENT OF TRUTH.
THOOM
THAT'S RIGHT.
GRR

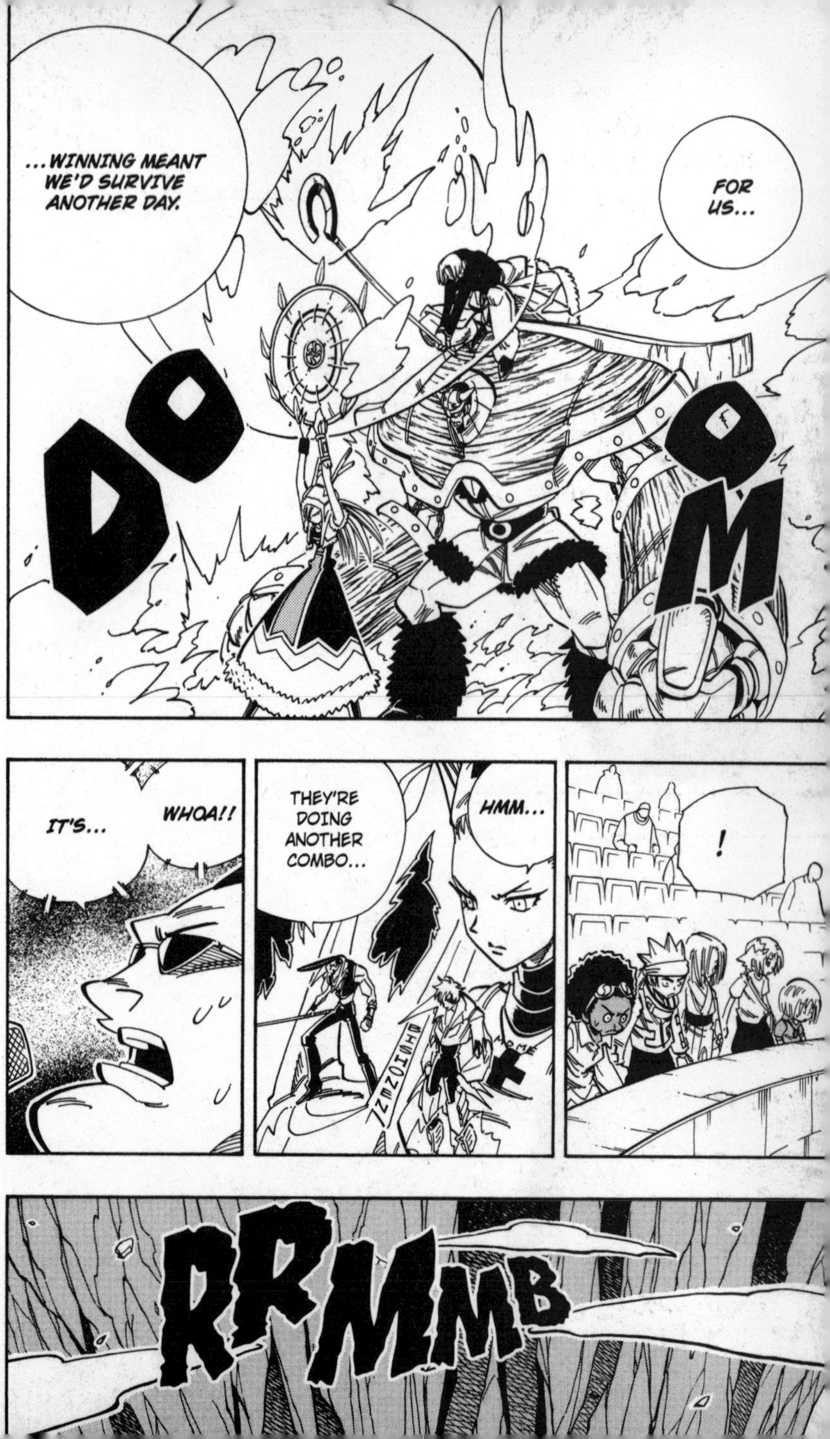
FOR US...
...WINNING MEANT WE'D SURVIVE ANOTHER DAY.
DOOM
!
HMM...
THEY'RE DOING ANOTHER COMBO...
WHOA!!
IT'S...
RRMMB

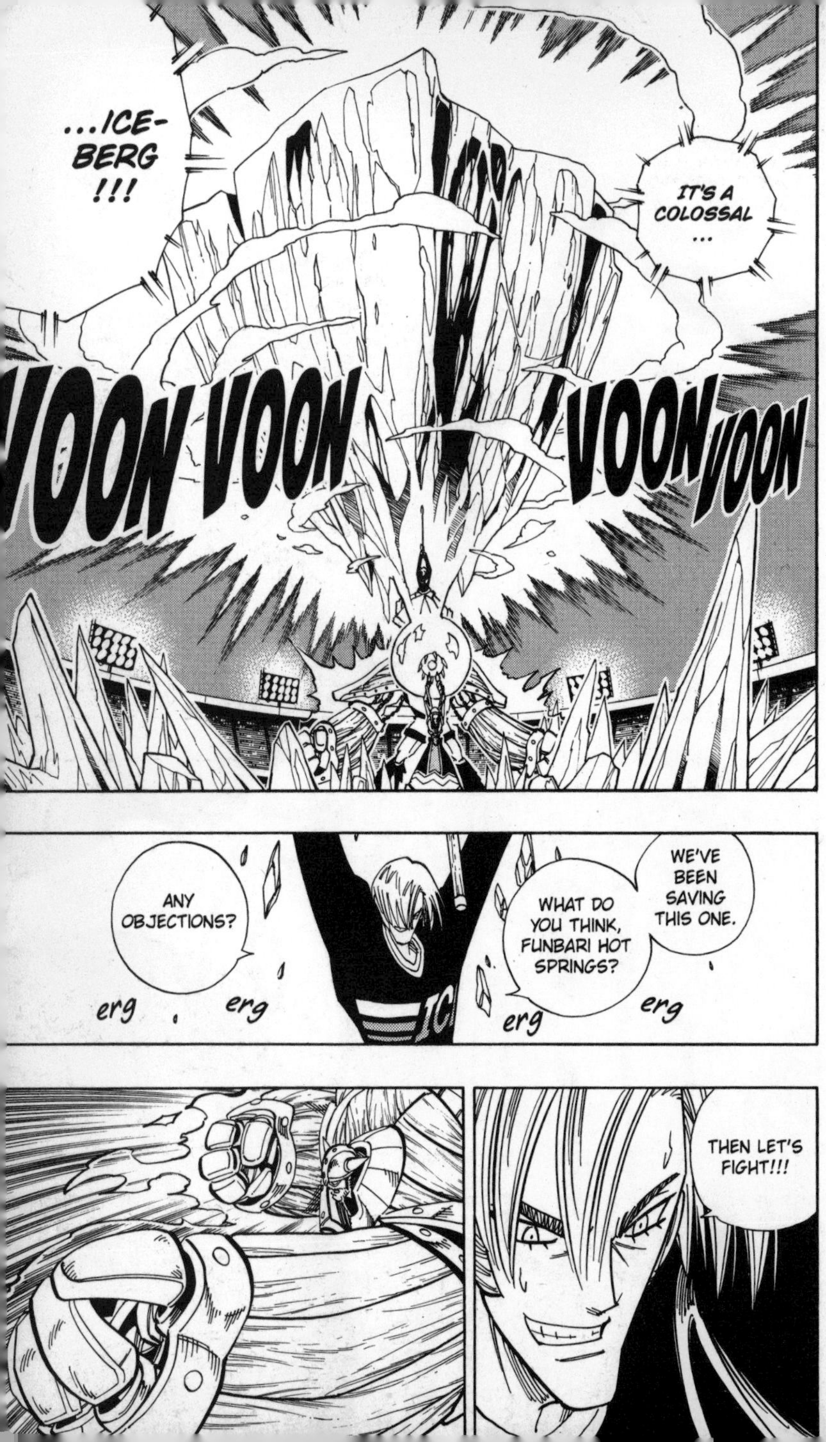
IT'S A COLOSSAL ...
...ICEBERG!!!
VOON VOON
VOON VOON
WE'VE BEEN SAVING THIS ONE.
WHAT DO YOU THINK, FUNBARI HOT SPRINGS?
ANY OBJECTIONS?
erg erg
erg erg
THEN LET'S FIGHT!!!

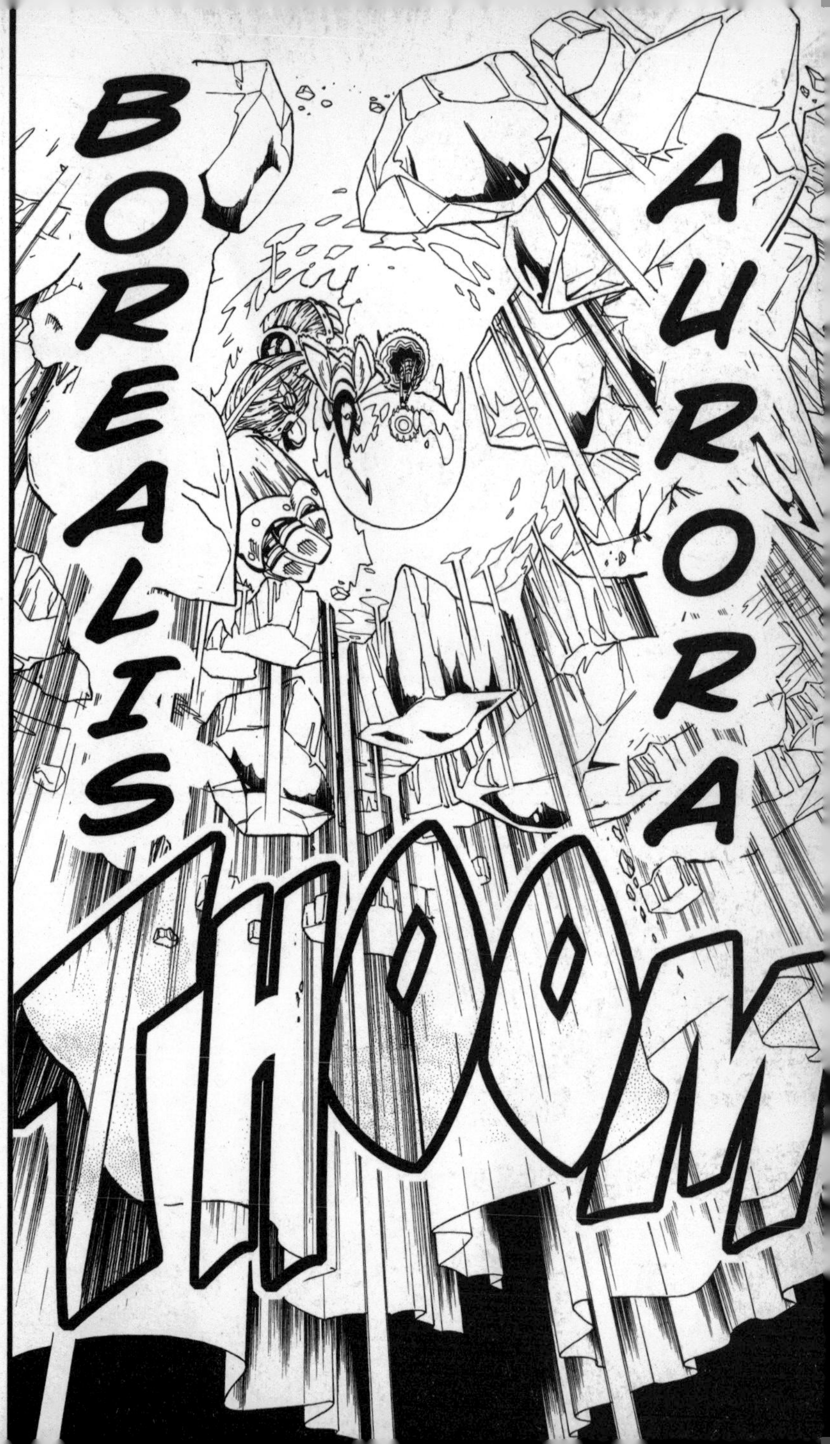
AURORA
BOREALIS
THOOM

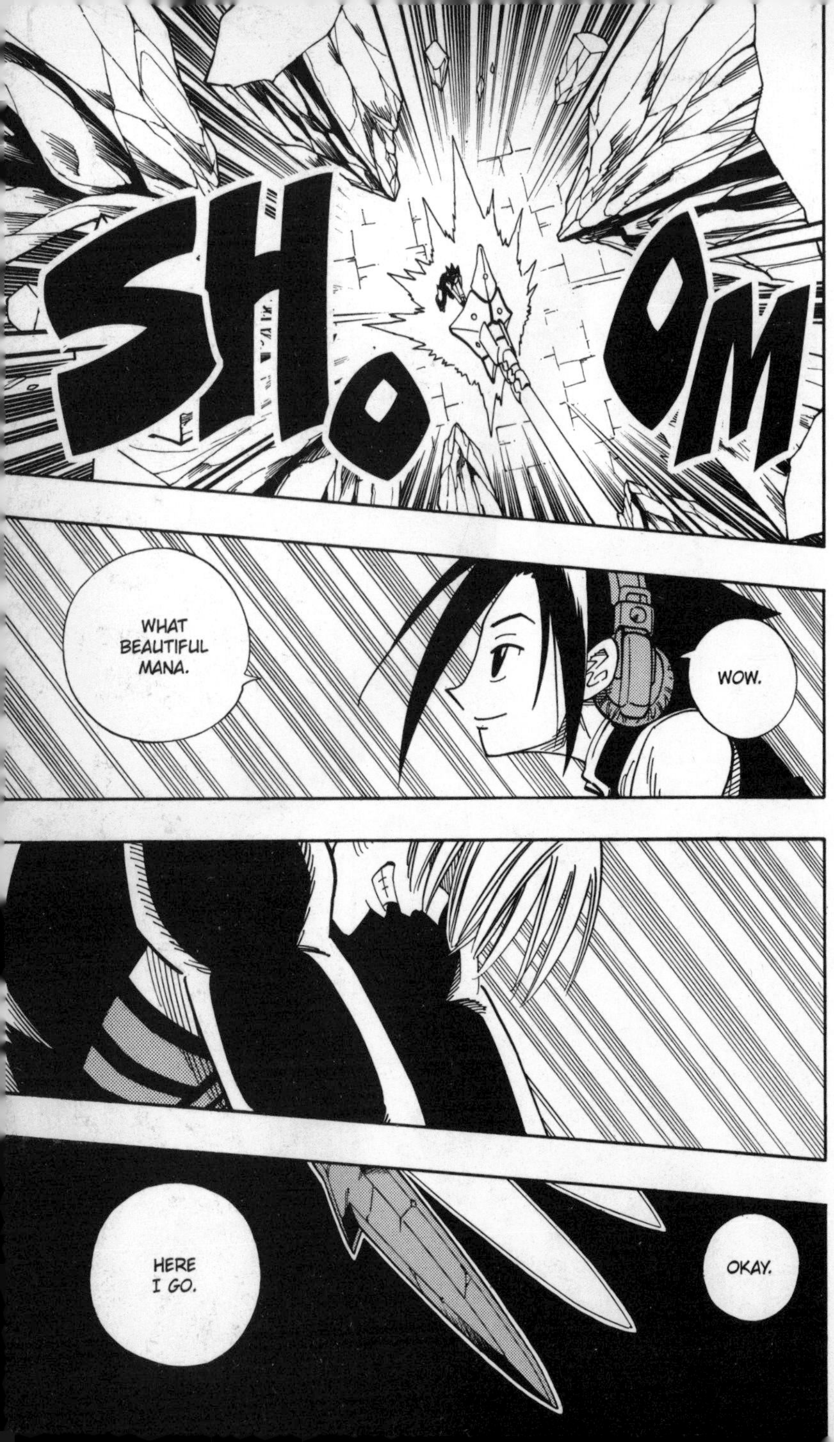
SHOOM
WOW.
WHAT BEAUTIFUL MANA.
OKAY.
HERE I GO.

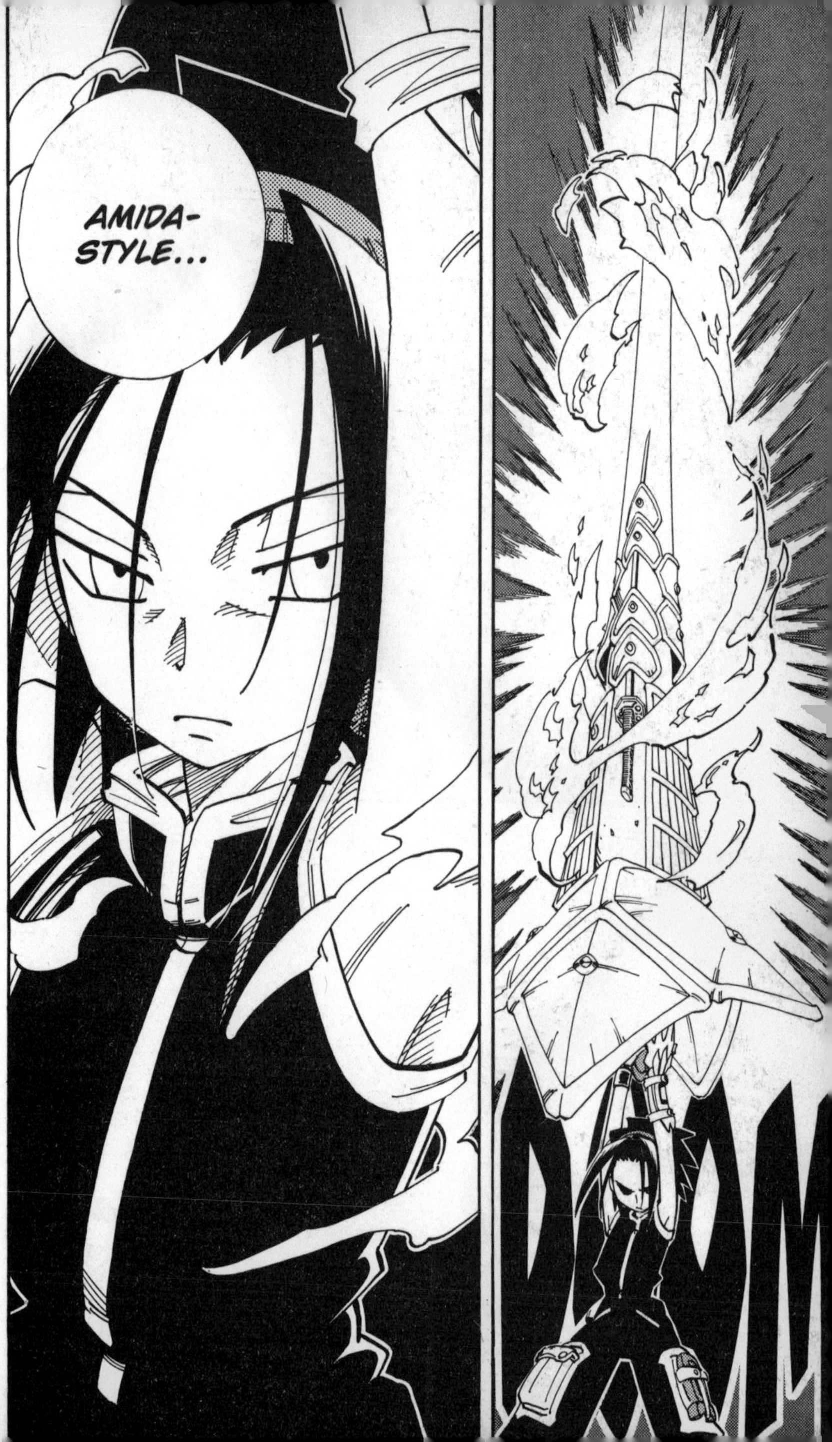
AMIDA-
STYLE...

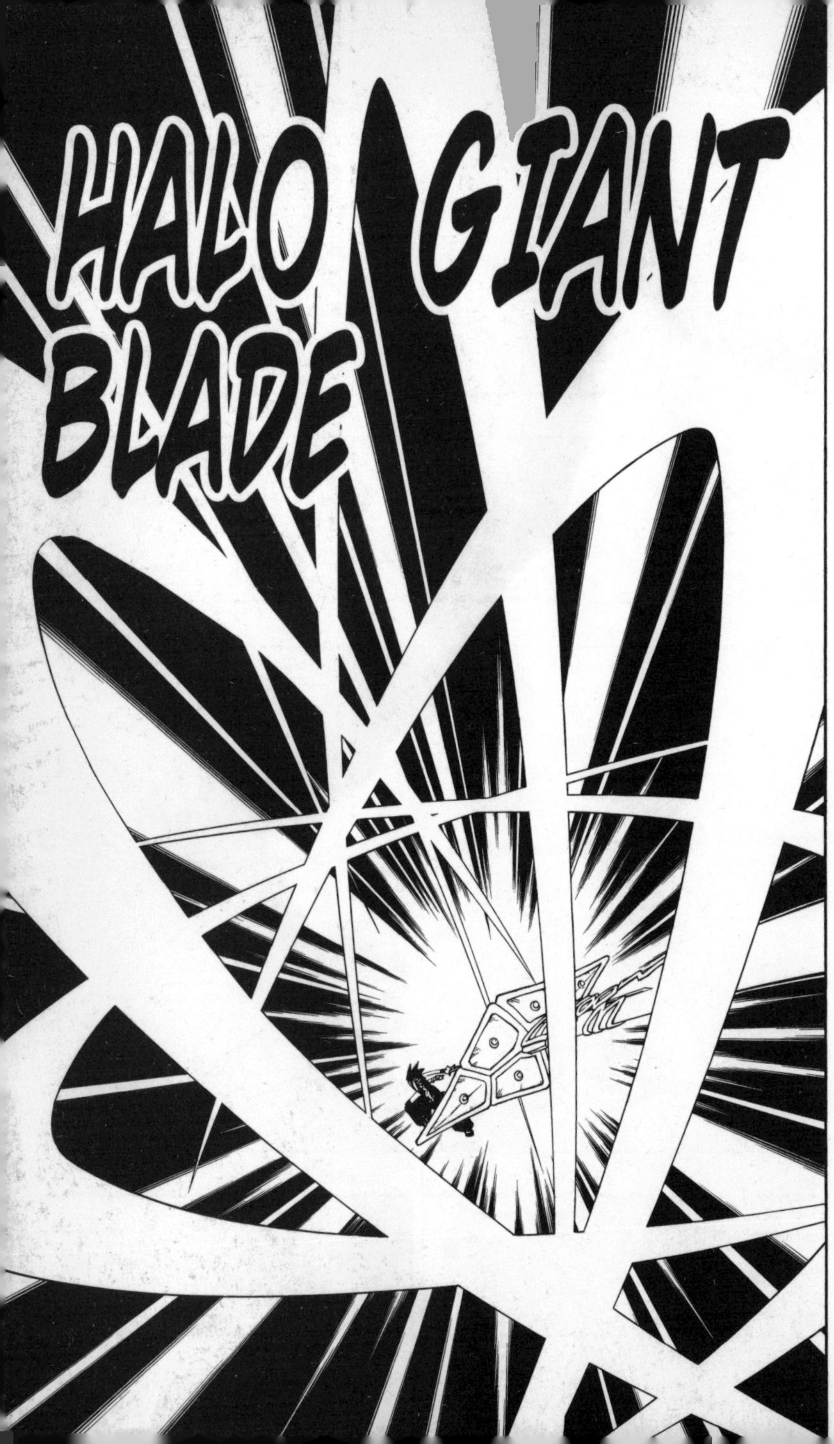
HALO GIANT BLADE

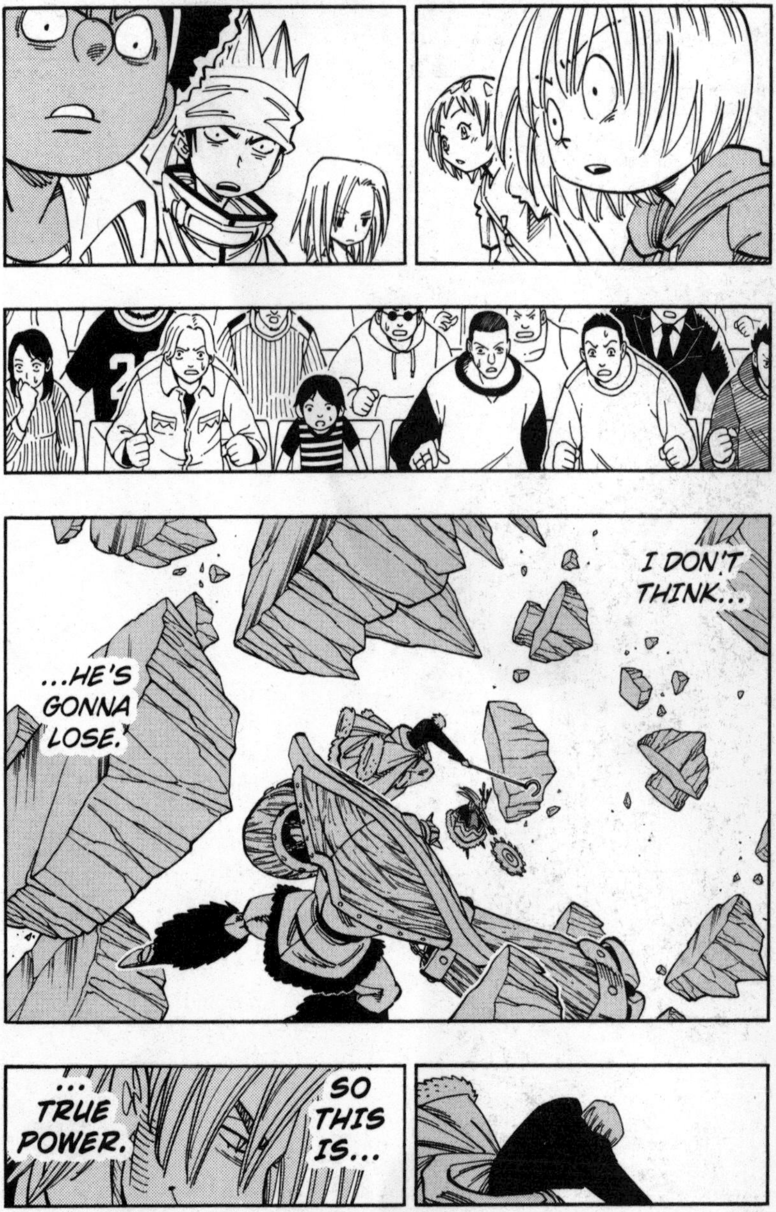
I DON'T THINK...
...HE'S GONNA LOSE.
SO THIS IS...
...TRUE POWER.

READ THIS WAY

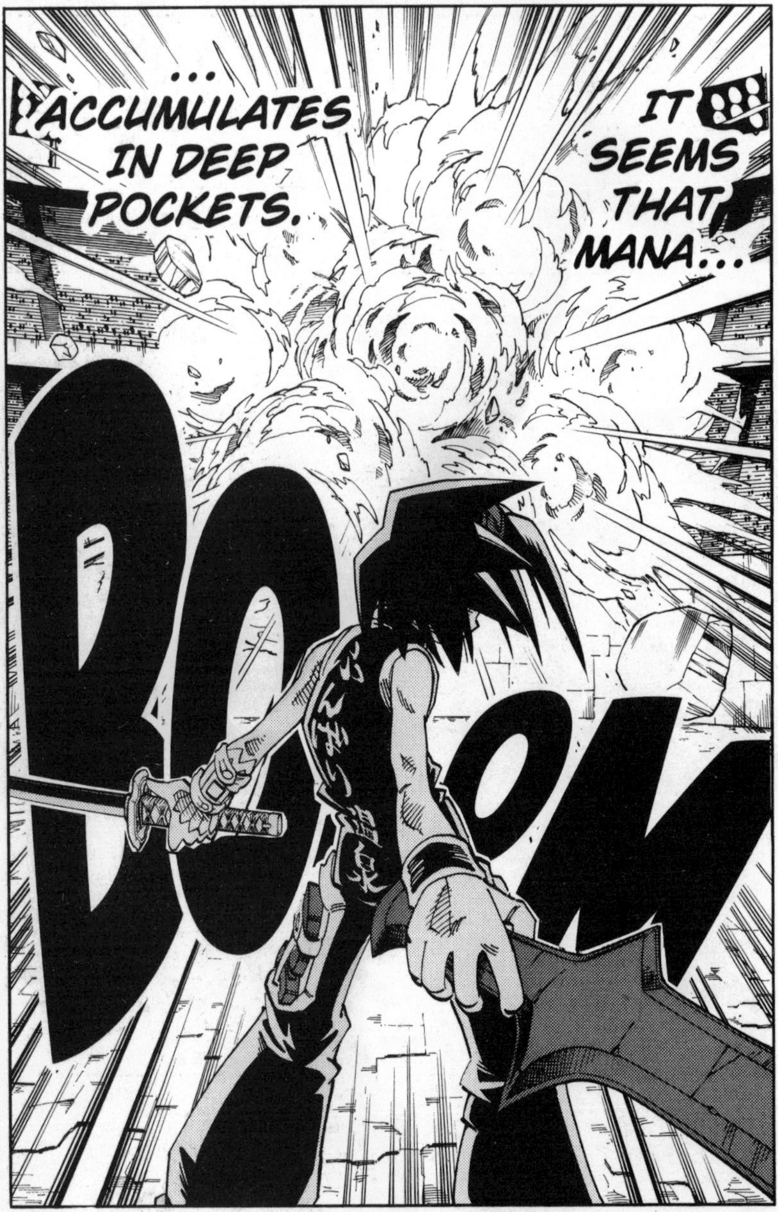
IT SEEMS THAT MANA...
... ACCUMULATES IN DEEP POCKETS.
BOOM

SHAMAN KING CHARACTER FILE No.78

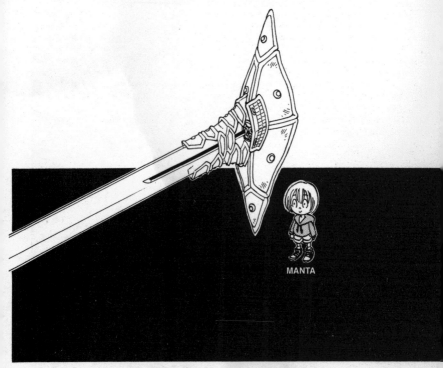

MANTA

OVER SOUL:

スピリット オブ ソード

SPIRIT OF THE SWORD

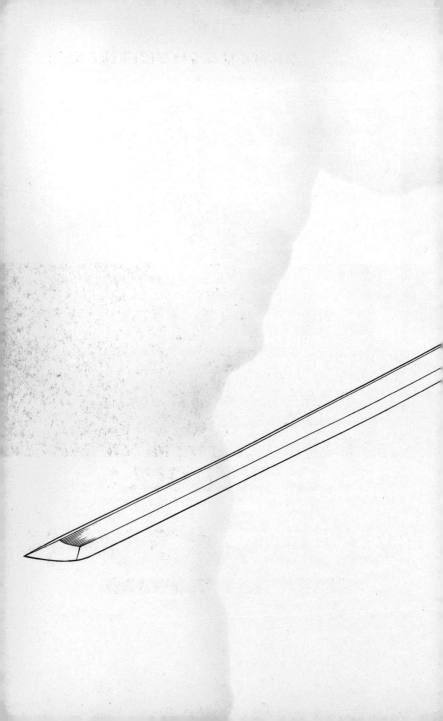

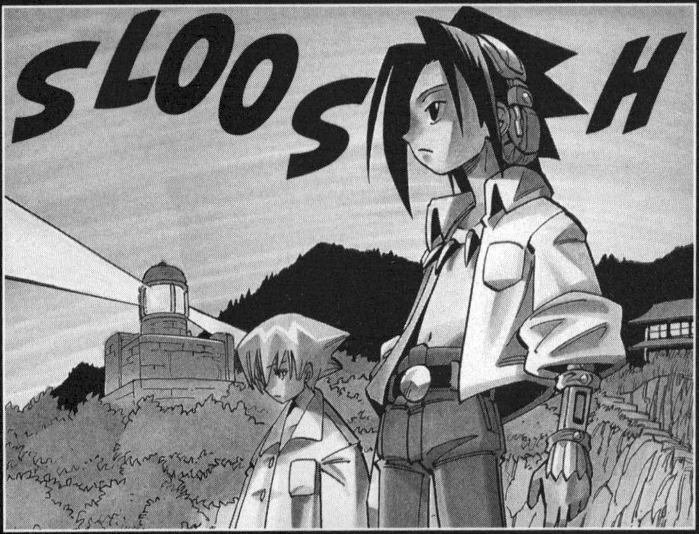
SLOOSH
H

IN THE NEXT VOLUME...

The X-Laws are determined to lure Yoh to their camp, Hao has his sights set squarely on Ren, and Lyserg discovers that the X-Laws may not be the steadfast allies he took them for...

AVAILABLE MAY 2008!

Shaman King

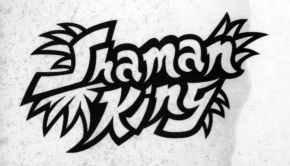

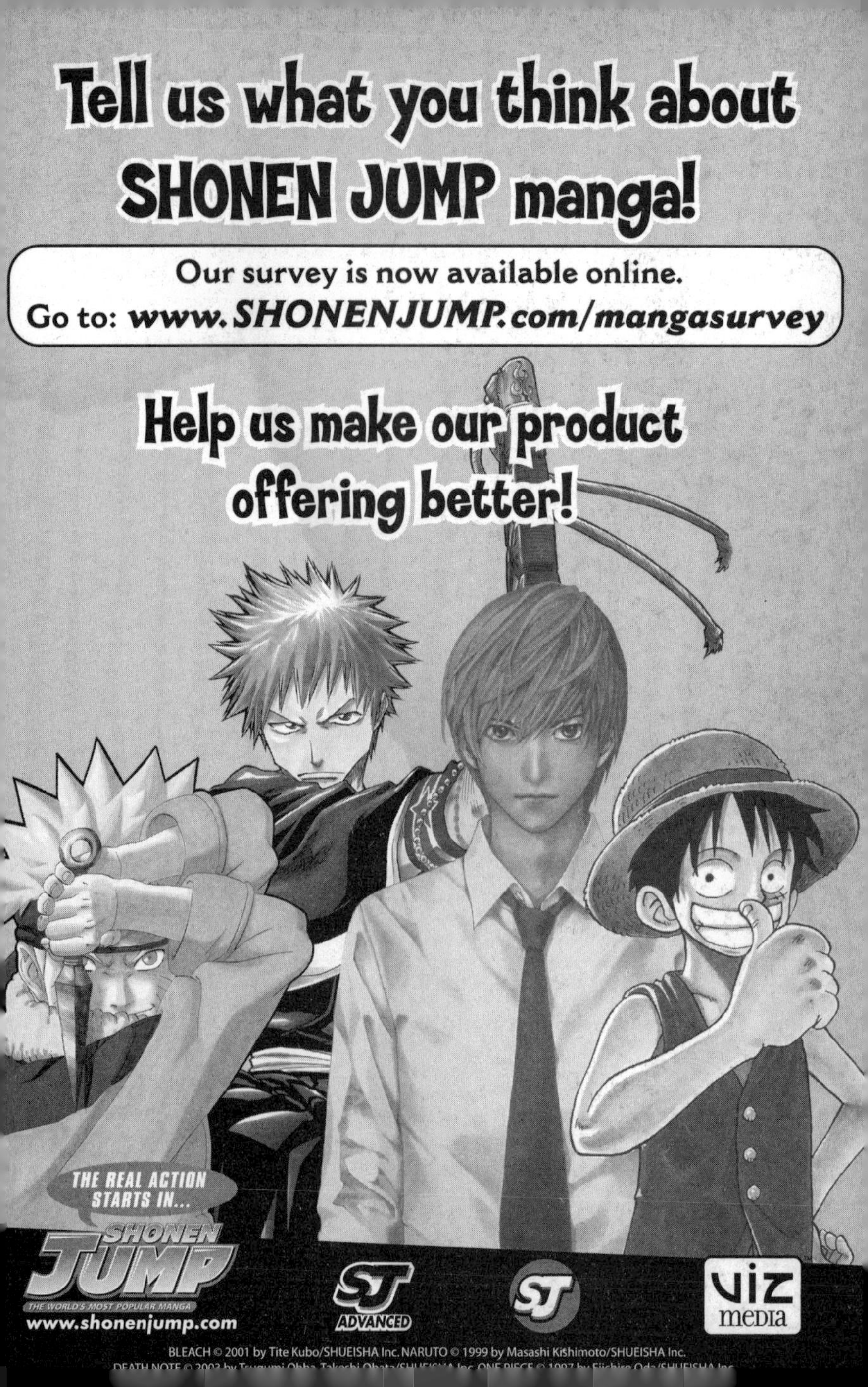

Tell us what you think about
SHONEN JUMP manga!
Our survey is now available online.
Go to: www.SHONENJUMP.com/mangasurvey
Help us make our product
offering better!
THE REAL ACTION
STARTS IN...
SHONEN JUMP
THE WORLD'S MOST POPULAR MANGA
www.shonenjump.com
SJ ADVANCED
SJ
viz media
BLEACH © 2001 by Tite Kubo/SHUEISHA Inc. NARUTO © 1999 by Masashi Kishimoto/SHUEISHA Inc.

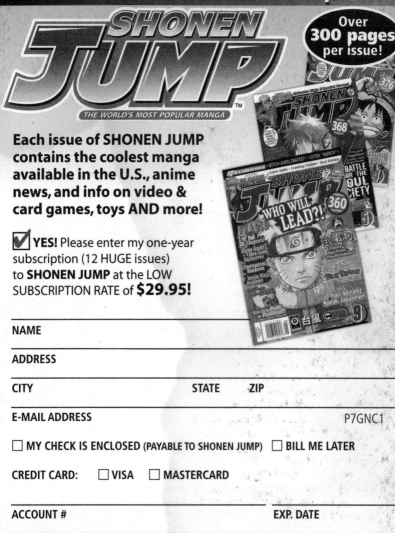